'The economics of earnings' analyses the wages th; the labour market laws and rules within which the conventional emphasis on point-in-time one-perio worker choice over the life-cycle – the human capital ...₃ ıramework, the book synthesises research results so as to point ... way to better labour market policies.

Government policy is often directed toward labour market issues such as education subsidies, training programmes, health and safety laws, and employment protection laws. By using models based on informed worker choice – the supply side – this book will assist concerned individuals in government, industry and academic study to evaluate and improve labour market policies and practices.

The economics of earnings

The economics of earnings

S. W. POLACHEK
State University of New York at Binghamton

and

W. S. SIEBERT
University of Birmingham

Published by the Press Syndicate of the University of Cambridge
The Pitt Building, Trumpington Street, Cambridge CB2 1RP
40 West 20th Street, New York, NY 10011–4211, USA
10 Stamford Road, Oakleigh, Victoria 3166, Australia

First published 1993

Printed in Great Britain at the University Press, Cambridge

A catalogue record for this book is available from the British Library

Library of Congress cataloguing in publication data

Polachek, S. W.
The economics of earnings / by S. W. Polachek and W. S. Siebert.
   p. cm.
Includes bibliographical references and index.
ISBN 0 521 36476 0 (hardback). – ISBN 0 521 36728 X (paperback)
1. Wages. 2. Occupations. 3. Labor market. 4. Labor economics.
I. Siebert, W. S. II. Title.
HD4906.P65 1992
331.2'1 – dc20   91–38731 CIP

ISBN 0 521 36476 0 hardback
ISBN 0 521 36728 X paperback

WD

Contents

		page
Foreword		xiii
Preface		xv

1 Introduction: the importance of life-cycle analysis — 1
1.1 What labour economics is about — 1
1.2 The life-cycle approach — 2
1.3 The static auction market — 5
    Pareto efficiency — 6
    Marginal productivity — 8
1.4 Long-term contracts — 12
1.5 The plan of the book — 15

2 The life-cycle human capital model — 16
2.1 Introduction — 16
2.2 The age–earnings profile — 16
2.3 The human capital model — 19
2.4 The Ben-Porath model — 22
2.5 Algebraic depiction — 30
2.6 Depreciation — 32
2.7 Conclusions — 33
Appendix 2.1 Present values and discounting — 35

3 Schooling — 39
3.1 Introduction — 39
3.2 Human capital specialisation — 39
3.3 The rate of return to schooling — 42
3.4 Differences in educational attainment — 45
    Supply and demand analysis — 45
    Transfers within the family – the Becker–Tomes model — 49

3.5 Individual differences in education: empirical examples   52
     Father's occupation and education   52
     Studies of twins and brothers/sisters   54
     A study of the proportion attending college, by state   57
3.6 Subsidising education   59
     Equity   60
     Efficiency   64
     Public choice   66
3.7 Conclusions   67
Appendix 3.1 Assessing family background effects using
     differences in brothers' and twins' education   68

4 Post-school investment   71
4.1 Introduction   71
4.2 Derivation of the earnings function   71
4.3 Regression estimates   74
4.4 Extensions   77
     General and specific training   77
     Extended earnings functions   82
     Ability – studies of twins   86
4.5 On-the-job training policy   88
4.6 Conclusions   91
Appendix 4.1 Deriving the earnings function   92

5 Labour supply   96
5.1 Introduction   96
5.2 Models of participation and hours   97
     The individual   97
     Married women's labour supply   108
5.3 Empirical results – women's labourforce participation   112
     Trends in participation and associated variables   113
     The participation, wage, divorce, fertility system   117
     Empirical studies   119
5.4 Male labour supply   127
     Elasticity of supply   127
     Negative income tax experiments   130
     Retirement   131
5.5 Conclusions   135

Contents

6 Gender in the labour market   137
  6.1 Introduction   137
  6.2 Demand-side discrimination   140
        Prejudice models   140
        Statistical discrimination   143
  6.3 Empirical findings on market discrimination   146
        Wage discrimination   146
        The crowding hypothesis   149
        Discrimination and competition   152
  6.4 The supply side   154
        Differences in tastes   154
        Intermittent participation and reduced human capital   155
        Intermittent participation and occupational choice   158
        Intermittent participation and the wage gap   160
        Estimating male and female capital stocks   163
        Monopsony and absenteeism   164
  6.5 Policy issues   166
        Current policy   166
        Comparable worth   168
        Appropriate policies to combat sex discrimination   171
  Appendix 6.1 Calculations of human capital stock for
    continuous and intermittent workers   172

**7 Compensating wage differentials and heterogeneous
    human capital**   174
  7.1 Introduction   174
  7.2 Theory   176
        A simple model   176
        The wage–job risk locus   180
        The wage–job atrophy locus   187
  7.3 The facts on compensating differentials   188
        Measurement difficulties   189
        The evidence   191
  7.4 Policy issues   202
        Workplace safety   202
        'Caring' and comparable worth   206
  7.5 Conclusions   207
  Appendix 7.1 How 'job protection' lowers wages, but raises
    the cost of capital   208
  Appendix 7.2 Omitted and mis-measured variables   209

8   Information and wages   210
    8.1 Introduction   210
    8.2 Search in the labour market   212
        A simple model   212
        The Stigler search model   216
        Sequential search – the optimal stopping rule   220
        The job offer production function   226
        Demand-side influences   230
    8.3 Empirical results   232
        Studies of reservation wages and unemployment   232
        A model of ignorance in the labour market   238
        Search and mobility over the life cycle   242
    8.4 Conclusions   247
    Appendix 8.1 Calculating the average maximum wage offer
        for the uniform distribution   248
    Appendix 8.2 Evaluation of $E(w/w \geq w^*)$ for a uniform
        distribution   249

9   Payment systems and internal labour markets   250
    9.1 Introduction   250
    9.2 The labour contract   251
    9.3 Piece rates and the principal agent problem   255
    9.4 Promotion as an incentive – the 'tournament'   258
    9.5 Efficiency wages   261
        The model   261
        Implications   263
    9.6 Deferred compensation   265
    9.7 Specific training   268
    9.8 Contracts and wage rigidity   271
    9.9 The role of trade unions   272
    9.10 Policy   273
    Appendix 9.1 Contracts and wage rigidity   275

10 Unionisation   278
    10.1 Introduction   278
    10.2 Union membership   279
        Time trends   279
        Economic factors affecting membership   284
    10.3 Union wage and employment objectives   290
        Monopoly models   290
        Off-the-demand curve models   294

Contents

10.4	Union wage and employment effects in practice	300
	Efficient bargains	300
	Insiders and outsiders	303
	Union effects on non-union workers	308
	Effects of unions on firms	312
10.5	Industrial democracy	322
10.6	The professions	326
10.7	Conclusions	329
References		330
Subject index		351
Author index		363

Foreword

The processes by which people develop their skills at school, at work, and through geographic mobility and job search are basic to an understanding not only of why their earnings differ, but to an understanding of a country's economic and social development as well. To be sure, other factors also influence earnings, for example, discrimination, trade union membership, inherited ability – or, simply, luck. But the importance of all these factors can be better assessed if the individual's skill development process and its consequences are understood. Moreover this process is important from the policy viewpoint, since many government policies influence skill acquisition either intentionally or unintentionally.

The basic merit of human capital theory for labour economics is its ability to handle analytically the heterogeneity of labour and the time-bound investment processes that play a role in creating heterogeneity. The concept of human capital is ancient, and has been eloquently stated by Adam Smith. However the steps towards a systematic economic analysis of human capital formation and its implications for labour economics were taken only three decades ago. Since then an extensive literature has grown up. In it, human capital analysis forms the basis for the study of the economics of education and training, of individual and group differences in earnings and earnings growth, of labour mobility and its consequences, and of firms' compensation policies.

This book summarises these theoretical developments, and their accompanying empirical results. It is a comprehensive and accessible analysis of the body of work on human capital and its wider implications for policy that has developed over the past generation.

JACOB MINCER

Preface

The study of the wages that people earn, the jobs that they do, and the labour market laws and rules within which they operate – the field of labour economics – has developed considerably over the last few decades. A major innovation has been the move from an institutional approach to an analytical setting. Two developments are noteworthy. The first is elaboration of the theory of rational choice. The focus has been changing from point-in-time one-period choice, to choice over the life cycle. People are now assumed to have the information and ability to optimise over a long-term planning horizon – this is the human capital revolution. Secondly the advent of large-scale micro-economic datasets, and the computer power to process these data, has enabled more satisfactory testing and exploration of the new theories.

At the same time government has become more powerful over the years, and government labour market intervention consequently more far reaching, and possibly more invasive. Much government policy is directed towards labour market issues, including education subsidies, training programmes, gender and race equality programmes, unemployment insurance laws, minimum wage laws, union protection laws, health and safety laws, and laws limiting the ability of firms to dismiss workers ('employment protection'). In the days when the government spent only 10% of the national income the reach of such labour market activity was less than nowadays when government spends 40% or more. So it is important to get the analysis right, and this is another reason why labour economics has grown in stature.

This book emphasises these new developments. Our aim is to present a synthesis of the main research findings in labour economics, emphasising the rationality of human beings – the human capital approach – and use these find-ings to point the way to better labour market policies. We aim to be as simple, yet as rigorous as possible. We hope these somewhat conflicting objectives have been met by using graphical methods based on suitable supply and demand curves, or production functions. In fact our analysis of problems as diverse as job search, education, and women's labourforce participation each centres on graphs based on special production functions. Mathematical derivations and other technical matters are placed where possible in appendices.

Our approach is firmly microeconomic, that is, it centres on the choices made by individual workers and firms. Government enters as setting the rules of the game, whether these be laws affecting labour contracts, or taxes and tariffs. We are concerned with government policy in this aspect. We are less concerned with government monetary and budgetary policies, such as affect 'aggregate' spending, or investment, or inflation, which we leave to macro-economics texts. What is required to be analysed is the impact of specific labour market and social policies. This is where the new research and the new human capital oriented models help, and consequently it is where we focus.

The book has grown out of our university labour economics and industrial relations courses. Hence the intended audience is those academically interested in labour markets and labour policy, many of whom will hopefully be going on to further study, and/or into personnel related positions in government or industry. The fact that our courses have been given in both America and Britain explains, in part, why we use empirical studies mainly relating to these two countries. However comparisons of two countries whose laws and trade unions have developed differently over time, and exhibit a somewhat different capitalist ethic, are interesting in themselves, and provide an additional useful hurdle for our models to negotiate. Nevertheless, as it turns out, the analytical tools apply well to both countries, despite their institutional differences. This leads us to believe that the theory of rational human choice, applied over the life cycle, will apply to other capitalist countries as well, though we leave tests of such applications to our readers.

While not implicating them in the results, we would like to thank Jacob Mincer for encouragement and comments on the education and training chapters, and Peter Sloane who kindly read the whole manuscript. Others who have given advice are John Addison, Robert Basmann, Ralph Bailey, Richard Barrett, Dale Belman, John Copas, John Heywood, Noel Kavanagh, Thomas Kneisner, Stanley Masters, Haim Ofek, Richard Perlman, Phillip Nelson, Hettie Pott-Buter and Bong Yoon. Our students who endured successive drafts include Archantis Pantsios, Curtis Simon, Yesook Merill, Jesse Levy, Russell Roberts, Elias Links, Feng-Fuh Jiang, Mark Regets, Phanindra Wunnava, Rajiv Mallick, Inseo Jeong, Charng Kao, and Byong Song. Patrick McCartan of Cambridge University Press provided editorial encouragement from the earliest days. Jenny Metcalfe helped with proof reading. Most of all we are grateful to our teachers Sir Henry Phelps Brown and Jacob Mincer not only for their encouragement over the years but because their insights and enthusiasm kindled our interest in labour economics. Finally we thank our families and friends for providing the atmosphere necessary to enable us to pursue this project.

1 Introduction: the importance of life-cycle analysis

1.1 What labour economics is about: who earns what and why?

Labour economics deals primarily with questions concerning the determinants of individual earnings power: Who works? What are their wages? What makes some destitute and others better off? With this knowledge we can better judge which policies will raise the national income and thereby help the average worker. We can also assess which policies to target towards particular groups, especially the least well off, and assist in reducing poverty.

As we will see, the wage system is an amazing and delicate system of prices. Table 1.1 shows how different these prices are for the various demographic groups. Women earn less than men, and black workers earn less than whites. For men, earnings increase with age, but at a decreasing rate. For women, earnings vary less with age. In addition, earnings and education are correlated, and earnings vary by occupation. The table even understates variation in pay because there seems to be wide differences in pay received by individuals working in the 'same job'. Our aim is to explain earnings variation.

In a competitive economy, wages should act as guideposts informing people which occupation to take, for example, or how long to stay at school, or when to change jobs. The outcome of such choices is hopefully to allocate each person to the job – or sequence of jobs – which best suits his or her talents. Consequently people are as well off as they can be, and the national income as large as possible. In such a world, moreover, influencing the wage system by taxes, or by trade unions, or by government laws (minimum wage laws, for example, or equal pay laws), adversely affects labour allocation and thus national income. If the wage–price system is already doing its proper job, many policies designed to alleviate poverty could make it worse.

To build up the competitive standard against which to judge wage variations such as those shown in table 1.1, it is necessary to use the life-cycle approach as well as basic supply and demand. The life-cycle approach deals with resource allocation over an individual's life, rather than solely with decisions of the moment. We have to take explicit account of the fact that the young expect to become old, and the old to retire, when making their decisions. Similarly the job choice of men and women in families is influenced by the mid-life child-rearing expectations of women. Complementing point-in-time analysis – 'auction' labour markets – with life-cycle models removes much that appears arbitrary in the distribution of wages.

Let us now consider the life-cycle approach in more detail, then turn to the more traditional point-in-time analysis.

1.2 The life-cycle approach

A life-cycle framework provides a fuller understanding of most central labour market issues. The following are some illustrations.

Labour supply deals with how much leisure individuals are willing to give up at any wage. Giving up leisure entails work, and work implies earnings. Life-cycle models however show that it makes a big difference whether wage changes are permanent or temporary. A transitory wage increase can induce larger increases in labourforce participation than permanent wage increases because a temporary wage increase does not make people feel much wealthier: it has no income effect to counteract the substitution effect. It is only when people feel permanently wealthier that they adjust by consuming more leisure (working less). For this reason, evaluation research using negative income tax experiment data can easily overestimate work disincentive effects by failing to account for the temporary nature of the experiment. These subjects are covered in chapter 5 below, on labour supply.

Minimum wages, too, involve life-cycle effects. Those who are unskilled, but lucky enough to find jobs at minimum wages, earn more than they otherwise would have. However, though initial wages rise for the new recruits, on-the-job wage growth tends to be diminished. The reason is that when a firm has to pay inexperienced workers more it must economise on fringe benefits such as training opportunities. An analysis which did not account for such considerations would overstate the effect of government minimum wage (and equal pay) laws, since it would appear that young workers' wages rose when in fact their lifetime wage prospects declined. This subject is covered in much more detail in chapter 4, on post-school human capital investments.

Unemployment: the unemployed tend to be predominantly unskilled. This is because the skilled tend to have more 'firm specific' training accumulated during tenure which makes them relatively more valuable in a recession. Skilled workers tend to require long-term contracts, as discussed below, to protect these investments. Consequently skilled workers tend to be the last fired. Young workers and workers who have accumulated fewer skills – for example black workers – are more likely to become unemployed.

Table 1.1. *Average weekly earnings*

	US 1982			UK 1983	
	Men	Women		Men	Women
Colour: White	$382 per wk	$244 per wk		£105 per wk	£67 per wk
Black	281	233		98	66
Age: 16–24	231	194		74	58
25–34	364	261		107	77
35–44	431	260		119	71
45–54	428	254		114	68
55–64	409	246		103	67
Education: <8 years	261	176	No grades	92	60
1–3 yrs high school	327	197	'O' levels	104	67
4 yrs high school	381	238	'A' levels	124	77
1–3 yrs college	422	279	Degree	153	111
4 yrs+ of college	525	351	Higher degree	179	131

Source: US – Mellor, 1984; UK – General Household Survey, 1983.

The link between human capital and unemployment is strikingly illustrated in figure 1.1, which shows the course of unemployment for blacks and whites in Britain. The interesting feature of the diagram is the much greater variability of unemployment for black workers. They are laid off first when a recession develops, as in the late 1960s and 1970s, then rehired first in expansion. A popular explanation of higher black unemployment rates would simply be 'discrimination'. But such an explanation could not account for the pattern of variability, though human capital theory can. Chapters 2 and 3 develop the human capital model and chapter 8 considers search theory and unemployment.

Even with unions, life-cycle effects are important. Unions increase pay for their members, but they also tend to reduce wage growth by requiring equal pay across all workers rather than rewarding the more productive. The consequence of these 'standard rate' policies is that unskilled workers and young workers, for example, receive a large wage increase if they obtain a union job, but at the same time are much less likely to obtain such a job. Firms respond to union wage standardisation by avoiding the less productive groups such as young workers. It is only as workers become more skilled and experienced that they have a chance of becoming employed in a union firm. These and other aspects of unionisation are discussed in chapter 10.

Gender: human capital investment decisions, based on life-cycle decision-making, can also be used to explain gender labour market differences. Arguably the most important reason that women earn less than men is the more intermittent career lifetime labourforce participation of women. Lifetime labourforce participation is also a factor in understanding sex differences in occupation distribution, so-called 'occupational segregation'. Since skills in some jobs, for example management, depreciate more quickly when not used than in more routine jobs, market forces will ensure that women are less well represented in managerial jobs. Again, the explanation is contrary to the popular view which is based on an idea of discrimination against women. Government policy, too, is based on theories of discrimination – hence the Equal Opportunity Commission and 'affirmative action' programmes. Gender issues and the importance of life-cycle approaches are discussed in chapter 6.

Market equilibrium is traditionally depicted as a unique price. In the labour market it is the price at which all labour offered is equal to the amount of labour sought. Similarly there are supply and demand curves in each of the other markets. Through Adam Smith's 'invisible hand' a multimarket equilibrium somehow emerges.

However although one implication of the market is the emergence of unique equilibrium prices, such an equilibrium is not always apparent. In reality there are many wages, many interest rates, and many rental rates. The problem is there is no one labour market, no one capital market, and no one land market. There are tremendous quality variations in land and labour, not to mention large risk variations in investments. These variations lead to many prices for factors of production. Understanding wage variations is one of the key problems labour economists face.

Our approach is more like physics and chemistry. We view labour as a complex structure built from basic molecules which we call human capital which serve as the building blocks of worker productivity. (In a sense this type of structure would hold for other markets as well since capital can be graded on the basis of risk, and similarly land can be graded.) In turn the market rewards human capital because those with greater amounts of human capital command more earnings.

This implies a more complicated market structure than usual. First there is a market for the very basic 'molecule', that is, for basic labour. Second, there is a market for units of human capital, 'eds' (p. 20). The market for basic labour is essentially a static market. However, since human capital is an investment whereby workers reap returns over many years, the rate of time preference becomes a factor. Of course since, at least at the margin, the time preference rate in equilibrium equals the interest rate, equilibrium in the capital market becomes intimately tied to equilibrium in the labour market so that a multimarket equilibrium evolves. This enables an individual to determine how much current income to forego to purchase human capital which in turn determines an individual's earnings over life.

One's earnings are determined both by the market wage for a unit of human

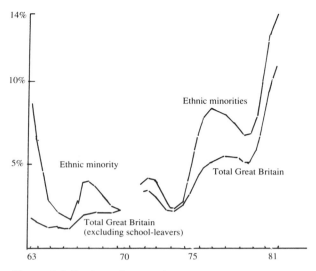

Figure 1.1 Registered unemployment rate among general population and ethnic minorities (moving average, males and females, 1963–81). *Source:* Brown, 1984, 272

capital as well as the amount of human capital one chooses. Human capital accumulation is determined on the basis of how much leisure and current earnings one foregoes in order to invest in future earnings power. This depends on interest rates determined in the capital market. Thus earnings are not determined in one market alone as most labour economics discussions indicate, but are a result of a multimarket equilibrium resulting from the simultaneous solution of all the factor markets.

The human capital model and its extensions are developed in the next chapters. But before doing this it is worth considering basic, static, labour market analysis in more detail. It is necessary to build up basic supply and demand concepts before moving on to the more involved life-cycle analysis.

1.3 The static auction market

The fundamental economic insight is that prices are set by supply and demand. Air is abundant, but diamonds are not. Despite air's intrinsic value, it is priced cheaply, because it is readily available. On the other hand, diamonds have a small supply relative to the demand for them, so they are expensive. The same is – or should be – true in the labour market. Fashion models have high earnings because great beauty is scarce relative to the demand for it (to help sell newspapers, or clothing and other goods, for example). Other, more useful workers, such as nurses, have low earnings because supply is large relative to demand. Many people are prepared to become nurses, in part because nursing does not require rare skills, and in part because nursing is a satisfying occupation – a 'vocation'. Lower earnings should be required to attract workers into such agreeable jobs, as will be discussed in chapter 7 on compensating wage differentials.

Traditionally labour markets are studied in a 'static auction' framework based on point-in-time supply and demand curves derived from individual utility and firm profit maximisation. Most labour economics problems are considered in this framework which ignores the life cycle (see Kniesner and Goldsmith, 1987). For example consider figure 1.2. The demand curve depicts the maximum hours of worker services firms are just willing to hire at any given wage. In the illustration this is L_1 at w_1, L_m at w_m and zero at any wage above A. At A we can assume wages equal the average product of labour so profits are zero. Any wage above A means profits are negative, so no-one would be hired. The demand curve is downward sloping because as wages fall more firms can afford to enter the market, and firms already in the market can afford to expand production. The demand curve is the 'marginal revenue product' of labour curve, as shown later.

The supply curve represents the maximum number of hours individuals are willing to sell to firms at any given wage. In the illustration, L_1 workers are forthcoming at wage w_1, and zero at wage G. At wages below G, everyone has better alternatives than working – they can be thought of as moving to other industries, or as working at home perhaps. Thus G can be taken as the lowest worker reservation wage in the market. Below this wage no-one would want to work. The supply curve is generally an upward sloping curve both because higher wages induce new entrants to the labour market, or the industry, and because higher wages will tend to induce those already at work to increase their hours. These issues are covered in more detail in chapter 5, and notions of the reservation wage are covered in chapter 8.

With free entry, full information, homogeneous workers, and many buyers and sellers of labour, equilibrium in the market occurs where hours supplied exactly equals hours demanded, i.e., point B. The equilibrium will be 'Pareto efficient'. Further, if firms are profit maximising, the wage will equal the marginal revenue product of labour, a measure of the worker's 'contribution' to the firm. Let us examine these concepts in turn.

Pareto efficiency

By definition, a Pareto efficient wage and employment combination is one which maximises welfare. Given such a situation, any change in the wage would reduce employment. While some would be better off, it can be shown

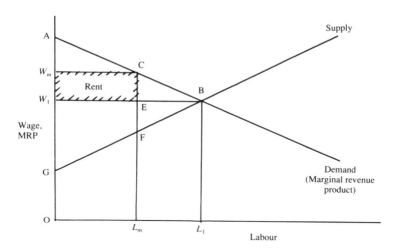

Figure 1.2 Workers' compensation and compensating wage differentials

that their gains would be smaller than the losses of those who lost their jobs. This important concept can be illustrated simply by using figure 1.2.

At the competitive wage w_1, producer surplus (or profit) is the triangle ABw_1. (This is explained in the next section.) Worker surplus is the triangle w_1BG. The square w_1BL_1O represents the wage bill, and the area GBL_1O represents the workers' opportunity costs of coming to work (what they could get elsewhere). Thus the triangle w_1BG is the amount over and above that required to get the workers to work, their surplus.

Now suppose that the wage is raised to w_m by minimum wage laws, for example, or union power. This is not a Pareto efficient move. It diminishes total welfare. The profit triangle diminishes to ACw_m, and employed workers' surplus increases by the cross hatched 'rent' rectangle w_mCEw_1. But the increase in the employed workers' surplus is not sufficient to compensate for the reduction in profits, and in workers' surplus of those who become unemployed. The triangle CBF is lost.

Another way of putting this is as follows: the gainers from the minimum wage have a gain:

G = area w_mCEw_1 (cross hatched).

The losers have a loss:

L = area w_mCEw_1 + area CBF.

L is greater than G by the triangle CBF. There have been analyses empirically calculating areas such as CBF, in the case of union-induced wage increases – see chapter 10.

In fact the net loss from the minimum wage policy is probably larger than triangle CBF. The reason is that the 'rent' rectangle need not be simply a transfer from profits to wages, but might itself be a loss. Union resources, for example, are required to lobby for the minimum wage policy. And firms will donate resources to lobby against the minimum wage policy. The situation is analogous to robbery. Robbery does not simply mean a transfer to the thief, because he has to expand resources to do the robbing, and householders have to spend money on locks and guards so as to deter theft. In equilibrium the rent square in figure 1.2 should simply equal the costs of obtaining/resisting that rent – be a further waste, in a word, to be added to triangle CBF.

The above applies to private firms, but in government or not-for-profit charities, the profit maximisation hypothesis obviously cannot hold. It is interesting, nevertheless, that there will still be a downward sloping demand curve for labour. This will be the result of the fact that, if the wage bill is constant, a rise in wages will mean fewer people are employed.

Be this as it may, it can be seen that the competitive wage, w_1, in figure 1.2 maximises the size of the producer and surplus triangles. Deviations from the competitive wage therefore decrease employee and employer welfare.

Marginal productivity

Where firms maximise profits, the wage will equal labour's contribution to the firm, as measured by the marginal revenue product (MRP). This proposition also has welfare connotations: workers are not exploited but paid, in a sense, an amount equal to their contribution to the firm.

A standard two panel diagram illustrating the wage = MRP proposition is given in figure 1.3. In the upper panel are shown the total revenue product (TRP) and total cost (TC) curves. The TRP curve is based on the production function, and takes the amount of capital in the firm as given. Product price is also given. The slope of the TRP curve gives MRP, as graphed in the lower panel. The area under the MRP curve up to L_0 in panel (b) gives the height of the TRP curve at L_0 in panel (a). Subtracting wages gives producer surplus (profits plus fixed capital costs) which is represented as the triangular cross hatched area in panel (b), or the two line segments in panel (a).

The total cost curve in the upper panel has a constant slope equal to the wage, and an intercept equal to the firm's fixed capital costs. We are assuming only two factors of production, and that raw materials costs have been netted out. The difference between TC and TRP gives profit. At maximum profit, given w_0, L_0 units of labour are hired, and the slope of the two curves is the same. This is shown in the lower panel, proving that $w = $ MRP. In the long run, if the

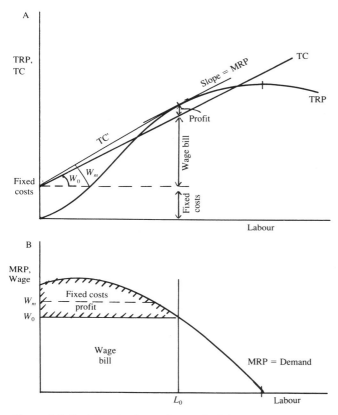

Figure 1.3 Deriving the demand curve for labour

wage is below w_m (when the firm just breaks even – TC' line), firms will attempt to adjust employment so as to remain on the MRP curve. Thus the MRP curve below w_m is the demand for labour curve.

The marginal productivity theory of wages will be our starting point in this book. Objections to the theory are often made on the basis that 'firms do not think like that'. But the proposition is simply a logical consequence of the given TC and TRP curves, and the assumption of profit maximisation – it matters little what firms think they do.

More serious is the objection that firms do not aim to maximise profits in fact. Yet where there is transferable private property, profit maximisation will be the natural outcome. Any firm which does not struggle to do as well as it can will be eliminated from the competitive race. Even where, for some reason, a firm is a monopoly supplier, the value of the monopoly will be greatest where profits are maximised. So the firm will be transferred from one owner (or group of managers) to others who can obtain the highest share price, that is, achieve the highest profit level. This is the takeover threat. Profit maximisation is therefore the outcome of transferability of property, coupled with human beings' desire for wealth.

Admittedly there remains the objection that the competitive process might work slowly, or that the costs of mounting a successful takeover are too great to make it much of a threat. Thus for quite long periods a firm with substandard 'slack' managers incapable of maximising profit, or anxious to achieve their own ends, will survive. Even here however wages will not be systematically below MRP. Wages will vary in a random manner above and below MRP, depending on the mistakes being made.

A case where wages will be systematically below MRP is where there is a single buyer of labour, 'monopsony'. Suppose we are analysing the company town. The position of that company is depicted in figure 1.4. The only difference between this figure and figure 1.3 lies in the TC curve, that of figure 1.4 having an increasing slope, the more labour is hired. The increasing slope of the TC curve embodies the assumption that, in a company town, if the company hires more labour, it will have to pay a higher wage. In the analysis of figure 1.3, the wage was given and constant, irrespective of the number of workers hired. If the company maximises profit it will hire L_0 workers, where MC = MRP, giving π_0 profit – read off the upper panel. At L_0 workers, the wage paid is indicated by the slope of the ray dashed in the upper panel. This slope is lower than MC, showing that the wage is lower than MRP, indicated in the lower panel. Were the firm to equate w = MRP, and hire L_1 workers, its profits would fall to π_1. Thus, where a firm has single buyer power, wages will be less than MRP.

Single buyer power can arise in many contexts. The company town example used above is presumably quite rare – though nurses are often faced with few hospitals in their town, and could be a case in point. But whenever workers are immobile their wages are likely to fall. An example could be illegal immigrant workers, who are afraid to move between jobs for fear of being arrested. Another example is married women, whose family responsibilities restrict their area of job search.

An important further example is the long-term contract. Where workers have a long association with a firm, they are more valuable in the firm than outside it, and this 'internal labour market' restricts mobility and might confer monopsony power on the firm. The implications of the internal labour market are discussed in detail in chapter 9. But it is worth noting here that long-term contracts are foreseen by both parties and mechanisms should develop (e.g., payment of severance pay) which will protect both sides. In these

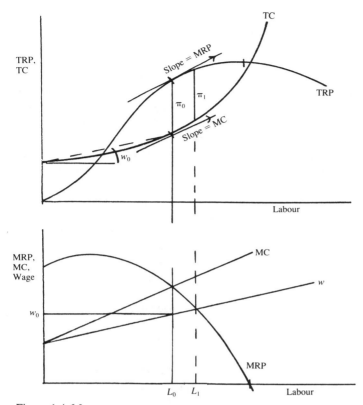

Figure 1.4 Monopsony

circumstances the *present value* of wages should equal the *present value* of marginal product.

Circumstances can also arise in which wages are higher than MRP. The possibility has been much discussed in the context of trade union collective bargaining. It can be shown that in certain circumstances it pays the two bargaining parties to move 'off' the demand curve, to a position above it. The argument, and evidence, is discussed fully in chapter 10 on unions. Suffice it to say here that the circumstances in which there is an 'off' the demand curve equilibrium are likely to be infrequent.

Another case in which wages are apparently greater than MRP arises in the case of highly paid managers and chief executive officers of prominent companies. These individuals receive annual salaries in the millions. Can their MRP be that high? One chief executive of a (failed) Savings and Loan company was able to arrange a salary of $8 million for himself. Clearly this was a case where wage was greater than MRP.

Theories of executive compensation, including the idea that executive pay and promotion might be a 'tournament', are discussed in chapter 9 on payment schemes. But it is worth repeating that the wage = MRP rule depends on the transferability of assets. If poorly managed companies cannot be taken over, or cannot be made bankrupt via new entry, then neither profit maximisation nor cost minimisation will occur. The US Savings and Loan industry has been heavily regulated, with new entrants and takeovers made more difficult, so consequently poor management has flourished. But whether such barriers to entry prevail widely is debatable, so we can still retain our marginal productivity theory of wages as a working rule.

Basic supply and demand analysis generally has strong predictive power. Shifts in supply or demand will affect wages and employment. A good example is Finis Welch's finding of strong wage sensitivity to supply shifts. Between 1957 and 1975 post-World War II baby boomers entered the labour market at unprecedented rates. As a result the young workers' labour supply increased, and their skill adjusted wages fell relative to wages of older workers.

Shifts in supply and demand also explain changes in blue-collar and white-collar wages. A draft deferment based on being in school was one way to avoid the Vietnam War during the 1960s and early 1970s. Partly as a result of this, the proportion of high school graduates going on to college soared in the 1960s leading to unprecedented college enrolments. This meant more white-collar and fewer blue-collar workers. The supply shift yielded increased blue-collar relative to white-collar wages, and resulted in a drop in the value of attending college – again a labour market supply and demand prediction (Freeman, 1976).

1.4 Long-term contracts

Although the backbone of most economic predictions, the simple supply–demand model is not always consistent with observation. For example, not all who want to work can find jobs. Business cycles are characterised by deviations in real GNP growth, typically declining 2% to 3% in recessions. Translating to an auction market framework, this implies that decreased aggregate demand should result in firms decreasing their labour demand. This would yield lower employment and wages, but should leave unemployment relatively unchanged – unemployment being frictional in the auction market framework. Adjustments should be a fall in wages and a fall in employment.

True enough, in recessions employment decreases by 2% to 3%. But both real and nominal wages are largely unaffected. On the other hand,

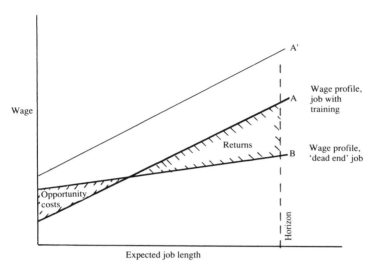

Figure 1.5 The long-term contract

unemployment shoots up. Indeed, in the 1982 recession US unemployment exceeded 10% and British unemployment was around 15%, the highest level since the great depression. Thus, contrary to auction market predictions, business cycles are characterised more by unemployment rate changes, less by employment changes, and very little by wage adjustments. Increased unemployment is an especially problematic result. Obviously there are other forces at work, creating wage rigidities and barriers to movement that hamper market equilibrating processes.

The main deficiency of the auction market view is its treatment of time. In the static auction framework all decisions are viewed at a moment, so that costs and benefits accrue instantaneously. But earnings benefits of education accrue throughout one's life. Job or geographic mobility has similar lifetime implications. Moreover the size of human capital investments both inhibit movement, and in turn stimulate long-term wage contracts (to protect the investment) which cause wage stickiness. When long-term implicit or explicit contracts are formulated between the worker and the firm, any one year's wages become impervious to short-term economic conditions.

The basic reasoning behind the long-term contract can be illustrated with reference to figure 1.5. We can imagine a worker deciding whether to change from his/her current 'dead end' job, with earning prospects B, to another job or region giving earnings profile A. Human capital theory posits that the individual will have to make an initial earnings sacrifice or investment in order to move to job A. The investment consists in the fact that job A starts on more unfavourable terms than job B. The initial period of low earnings, shown shaded as opportunity costs, is counterbalanced by a later period of high earnings, the returns. The two profiles must cross. If they did not, so that the job with the higher increase in earnings also started better, for example earnings profile A', then everyone would move to job A'. The consequence would be that wages in A' would be bid down until the profile became similar to A. The equilibrium relationship between profile A and profile B is such that the present value of returns equal the present value of the costs, both discounted at the market rate of interest – this is shown in chapters 2 and 3.

The investment implications of job changing and/or training – of labour mobility in its broader sense – bring human capital theory to the core of labour market analysis. Labour mobility is fundamental to the process of labour allocation and wage determination. Obstacles to mobility cause unemployment and dispersion in wages for the same job. The size and uncertainty of human capital investments make formidable obstacles to mobility, and labour market devices such as the long-term (implicit) contract and the 'internal labour market' have developed to ameliorate the obstacles. In other words, people enter into long-term contracts with firms so both sides can be protected when investing in knowledge specific to the firm (which would be of little value elsewhere).

The market for human capital is inherently imperfect, because human capital investments are not good loan collateral. Hence borrowing to finance training or migration is expensive or impossible. The poor are consequently less able to migrate and change jobs, and are more subject to structural unemployment. To counter such capital market imperfections the state some-times advances soft loans or subsidies for training. This is the solution widely adopted for school and college training.

Another solution is for firms themselves to share all or part of the training investment. Such sharing takes the form of workers being paid more than their marginal product during the training period, and correspondingly less after-wards. In terms of figure 1.5, with firm sharing, the individual's opportunity costs and returns are both reduced, and the wage profile for job A becomes more like that for job B, though the profile of marginal product in job A remains unchanged. Such sharing implies a long-term understanding or implicit contract with rules designed to protect both parties' investments – the internal labour market. The situation is similar in principle to indentured labour in the old days. Then firms would pay workers' transport expenses and main-tenance in return for a specific labour contract lasting several years, the low pay in this period recouping the employer's initial expenses.

In sum, life-cycle analysis improves our understanding of the 'supply side', of the determinants of worker skills, or worker allocation among jobs (a different aspect of the same thing, because a skilled worker in an unskilled job is effectively an unskilled worker). It can be seen that life-cycle analysis provides a rationale for government intervention on the supply side. Programmes to subsidise education, training, and regional mobility are justified. If this is not done, the poor – who have no savings to finance self-investment, and who cannot borrow because of the nature of human capital – will be disadvantaged.

The truths of basic supply and demand nevertheless remain, in particular the truth that interfering with wages is counterproductive. But we hope in this book by explaining human capital analysis to enrich those basic truths.

1.5 The plan of the book

The book is organised so that the basic human capital model is described first, in chapter 2. Then in chapter 3 we apply the model to the case of the educational decision. Chapter 4 continues with applications, this time in the field of post-school investment decisions, that is, training.

The participation decision, and other dimensions of traditional labour supply are considered in chapter 5. The more complicated issues of female labour supply – having as it does a strong life-cycle aspect – is reserved for chapter 6, on gender in the labour market. This chapter also analyses reasons for differences in pay as between men and women.

Various aspects of pay differentials are the focus of the next three chapters. Chapter 7 considers compensating pay differences for good and bad job characteristics. Chapter 8 analyses job search, and the problem of information collection – and consequent pay differences for identical jobs and/or people. Chapter 9 takes up the issues of labour contracts, including efficiency wages, 'tournaments', and specific capital investments as a means of monitoring and motivating workers.

The final chapter, chapter 10, considers trade unions. There is a general treatment of the main union issues, including the effect of union activity on the pay of non-union workers. The chapter also includes a section on the professions (doctors, lawyers), which form union-like bodies to help set their members' pay and conditions. Like unions, these organisations are able to restrict entry as a consequence of the special legislative protection which they receive, so similar policy problems arise.

2   The life-cycle human capital model

2.1 Introduction

The life-cycle model concerns individual investment decisions. It forms the core of human capital theory which deals with the acquisition of earnings power so crucial to understanding earnings differences. In this chapter we concentrate on two earnings patterns. The first pattern is that earnings rise with age, but at a diminishing rate so that younger workers' wages rise more quickly than older workers' wages. The second pattern is that earnings rise with education so that college graduates earn more than high school graduates, and in turn high school graduates earn more than primary school graduates. These observations are prevalent in data not only for the US and England, but also for all countries for which earnings data are available. The two patterns are universal and hence worthy of an explanation.

The chapter sets the stage by presenting statistical evidence. It then explores the life-cycle human capital model graphically, and ends by depicting the model algebraically.

2.2 The age–earnings profile

Earnings generally rise with age at a decreasing rate. This can be illustrated graphically in what is called an age–earnings profile as shown in figure 2.1. Typically age or labourforce experience is measured along the horizontal axis, and earnings along the vertical axis. The relationship between the two is depicted by the concave graph. Earnings rise quickly at young ages, but growth tapers off so that a peak is reached at about age fifty-five, and then earnings decline.

To make such a graph one ideally should have cohort data. Cohort data are information for a given generation of individuals each year of their life. Accumulating such data entails following the individuals over a forty-five year time period, for example, and hence is costly and time consuming. Asking

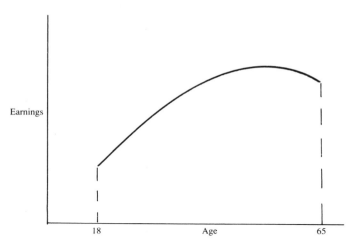

Figure 2.1 An age–earnings profile

individuals retrospectively historical questions about prior earnings often leads to erroneous data caused by problems of recalling the past. Further, even if one were to successfully conduct such a cohort earnings survey, the data would necessarily be incomplete since the young would not have had the opportunity to have worked long enough to yield a complete work history. Even the University of Michigan's Panel Study of Income Dynamics, which follows individuals over a twenty year period (since 1968), does not have enough datapoints to give complete work histories. Therefore earnings profiles are most often constructed using cross-sectional data.

Cross-sectional data are data collected from a random population at a point in time. Such data contain information for various population groups: whites, blacks, males, females, Hispanics, urban, rural, highly educated, etc. We will concentrate in this chapter on white males, and deal with other groups in later chapters.

The profile itself is computed by taking average earnings at each age for a particular demographic group – though researchers concerned with obtaining 'smooth' profiles often compute 'moving averages' of the wage rates. When using cross-sectional data it is usually assumed that the cross-section is equivalent to following an individual over his or her lifetime. This means that all individuals within the particular demographic group under study should be considered identical so that the earnings profile can be taken as depicting the change in earnings as a given individual moves through life.

Figure 2.2 depicts a set of age–earnings profiles for eight schooling groups. These profiles are not smoothed by moving average techniques and thus

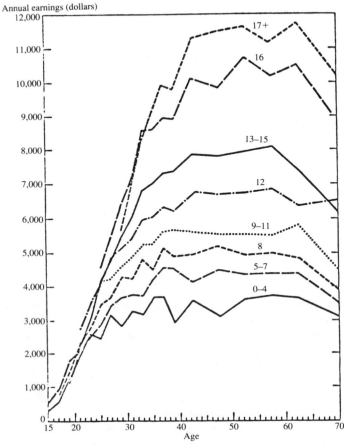

Figure 2.2 Age–earnings profiles of white non-farm men by schooling level, 1959.
Source: Mincer, 1974, 66

oscillate a bit more than the smooth hypothetical age–earnings profile depicted in figure 2.1.

The bunching of profiles in the lower left of the figure arises because those with higher levels of schooling begin work at later chronological ages. Those with low schooling but more work experience often find their wages have risen to the entry wage of the better educated. Partly for this reason one gets a clearer picture of life-cycle wages by concentrating on experience–earnings profiles. Figure 2.3 is such a diagram. Rather than age, experience is on the horizontal axis.

Annual earnings (dollars)

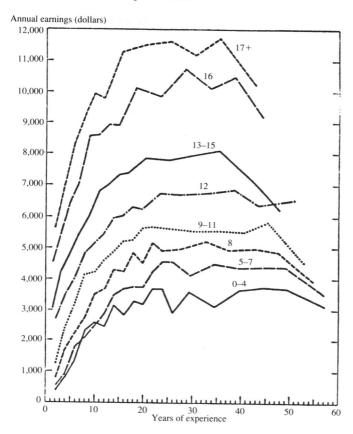

Figure 2.3 Experience–earnings profiles for white non-farm men by schooling level, 1959. *Source:* Mincer, 1974, 67

In figure 2.3 the two earnings patterns alluded to earlier are eminently clear: (1) earnings rise with age at a diminishing rate and (2) earnings profiles are higher the higher one's level of schooling. In the remainder of this chapter, we shall develop the life-cycle human capital model to find out why these patterns emerge.

2.3 The human capital model

Human capital theory explains earnings in terms of job skills acquired in school and on the job. The basic point is that a current earnings sacrifice or cost is incurred in order for a future benefit. This is the definition of an investment.

Were a current cost incurred for a current benefit, the expenditure would fall in the category of consumption. Investment in people is termed investment in human capital by analogy with investment in machinery, which is called physical capital.

Just as there is difficulty in measuring physical capital, since the value of a machine depends on the discounted future profits from the machine, not on some historic cost ('book value') of the machine, so there are questions concerning how to measure human capital. Here we deal with human capital abstractly, and assume a measure of human capital, namely 'eds', just as economists have invented 'utils' to conceptualise utility. Eds represent skill units – degrees, qualifications, on-the-job experience – acquired by individuals throughout life. One's stock of human capital at any age is related to the number of eds purchased at each age, so that the stock of human capital is the sum of human capital purchased in all prior years (minus depreciation which we shall discuss later). An individual's earnings are proportional to his or her human capital stock, the factor of proportionality being the wage or 'human capital rental rate' per ed. The greater one's human capital ed accumulation, the higher one's earnings.

If the human.capital model is to be applicable to the two questions raised in this chapter, we need to demonstrate that 'eds' are purchased at different rates over the life cycle. For earnings to rise more quickly at younger ages, human capital purchases would necessarily have to take place in greater amounts for the young relative to the old. And for earnings increase to slow down as a person ages, human capital purchases have also to taper off as one ages. Similarly human capital acquisition needs to be positively related to schooling. In order to assess these propositions concerning human capital acquisition we need to establish motives for buying human capital, so that the problem can be studied within a framework of rational choice.

The dichotomous investment decision

Imagine two hypothetical age–earnings profiles such as those shown in figure 2.4, depicting choices for an eighteen year old individual, say. The figure shows two possible choices: to go to work or to go to school (college) for at least another year. If one works it is possible to earn $G initially and then have earnings rise to the profile Y(high school). On the other hand if one obtains an extra year of college, one would have zero earnings in the first year, and incur direct costs of tuition, books, etc., thus ending up with negative earnings, −$C, between age eighteen and nineteen. However, after age nineteen, earnings profile Y(college) would ensue. Going to school enhances future earnings by the vertical distance between OA and OB, yet has a direct cost depicted by the two areas comprised of the direct outlay

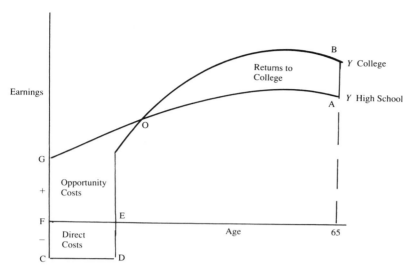

Figure 2.4 Earnings profiles for high-school and college

on books, tuition, etc. (area DEFC), and indirect opportunity costs (area GFEO).

Deciding whether to invest requires comparison of the 'present value' of future benefits with direct costs. Benefits consist of the difference between the two earnings profiles, ΔY, from age nineteen to retirement. The present value of this stream of benefits discounted at rate i, PV(i), is approximately (see appendix):

$$PV(i) \cong \Delta Y/i.$$

Investment should occur as long as costs, C, are less than the present value of benefits:

$$C < \Delta Y/i.$$

For example if $\Delta Y = \$2,000$ and $i = 10\%$, the cost of going to college would have to be less than $\$20,000$ ($= 2,000/0.1$).

The investment criterion is more usually stated in terms of the 'internal rate of return' (IR) – that discount rate that equates cost and present value of returns (see appendix):

$$PV(IR) = \Delta Y/IR = C.$$

On this criterion, if IR is greater than the market rate of interest plus a risk premium, then the investment is worth buying. A 'demand for education' curve can be drawn up, relating *IR* to years of investment – the first years having a high *IR* (because foregone earnings costs are low, while the benefits of learning to read and write are large), and later years having a lower *IR*. Education is bought so that the *IR* on the final year equals the appropriate market rate of interest. This is discussed in more detail in the next chapter.

Divisible investment

Human capital investment does not always take place at school. Nor is human capital investment always an indivisible type of decision in which people devote themselves only to full-time investment. Often investment opportunities come in smaller units: one can go to school part time, one can take an adult education course, or one can train 'on the job' while simultaneously working. Many jobs, such as a management trainee or an accountant, offer wide training opportunities. Other occupations such as cab driver or waiter are more 'dead end' – they offer little incentive to train on the job as the job is simpler and it changes less quickly. Nevertheless individuals even in these jobs can opt to train, either on the job, or off it (at night school for example).

In the human capital model individuals are envisaged as spending some time and effort in improving themselves at every stage of their lives. The amount of time and effort will vary, being greater for youthful individuals, and for individuals just starting a job. The method of self-investment will also vary. Sometimes it will take the form of formal training courses, at other times it will consist of taking jobs which offer learning opportunities – 'on the job' training. The different types of training will be covered in later chapters. Here we are interested in laying down the broad outlines of the investment process, the basic imperatives, as it were, to which all people must respond.

How does one know whether to invest on a full-time or part-time basis? The problem is difficult but was first tackled by Yoram Ben-Porath in a classic article written in 1967.

2.4 The Ben-Porath model

Essentially Ben-Porath claims that in every year of one's life, one invests in oneself – buys eds – in accordance with the benefits and costs of buying the eds at that stage of the life cycle. Benefits are equal to the present value of the extra wages obtainable from the incremental unit of training. Costs are primarily the foregone earnings entailed in diverting one's time to acquiring that incremental unit. Ben-Porath assumes that individuals behave much like firms. Just as firms produce so that marginal cost equals marginal revenue, so individual investors purchase human capital up to the point that marginal cost equals (the present value of) marginal gain.

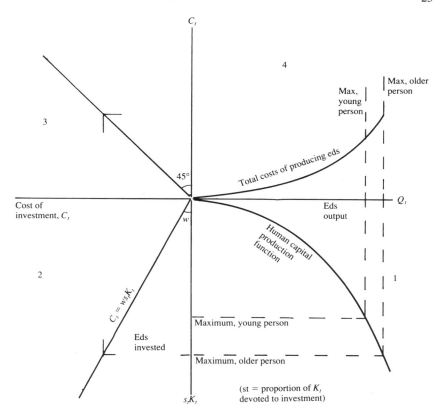

Figure 2.5 The human capital production function and the total cost of producing eds

Let us consider the costs side first. The elements of the model are laid out in figure 2.5. The central component is the 'human capital production function' given in quadrant 1. Eds are produced every year, Q_t, and the input is the human capital the person diverts from the market into self-investment. We measure this input as $s_t K_t$, where s_t is the proportion of human capital stock, K_t, diverted from earnings. In other words, the person can use his or her eds to earn money in the market, or use the eds to study and produce further eds. A simple human capital production function is:

$$Q_t = (s_t K_t)^b,$$ (2.1)

where $0 < b < 1$ is an 'ability' parameter. The individual's decision problem is to choose s_t every year.

Note that since s_t cannot be greater than unity, the maximum Q that can be produced in any given year, t, is limited by the existing capital stock, K_t. However, since K_t grows with age (assuming investment continues), the maximum possible output of human capital, Q, grows with age. This growth in the maximum is indicated on the diagram, and illustrated in table 2.1. Table 2.1 shows an individual with an assumed initial stock of human capital of 100 'eds', and an exponent, b, equal to 1/2. The first column shows possible human capital output in this initial year for different investment time fractions, s_t. Thus human capital increases by 7.07 units per period with investment time intensity $s_t = 50\%$, for example. It can increase at most by 10 units with maximum time intensity, $s_t = 1$. With maximum investment in the first year, the stock of eds would increase by 10. Then at the beginning of the next time period the individual would have 110 eds, and if he or she continued to invest full time the maximum production of eds would be 10.49 units. Particularly at young ages, as we will see, this upper limit on the amount that can be invested will be important.

It might seem strange to have eds both as an input and as an output. An analogy would be the case of corn. Corn can be either eaten, or saved and used as seed for next year's crop; that is, corn can either be consumed or invested. In the same way we take it that eds can be consumed (by renting them in the market) or invested so as to produce further eds.

Investing the eds to produce further eds has a foregone earnings cost (and perhaps direct costs such as the purchase of books and training materials, which we ignore for simplicity). The foregone earnings cost, C_t, is the wage per ed, w, multiplied by the number of eds directed away from the market and towards investment:

$$C_t = ws_tK_t. \tag{2.2}$$

This function is graphed in quadrant 2.

Using the 45 degree line of quadrant 3 to map dollar costs over to quadrant 4, we then have in quadrant 4 what we want: the total cost function for producing eds. Notice how, when the maximum Q_t is reached, the cost function ends (dotted vertical line). This maximum will move outward with age, as already explained.

The formulation of the human capital production function emphasises the individual's own resources. Borrowing funds for self-investment is assumed to be unimportant – as is realistic, since human capital is not good collateral for a bank loan (see next chapter). More restrictively, there might appear to be no role for family funds to enter the investment decision model – yet such funds are likely to be vital in the early years, in that wealthy families can afford to wait longer for their children to become self-supporting. However family wealth can be shown to have a role in the model in that a wealthy family will

Table 2.1. *Illustrative human capital production function*

s_t	$K_0 = 100$ Q_0	$K_1 = 110$ Q_1	$K_2 = 120.5$ Q_2	$K_3 = 131.5$ Q_3
0	0	0	0	0
0.1	3.16	3.32	3.47	3.63
0.2	4.47	4.69	4.91	5.13
0.3	5.48	5.74	6.01	6.28
0.4	6.32	6.63	6.24	7.25
0.5	7.07	7.42	7.76	8.11
0.6	7.75	8.12	8.50	8.88
0.7	0.37	8.77	9.18	9.59
0.8	8.94	9.38	9.82	10.26
0.9	9.19	9.25	10.11	10.88
1.0	10.00	10.49	10.98	11.47

Notes: Human capital production function assumed:

$$Q_t = (s_t K_t)^b, \text{ where } b = 1/2$$

Q_t = output of capital
s_t = fraction of human capital stock (K) devoted to production of further capital = portion of time devoted to study in a year.
b = 'ability' parameter, $0 < b < 1$ (if $b = 1$ there are no diminishing returns).

apply a lower discount rate when evaluating the benefits of investment. This will lead to more investment, as is now shown.

On the benefits side, the benefit of an extra unit of human capital is the present value of the stream of future wages, PV(w, i), which that unit will bring. The stream goes on until retirement, age sixty-five, say. Thus benefits, B_t, are:

$$B_t = \text{PV}(w, i)\, Q_t \tag{2.3}$$

$$= \frac{w}{i} (1 - \frac{1}{(1+i)^{65-t}})\, Q_t$$

$$\cong \frac{w}{i} Q_t \text{ when a person is young (t small)}$$

$$\cong 0 \quad \text{when a person nears retirement ($t \cong 65$).}$$

The above is a simplification because future benefits are not known with certainty (see Levhari and Weiss, 1974 and Warren and Snow, 1990). Also, the retirement age is itself chosen (see chapter 5). However it is a useful starting point. The benefits schedule is shown in the top panel of figure 2.6, which also includes the total cost function already derived. The benefits schedule is a straight line from the origin. The slope is steeper for young than old workers because the present value of a unit of human capital is greater for younger workers. The slope will also be steeper if the discount rate, i, is low – that is, if the person can afford to wait. This position, as mentioned above, is more likely to characterise individuals from wealthy than poor families.

Where the difference between total benefits and costs is greatest gives the surplus maximising output of human capital. As drawn, this is output Q_1 for the young person. At Q_1 the slopes of the benefit and cost curves are equal, that is, marginal benefit equals marginal cost. This is shown in a different way in the bottom panel, which graphs the marginal benefit and marginal cost curves.

Because the present value of a unit of human capital is greater for young than old workers, the optimum output of human capital falls over the life cycle. As the benefit curve in the upper panel of figure 2.6 falls with age, so the marginal benefit curve in the lower panel declines. Assuming the marginal cost curve remains unchanged with age, the MB curve simply slides down the MC curve. Two positions are shown in figure 2.6, with Q_1 for the younger worker, and Q_2 for the older.

Not all individuals have the same marginal cost and marginal benefit curves. Presumably those individuals with greater abilities would find it cheaper to 'produce' human capital. For example, clever people might find that it takes less time to learn calculus in school or management techniques on the job. For them the marginal cost curve would be lower, and greater amounts of human capital would be purchased.

Let us now follow a typical man through his life (women's intermittent labourforce participation makes their earnings profile more complicated – this is analysed in chapters 5 and 6). Assume for simplicity that the marginal cost curve does not vary as an individual gets older – except that the vertical section indicating maximum Q_t shifts out with age. During the initial years, the present value of gain for each unit of investment is relatively high, and maximum Q_t low – so the individual will be at a corner, producing as much Q_t as possible, that is, choosing a time investment fraction, s_t, of unity (no time spent earning). Then, as the individual ages, the maximum shifts outwards, and the marginal benefit curve shifts downwards. It shifts continuously until the year in which he retires, and in that year the present value of the marginal gain curve coincides with the horizontal axis. In that year, the last year of his work life, investments in market earnings power have no value (from an investment viewpoint – though they might still be undertaken for reasons of enjoyment, i.e., consumption reasons) since he plans to cease working.

Figure 2.7 translates these investment patterns into a life-cycle investment curve and corresponding human capital stock curve. The figure also shows the time path of s_t, the fraction of time spent investing every year. According to our argument, the amount of investment in eds, Q_t, increases for a period since

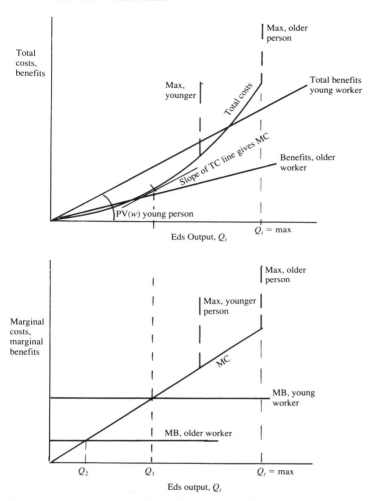

Figure 2.6 Total and marginal benefits and costs of producing eds

initially human capital is a very profitable investment, but the individual cannot produce enough of it, and so chooses $s_t = 1$. Q_t then declines continuously as one gets older reaching zero at retirement. Accumulated human capital is computed by adding the annual investments. The process of adding yearly human capital investments yields a stock of human capital curve, K_t, as depicted in figure 2.7. Note that the stock of human capital increases quickly in the period when $s_t = 1$, then more slowly in middle age, and stops increasing at all when one is old. In fact, ignoring depreciation (see below) human

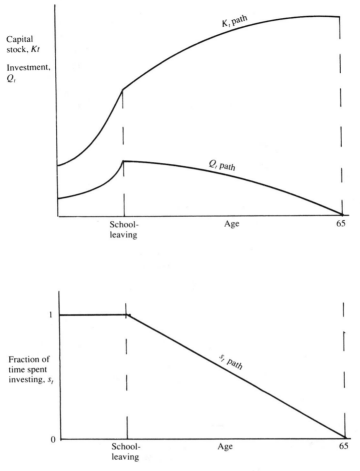

Figure 2.7 The production of human capital and the stock of human capital over the life cycle

capital stock peaks at retirement and reflects a concave function looking very much like the age–earnings profiles depicted earlier in the chapter.

This should be no surprise: earnings in the market place are determined on the basis of one's accumulated human capital stock. Human capital stock and earnings are related in the following way. Define potential earnings, E_t, as the most that an individual aged t could earn if he spent all his time working. Earnings in this case would be equal to the product of the stock of human capital accumulated over past investments, K_t, and the wage rate per unit of

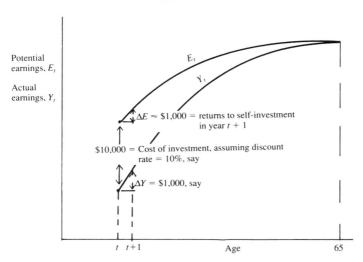

Figure 2.8 The relation between actual (Y) and potential (E) earnings

human capital, w. w is given by the market, and is assumed constant over life and independent of the stock of human capital. Thus:

$$E_t = wK_t. \tag{2.4}$$

Then observed earnings, Y_t, equals potential earnings minus the foregone earnings cost, C_t ($= ws_tK_t$), of human capital investment in that year:

$$Y_t = E_t - C_t \tag{2.5}$$

$$= wK_t(1 - s_t).$$

For example, if we measure eds so that the wage per ed is $1 per ed per year (say), then potential earnings follow a path the same as the capital stock path, and actual earnings are related to potential earnings by the fraction $(1 - s_t)$. As illustrated in figure 2.8, observed earnings are much smaller than potential earnings (and the value of the individual's capital stock) early in life, when s_t is large, and the gap tapers to nothing as s_t declines.

It is instructive also to link potential and actual earnings using the internal rate of return. When investment costs, C_t, are incurred, the value of human capital and thus of potential earnings is increased by some amount ΔE_t. The relationship between the two is given by the internal rate of return, IR, which should equal some market rate of interest, i, in equilibrium:

$$\Delta E_t/C_t = IR \cong i.$$

For example if $1,000 of earnings is foregone by going on a training course, so

$C_t = \$1,000$, and capacity earnings are increased by $200 a year as a result of the course, so $\Delta E_t = \$200$, then $IR = 20\%$. This is a very good rate of return, so more investment should be undertaken until IR comes down to about $i = 10\%$, say. Once this happens, given that $Y_t = E_t - C_t$, we have:

$$Y_t = E_t - \Delta E_t/i,$$

and:

$$E_t - Y_t = \Delta E_t/i.$$

However, $\Delta E_t \cong \Delta Y_t$, as figure 2.8 shows. Therefore the gap between potential and actual earnings can be written:

$$E_t - Y_t = C_t = \Delta Y_t/i. \tag{2.6}$$

This is an important equation, because it shows that we can simply build up a person's *potential* earnings profile using that person's *actual* earnings profile. The equation shows that the increase in observed earnings in a given year, divided by a suitable discount rate ('capitalised') allows us to assess the amount that person invested in himself or herself in that year, and therefore his/her hypothetical potential earnings. Suppose, for example, that a man was earning $10,000 at the beginning of the year, his pay increased by $1,000, and the discount rate is 10%. Then, from equation (2.6), his self-investment in new skills during that year must have been approximately $10,000 (= 1,000/0.1), and his potential earnings $20,000.

2.5 Algebraic depiction

It is useful to collect together the equations we have used above, and derive some algebraic results.

We have already (equation 2.4) defined potential earnings, E_t, as the amount an individual aged t could earn by spending all his time working:

$$E_t = wK_t.$$

The path of E_t is therefore determined by the path of K_t, which is in turn determined by how much one invests during the year, that is, the path of Q_t in figure 2.7. This is seen algebraically: from the definition of E_t it follows that:

$$\partial E_t/\partial t = w\partial K_t/\partial t = wQ_t.$$

To explain movements in E_t we must thus analyse movements in investment, Q_t.

We can depict the process of human capital creation by means of a production function such as that used in figure 2.5. For illustration we use a simplified version of the Cobb–Douglas production function as suggested in equation (2.1) above. We assume capital created in any year, Q_t (which equals the rate of change of capital stock from year to year) is related to the fraction of time, s_t, devoted to enhancing one's existing skill level. K_t. Investment effort, s_t, is measured as a proportion of total time available and hence can vary from zero to one. Thus:

$$Q_t = \Delta K_t / \Delta t = (s_t K_t)^b,$$

where b is a constant less than unity depicting 'ability'.

From the production function, it is possible to derive cost curves for the production of human capital. Since the cost of producing human capital is the foregone earnings cost of taking time away from work to produce the human capital, total costs can be computed as opportunity costs. Thus as noted in equation (2.2) above, total dollar costs of producing human capital at age t, C_t, are:

$$C_t = w s_t K_t.$$

This cost function can be expressed in units of human capital Q_t. From the production function we have:

$$s_t K_t = Q_t^{1/b},$$

so:

$$C_t = w Q_t^{1/b}.$$

This implies a marginal cost function:

$$\partial C_t / \partial Q_t = \frac{w}{b} Q_t^{(1-b)/b},$$

which, it must be remembered, becomes vertical when $s_t = 1$ (see figure 2.6).

The benefits curve is (equation (2.3) above):

$$B_t = \frac{w}{i} \left(1 - \frac{1}{(1+i)^{65-t}}\right) Q_t,$$

and the marginal benefits curve is:

$$\partial B_t / \partial Q_t = \frac{w}{i} \left(1 - \frac{1}{(1+i)^{65-t}}\right).$$

At any age, optimal investment is determined by equating marginal cost and marginal benefits from investment. Thus setting $\partial C_t / \partial Q_t$ equal to $\partial B_t / \partial Q_t$ yields:

$$\frac{w}{b} Q_t^{(1-b)/b} = \frac{w}{i} (1 - \frac{1}{(1 + i)^{65-t}}).$$

Solving for Q_t gives:

$$Q_t = \left(\frac{b}{i} (1 - \frac{1}{(1 + i)^{65-t}}) \right)^{b/(1-b)}. \tag{2.7}$$

Equation (2.7), shows us that human capital output, Q_t (and thus earnings) depends upon i, b, and t. Looking first at the discount rate, i, we see that Q_t is smaller the higher is i. In other words individuals facing high discount rates will invest less, accumulate less capital, and consequently have a lower growth in earnings over their lives. In the next chapter we will see that poor families face higher discount rates, and hence can be expected (on the basis of the human capital model) to accumulate less capital. This is the equity basis for subsidising education.

Also according to equation (2.7), Q_t rises with b, the indicator of 'ability'. The more able accumulate more human capital. This seems plausible – a higher b lowers the marginal cost curve in figure 2.6, and causes more Q_t for a given MB curve. However, the more able need not remain at school (full time investment) longer than the less able. Equation (2.6) only holds when MC can be equated with MB. But during the schooling period, as we have seen, MB is greater than MC because the MC curve reaches a maximum. This maximum shifts out with age. It is possible that the maximum shifts outward more quickly for the more able people, and so their period of schooling (though not their output of Q_t) is in fact shorter than average.

Finally, whatever the value of b and i, Q_t decreases as t increases. Eventually Q_t falls to zero at the age of retirement, when $t = 65$. In sum, the capital stock – and potential earnings – grows more quickly with high b, less quickly with high i, and, after an initial period of swift increase, increases less quickly with age.

To derive actual pay, Y_t, subtract investment costs, C_t, from potential earnings, wK_t. Thus:

$$Y_t = wK_t - ws_tK_t = w(1 - s_t)K_t.$$

Since K_t is increasing and s_t decreasing over the life cycle, observed earnings must increase, and the rate of increase of observed earnings must exceed the growth in capacity earnings (see figure 2.8).

2.6 Depreciation

The earnings profile of figure 2.8 peaks when one is about to retire, yet the earnings profile of figure 2.1 peaks slightly before retirement age and then is negatively sloped. Why the inconsistency?

Skills depreciate and often become obsolete. What this means is that one's stock of human capital can deteriorate with age. How often do we wish that we remembered everything we learned in our freshman courses? It is the forgetting of skills, the obsolescence of skills, and perhaps the decline in health which cause depreciation. Few estimates of depreciation exist. Thus one would be hard pressed to postulate just how depreciation varies over the life cycle. Nevertheless, it is intuitively plausible to hypothesise that depreciation of skills probably increases with age. Depreciation can be illustrated graphically (a mathematical analysis is given in the appendix to chapter 4).

Figure 2.9 depicts depreciation as well as the entire investment/earnings process. On the top half is investment and on the bottom are earnings profiles. Curve C_t is the (gross) investment path, and depends on Q_t. The upward sloping curve, $D_t = \delta PK_t$, represents depreciation for each year, where δ is the depreciation percentage and PK_t is the dollar value of human capital. For example, given that $w = \$1$ per year is the rental rate of an ed, $P = w/i$ is the capitalised value of an ed, and P can be thought of as the price of human capital. Thus, if $i = 10\%$, then $P = \$10$. If the number of eds is $K = 20$, then the earnings stream is $\$20$ ($= iPK = wK$), and the dollar value of eds is $\$200$ ($= PK$). If $\delta = 3\%$ a year then $D = \delta PK = \$6$.

The difference between investment and depreciation is net investment, C_{nt}. Thus $C_{nt} = C_t - \delta PK_t$. Net investment equals zero when depreciation equals gross investment. Net investment is negative when one's capital stock depreciates more quickly than it appreciates. This occurs when depreciation exceeds gross investment (see the appendix to chapter 4).

Potential earnings, when depreciation is zero, rise continuously as depicted in figure 2.8. When depreciation is non-zero, potential earnings peak when net investment is zero. Beyond this point capital stock is declining as depreciation exceeds investment. Thus earnings decline from this point on. As in figure 2.9 observed earnings can be obtained by subtracting investment costs from E_t. Again, as investment costs go to zero, both earnings streams converge.

2.7 Conclusions

Observed earnings profiles are concave. They rise initially at a rapid rate, then at a decreasing rate,·finally peaking and then falling. The chapter develops a life-cycle human capital investment model to explain these patterns. Earnings are related to skills and skills are acquired through human capital investment both in school and 'on the job'. As skills accumulate over life, earnings rise in direct proportion to accumulated human capital. The finite life constraint governs incentives for investment. Older workers about to end their work life by entering retirement have few years in which to reap investment gains. Young workers with a whole work life ahead have many years in which to reap

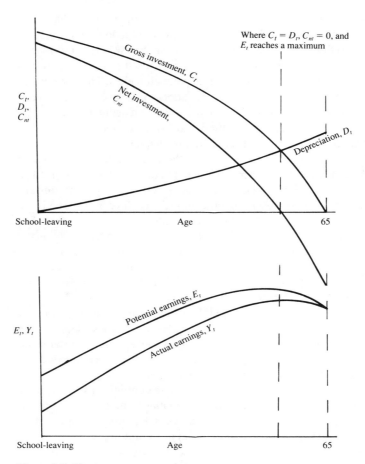

Where $C_t = D_t$, $C_{nt} = 0$, and E_t reaches a maximum

C_t, D_t, C_{nt}

Gross investment, C_t

Net investment, C_{nt}

Depreciation, D_t

School-leaving   Age   65

E_t, Y_t

Potential earnings, E_t

Actual earnings, Y_t

School-leaving   Age   65

Figure 2.9 The investment–earnings process

gains. Therefore the young invest more heavily, thereby accumulating human capital at a more rapid rate – initially at an increasing rate. Over the life cycle total capital stock is theorised to rise at a diminishing rate, peaking some years before retirement, then depreciating.

Potential earnings are proportional to capital and thus mirror the time profile of accumulated human capital assets. Observed earnings differ from potential earnings by the amount the individual is investing, and considerably understate potential earnings early in the life cycle. Concavity of the earnings profile has thus been explained. We leave for the next chapter the question of why education raises the height of earnings profiles.

Appendix 2.1 Present values and discounting

The simplified annuity formula

Suppose an investment is expected to bring in $1,000 a year over a certain period, say four years. By using the formula for calculating present values we can work out what this investment would be worth now as a capital sum. To calculate present value requires 'discounting' the future stream of returns. The rate of discount usually used is the market interest rate since this shows the opportunity cost of funds. The estimated present value of the investment is then compared with its asking price to see if it is worth making.

Data for an illustrative calculation are given in table A2.1. This applies the present value formula using two discount rates, 5% and 10%, to an investment providing $1,000 per year income for four years. The present value formula is:

$$\text{PV}(i) = \frac{Y_1}{(1 + i)} + \frac{Y_2}{(1 + i)^2} + \frac{Y_3}{(1 + i)^3} + \ldots + \frac{Y_t}{(1 + i)^t},$$

where $\text{PV}(i)$ is the present value of the income stream discounted at interest rate i measured in decimal points, i.e., 5% is written as 0.05; $Y_1, Y_2, \ldots$, etc. is the income received each year; t is the number of years over which income is expected to be received.

In the example of table A2.1, $t = 4$, and $Y_1 = Y_2 = Y_3 = Y_4 = \$1,000$. The present value of the investment can be seen to be $3,546 if $i = 0.05$, and $3,169 if $i = 0.10$.

The present value formula above can be written more simply where the income (Y) received is the same each year as in our example. The formula is then called the 'annuity' formula:

$$\text{PV}(i) = (Y/i)(1 - 1/(1 + i)^t).$$

This is derived as follows. Using the basic formula and assuming $Y_1 = Y_2 = Y_3 = \ldots = Y_t = Y$, we can write

$$\text{PV}(i) = Y[1/(1 + i) + 1/(1 + i)^2 + \ldots + 1/(1 + i)^t].$$

The expression in square brackets is a 'geometric progression' (GP) with each succeeding term multiplied by a common factor, $1/(1 + i)$. The formula for taking the sum of a GP is:

$$A(1 - F^t)/(1 - F),$$

where A is the first term ($1/(1 + i)$ in our case), t is the number of terms, and F is the common factor (also $1/(1 + i)$ in our case). Substituting into the formula gives:

Table A2.1. *Present value of $1,000 per annum received for 4 years, at various discount rates*

Return	$1/(1 + 0.05)^t$	5%	$1/(1 + 0.10)^t$	10%
$1,000 at end of				
first year, $t = 1$	0.952	$952	0.909	$909
$1,000, $t = 2$	0.904	$907	0.826	$826
$1,000, $t = 3$	0.864	$864	0.751	$751
$1,000, $t = 4$	0.822	$822	0.783	$783
Present value		$3,546		$3,169[a]

Note:
[a] Notice how $3,169 can also be derived from the annuity formula, $PV(i) = (Y/i)(1 - 1/(1 + i)^t)$ using $i = 10\%$ and $t = 4$. Thus: $PV(10\%) = (\$1,000/0.01)(1 - 1.1^{-4}) = \$10,000 (1 - 0.68) = \$3,169$.

$$PV(i) = (Y/i)(1 - 1/(1 + i)^t), \text{ as above.}$$

This formula becomes simpler still if t is large, say, above 30, because then the last term in the brackets becomes approximately zero. For example if $i = 10\%$ and $t = 30$ then $1/(1 + i)^t = 0.054$; and if $t = 50$, $1/(1 + i)^t = 0.0085$. So if t is greater than thirty years we can write:

$$PV(i) \cong Y/i.$$

Thus $1,000 received for thirty years and discounted at 10% would have a present value of approximately $10,000. This is the *simplified annuity formula* and is used frequently in human capital analysis.

Notice how the present value of an investment is higher: the higher are the annual returns from the investment (Y), the lower is the discount rate (i), and the larger is the period over which the returns are forthcoming (t). This is what you would expect using common sense. The question we now face is what discount rate should be used to compute the PV: To answer this we have to bring the asking price of the investment into the analysis, and also consider what alternative investments are available.

Investment appraisal

Continuing with the example of table A2.1, suppose that the asking price (C) of the investment were $3,546. We know that $PV(5\%) = \$3,546$, so the problem is whether to buy the investment. Whether we buy the investment or not depends on whether we can get more than 5% on our money elsewhere.

The rate of discount usually used to evaluate investments (the criterion rate of discount) is the market rate of interest. For example suppose that 10% was being offered for funds deposited at the local bank. Then $3,169 deposited at the bank could provide $1,000 per annum for four years – with nothing in the account at the end of the period. The reasoning is as follows: deposit $3,169 at the beginning of year 1. By the end of the year it has grown to $3,169 + $317 = $3,486. Pay out $1,000. The beginning balance in year 2 is then $2,486 which grows to $2,486 + $249 = $2,735. Pay out $1,000. The beginning balance in year 3 is then $1,735 and the process continues. At the end of year 4 exactly $1,000 remains to be paid out.

This $1,000 per year for four years at an initial cost of $3,169 is better than an investment which costs $3,546 for the same income stream. In fact only if the price of the investment fell to $3,169 would it even be worth contemplating. And since human (and industrial) investments are risky, while the local bank is not, the price would have to fall considerably below $3,169 before it were worth buying the investment given market interest rates of 10%.

Before going any further it is necessary to define the 'internal rate of return' (IR) on an investment. The IR is a special rate of discount:

$$PV(IR) = C.$$

In other words the internal rate of return ('rate of return' for short) is that rate of discount which makes the present value of income from an investment equal the investment's asking price. For example in table A2.1 the IR for the investment if $C = \$3,546$ is 5%. If C dropped to $3,169 the IR would rise to 10%.

When working out whether to buy an investment or not, that is, when 'appraising' an investment, it has to be determined whether the investment's IR is greater than the market interest rate (r) plus an appropriate risk premium (p). In symbols the rule is:

if $IR > r + p$, buy the investment;
if $IR < r + p$, do not buy.

We know that $C = PV(IR) = Y/IR$ so that $IR = Y/C$ using the simplified annuity formula. Therefore it follows from the above rules that, if an investment is to be bought:

$$Y/C > r + p.$$

For example if the market interest rate were 10%, and the risk premium 5%, Y/C would have to be greater than 15%.

The investment rule can be translated into just a comparison of the asking price and the present value of returns. The present value of the returns evaluated at a discount rate of $r + p$ is:

$$PV(r + p) = Y/(r + p).$$

If $Y/C > r + p$ in accordance with our previous rule, then $Y/(r + p) > C$ and therefore $PV(r + p) > C$. Thus if the present value of the returns discounted at the market interest rate plus a risk premium is greater than the case price, the investment should be considered.

Why discount the future?

Two answers to this question are generally given. The first is that individuals as consumers prefer present satisfactions to future satisfactions. The average person has a 'positive time preference' in the jargon, or, to put it in another way, he or she discounts the future at some rate. In order to persuade people to save and lend their money to business a positive rate of interest has therefore to be given. Thus for $100 given up now, $110 has to be promised in the future if people discount the future at 10% per annum.

The other answer to the question relates to the productivity of investment. By investing in machinery we can make $100 invested now grow into $110 next year (or more or less depending on the quality of the investment). It is because more can be produced with machinery than without, that businessmen can in fact pay potential savers a sufficient rate of interest to make them overcome their time preference and save.

Notice that in all the above we have been ignoring inflation, that is, taking real and money rates of interest as equal. In practice rates of interest are quoted in money or 'nominal' terms. The relation between the real and nominal rate of interest is approximately:

$$r = M - \Delta P/P,$$

where r is the real rate of interest, M is the money rate of interest, $\Delta P/P$ is the rate of inflation. The long-term real rate of interest is probably 3% to 4% (this was the rate assumed by economists in the eighteenth and nineteenth centuries, before inflation). If inflation is about 10%, then the nominal rate of interest is 13% to 14%. Given a nominal return on your investment you subtract the rate of inflation to get the real return.

3   Schooling

3.1 Introduction

In chapter 2 earnings profiles were introduced. It was argued that these profiles were related to human capital stocks accumulated over the life cycle. Human capital stocks were determined by individuals rationally choosing the proportion of time devoted to investment at each age. A rationale based on the finite life constraint served as reason for greater specialisation in investment activity for the young compared to the old. This led to greater human capital accumulation at young ages and hence a concave earnings profile.

In this chapter we concentrate on the initial life-cycle phase. Here specialisation occurs so that individuals literally spend all their time devoted to human capital investment. Such specialisation is defined as schooling. The questions we ask are: How does one picture potential earnings during the schooling phase? Can the returns to schooling be analytically measured? Why do individuals differ in their amounts of school? And finally, what role does government policy play in influencing both the levels of schooling across the population and the returns to the educational process?

3.2 Human capital specialisation

It is useful to define 'schooling' as being the period in which 100% of one's time is devoted to earnings enhancement. Recall the human capital production function described in chapter 2 and illustrated in table 2.1. The production function shows the amount of human capital created as a function of one's time investment fraction, s_t, holding constant innate ability and initial capital stock. Because the time investment fraction can at most be 100%, human capital output, Q_t, has an upper bound. This upper bound is depicted in figure 3.1. As drawn, the marginal benefits of investment are so high that we obtain equilibrium on the vertical region of the marginal cost curve, implying full-time investment. This must be true during all years in which the individual is going to school.

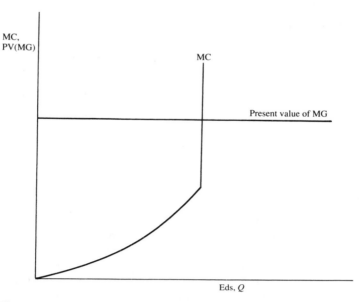

Figure 3.1 Marginal cost and marginal gain curves for human capital in the school period

In any year at school, one's human capital stock rises in accordance with one's success that year in school, and this enhances the maximum Q_t that can be created in following years. The increased human capital production capacity attributable to schooling is reflected in the cost curves associated with human capital production. As one's human capital stock grows, one's capacity for production grows and hence, the vertical segment of the marginal cost curve in figure 3.1 shifts to the right.

The movement of the marginal cost and marginal benefit curves during the schooling period is illustrated in figure 3.2. The MCLR curve is the long-run marginal cost curve for producing human capital under the assumption that there exist no time or human capital stock constraints. Thus, if one were not bounded in any way, marginal costs of human capital production would be determined by MC. However, two constraints exist for any individual. First there is the constraint that the investment fraction, s_t, cannot be greater than 100%. Secondly that the capital available for investment is limited to the capital that one has accumulated in previous years. The way the marginal cost curves MC_1, MC_2, etc. . . . , move outwards reflect the progressive relaxation of these constraints on marginal cost.

The marginal gain from investment curves are depicted by the horizontal

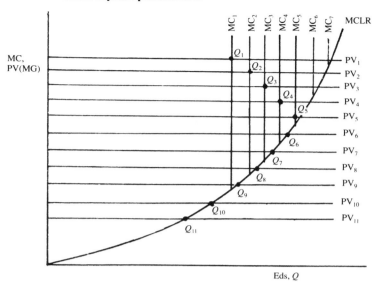

Figure 3.2 The sequence of human capital outputs during and after school

line segments PV_1, PV_2, . . . , PV_{11}. As was discussed in the last chapter, these curves necessarily become lower with each year due to the finite life constraint. Equilibrium investment in each year is determined by the intersection of marginal cost and marginal gain curves for each year. Hence, investment in period one reflects the optimal investment determined by equating MC_1 with PV_1. Similarly, investment in period two is obtained by equating MC_2 with PV_2. The optimal quantities of human capital produced are traced out by the appropriate intersection of these curves and depicted in figure 3.2 by the equilibria Q_1, Q_2, . . . , Q_{11}. Note that in the initial periods the optimal quantity of investment increases, but that after period five it declines in a regular fashion.

The number of years in school can be determined by the number of years in which the equilibria fall on the vertical marginal cost segments. In figure 3.2, the individual obtains five years of schooling. In each of these five years, the equilibrium occurs on the vertical portions of the marginal cost of investment curves. Only beginning with period six is an equilibrium reached on the long-run marginal cost curve. In period 6 the individual has left school.

Certain earnings profiles are implied by the investment paths of figure 3.2. Actual earnings will be zero while one is in school, then jump upwards when one has one's first job, then continue increasing, but at a decreasing rate. 'Capacity earnings' will be higher than observed earnings and – after school –

rise at a slower rate. During school however capacity earnings rise at an increasing rate.

3.3 The rate of return to schooling

Schooling is an intra-marginal decision. It comes about when individuals are not able to equate marginal costs and benefits of investment, but instead are on the vertical region of the MC curve. This implies that individuals would rather invest more than they do, but are constrained by limited time resources. As such, for each unit of schooling bought the present value of marginal gain exceeds marginal cost. This has two implications: (1) that the benefits of each year of schooling, at least up until the last year, exceed the costs, and (2) that the gap between benefits and costs diminishes for each year of schooling. These implications can be cast in terms of a benefit-to-cost ratio.

Define the ratio of schooling benefits to schooling costs as the rate of return to education. Theory then dictates, first, a rate of return exceeding the market interest rate, and second, a diminishing rate of return per incremental year of schooling. Thus, the benefits of elementary school exceed those of high school, college, and so on.

Let us be more rigorous. Figure 2.4 of chapter 2 depicts a typical age–earnings profile for a high school and a college graduate. In that figure, extra earnings were depicted as the gains from extra schooling while the foregone earnings were depicted as the costs. An 'internal rate of return' was defined as that interest rate which just equated the costs and benefits of education. Thus the interest rate that equates the present value of the returns to costs is the internal rate of return.

More technically, the internal rate of return can be computed as follows. The stream of extra income from s years of schooling is:

$$w\Delta K_s = w(K_{t+s} - K_t), \tag{3.1}$$

where K_{t+s} is the stock of eds after s years, K_t is the stock prior to beginning the s years, w is the wage rate per ed (human capital rental rate). Remember that $w\Delta K_s$ is a monetary amount per unit time, say per year. This implies that in each and every year after gaining the s years of education one's earnings are enhanced by $w\Delta K_s$ per year.

Costs are equal to foregoine earnings plus direct costs of investment (books, fees). Denote the cost of s years schooling as C_s. To compute the internal rate of return on the s years of investment, r_s, set C_s equal to the present value of the gains discounted at rate r_s (remember the annuity formula), thus:

$$C_s = w\Delta K_s/r_s,$$

or:

$$r_s = w\Delta K_s/C_s. \tag{3.2}$$

A further year of schooling would normally have a lower rate of return for a given individual (we are ignoring indivisibilities caused by the fact that education courses last a fixed number of years, so buying just one year might be impossible). Marginal costs rise as one invests in the production of more eds because we assume there are diminishing returns to human capital production (remember the human capital production function). An extra year in school also slightly reduces one's labour market period, and thus the present value of the income gain from the year. So the internal rate of return to $s + 1$ years of education is:

$$r_{s+1} = w\Delta K_{s+1}/C_{s+1}, \tag{3.3}$$

where K_{s+1}, C_{s+1} are the returns and costs respectively of $s + 1$ years of education. We expect that while the individual remains at school:

$$r_s > r_{s+1} > i, \tag{3.4}$$

where i is some 'market' interest rate (see below). Eventually, however, by the n-th year of schooling we will reach equality:

$$r_n = i. \tag{3.5}$$

The individual will then stop this form of investment, and so end the period of full-time education.

Take a numerical example as an application. Assume that the starting wage for a given college graduate is \$22,000, while her wage as a high school graduate would be \$15,000. Also assume that this \$7,000 differential between college and high school is perpetuated over the life cycle. This implies that the present value of gains from college equals \$7,000/i. As for the costs, nowadays the cost of four years of college can be about \$7,000 per year for direct costs, and \$15,000 per year for indirect costs. For four years of schooling (and neglecting the discounting of costs), the full cost of schooling would be \$22,000 per year, or \$88,000. According to equation (3.2), the internal rate of return on four years of college, r_4, can be computed as \$7,000/\$88,000 or about 8%. This figure is well above the long-run real rate of interest which is about 3% to 4% – though we should be careful to note that it is a rough estimate. This individual would stay on further years at college until the return on the marginal year was about 3% or 4%. (This reasoning ignores complications such as allowing for risk, which we take in below.)

Many studies compute aggregate rates of return to education. These entail computations for various population strata, such as for blacks compared to whites; for males compared to females; for specific types of education, such as for medical education compared to professional and trade schools; as well

Table 3.1. *Primary, secondary, and higher education: private rates of return*

Country	Year	Primary	Secondary	Higher
Australia	1976			16.4
Belgium	1960		17.1	6.7
Canada	1961		11.7	14.0
Denmark	1964			7.8
France	1962	14.3	11.5	9.3
	1976	13.5	10.8	9.3
Germany	1964			4.6
	1978		6.5	10.5
Great Britain	1971		14.0	27.0
	1978		11.0	23.0
Italy	1969		17.3	18.3
Japan	1967			10.5
	1980			8.3
Netherlands	1965		8.5	10.4
New Zealand	1966		20.0	14.7
Norway	1966		7.4	7.7
Sweden	1967			10.3
United States	1969		18.8	15.4
	1976		11.0	5.3

Source: Psacharopoulos, 1985, appendix A-1.

as for a host of other groups for which rate of return estimates are possible. As an example table 3.1 provides private rate of return estimates by country and education level.

What is interesting is that the rate of return estimates seem reasonable in terms of magnitude. Rates of return to primary education are relatively high, (at least in France), then the rates tend to decline with increasing levels of education. At the higher education levels, rarely does a rate of return exceed 20%, and rarely are there negative returns. This is consistent with the theory of investment already discussed. Nevertheless, despite the uniformity of computed rates of return, certain variations exist (British rates of return as illustrated are 11% for secondary, and 23% for higher education, but in fact most British studies do not have this peculiar reversal). This is not unnatural and as shall be explained shortly, comes about primarily because of population heterogeneity in the costs and benefits of financing investments. Put differently financing costs, abilities and other factors vary across the population so as to yield varying rates of return.

'Public' rates of return to education can also be computed. These differ from private rates of return primarily in including the full costs of tuition. The

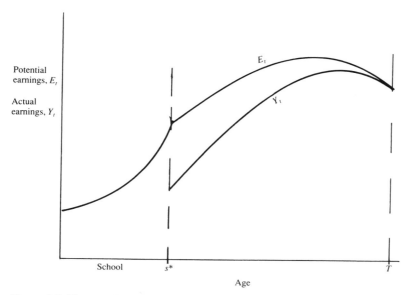

Figure 3.3 The actual and potential earnings profiles over the lifetime

productivity (increased earnings) payoff from the public point of view should also be computed pre-tax, rather than post-tax. Because public costs are higher than private costs, public rates of return to education are generally lower than private rates. A British government computation of the public rate of return to university level education put it at 5%, compared to a 22% private rate (Department of Education, 1988, 40). This might be thought to be economically efficient since the state can (and should) apply a lower discount rate than private individuals. However it could be that the state earns a low rate of return on its education investments because public education programmes are over-expanded since powerful pressure groups (teachers' unions, public officials) stand to gain from a large education sector. We take up the issue of public policy in a later section; let us now consider the reasons for differences in educational attainment.

3.4 Differences in educational attainment

Supply and demand analysis

Why do individuals differ in their amounts of school? This is an important question for several reasons. In the *first* place it seems that those who are well educated earn considerably more than those who are not. Exactly how much more is a matter of controversy into which we will inquire – but there is no doubt about the effect. *Secondly*, given that education influences pay, there is the point that government policy might be able materially to help the disadvantaged. Education is heavily subsidised in both America and Britain. A reason advanced for the subsidy is that it represents a concrete way in which the taxpayer can help the poor – by improving skills. We will consider this topic in the last section of this chapter.

Thirdly, the question of differences in educational attainment is interesting because of the light it throws on the different opportunities and abilities of individuals. Since education increases pay, what stops all people becoming equally well educated? Presumably the benefits and/or the costs of spending extra years at school differ among individuals. In particular, as we will see, individuals from poorer families are likely to spend less time at school. Individuals born poor thus tend to become poor themselves – there is 'positive feed-back', so poverty is transmitted across generations.

Looking at variations in the demand for education, we might expect cleverer individuals to stay at school for longer. Such individuals could have a lower MC curve and/or a higher and more slowly declining sequence of PV curves, and thus have a longer period of disequilibrium. Looking at the MC curve, its shape is determined by the human capital production function and the wage rate per ed. An individual with high ability might be expected to have a higher production function and consequently lower marginal costs (see figure 2.5 in chapter 2). However this is not certain because strictly speaking the human capital production function does not relate to years spent in school. It relates ed inputs to ed outputs. Over a given year a more able person will invest more inputs and get more out. His/her capital stock and value of earnings foregone will increase more rapidly than for the less able, and he/she might leave school earlier. In terms of figure 3.2, the vertical section of the MC curve for the able person is to the right of that for the less able, and disequilibrium will last for a shorter period of time. If the MC curve simply has a shallower slope, however, the able person will stay at school longer.

Looking at the PV curve, this depends on $w\Delta K$, the earnings increment subsequent to a school investment, and the discount rate. The higher is $w\Delta K$ and the lower the discount rate the higher will be the PV curve and the longer the school period. As shown by equation (3.1), $w\Delta K$ depends on w and the eds produced in the school course. An able person could produce more eds and thus experience a higher ΔK. This would be a factor predisposing cleverer pupils to stay at school longer. Also a person with 'connections', or good information might achieve a better w than average (in chapter 8, on information, we drop the assumption that w is constant across individuals). He or she will stay longer at school for this reason – though a high w will also shift the MC curve upwards.

In sum, we can only say that the more able will (probably) stay at school longer, as will those who enjoy learning. We can view these factors as constituting the 'demand' for education. Further, those who face lower interest rates or who have access to student loans or grants, will stay at school longer. This is the 'supply of funds' side of the model.

We have not spoken much about the desire to be educated for its own sake, that is, the consumption benefits of education. Clearly an individual who enjoys school will stay on longer. The education of the parents might have a role to play here, in promoting academic values. A person viewing school in part as a consumption opportunity can be pictured as discounting the returns from education at a lower rate, and being prepared to borrow more than purely financial considerations would imply. However the fact that the rate of return to college education does not appear to be widely different from physical capital returns militates against a simple consumption explanation of education (Lazear, 1977).

Let us now consider in more detail the supply of funds. We should note in the first place that it is difficult to raise money to finance human capital acquisition, since such capital does not serve as good collateral for a loan. Most legal systems will not permit employers and workers to agree to bind themselves to a specific labour contract. In the absence of such a contract loans cannot be easily secured. Banks will lend some money, but at high rates of interest, and the sums involved will be small in relation to the profit from education that a student can reasonably expect. Generally the government has to step in to guarantee such loans. Another factor making commercial loans hard to come by is the youth of students. They do not yet have a track record. Leaving aside government, sources of funds for education are therefore limited to personal savings, or to family donations.

An individual who has to finance his or her education out of savings is likely to apply a high discount rate. Abstinence is not easy. The poorer a person the more difficult abstinence becomes – in accordance with the principle of the diminishing marginal utility of money, which here implies that the marginal utility of money will increase as less is held. On the other hand, a person who can rely on family donations will apply a low discount rate – such a person's family foregoes interest at the bank deposit rate (say), which is lower than the rate which banks charge on loans. There is also the point that families might think it prudent to bequeath human rather than physical capital to their children, and will therefore 'subsidise' its acquisition. Human capital is less likely to be squandered, perhaps – particularly if we remember that parents are in a good position to assess the propensities of their offspring.

The above factors all point to the (implicit) cost of funds being lower for

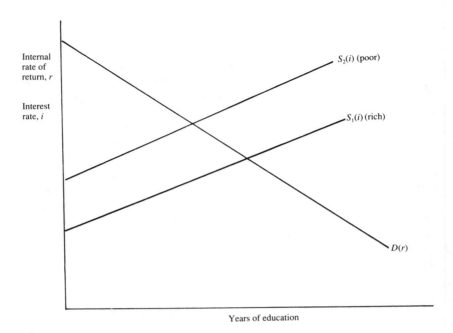

Figure 3.4 Supply and demand determination of education

children from better-off families. We would expect such children to stay at school for longer because it is cheaper for them to do so. The arguments summarised here form the basis of the equity argument for the state subsidising the education of children from poor homes.

Figure 3.4 illustrates the position using supply and demand curves. The supply curve shows the supply of funds to be a function of the discount rate, i, employed by the individual. The poor will face higher discount rates other things equal – indicated as curve S_2. The demand curve shows the internal rate of return to education, r, as a function of the number of years of education. It is downward sloping because of the assumption of diminishing returns to education. Once i becomes equal to r the individual leaves school, as shown in equation (3.5). According to this diagram children from poor homes should experience higher rates of return to education than children from rich families – there is some evidence that they do (see Siebert, 1989).

Summarising the supply of funds side, this depends on family funds, student aid, and the general availability of funds. This last variable we can think of as being indicated by the general level of interest rates: if interest rates are high, then credit is tight, and vice versa. Of all these factors we have argued that

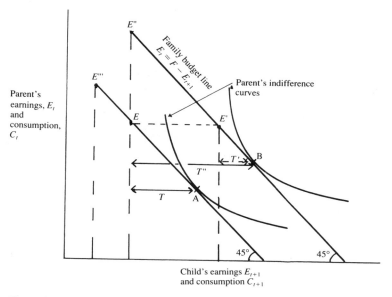

Figure 3.5 Transfers within the family

family funds have the most impact, though student aid has become increasingly important over time as government student subsidies have become more widespread.

Transfers within the family – the Becker–Tomes model

As we have noted, parents make the main decisions about their children's education, and – despite government subsidies – are the main source of funds. Children from poorer families therefore receive less human capital investment. The higher cost of funds for the poor is a major source of inequality of opportunity, and hence of transmission of inequality across generations. It is therefore useful to consider the determinants of income transfers between parents and children more closely.

The basic Becker–Tomes (1979) model is illustrated in figure 3.5. The parent's utility curves (let us assume only one parent) are shown with respect to his/her consumption and his/her (only) child's consumption. The diagram is meant to relate to 'lifetime' consumption and earnings, so we can represent everything in one period. The parent is an altruist (values the child's consumption), and so makes income transfers to the child – but these transfers will also depend on the child's own earnings.

The family budget constraint, F, is the sum of the child's earnings, E_{t+1}, and the parent's earnings, E_t:

$$F = E_{t+1} + E_t,$$

which is a line with -45 degrees slope as shown (ignoring discounting of the child's income for simplicity). The child's consumption, C_{t+1}, is equal to his/her income plus transfers, T, from the parent:

$$C_{t+1} = E_{t+1} + T.$$

Similarly the parent's consumption equals his/her income minus his/her transfers, $C_t = E_t - T$. So we can write:

$$F = C_{t+1} + C_t,$$

which is the same -45 degrees sloped line – the parent moves up and down it by varying transfers, T. Starting from point E, for example, with the given indifference curve, the parent will transfer T, moving to point A. The transfer will not only be food and clothing for young children, but also expenses for education, and perhaps, later, inheritances.

The figure can be used to illustrate several aspects of intergenerational transfers. *Firstly* a clever child will receive a smaller transfer (schooling investment, say), given the parent's income, than a dull child. This is because the clever child will be seen by its parents as earning a lot in later life, and therefore not needing so much from the family. To demonstrate, suppose the budget line starts from E', with higher child's income but the same parental income. The new equilibrium will be at B, and B will normally be north-east of A (child's consumption is a normal good for the parent), so the transfer, T', will be smaller. Within the family, parental transfers tend to be equalising.

Secondly, increased parental income will increase transfers to the child, but the increase in transfers will be less than the increase in parental income. The proportion of income given by parents in the form of educational finance for their children will tend to decline as parents become richer. This is a factor making for 'regression to the mean', that is, making children of the rich less rich (and children of the poor less poor) than their parents.

The concept of regression to the mean is illustrated in figure 3.6. Suppose the relation between parent's and child's earnings is given by:

$$E_{t+1} = a + bE_t.$$

The regression line has slope b, and cuts the 45 degree line at the average income level $\bar{E}$, assuming that average incomes are unchanging over the generations. If b is less than unity and a is positive, then equality falls with time, that is, there is regression towards the mean. Therefore b measures the extent to which the children of rich parents tend to be less rich than their

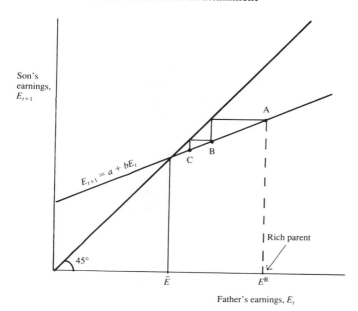

Figure 3.6 Regression towards the mean

parents. (The concept began with analysis of heights: children of tall parents tend to be less tall, so regress towards the mean.) For example, start with a rich parent, with earnings E_R; the child's income can be read off the regression line as A, and his/her child will have a child with earnings B, and so on to C until the mean is reached. It can be seen that the closer is b to unity, the closer is the regression line to the 45 degree line, and the lower is 'intergenerational mobility'. In a 'classless society' we want a low b.

Thirdly, returning to figure 3.5, while richer parents will make larger transfers to their children, the importance of transfers in the form of educational expenditures is lower for richer families. There is only so much education you can give your child, no matter how wealthy you are. Once the rate of return on a child's education has reached the rate of return on physical capital, the parent will make further transfers in the form of physical capital. There is thus a limit to how unequal the education distribution can be, and a limit therefore to education as a source of earnings inequality. This limit is a further factor reducing b in figure 3.6, and speeding up regression to the mean.

Finally, forced transfers from parent to child, or vice versa – that leave family income unchanged – will not affect either's consumption. Take point E''' in figure 3.5, which is on the same family budget line as E, and represents higher parent's income with the child's income lowered by an equal amount.

Equilibrium is unchanged at A, because the parent simply transfers more. For example, transfers from the child to the parent will be matched by increased voluntary transfers the other way – from parent to child. Thus a big national debt need not favour parental consumption at the cost of burdening later generations with taxes, because parents will increase their savings and transfers to children – the 'Ricardian equivalence theorem' (the theorem states that government bonds are not net wealth, i.e., that people feel no better off if the government borrows than if it increases taxes – see Barro, 1989, for a recent discussion).

Similarly, taxing parents to subsidise children's education will mean that parents try to reduce their voluntary transfers in other ways, for example by reducing their private educational expenditures. Clearly these countervailing parental decisions can frustrate government attempts to target educational expenditures at poorer families (and so increase regression to the mean), as we will see when discussing policy.

3.5 Individual differences in education: empirical examples

Father's occupation and education

It is worth starting with a picture of the relationship between family background and education. Such a picture is given in table 3.2 for males in Britain and America. We want to compare the two countries, since a finding of similar family background importance in two different countries is a stronger result. The table uses father's occupation as the measure of family background. It would have been preferable to use 'family wealth', but this is difficult to measure. In fact the occupation of the head of the household is not such a bad measure of that family's long-term wealth.

The table uses an 'education index' rather than years of education. The index is the person's years of education multiplied by 0.05, which was the rate of return to education (estimated from a full earnings regression) in the two samples. The index was also adjusted for whether the person had a university degree or higher degree, and whether he had been to a selective school in the British case. But these adjustments were not large and need not detain us. The index translates education increments into pay increments.

The first coefficient in table 3.2 under the UK column, 0.173, shows that a person with a professional category father had an education that was significantly higher than a person with a father in the base category (foreman or skilled manual). His extra education increased his pay by about 17.3%. Similarly, a person with a professional father in the US had more education than the base category, so that his pay was 14.5% higher on average. Looking

Table 3.2. *Regression of education index on father's occupational category, white non-farm males, 1972, 1973*

Father's occupation		UK		US
Professional		0.173*		0.145*
Employer or manager		0.117*		0.125*
Clerical or sales		0.079*		0.077*
Foreman or skilled manual		—	Base	—
Semi-skilled		−0.013		−0.007
Labourer		−0.037*		−0.066*
Farmer or farm manager		0.014		−0.048
Member of armed forces		0.036*		−0.018
	N	4647		1311
	R^2	0.134		0.128

Notes: *denotes coefficient significantly different from zero at the 5% level.
Sample: White male heads of household, outside agriculture.
Education index: This is the person's years of education multiplied by 0.05, the rate of return to education in the two samples. For example, a person with ten years of education would have an index value of 0.5 (= 10 × 0.05). His earnings would be approximately 50% greater as a result of the education. The coefficients therefore show the effect of education on pay.
Source: UK – General Household Survey, 1972; US – Panel Study of Income Dynamics, 1973.

at the other end of the scale, respondents with labourer fathers have lower education levels: in the UK they earn 3.7% less than the base category due to less education, and in the US about 6.6% less.

Comparing the two countries we see quite a similar pattern of coefficients, with children from families headed by a professional having the most education grading down to those with labourer fathers having the least. Children from poor backgrounds are as backward relative to the better-off children in the American sample as in the British. In the UK the difference in expected income on the basis of education alone as between a labourer and a professional worker's child is .173 + .037 = .210, i.e., the latter would earn 21% more than the former. The equivalent figure for the US is almost the same, .145 + .066 = .211. We interpret this as indicating that children from poorer families are less well able to afford lengthy periods at school. It is interesting that two countries, with different methods of state education subsidy, give such similar results for the importance of family background for educational attainment.

Studies of twins and brothers/sisters

Studies of brothers and sisters are interesting because brothers and sisters come from the same family, which allows us to hold constant a more comprehensive measure of family background than simply father's occupation. If one brother/sister differs in educational attainment from another brother/sister this is not likely to be due to important differences in home environment, or differential access to funds for education (though parents could spend more on educating their less clever children as noted above). Differences in education as between pairs or brothers/sisters are likely to be mainly due to differences in ability. However, if identical (monozygotic) twins are compared this also rules out any genetic variation (such as might lead to differences in ability). Differences in identical twins' education can be attributed to errors in measuring education, or to 'luck'.

In terms of the supply and demand curves of figure 3.4, the family wealth factor impacts on the supply curve, while the ability (genetic) factor impacts on the demand curve. Assessing the importance of these two sources of variation, shows us whether it is 'inequality of opportunity' which causes education differences, or inequality of ability. Government policies are designed to equalise education opportunities (the same supply curve for all). These policies will have less of a role to play if in fact it is differences in ability which drive educational attainments.

Before turning to the data let us construct a model which will allow us to proceed from the measured correlations between brothers'/sisters' education to the unobserved 'family background' factor, B. Suppose one of the pair has:

$$U = mB + v, \qquad\qquad\qquad (3.6)$$

where U is educational attainment and v is the error term. The other party has:

$$U' = mB + v'.$$

This simple model assumes each brother/sister has the same link, m, between B and U. As for complications such as differences in ability, this problem can be avoided by assuming B includes ability that is a consequence of background. Remaining elements of ability are not correlated with B, and are included in the error term (see appendix for a fuller explanation).

The measure of education can be years at school, E. It is usually best to transform this variable thus:

$$U = (E - \bar{E})/\sigma_e,$$

where $\bar{E}$ is average education for the sample, and σ_e is the standard deviation of education in the sample. This means that the mean of U will be zero, and its standard deviation will be unity, which is convenient. We can think of the unobserved family background variable being calibrated in this way, too, with mean zero and standard deviation unity – this is the least arbitrary choice of units.

Now calculate the correlation between U and U' for a sample of pairs or brothers (or sisters), or identical twins. It can be shown (see appendix) that the correlation coefficient, $r_{uu'}$, is related to m as follows:

$$r_{uu'} = m^2.$$

(3.7)

Thus the root of the correlation coefficient measures m. For example if the correlation between brothers/sisters is 0.81, then $m = 0.9$. This means that if the family has a B value one standard deviation above average, the children have an education level 0.9 standard deviations above average.

Table 3.3 gives some illustrations of pairs of sisters having different correlations between their educations. Example 1 illustrates the technique, using a perfect correlation. Example 2 illustrates the point that the mean of the variable under consideration does not affect the value of the correlation. Example 3 shows that the correlation coefficient and the regression slope need not be the same. (In fact however, when comparing pairs of brothers or sisters the correlation and the regression slope will have the same value because the standard deviation of education for brother/sister 1 will be the same as the standard deviation for brother/sister 2, since the ordering is arbitrary.)

We can also show that the error variance, σ_v (a measure of the scatter of the observations around the regression line), and the correlation coefficient add up to one:

$$1 = r_{uu'} + \sigma_v.$$

(3.8)

In other words, the higher the correlation coefficient, the smaller must be the error term in (3.6). The correlation coefficient can be thought of as measuring the proportion of variation in education 'explained' by common family background. A correlation of 0.8, for example, implies that 80% of variation in education is related to variations in family background, B, leaving 20% to be explained by other factors.

Table 3.4 gives the results of comparing brothers' education levels in different samples. The correlation coefficients are around 0.54 for brothers and non-identical twins, though higher, 0.76, for identical twins. In accordance with equation (3.8), we can take the 0.54 figure as indicating that the full effect of brothers' shared background explains 54% of differences in brothers' educational attainment. This is considerably higher than the 12% to 13% explained by father's occupation alone, as we would expect. The higher correlation between identical twins, 0.76, presumably indicates the effect of the twins' extra genetic resemblance in abilities and tastes.

It is possible to do a back of the envelope calculation, breaking down the

Table 3.3. *Illustrative correlations between pairs of sisters in four families*

Example 1: Perfect correlation, regression slope unity

	Sister 1	Sister 2
Family: 1	0	0
2	0	0
3	1	1
4	1	1

Example 2: Zero correlation (even though mean is 10.5)

	Sister 1	Sister 2
Family: 1	10	10
2	11	10
3	10	11
4	11	11

Example 3: Correlation = 0.71

	Sister 1	Sister 2
Family: 1	0.3	0
2	0.8	0.5
3	0.3	0.5
4	0.8	1

Note: Correlation, r, between x and y is:

$$r = \text{cov}(x,y)/\sigma_x\sigma_y, \text{ where } \text{cov}(x,y) = \Sigma\, x\,y/N - \bar{x}\,\bar{y},$$

where cov (x,y) = covariance between x and y, and σ denotes standard deviation. The slope, b, of a regression of x on y is:

$$b = \text{cov}(x,y)/\sigma_y^2 = r\,\sigma_x/\sigma_y.$$

Thus $r = b$ if $\sigma_x = \sigma_y$. In example 3, regressing sister 1 on 2 (2 on 1) gives $b \cong .5$ ($b \cong 1.0$).

family background effect into its nature (genes) and nurture (family wealth) components. The best way to do this is to compare identical twins who have been reared apart. In such circumstances the pairs share all their genes, but no family environment, so it is possible to work out the effects of genes alone. Unfortunately such results are not available for education – but IQ comparisons have been made for pairs of identical twins reared apart. The results of such comparisons are included in table 3.4 for the sake of interest. It can be seen that the IQ correlation for identical twins reared together is not much higher than the correlation for twins reared apart, implying that family wealth as such is not a very important determinant of IQ. Genes alone explain about 70% of the variation in IQ for this sample of forty pairs of twins.

From the education data we have, however, it is possible to make the computations illustrated in figure 3.7. Starting with the factors of measurement

Table 3.4. *Correlations between brothers' IQs and education levels*

	Correlation coefficient
Education levels	
NORC sample of brothers	0.528
Project talent sample of brothers	0.546
NAS/NRC twins: non-identical	0.54
identical	0.76
IQ	
Minnesota identical twins: reared together	0.83
reared apart	0.71

Sources: Corcoran, Jencks, and Olneck, 1976; Taubman, 1976; Bouchard, Lykken, McGue, Segal, and Tollegen, 1990.

error and luck, we would assess their contribution to variation in education as 24%. This is simply the difference between a perfect correlation, and the correlation we observe for identical twins brought up together, and who must have the same genes and family upbringing. As for the genetic factor, a view on this is provided by the difference in the correlation between brothers, and identical twins. Brothers (and non-identical twins) share half their genes, on average, while identical twins share all their genes. So the increase in the correlation from 0.54 to 0.76 can be attributed to the extra 50% of genetic similarity. If there were no genetic similarity, on this reasoning, the correlation should fall to 0.32, what we would observe for unrelated individuals brought up together. The difference between 0 and 0.32 then gives the contribution of family background excluding genetic factors.

A somewhat more respectable method of allowing for ability is outlined in the appendix. But our simple method gives quite similar results. In any case, whatever might be thought of attempts to separate genetic influences from family wealth influences per se, the fact is that studies of brothers/sisters and twins indicate family background, broadly interpreted, is probably as important a determinant of educational attainment as ability differences (though admittedly a recent study by Behrman and Taubman finds ability to be considerably more important than inequality of opportunity – 1989, 1427). There thus appears to remain considerable inequality of opportunity, despite government policies.

A study of the proportion attending college, by state

The influence of family wealth on educational attainment enters primarily as a supply-side factor, reducing or increasing the cost of educational funds to the student, other things equal. Also entering on the supply side will be availability of student aid, and prevailing market interest rates. On the demand side will enter factors such as average returns currently received by previous investors in education, ability, and 'tastes' for education. Such tastes might be developed in better-off families, particularly if the parents are educated – which suggests parents' education as a determining factor.

Such a model has been tested by Michael Tannen using college attendance by state. His dependent variable is the proportion of male residents of a state aged fourteen to twenty-four attending college in 1959 and 1969 (*PS*). He makes this fraction dependent on the demand and supply variables we have mentioned, in particular:

(a) foregone earnings costs of attending college, proxied by average incomes of males aged fourteen to nineteen (*FC*);
(b) direct costs of college attendance, measured by average student fees less average scholarship aid (*DC*);
(c) financial returns from college, measured as the difference in incomes between college and high school graduates in the twenty-five to forty-three age group, with 20% subtracted from the difference to allow for the presumed greater ability of college students (*R*);
(d) family wealth, measured as the average value of housing (*W*);
(e) parents' education, measured as average level of schooling of males aged forty-five to fifty-four (*PED*);
(f) market interest rate, measured as the average interest rate paid on deposits at savings and loan institutions (*i*);
(g) natural ability – assumed not to vary by state.

In the estimated equation all the variables are significant and have the expected sign (1978, 495). Elasticities (percentage change in proportion attending college consequent on percentage change in the independent variable, other variables constant) are as follows:

FC	*DC*	*R*	*W*	*PED*	*i*
-0.427	-0.264	0.154	0.365	1.01	-0.931

It can be seen that costs, both foregone (*FC*) and direct (*DC*), are negatively associated with the proportion attending college, as expected. Returns (*R*) are significantly positively associated, family wealth (*W*) and parental education (*PED*) are positively associated, and state interest rates (*i*) are negatively associated with college attendance. This is all exactly as expected.

The size of the elasticities gives an idea of the sensitivity of college attendance to percentage changes in the independent variables. According to this indicator college attendance is most sensitive to parents' education, and to the interest rate. The elasticity of college attendance with respect to direct costs is however on the small side, -0.264. This has some importance for policy

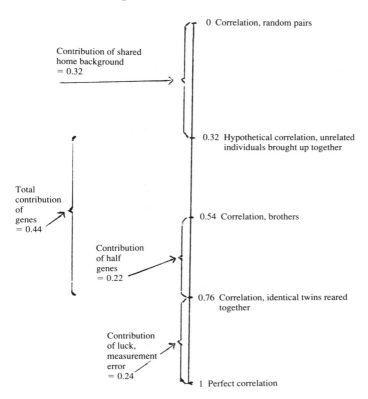

Figure 3.7 Schematic breakdown of the effects of nature and nurture on education

since subsidising direct education costs is a major method of encouraging college attendance. According to this figure an increase of 10% in average tuition assistance would only increase the proportion at college by 2.6% other things equal. To further consideration of student aid we now turn.

3.6 Subsidising education

The involvement of the state in education raises many interesting issues in political economy. In most developed countries elementary education is both compulsory and free, in the sense that the pupil does not have to pay tuition fees. The same goes for some years of high school. Then at the college level the subsidies continue, with subsidised tuition, soft loans, and even – in Britain – maintenance grants. In Britain and America education expenditures take up the major part of local government finance. Measured as a proportion of national income, government expenditure on education is generally about as large as that on defence. The question is, why is there so much state involvement? – it was not always that way. A second question is what are the consequences of the subsidies for education expansion and income redistribution?

Equity, efficiency, and public choice reasons can be advanced for the policy of subsidising education. Equity is involved because, as we have noted, since an education investment is not good collateral for loans, those from poor families will be at a disadvantage in making such investment. It might be thought equitable to direct money away from the better off so as to equalise opportunity. Economic efficiency is involved because education might have external benefits. Since such benefits are not captured by the student there will be underinvestment in education in the absence of subsidies. Externalities that might be mentioned are the effect of education in encouraging voting, and its making of a more homogeneous population with common values (Protestant values were initially stressed in Scotland, for example).

Public choice issues arise because teachers are a well-organised pressure group. It is in the interests of teachers to expand their job prospects by pressing for subsidies and compulsory education. The interests of taxpayers who are dispersed and ignorant will tend to get trampled under. This can be seen to be so particularly since teachers might be said to have plausible 'cover stories' in the form of the equity and efficiency arguments already mentioned. We now consider the above reasons for subsidising education, and the evidence, in more detail.

Equity

It is interesting to note that both the United States and England introduced fee-less elementary schooling on a nationwide basis at about the same time last century, 1867 and 1870 respectively. Scotland has had a subsidised system from as early as 1696 (see West, 1967, 1975). Teachers' groups and the educational bureaucracy played a prominent part in the passing of the legislation. For example, in New York State in the 1840s we see the Onondaga County Teachers Institute campaigning for a Free School System (West, 1967, 108).

It is in fact quite difficult to increase education expenditures made by poor families even though, as we have emphasised above, there is an equity case for such an increase. The difficulties arise firstly because the subsidies might not go to the poor, but to other less-deserving groups. Free education is not means tested. Moreover those eligible for subsidised higher education are only those who have successfully completed the lower education courses – who tend to be middle class.

Then secondly there is the fact that subsidies might to a large extent be

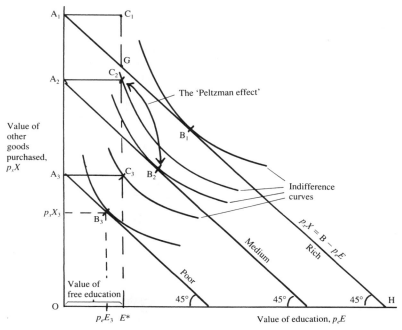

Figure 3.8 The Peltzman effect

matched by a withdrawal of private purchases, leaving the situation unchanged (but with a larger bureaucracy). We noted this possibility above when analysing the Becker–Tomes model of within-family transfers in figure 3.5. However the position can be illustrated in another way, and in fact goes by the name of the 'Peltzman effect' (see Peltzman, 1973).

The Peltzman effect, whereby some families spend *less* on education after the state introduces an education subsidy, is illustrated in figure 3.8. The subsidy considered here is a subsidy 'in kind', that is, the state does not give money, but rather subsidises schools. Families either send their children to the state school, or they do not, in which case they lose the subsidy; they cannot obtain the monetary equivalent. Three budget lines are illustrated, for a rich, a middle-income, and a poor family. They are of the form:

$$B = p_e E + p_x X,$$

where p_e and p_x are the price of education and other goods, and E and X are the amounts of education and other goods. This can be rewritten:

$$p_x X = B - p_e E,$$

Table 3.5. *Example of the distributional consequences of free state education*

Number of families	Income class	Before intervention		After intervention		
		Education per family	Total exp. on education	Value of free ed. per family	Total exp. on education	
					Public	Private
2	$100	$10	$20	$12.5	$25	0
6	200	20	120	12.5	75	0
2	300	30	60	—	—	60
			200		160	

Source: West, 1975, 195.

giving the budget lines of -45 degrees slope as shown. The poor family's budget line, for example, starts at A_3, and the family is in equilibrium at B_3, buying p_eE_3 education and p_xX_3 of other goods.

Now suppose that the government offers a certain value of education services (OE^*) free at the state school or university. The poor family would be better off moving to the corner C_3. The middle-class family would also move to a corner, in this case at C_2. However the move from C_2 to B_2 means that the children of this family are in fact getting *less* education than before. The rich family would remain at B_1. Depending upon the numbers of poor and middle-income families, it is possible that providing free education will have little effect on total education expenditures, and could even reduce them.

We might also note – if we think of the diagram as applying simply to higher education for the moment – that people not eligible for higher education will have horizontal indifference curves. They will be at points such as A_1 or A_2, and not benefit from the scheme; though they will be taxed to pay for it.

To illustrate the 'Peltzman effect' let us take the example in table 3.5. There are assumed to be ten families of equal size, with the given income distribution. Families are assumed to spend 10% of their incomes on education as shown in the third column, and total education expenditures are $200. Now we suppose that free education worth $12.5 per family is made available at government schools. Poor families will accept. Middle-income families will also accept since they must choose between private or public school: to take the former would mean giving up $12.5 to gain $7.5. Middle-income families become less educated – the Peltzman effect. (In fact, the table's emphasis on monetary values is a simplification; the Peltzman effect also depends on preferences, as figure 3.8 makes clear.) The rich families continue using private schools. The

Table 3.6. *Education expenditures as % of GNP, before and after free education*

	Remarks	GNP per capita 1890–99 = 100	Share of education expenditures
England and Wales			
1833	No government subsidy No compulsion	$84	1.0%
1858	Predominantly private and church aided No compulsion	108	1.10
1870	— English Education Act —		
1882	1/3rd of students in schools at reduced fees. Compulsion	151	1.06
United States			
1860	Common school system with fees a significant element in several stages. Typically little compulsion	137	0.80
1867	— 'Free School Act' —		
1880	Fees largely abolished. About 14 states have compulsion	159	1.10
1900	Compulsion and free nearly everywhere	202	1.70

Source: West, 1975, 201.

consequences of this scenario are shown in the last two columns. Most of the public education funds are now going to the middle group (75 out of 100), and total education spending has fallen from 200 to 160.

Considering the evidence, table 3.6 shows some interesting figures for England and America in the nineteenth century when the free school system was established. The picture before and after free school is presented. Looking first at England we see that the English Education Act apparently made very little difference. Public provision seems simply to have substituted for private. The same holds true for the United States, at least between 1860 and 1880. After 1880 the share of education in GNP did increase, but it should be noted that GNP per capita also markedly increased during this period. This latter factor, rather than government subsidies, might be the main factor responsible for the increase in education expenditures. This seems likely because we know that prior to the Free School Act most children were in any case at school (West, 1967, 106), so there was little the Act could do.

Looking at higher education, the subsidy system seems inequitable as presently organised. In the US it has been calculated that families of students at the Universities of California and Wisconsin in 1964 had average incomes about 50% higher than families of non-students (Peltzman, 1973, fn. 17). The subsidies received by these students were two (Wisconsin) or five (California) times as great as the average state taxes paid by their families (Peltzman, 1973). In England a similar picture can be drawn. Each year the Central Statistical Office publishes estimates in Economic Trends of taxes paid and benefits in cash and in kind received by families according to family income. The richer families receive the higher education benefits. Thus it seems that the prevalent method of subsidising education, by providing education free at government run schools and universities, is not a very effective means of reducing education inequality.

There is also the point that state education promotion policies could be an *effect* rather than a cause of better education. It might be that only after most of the electorate have reached a certain standard do they vote for measures aimed at making that standard (or something like it) a minimum. Landes and Solomon (1968) have analysed compulsory schooling laws from this viewpoint. Two States had compulsion in 1870, fourteen by 1880, and most by 1900 (twelve to twenty weeks school a year were required, up to the age of fourteen and sixteen). They show that those states which had a high proportion of children in school in 1870, *prior* to the passing of the laws in most states, were first to pass such laws – the correlation between proportion in school in a state *in 1870* and the date of the state law is -0.8 (1968, 87).

It thus seems as though the laws to encourage education were in fact a consequence of education. Yet, if states pass laws only to coerce a minority into school, one wonders what the aim is of the laws. The authors give as a possible reason the fact that teachers and school officials gain from the laws (1968, 87). Such laws are likely to mean a steadier income, and so a rise in the number of teachers and officials – we take this up in the section on public choice, below.

Efficiency

If education has external benefits or costs, then the social benefits and costs of education will not be the same as private benefits and costs. For example, more widespread education might encourage voting and so promote democracy, or reduce crime, or subject individuals to a uniform process of socialisation and so promote a benign sense of national identity. This is what Adam Smith in fact believed. He said: 'In free countries where the safety of government depends very much upon the favourable judgement which the people may form of its conduct, it must surely be of the highest importance that they should not be disposed to judge rashly or capriciously concerning it', and, therefore, 'the state derives no inconsiderable advantage from their instruction' (Smith, 1776, vol. II, 309). But these external benefits will not be captured by a mere comparison of the earnings of more with less educated individuals. Such a comparison would understate the 'social' benefits of education. Since individuals when making education choices are necessarily only interested in the private benefits of education there will therefore be too little education investment, so the argument runs.

But – ignoring the issue of empirical verification for the moment – there are arguments going the other way. It has been said, for example, that 'college degrees have been used as a means to allocate the cushy jobs regardless of the relevance schooling may have to the work'(Levitan, 1981, 146). The implication is that there has been too much education investment. One major strand of literature contends that education can be used by employers primarily as a 'screen' to sort out those with high ability. It is necessary to posit a large amount of employer ignorance. Then those who are uneducated will be passed over, even if they are able, in favour of those who are educated. Everyone will then be caught up in a competitive race for qualifications, with the attendant waste.

A way of testing the screening argument is to consider situations where employer ignorance is low, and see if there is then less education overinvestment. One such situation is where a person is self-employed: individuals have an advantage in gauging their own abilities. In fact we do find that the self-employed have lower levels of educational attainment than the employees, other things being equal (Wolpin 1977, table 1). At first sight this appears to bear out the screening idea. However, it should be remembered that the self-employed generally undergo a long period of training in 'the school of hard knocks'. The lucky ones are employed in the family firm and learn from a relative, a form of apprenticeship. If we are going to compare employees with the self-employed we should include the on-the-job training of the latter. The easy test of the screening hypothesis therefore proves to be inconclusive.

Even if the idea of positive externalities from education is accepted, there remains the question of whether state production of schooling is the appropriate way of capturing these externalities. Private schools with subsidised entry for lower income families is likely to be a better method. A decentralised system of independent, competing schools would have lower costs and be more responsive to consumers for the same reason that competition makes firms in any industry more attentive to their customers. A state-wide system raises problems of weeding out poorly managed schools, and poor teachers. There is the zoning which limits parents' ability to desert the poorer schools; there is the bureaucracy of a centralised system; there is the increased tendency for teachers to please themselves when they are released from the need to please the parents. Higher administrative costs, lower output per teacher, and poor quality product might make the costs of government intervention outweigh the benefits of capturing positive externalities.

In any case, looking at the question of the empirical magnitude of the external benefits of education, little testing has been done. Hansen and Wiesbrod's well-known work on the benefits and costs of higher education merely lists some possible benefits (1968, 36–8); no empirical magnitudes are calculated because of the difficulty of doing so. Kenneth Greene *et al.* (1974, table 5) take it as reasonable to assume that no portion of higher education expenditures have external benefits, and 20% of elementary and secondary education expenditures have external benefits. However, they stress that these assumptions have little factual basis.

Public choice

Education subsidies are the result of a political struggle, it must be remembered. In such a struggle people naturally ask first 'how will it benefit me?'. The social reason for government intervention which we have been considering above need not be the reason that particular policies are followed. The social reasons might nevertheless be used in the public debate as a cloak or 'cover story' for special interest groups. These special interest groups are the teachers and the bureaucrats in government who have budgetary responsibility for education authorities. These groups are not neutral organisations following the will of the people.

It must be remembered that the suppliers of educational services generally have a monopoly on the supply of information to the government. It is plausible to assume that this power is used to advance the interests of the suppliers, in particular to increase their budgets. We have seen a possible example of this above, in the way compulsory school legislation tended to lag rather than lead educational standards. Bureaucracies will aim to exaggerate the demand for their services and play down the costs of their policies. Efforts to measure the performance of the public educational sector will be met by the response that output cannot be measured, and that the education of future generations should not in any case be subjected to cost-benefit analysis. It must be remembered that special interest groups derive their livelihood from their sector's growth, whereas for the voter they are a minor expense. Thus the voters have little incentive to become informed (they are rationally ignorant), and are no match for the producers. The producers will naturally protect 'their' sector, and will have little incentive to improve efficiency (see also Dowd *et al.*, 1991).

Education vouchers (or tuition tax credits) are a case in point. Instead of the government subsidising education by providing free schools, the voucher idea is that parents be issued with vouchers (looking like cheques) which they would present at the school of their choice every term, for example. Schools would therefore have to please parents. These vouchers have been vigorously opposed by teachers' unions and by central government because of fears of a large consequent expansion in private schools. A US nationwide poll in 1981 in fact found that about 25% of the parents questioned with children in state schools would transfer them to private schools if offered tuition tax credits of $250 to $500 per year (West, 1982, 24; see also Seldon, 1986). The expansion in private schools would diminish the power of teachers' unions, and of the central government bureaucracy. But a more efficient competitive system would be beneficial for society. By subsidising education using vouchers we would get more teaching output for our tax dollars.

3.7 Conclusions

In this chapter we have considered the formal schooling phase of an individual's life; the period when he or she is self-investing full time. We have attempted to measure the financial returns to investment, to answer why some individuals stay at school longer than others, and to explain why so much schooling is 'produced' by the state.

We have found that private rates of return to investment in education correspond broadly to rates of return on other assets. This supports the idea of treating schooling as an investment decision. We have also found that family wealth is an important determinant of how much education an individual obtains. Again this is best interpreted in an investment framework: human capital being a peculiar type of capital which will not stand easily as collateral for a loan, so that people cannot borrow much to finance its acquisition. The advantages of the better-off in human capital acquisition provide an argument based on egalitarianism for government subsidies for education.

The last section of the chapter considered the issues raised by government subsidisation – whether the subsidies reached the poor, and whether the dominant form of the subsidies (state-run schools, provided free of charge) could be improved. Our conclusions were that the poor were not much helped by the subsidies (which tended to be appropriated by the middle classes), and that a voucher or tax credit system could be a better way of delivering the subsidy. This needs more research.

Appendix 3.1 Assessing family background effects using differences in brothers' and twins' education

We suppose that education, U, is determined by 'family wealth', B, 'ability', Q, and other factors, e. Let us suppose that U, B, and Q are measured in units such that they have zero mean and unit variance.

In the simplest model we ignore the distinction between B and Q, and simply assume that B contains Q (B is a broad measure of family background). Let:

$$U = mB + v \quad \text{for one member of the pair, and}$$
$$U' = mB + v' \quad \text{for the other member.}$$

We assume that B and v or v' are uncorrelated, and v and v' are uncorrelated.

Now calculate the relation between U and U' for a sample of pairs of brothers/sisters or twins. The correlation coefficient is defined as:

$$r_{uu'} = \text{cov}(U,U')/\sigma_u\sigma_{u'}$$
$$= \text{cov}(U,U') \text{ since } \sigma_u = \sigma_{u'} = 1.$$

Now $\text{cov}(U,U')$ is:

$$\text{cov}(U,U') = \text{E}(mB + v)(mB + v') - \bar{U}\bar{U}'$$
$$= m^2\text{E}(B)^2 + m(\text{E}(B,v) + \text{E}(B,v')) + \text{E}(v,v')$$
$$= m^2\sigma_B^2 = m^2,$$

since $\text{E}(B,v) = \text{E}(B,v') = \text{E}(v,v') = 0$ by assumption, and $\sigma_B^2 = 1$. Thus $r_{uu'} = m^2$.

We can also calculate that the variance in educational attainment is:

$$\sigma_U^2 = \text{E}(mB + v)^2 - \bar{U}^2$$
$$= m^2\sigma_B^2 + \sigma_V^2.$$

Thus, $1 = m^2 + \sigma_v^2$, since $\sigma_U^2 = \sigma_B^2 = 1$. Therefore:

$$1 = r_{uu'} + \sigma_v^2,$$

which shows that the error variance and the correlation coefficient add up to one.

Now let us take the more revealing model which distinguishes between family wealth (nurture), and ability (nature). In this case:

$$U = aB + cQ + e \quad \text{for one member of the pair, and}$$
$$U' = aB + cQ' + e' \quad \text{for the other member.}$$

We assume that B, Q, and Q' are uncorrelated with e and e', and e is uncorrelated with e'. Then the correlation between brothers' education is:

$$r_{uu'} = \text{cov}(U,U') = E(aB + cQ + e)(aB + cQ' + e')$$
$$= a^2 + 2acr_{BQ} + c^2 r_{QQ'},$$

where r_{BQ} is the correlation between background and ability for an individual; $r_{QQ'}$ is the correlation between brothers' ability. We have assumed Q is that ability which is independent of background, so $r_{BQ} = 0$. Also $r_{QQ'} = 1$ for identical twins, presumably. (Note Bouchard et al. give the IQ correlation for identical twins brought up together as 0.83 – see text table 3.4. However given the measurement error in IQ testing, for example the same individual tested on successive occasions only correlates about 0.9 with his/her previous scores, the 0.83 figure can be taken as insignificantly different from unity.) So we have:

$$r_{uu'}^b = a^2 + c^2 r_{QQ'}, \text{ for brothers} \tag{1}$$

$$r_{uu'}^{mt} = a^2 + c^2, \text{ for identical twins reared together} \tag{2}$$

$$r_{uu'}^{ma} = c^2, \text{ simply, for identical twins reared apart.} \tag{2'}$$

(2') follows, since there can be no family wealth effect for twins reared apart.

In addition, we have an equation for the variance of education:

$$1 = \sigma_U^2 = E(aB + cQ + e)^2$$
$$= a^2\sigma_B^2 + c^2\sigma_Q^2 + 2acr_{BQ} + E(e, e')$$
$$= a^2 + c^2 + \sigma_e^2, \text{ given } r_{BQ} = 0. \tag{3}$$

This gives the 'shares' of background, intelligence, and other factors determining education.

There are three equations in four unknowns, a, c, $r_{QQ'}$, and σ_e. So one unknown has to be fixed or estimated. There exist data on correlations between brothers' IQs, which might be thought to measure $r_{QQ'}$. These correlations are about 0.5 (see Corcoran, Jencks, Olneck, 1976, 434). However IQ is influenced by background. Taking that element of Q which is independent of background must give a lower correlation. Below we will calculate results for $r_{QQ'} = 0.5$, $r_{QQ'} = 0.25$ and $r_{QQ'} = 0.1$.

As noted in the text, $r_{uu'}^b = 0.54$, and $r_{uu'}^{mt} = 0.76$ (unfortunately we do not have a figure for $r_{uu'}^{ma}$). Using $r_{uu'}^{mt}$ in equation (3) gives the error contribution, $\sigma_e^2 = 0.24$. Rewriting (3) in terms of $r_{uu'}^b$, gives

$$1 = r_{uu'}^b + c^2(1 - r_{QQ'}) - \sigma_e^2$$
$$= 0.54 + c^2(1 - r_{QQ'}) + 0.24.$$

From this equation we can calculate c and then a for different values of $r_{QQ'}$.

Thus:

	'genes'	'family wealth'	luck
if $r_{QQ'} = 0.5$	then $c^2 = 0.44$	$a^2 = 0.32$	$\sigma_e^2 = 0.24$
$r_{QQ'} = 0.25$	then $c^2 = 0.29$	$a^2 = 0.44$	$\sigma_e^2 = 0.24$
$r_{QQ'} = 0.10$	then $c^2 = 0.24$	$a^2 = 0.52$	$\sigma_e^2 = 0.24$

(IQ– Bouchard (1990): $c^2 = 0.70$, $a^2 = 0.1$ to 0.15, $\sigma_e^2 = 0.15$ to 0.2.)

The contribution of differences in family wealth to differences in education is measured by a^2, and c^2 is the contribution of that element of intelligence which is not associated with wealth. As the intelligence of brothers becomes less correlated, so similar ability becomes less able to explain similarity in education. This explains why the contribution of shared family wealth rises as $r_{QQ'}$ falls. Wealth can never explain more than 54% in this model, since the contribution of ability (genes) tends to 22% and we know – from identical twins – that there is an error term of 24%.

4 Post-school investment

4.1 Introduction

According to human capital theory, we can in general almost always earn more than we do. The difference between actual and potential earnings corresponds to the sacrifice we incur by learning on-the-job so as to ensure future earnings growth. The fact that we receive an earnings increment in any year is taken to be the return to on-the-job learning costs. Assuming the earnings increment represents a permanent addition, its present value is a measure of the size of on-the-job learning costs.

However, post-school investment in training – the gap between actual and potential earnings – is not constant each year. It ordinarily diminishes over the life cycle. If the link between earnings growth and past human capital investments is accepted, lower earnings growth must imply lower investments. Thus the old generally invest less than the young.

This chapter deals with the incorporation of post-school investment into an empirical framework so that earnings functions can be estimated, and the plausibility of the hypothesis that individuals rationally plan over their life cycles can be considered. The next section of the chapter derives a statistical formulation based on the work of Jacob Mincer (1974) which, when applied to real world data, can be used to test the validity of life-cycle models. The third section then presents some regression estimates using this specification. The fourth section considers extensions to further variables, and to the theory of general and specific training. Implications concerning vocational training policy follow.

4.2 Derivation of the earnings function

The life-cycle model predicts that investment in human capital will be a monotonically declining function of age. This means that human capital stock is accumulated at a diminishing rate. On the assumption of a given human capital rental rate, the result is a concave earnings profile. We seek now to derive an empirical formulation which can be applied to data so that tests of the life-cycle hypothesis can be made.

Start by recalling some definitions: C_t is the dollar expenditure on net human capital investment in any time period t (see appendix 4.1 for the difference between net and gross investment); E_t is potential earnings, and Y_t is observed earnings. E_0 and Y_0 represent potential and observed earnings in the initial time period. Earnings in period 1 can be expressed in terms of prior investment. Assume a dollar investment of C_0 during the initial year. Investment theory dictates that potential earnings in the following year would be augmented by the returns on initial investment rC_0. Thus:

$$E_1 = E_0 + rC_0.$$

Similarly, potential earnings in period 2 would equal earnings in period 1 plus the returns on investment. Thus:

$$E_2 = E_1 + rC_1 = E_0 + rC_0 + rC_1.$$

In general $E_t = E_0 + r\Sigma_{i=0}^{t-1} C_i$.

In any time period, dollar investment equals potential earnings minus observed earnings. Thus:

$$C_t = E_t - Y_t.$$

Empirically, it is difficult to observe dollar investment. No direct data are readily available on either direct or individual post-school investments. For this reason we must rely on creating a measure of the time involved in investment.

Recall from chapter 2 that s_t represents the proportion of one's time spent investing. This is what Mincer calls 'time equivalent investment', and can be expressed as:

$$s_t = C_t/E_t,$$

indicating the fraction of potential earnings, E_t, one foregoes to accumulate human capital. As indicated in chapter 2 this definition is plausible when there are no direct investment costs, i.e., when all investments have only a time component. In this case all investment expenditures are solely foregone income, so that the proportion of potential earnings foregone reflects the proportion of one's available time spent investing. In a world where it is impossible to borrow for human capital investment, all expenditures on such investment must be earned by the individual concerned. In this case, it is simply foregone earnings which finance the investment.

Substituting s_t for C_t yields:

$$E_1 = E_0 + rs_0E_0 = E_0[1 + rs_0]$$

$$E_2 = E_1 + rs_1E_1 = E_1[1 + rs_1]$$
$$= E_0[1 + rs_0][1 + rs_1]$$
$$E_t = E_0[1 + rs_0][1 + rs_1]\ldots[1 + rs_{t-1}]$$
$$= E_0 \prod_{i=0}^{t-1}[1 + rs_i].$$

Taking the logarithms of both sides yields:

$$\ln E_t = \ln E_0 + \sum_{i=0}^{t-1}\ln[1 + rs_i].$$

However, $\ln[1 + x] \cong x$ when x is small. Thus, the above equation can be written as:

$$\ln E_t = \ln E_0 + r_s \sum_{i=0}^{t-1}s_i, \tag{4.1}$$

since rs_i, the product of two fractions, is small.

The term s_t represents time equivalent investment, namely the proportion of time in each period spent investing. During school, s_t equals one since schooling is essentially a full-time task, but after formal schooling ends s_t declines becoming zero at retirement – recall figure 2.7 in chapter 2. Thus, s_t can be divided into two segments: (1) a full-time schooling period and (2) a post-schooling period. It follows that equation (4.1) can be written:

$$\ln E_t = \ln E_0 + r_s \sum_{i=0}^{S}s_i + r_p \sum_{i=s+1}^{t-1}s_i,$$

where S represents years of schooling, r_s is the rate of return to schooling, and r_p is the rate of return to post-school investment (presumably $r_s = r_p$ in competitive equilibrium for the marginal year of school).

We simplify this equation. Firstly, since $s_t = 1$ during the schooling phase, $\sum_{i=0}^{S}s_i = S$, implying:

$$\ln E_t = \ln E_0 + r_sS + r_p \sum_{i=1}^{t-1}s_i. \tag{4.2}$$

Secondly we assume that post-school investment, s_i, declines monotonically with experience. If s_i decreases over the life cycle, then the accumulated value of eds, that is, the human capital stock, must increase at a decreasing rate and so must earnings – the return on the capital stock. One function that approximates this non-linearity is a parabola, for example, $at + bt^2$ where t is post-school experience. This results in the basic earnings function (see appendix 4.1). (See Murphy and Welch, 1990, for experiments with cubic and quartic functions.)

$$\ln E_t = \ln E_0 + rS + \alpha rt - brt^2. \tag{4.3}$$

Recall that E_t is potential earnings. Observed earnings equals that fraction of potential earnings used for work. This fraction is $[1 - s_t]$. Thus, $Y_s = E_t[1 - s_t]$, and $\ln Y_t = \ln E_t + \ln[1 - s_t]$. It can be shown that accounting for

$\ln[1 - s_t]$ affects the earnings specification merely by rotating downward the earnings function – see for example figure 2.9 in chapter 2. As such, the parabolic specification remains appropriate. Thus, the typical earnings function is:

$$\ln Y_t = a_0 + r_s S + a_1 t + a_2 t^2, \tag{4.4}$$

which is fitted to data by statistical regression analysis. For details on how (4.4) is derived, and the meaning of coefficients, a_0, r_s, a_1, and a_2, see appendix 4.1.

4.3 Regression estimates

Table 4.1 contains earnings functions estimated by Jacob Mincer using 1960 US census data. To start, let us concentrate on equation (b) and interpret each of the coefficients, as they are important in understanding the earnings process. Begin with the schooling coefficient: 0.107. This is known as the 'rate of return' to schooling. In reality it is merely the derivative of the $\ln Y$ with respect to schooling, and reflects the impact of one extra year of school on the log of earnings. The coefficient approximates the per cent increase in earnings resulting from one extra year of school – here, for each extra year of schooling earnings rise by about 10.7%.

To see how the coefficient on S can be interpreted as a rate of return, hold t constant and compare two individuals, one with S years of schooling and the other with four more years, for example, that is $S + 4$ years. Thus we have:

$$\ln Y_s = a_0 + rS + a_1 t - a_2 t^2$$

and

$$\ln Y_{s+4} = a_0 + r(S + 4) + a_1 t - a_2 t^2.$$

The difference in their earnings is:

$$\ln Y_{s+4} - \ln Y_s = 4r.$$

However, using the approximation:

$$\ln X - \ln Y = (X - Y)/Y$$

(e.g., $\ln 110 - \ln 100 = 4.7 - 4.6 = 0.1 = (110 - 100)/100$) we can write:

$$\ln Y_{s+4} - \ln Y_s = (Y_{s+4} - Y_s)/Y_s = 4r.$$

As can be seen, $Y_{s+4} - Y_s$ is the extra earnings from the four extra years of education, and $4Y_s$ is foregone earnings cost of these four extra years. Thus we can write:

Table 4.1. *Basic earnings functions*

Equation (a) $\ln Y = 7.58 + 0.070S$	$R^2 = 0.067$
Equation (b) $\ln Y = 6.20 + 0.107S + 0.081t - 0.0012t^2$	$R^2 = 0.285$
Equation (c) $\ln Y = 4.87 + 0.26S - 0.003S^2 - 0.0043tS + 0.148t$	
$\quad\quad\quad\quad - 0.0018t^2$	$R^2 = 0.309$

Notes:
$\ln Y = \log_e$ annual earnings,
S = years of schooling,
t = experience measured as age minus education minus 6,
R^2 = measure of goodness of fit.
Data: 1960 US Census of Population, 1/1000 sample.
Source: Mincer, 1974, 92.

$$\frac{Y_{s+4} - Y_s}{4Y_s} = \frac{\text{returns to four extra years of education}}{\text{costs of four extra years of education}} = r.$$

So r can reasonably be taken to be a 'rate of return' to the four years' investment in education.

The coefficients on t and t^2 indicate whether the earnings function is concave. A positive coefficient for t and a negative coefficient for t^2 imply concavity. This can easily be seen by noting that the slope of an age earnings profile is merely the derivative $\partial \ln Y/\partial t$. The second derivative indicates the rate at which the slope is changing. If the second derivative is negative this implies that the slope of the earnings profile is diminishing. For the earnings function depicted by equation (b) in table 4.1, $\partial \ln Y_t/\partial t = 0.081 - 0.00024t$. For $t < 33.75$, this is positive. The second derivative is -0.0024 which is negative. Thus, earnings rise, but at a diminishing rate, peaking at experience level 33.75.

The intercept term (6.2) depicts the logarithm of earnings for an individual with no school or experience. The antilog of 6.2 is about 500. This seems low for annual earnings even for a non-schooled individual just starting out in the workforce. In part the low figure is because the data relate to 1960, and in part it is due to the fact that we are extrapolating outside of the sample space – very few individuals have no schooling. If we were to take the average schooling level to be about twelve years, then one would have to augment log earnings by 0.107×12. Log earnings would then be 1.28 + 6.2 or about 7.5. This translates to about $1,800 which is in the neighbourhood of 7,200 1985 dollars, comparable to the minimum wage (about $3 an hour at that time), which would be expected for the worker with no experience. Thus, the figures are reasonable.

For higher levels of schooling, the earnings profile is shifted up by 10.7%

per year of schooling. Given this specification, each of the profiles peak at about thirty-seven years of experience. This can be translated to age by adding in years of schooling plus the initial number of years before which one entered school. Thus, for someone with twelve years of schooling, the profile peaks at about $38 + 12 + 6$ which is fifty-six years.

The earnings function specification just analysed is not the most general nor for that matter is it the only one used in empirical analysis. Consensus seems to exist that a log-linear specification is the most appropriate. But even among log-linear models there are variations. Equation (a) in table 4.1 is a simplification in that 'on-the-job training' is neglected. Here the log of earnings is related solely to schooling level. The third specification in table 4.1 is more general in that it not only incorporates schooling and experience, but looks at 'interactions' between the two. Even this is not the most general specification, but both these and others warrant at least some attention here.

In equation (a) only an intercept and a schooling coefficient are reported. Note that both coefficient values are different from the ones already discussed in equation (b). The difference in coefficients is interesting and illustrates the importance of taking care to appropriately 'specify' statistical equations such as earnings functions.

To illustrate the importance of including experience in the earnings function, compare two individuals both of the same age. Two thirty year olds would suffice. Let one individual have sixteen years of schooling. Let the other have twelve. The sixteen year individual would on average then have at most eight years of experience (the possible work years from graduation at age twenty-two to age thirty). The other, with twelve years of school, would have at most twelve $(= 30 - 12 - 6)$ years of experience. Both schooling and experience increase earnings. In comparing these two individuals, one has more schooling but less experience. Fitting an earnings function relating earnings only to schooling neglects the fact that the more educated have on average less experience. Thus, this earnings function mistakenly neglects to account for experience differences for individuals who are of the same age but have different schooling levels. For this reason the first equation understates the true returns from schooling.

Moreover, neglecting experience implies that experience has no effect on earnings so that the experience–earnings profile is completely flat. Dropping experience from the statistical regression model forces a flat earnings profile at the point of average earnings for both the young and old. Consequently the intercept now represents average earnings across all experience groups instead of initial earnings for the young. This explains why the intercept term in the first regression surpasses that of the second.

Now consider earnings function (c) in table 4.1. Here two modifications are made to the standard function. First, schooling is expressed as a quadratic having an S and S^2 term instead of simply years of schooling; and second, an 'interaction' term ($t.S$) defined as the product of experience and schooling is added.

The quadratic schooling term allows non-linearities in the rate of return to schooling. Recall that $\partial \ln Y / \partial S$ measures the per cent increase in earnings for each extra year of schooling. In the linear case of equation (b) this derivative is measured by the schooling coefficient alone. In equation (c) there are two schooling coefficients, and the derivative equals the first coefficient plus twice the second coefficient. For this case the return to schooling is $0.26 - 0.006S - 0.0043t$. This implies a diminishing rate of return with increased school (as predicted in chapter 3), as well as with increasing experience. For an individual with zero years of experience and ten years' education, the rate of return to an extra year of schooling is $0.255 - 0.0058(10) = 0.197$ or 19.7%. Yet the rate of return would only be 16.2% for an extra year for new labour market entrants with sixteen years of schooling. In short, specification (c) indicates a declining marginal rate of return as years of schooling rise – the marginal value of the last year of schooling is smaller for each extra year of school. We also see that the marginal rate of return to schooling diminishes for older (more experienced) individuals. Such higher rates of return to schooling for the young may reflect higher returns for 'newer vintage' schooling.

The interaction term specification also allows the age–earnings profile slope to vary with schooling. Recall that the derivative of the earnings profile with respect to experience measures the rate at which earnings rise over the life cycle. Whereas in the previous equation this slope diminished solely with experience, now the slope is also related to schooling level. Here, $d \ln Y / dt = 0.148 - 2x.0.0018t - 0.0043S$. This means that earnings profiles increase more slowly the greater one's schooling. Since this result is clearly at variance with the facts (recall figures 1.2 and 1.3 in chapter 1), a yet more complicated specification is evidently needed, allowing curvature as well as slope to vary with schooling.

Other modifications to the earnings profile are possible. Most common are the inclusion of further exogenous variables known to affect earnings. These include such variables as region (north, south, east, west), city-size, gender, race, health, occupation, industry, and measures of family background. In addition, interaction terms between these variables as well as the others already studied are possible. To these variables we now turn.

4.4 Extensions

General and specific training

According to the human capital model we have been discussing, people 'pay for' their own training by accepting lower wages in jobs which provide training. A job which provides training will be less well paid than a job which does not. If this were not the case, so that career jobs offered higher pay than 'dead-end jobs', no-one would take the dead-end jobs.

The position is illustrated in figure 4.1 which shows various possible earnings profiles associated with periods of on-the-job training. On-the-job training is seen simply as part-time education, located in a factory or office rather than a school or college. Because on-the-job training is part time, the trainee has positive earnings equalling marginal revenue product as a trainee. However the trainee incurs opportunity costs in the same way as he or she would have done when at school. Later on there is a payoff in terms of increased earnings. The payoff, k, and the opportunity costs, C, have to be related in exactly the same way as for full-time education:

$$k/C = \text{IRR} = i,$$

where IRR is the internal rate of return, and i is some market interest rate (plus a risk premium).

In figure 4.1 the profiles are drawn straight for simplicity, and the jump in the profile on completion of training is related to the amount of training. Training after all is meant to increase an individual's marginal revenue product. Thus the 'no training' profile is flat for the whole time the individual is with the firm, the 'some training' profile A'B'C'D' has a small jump, and profile ABCD indicates the largest amount of training. However all profiles have to cross the 'no training' profile, ensuring that opportunity costs are precisely balanced by returns, so as to give an internal rate of return equal to the market interest rate. A profile such as XYZV (dashed), while it increases an individual's productivity, provides no payoff, so the course of training it represents would be abandoned.

We thus imagine a firm as having a portfolio of possible job sequences – beginning with a training slot, and ending with a skilled job. Each job sequence has its corresponding earnings profile. Individuals choose among sequences in accordance with their tastes, abilities, and willingness to forego income, just as with full-time education. Indeed some traineeships involve very low incomes initially (see ABCD) since initial productivity is low for such trainees, just as with school. Raising wages via a minimum wage law will disrupt such training, as we will see.

But the question might be asked: why does the employee shoulder all the training costs, and not the employer? Why is training not an expense for the firm? The answer is that sometimes the worker bears all training costs, and sometimes the firm shares part of the costs. But whatever the arrangement, the workers' earnings profile will reflect how much training he or she has paid for.

To expand, two types of training are generally distinguished: 'general' and 'specific' training. General training raises a worker's productivity outside the

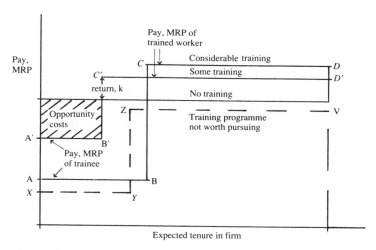

Figure 4.1 Various on-the-job training earnings and productivity profiles

firm as well as within it; it raises the worker's alternative wage. Schooling is a form of general training. An example in the industrial field would be the employee in the insurance company who learns the principles of insurance and how to assess risks. The knowledge makes him or her a more useful employee to all companies in the industry. It would not make sense for the employer to pay for the training in such a case (offer a wage higher than marginal product while training) because, once trained, there would be nothing to stop the employee leaving.

Specific training is where the worker learns something which is of value only in the given firm. His or her marginal product is not raised outside the firm. To continue our example of the insurance company employee, specific training would for example involve learning about the preferences of the company's particular clients. Information such as this would be of little value outside the firm, so the employee's alternative wage is not altered. In such a case the firm would bear some of the. training costs and correspondingly collect some of the benefits. The firm would not bear all the costs however. It is sensible to have the worker share in the investment so as to provide an incentive to stay on.

The two types of training are contrasted in figure 4.2. The upper panel shows the position for general training using flat wage profiles for simplicity. The worker's training costs are the earnings foregone while training (area C), and the returns are the increased wages after training (area R). Since wage always equals marginal product the employer neither bears any costs nor reaps any returns.

The lower panel shows specific training. Here the worker and employer are pictured as equally sharing the costs and returns to training. The employer's training costs (area C_E) are represented by the fact that the marginal product of the trainee, MP_0, is less than the trainee wage, W_0 – which is in turn less than the trainee's alternative wage W_A, so that the trainee pays something, too (area (C_W). The return of the employer (area R_E) is given by the divergence between the trained person's wage, W_1, and marginal product, MP_1. The return of the worker (area R_W) is given in turn by the fact that the wage in the firm is greater than the alternative wage, W_A.

It is interesting to note that in the specific training case the marginal productivity theory of wages does not hold – the worker is never paid the value of his/her marginal product! However it can be shown that the present value of wages will equal the present value of marginal product. So the theory is rescued in present value terms at least.

The proposition can be demonstrated with figure 4.2 (lower panel). The present value of the marginal product stream, PV_{MP}, is:

$$PV_{MP} = MP_0 + MP_1/i,$$

where MP_0 is marginal product while being trained, MP_1 is marginal product once trained, and i is the interest rate. We are assuming that MP_0 continues for a short period, and so does not need to be discounted, and use the simplified annuity formula to discount MP_1 (thus assuming MP_1 will continue for a long time). Similarly, the present value of the wage stream, PV_W, is:

$$PV_W = W_0 + W_1/i.$$

If the two present values are equal we have:

$$W_0 - MP_0 = (MP_1 - W_1)/i.$$

This states that the costs of the investment for the firm are equal to the present value of the returns discounted at the interest rate, which will be true if there is competition.

However, whether a worker is specifically or generally trained, the basic factor relevant for the wage is the amount of training he or she has paid for. The fact that in the specific training context the employer pays for a proportion of training costs does not matter for the worker, since the firm will collect a corresponding proportion of the returns (Kuratani, 1973). An earnings profile rises because of prior investments made by the worker, and it does not really matter whether these investments are in specific or general training.

Specific and general training have different time horizons however. The relevant horizon for general training is the worker's age until retirement. But for specific training the horizon is the worker's expected tenure with the firm. In deciding on how much specific training to invest in therefore, the worker

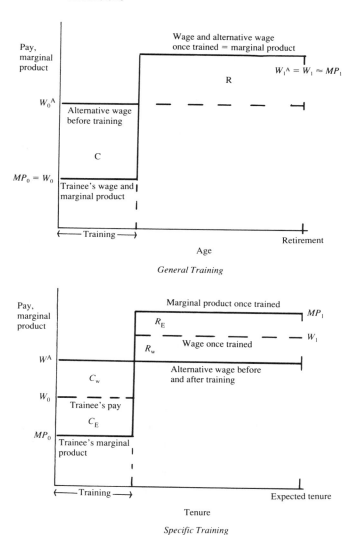

Figure 4.2 General and specific training contrasted

(and the firm) has to calculate how long he or she is going to remain in the firm. The extra risk here would probably prompt a higher required return for specific rather than general training.

Just as general training investments are proxied by total years of experience in the workforce, so specific training often is proxied by years with the current employer. A year of experience obtained prior to the current job will have involved both general and specific training, but it is only the previous general training (by definition) that is reflected in the current wage. Holding total experience (and thus general training) constant, the way one's wage grows in the current job can reflect the extent of firm-specific investments. The coefficient on tenure should reflect the amount of and return to specific investment, given experience; and the coefficient on experience should measure the amount of and return to general investment, given tenure.

Linking an individual's specific training investments (and thus productivity on the job) to the coefficient on tenure is not the only logical explanation of why earnings might increase with tenure. For example there is the 'job match' hypothesis: individuals who remain with a firm a long time are those who have found a job which matches their talents. It is not as though they have learned much on the job, simply that, by a process of selection, we naturally observe the better job matches in the longer jobs. These and other arguments are examined in chapter 9 which analyses in more detail what goes on inside firms ('internal labour markets'). For the moment we can take the specific training interpretation of the tenure coefficient as a reasonable simplification.

Extended earnings functions

It is useful at this point to consider the simultaneous effect of some of the variables discussed above. In table 4.2 are presented the results of including all these variables, plus some others. Results both for the US and for the UK are given for the sake of interest. Note, such an equation forms the basis of many areas of economic concern. For example, regional economics deals with regional variation in earnings. Urban economics deals with city-size wage gradients. Industrial economics deals with industry–occupation wage differentials. Discrimination economics deals with racial, sexual, and ethnic wage differentials. Health economics deals with the impact of various illnesses on earnings potential. In short, each of these factors are important in understanding the earnings distribution.

Discussing the variables in turn, take first the sex variable. The coefficient has a percentage interpretation since the dependent variable is in log terms. Thus in America a male has earnings about 35% higher than a female, holding all other variables in the table constant. In Britain the figure is even higher, 49%. This is not the best way to test for differences in earnings between the sexes, since we assume that the coefficients on all the other variables are the same for the two sexes – for example, that the return to years of education is the same. Still, there is no doubt a large difference. This matter is considered in detail in chapter 6.

The next variable is intended to demonstrate the effect of marriage on

Table 4.2. *Extended earnings functions, US and UK 1972*

Dependent variable: ln annual earnings	US	UK
Constant	6.01	4.30
Sex (1 = male)	0.351	0.493
Marital status (1 = married)	0.196	0.090
Colour (1 = black)	−0.191	−0.054
Years of education	0.077	0.062
Experience	0.033	0.027
Experience squared	−0.00006	−0.00004
Tenure level < 1 year with firm	Base	Base
1 to 3.5 (5 for UK)	0.187	−0.036[a]
3.5 (5) to 10	0.237	0.024[a]
10 to 20	0.293	0.067
over 20	0.279	0.117
Hours worked per week	−0.001[a]	0.004
Weeks worked per year	0.021	0.031
Poor health (1 = yes)	−0.095	−0.050
Attended selective school	n.a.	0.147
Working in north-east	0.061	n.a.
south	−0.126	n.a.
rest of US	Base	n.a.
Working in city (1 = yes)	0.199	n.a.
Union member (1 = yes)	0.167	n.a.
R^2	0.462	0.450

Notes:

[a] All variables are significant at the 5% level or more, except these.

The sample consisted of heads of household, aged 20 to 66, in work, working more than 30 hours a week, and employed at least 10 months of the year.

Sources: US – Panel Survey of Income Dynamics, 1972; UK – General Household Survey, 1972.

earnings. The coefficient shows that in both countries married individuals earn more than single, other things equal. This is in fact a misspecification: we should allow the marital status coefficient to differ according to sex. While married men earn more than single men, married women earn less than single men. As an example of this technique, interacting marital status, MAR, and sex, SEX, we have in the case of the UK:

ln Pay = 0.47SEX − 0.25MAR + 0.35MAR × SEX − other variables.

Single women are the base category (zero for MAR and SEX); single men earn

47% more, married men earn 57% (= 47 − 25 + 35) more, and married women earn 25% less than single women. As can be seen, married men earn considerably more than single men holding age and education constant. Married women on the other hand earn less than single women and single men. We will consider the case of women next chapter, so here let us concentrate on married men.

Married men could earn more than single men because they were intrinsically more able than single. It can be argued that those with high market productivity benefit more from the division of labour that marriage brings than those with low market productivity (Benham, 1974). Having a wife enables the expert salesman, for example, to be on the road for longer. Marriage thus 'sorts' the higher productivity from the lower productivity males.

An alternative explanation is that marriage makes self-investment cheaper. Once a man gets married he accumulates more human capital and thus earns more. It could be cheaper to self-invest once married if the wife finances her husband's 'lean years' (Polachek, 1975; Neumark et al., 1991). It would also be cheaper if married men worked more hours than single men (they do), so they could spread a given quantity of investment over more hours of work.

It has been found that single men, once they get married, have a faster rate of wage increase than when they were single (Kenny, 1983). These results are based on observations of men before and after marriage. Since the man himself does not change, only the incentives he faces, the implication is that it is the incentives that are important. Moreover, the difference between wage growth as between married and single becomes smaller the later a man marries. This also makes sense from the investment point of view since differences in investment should play a smaller role as one ages.

The colour dummy shows blacks earn less than whites, *ceteris paribus* − about 19% less in the US and 5% less in the UK. It is worth noting that the equation relates only to individuals who are in full-time, non-seasonal employment. Many black workers and female workers, whose search for employment is not successful for various reasons, are thereby excluded. Such workers would have expected earnings lower than the included groups, so the difference in expected pay by colour could be higher than that shown (see chapter 8 for more analysis of the effect of job search on pay).

The next variables relate to education, experience, and tenure. The return to education is the coefficient on the education variable as has been discussed already. The figure, 6% to 8%, is somewhat lower than that considered in table 4.1. But there might be some influence of education on other independent variables such as health, weeks worked per year, and whether working in a city. This is demonstrated by the fact that, if these are excluded, the coefficient in education increases by about a percentage point.

The coefficient on experience is meant to show the returns to general training prior to the present job, and the coefficients on the various tenure levels show returns to training within the company. The base for comparison is taken as the group who have just joined the firm with tenure less than one year. Those in the next category, with about two and a half more years (four for the UK), then show a large increase in earnings in the US sample – this group earns 18.7% more than the base group – but no increase in the case of the UK. Instead of increasing at a decreasing rate, the UK tenure profile seems to go on increasing which is a puzzle. Taking the US tenure coefficients, it is instructive to do some exercises. Assuming midpoints for the various tenure levels and then fitting a quadratic we find ln pay $= .0.04T - 0.001T^2 +$ other variables, where T is number of years of tenure ($T = 0$ signifies the base category). The parabola here is more peaked than for years of experience, which is sensible given the shorter horizon for investments associated with any given firm.

The union membership effect can be assessed with the US sample. If an individual is a union member, the coefficient is 0.167. This indicates that union members earn about 16.7% more than non-members, other things equal. We will consider in detail the implications of union membership for pay in chapter 10.

Looking at the remaining variables in the equation we see that poor health enters with a negative coefficient as might be expected. Living in the southern states of the US also has a negative effect. Working in a city has a positive effect (though the variable does not seem important in the UK, outside London) presumably because of the better job matches that can be made in a city due to greater opportunities there. We also have a variable for attending a 'selective school' in the UK regression. This is one of a range of education quality variables which might have been included.

The earnings function could have been extended even further. Some investigators include the individual's occupation and industry. The question then becomes more restrictive: what determines pay given occupation/industry? In most cases however we would rather not take so much as given – the question of why an individual lands up in a particular occupation cannot really be divorced from their pay. However occupation might exert an independent effect, in the sense that some occupations have higher non-pecuniary rewards than others (teachers have longer vacations for example). This aspect of compensating differentials will be considered in chapter 7.

Then there are variables relating to a person's family background. Family wealth, religion, father's and mother's education, the size of the family have all been studied as determinants of an individual's earnings. As we have seen, such variables are important in determining how much education a person obtains. In the simplest model the effects of family background are exhausted once the individual finishes education, and begins to fend for himself or herself in the labour market. More realistically however we can imagine family support and 'connections' as helping one all through one's life (Laband *et al.*,

1985). This is difficult to prove however because of difficulties in measuring family background as we have already seen in the case of education. One approach is again to analyse twins, or brothers and sisters, who have had the same up-bringing by definition.

The problems of holding constant the effects of background is similar to allowing for differences in 'ability'. Ability is difficult to conceptualise and measure. Once again a profitable way seems to be to use twins. Measures of 'intelligence' exist it is true. But the difficulty with these measures is that they are heavily influenced by education as well as being controversial in terms of content. Another method is to use panel data: ability is held constant since we are following the same individual over time (for example see Ashenfelter and Card, 1985). Sometimes it is also possible to randomly divide the population into control and experimental groups (for example using the US draft lottery, see Angrist, 1990).

Ability – studies of twins

The same methods employed to analyse twins' education (chapter 3, table 3.4) can be used to analyse twins' incomes. The basic study here is by Paul Tabuman (1976) who was able to collect data on the incomes of 1,000 pairs of white male identical and 1,000 pairs of non-identical twins. These twins were all approximately forty when interviewed, so variation in age is removed from the data.

The main data are again in the form of correlations. The correlation between an identical twin's income and his brother's income is 0.545. The correlation between non-identical twins' incomes is 0.30, which is similar to the figures that have been found for brothers (Jencks (1979) takes figures of 0.15 and 0.35 as fair estimates for brothers). The correlation between incomes of pairs of randomly selected individuals should be zero.

In an intuitive sense we can say that the correlation between the incomes of brothers and non-identical twins is raised from zero to 0.30 in part by the fact that brothers share a common family environment when they are being brought up and in part by the fact that they share their genes (the genes, that is, that can vary between people). The correlation then rises further, from 0.30 to 0.545 when we move to a comparison of identical twins – who have a common home environment, and share all their genes. The correlation would rise from 0.545 to unity if identical twins had identical lives in addition to identical childhood environments and genes. The difference between 0.545 and unity is a measure of how dissimilar the lives of otherwise identical people are by the time they have reached forty. It is largely a measure of luck or chance cumulating over forty years.

The correlation between incomes of various types of pairs can be thought of as showing the contribution of whatever the pairs have in common to 'explaining' the variance of incomes in the population. Randomly selected pairs have nothing in common, so their income correlation is zero. The 0.545 correlation for identical twins implies that factors arising from the home environment and from genes explains 54.5% of the variance in earnings (see the appendix to chapter 3 for an explanation of correlations). Non-systematic factors explain the remaining 46%. According to this reasoning, our regressions in the previous section, however well specified, would never be able to explain more than 54.5% of the variation in individuals' incomes.

On the ability issue, one way of looking at ability is to identify it with possession of certain types of genes. Since one's genetic make-up is given and exogenous, such a view has the merit of distinguishing ability from training. The 0.245 difference in the income correlations of non-identical and identical twins, 0.30 and 0.545, then shows the effect of being exactly alike, rather than half alike in genetic make up. One might crudely calculate that, if there were no genetic similarity, the correlation between non-identical twins would be diminished by 0.245, and become about 0.05. Then the contribution of family wealth to explaining income variation would be only 0.05, the contribution of genes would be 0.49, and the contribution of chance would be 0.46. In fact, the simpler models achieve these very figures.

These figures may be compared to the earlier breakdown for education, illustrated in figure 3.7: family background explaining 32%, genes 44%, and chance/measurement error 24% of the variation in education. The fact that family wealth is so much less important in explaining pay than education, while genes remain equally important for both is interesting. Since education appears to be such an important determinant of pay (for males of the same age), and family wealth is linked to education, we might have expected family wealth to have more impact on pay. If the estimates are to be believed, family wealth effects fade into the background by the time one is forty, but genes continue to be important – which is perhaps not so implausible. However such a conclusion is disappointing for educationists, because it implies that education policy has little long-run effect on income distribution.

The preceding measurements are not however meant to be taken as a serious foray into the 'nature versus nurture' debate. Rather it is intended to show how difficult it is to come to grips with the concept of ability. Moreover, it is perhaps not worth trying to separate ability from training, or the environment. Einstein, if he had been born fifty years earlier, might not have been able to think up the theory of relativity because the field did not exist. He might then have lived out his life as a technical officer in the Swiss Patent Office. His intelligence needed the right environment in which to bloom. Nevertheless, experiments with twins are always fascinating, and we have certainly not heard the last of the 'ability' issue.

4.5 On-the-job training policy

According to human capital theory it is possible to assess the amount of training investments a worker is making in any year by looking at the rate of increase in his or her earnings in the next year. We have already shown this in a simple way – ignoring depreciation – in chapter 2 (equation (2.6) and figure 2.8). Strictly speaking, the relationship is between *potential* earnings, E_t, and *net* investment (see appendix 4.1):

$$\Delta E_t/i = C_{nt}. \tag{4.5}$$

We can approximate ΔE_t as ΔY_t (remember figure 2.8), and so calculate C_{nt}.

Take for example equation (b) in table 4.1 and consider the case of workers in their first year in the workforce, so $t = 1$. The slope of the $\ln Y$ profile here is:

$$\partial \ln Y_1/\partial t = 0.081 \cong \partial \ln E_1/\partial t.$$

Therefore, since $\partial \ln E_1/\partial t = (\partial E_1/\partial t)(1/E_1)$:

$$\Delta E_1/E_1 = 0.081,$$

that is, capacity earnings increase about 8% in the first year on the job. Assuming the discount rate, i, is 15% (i includes interest, depreciation, and inflation), then net investment in the first year is:

$$C_{n1} = \Delta E_1/i = 0.081 \, E_1/0.15 = 0.53 E_1.$$

In other words, in this example, net investment would be 53% of capacity earnings in the first year of work.

Making an assumption about depreciation we can also figure out what gross investment is, and estimate actual earnings as a fraction of potential earnings. Gross investment, C_{gt}, is (see appendix 4.1):

$$C_{gt} = C_{nt} + \delta P K_t,$$

where δ is the depreciation fraction, $P = w/i$ is the value of a unit of capital, and K is the number of units of human capital. Since $E_t = wK_t$ we can write:

$$C_{g1} = 0.08 E_1/i + \delta E_1/i = (0.08 + \delta) E_1/i.$$

The difference between actual and potential earnings in any year represents the gross investment that is made in that year:

$$C_{gt} = E_t - Y_t.$$

Therefore:

$$(E_1 - Y_1)/E_1 = (0.08 + \delta)/i.$$

Table 4.3. *Estimates of the value of on-the-job training, men, 14–24, US 1966–9*

	White	Black
Hourly actual wage	$2.14	$1.57
Value of on-the-job training*	1.42	0.87
Estimated full wage	3.56	2.44

Note: *Value of on-the-job training is estimated as in figure 2.8, by taking a wage growth figure for young men. The present value of the earnings increment, using a discount rate of 10%, is an estimate of human capital investments made by the young men.
Source: Lazear, 1979a, 557.

If we take $\delta \cong 2\%$ a year (as is suggested by studies of the way earnings decline after periods out of the workforce), then $Y_1/E_1 \cong 1/3$. The suggestion is therefore that the average new entrant invests about 2/3 of his or her potential earnings in human capital.

The above is an example. In an accurate study however the implication that training opportunities are important for young people remains. Thus Lazear, in a study of young men aged fourteen to twenty-four, finds the results given in table 4.3. For young white men, for example, the actual hourly wage was $2.14. However, the value of on-the-job training investments were estimated as $1.42, giving a 'full' wage of $3.56. The value of training investments corresponds to 40% of the full wage. The corresponding figure for young black men can be seen to be nearly as high, 36% – though this does not appear to hold for later decades (see below).

An important policy implication follows from the above. High youth wages – whether caused by minimum wage legislation or union collective bargaining – prevent workers from having the opportunity to take a low wage job now in return for training which gives them higher pay in the future. This effect is significant mainly at the younger ages when most self-investment occurs. For example, looking at figure 4.1, suppose that a payment of a low wage such as that indicated by A were 'illegal', and that a higher wage had to be paid instead. Because of such minimum wage legislation firms cannot make available training slots having low initial wages and later higher wages. Firms will tend to opt for profiles such as A'B'C'D'. In other words the increase in pay will be smaller, implying few training opportunities (i.e., fewer steeply sloped earnings profiled jobs) for young workers. The worker's full wage including the value of training would actually have been reduced.

In sum, normally the full pay of young people will be much higher than their observed pay. Minimum wage laws, or affirmative action laws requiring higher levels of pay for minorities, can disrupt the process whereby a worker can accept lower pay in return for training.

Estimates of the magnitude of this effect have been made. For example, it has been estimated that the rate of increase of wages of teenage American workers was lowered by 20% when US minimum wages were increased from $1.25 to $1.60 in 1967/8 (Hashimoto, 1981). This would also reduce investment, C_n, by 20% using equation (4.5) above. The reduction would occur during the years that the minimum wage was a constraint, the teenage years for example. For those that were made unemployed as a result of the minimum the loss would naturally be greater, including not only the loss of a money wage but also of training opportunities worth nearly as much again.

Leighton and Mincer (1981, table 2) have a similar result, finding that minimum wages diminish wage growth of unskilled workers. More specifically, they show that workers with less than high school education have lower wage growth in states whose average wages are closer to the minimum wage (and in which the minimum wage therefore has more impact). The effect is not evident for workers with more than a high school education, as might be expected, since these workers are generally paid much more than the minimum. Backing up an on-the-job training interpretation of these results, workers were also less likely to say they were 'learning things on their job' (that is, undergoing on-the-job training, OJT) in states with wages close to the minimum (1981, 168).

Anti-discrimination laws appear to have had a similar effect, deterring training, in this case, of young black workers. The Lazear (1979a) study referred to above (see table 4.3) finds that by 1973–4 the black–white estimated full wage gap had widened, even though the observed wage gap had narrowed. Over the period 1966–74 it seems therefore that the value of OJT had increased more for white youths than for black. An explanation for this could be the affirmative action legislation which caused employers to raise wages. In terms of the specific training diagram of figure 4.2, the laws would push up W_0 and so reduce area C_W, the worker's training costs. If the employer did not react, his training costs, area C_E, would increase. Presumably the employer would resist however and try to preserve the equitable sharing of costs. He would therefore put the young worker on jobs with a higher current value to the firm (higher MP_0), so reducing the training investment. In the limit, if W_0 were made equal to W_A, all training could be deterred. This shows the perils of fixing wages.

Countries such as Germany, where youth training is widely regarded as successful, have relatively low youth wages. In Germany, trainees receive only 30% to 40% of the adult rate, compared to 80% to 100% in Britain (Casey, 1986). Correspondingly, Prais and Wagner (1988) find skill differentials to be much more compressed in Britain than in Germany. Often policy-makers tend to blame firms for not training workers more intensively, and attempt to legislate to force firms to allow workers to attend training courses during working time. For example, the European Commission's Social Charter of Fundamental Workers' Rights, which is meant to become law by 1992, proposes vocational training courses 'during working time'. Such a policy forces up firms' costs. Since nothing is done to address the problem of high trainee wages, the policy would cause firms to avoid hiring workers in need of vocational training, and actually work to reduce training (see Addison and Siebert, 1991, for an analysis of the Charter).

4.6 Conclusions

The chapter has concentrated on explaining the curvature of the age–earnings profile. We argued the curvature results because early in people's lives they forego income in order to train. Later in life people spend less on training, and are recouping the costs of past training, so their incomes are higher.

The merits of this explanation can be judged in various ways. First, it is logical to suppose that individuals invest in themselves by foregoing income, and that these investments decline with age. Second, the explanation gives an interpretation to earnings function coefficients, linking them to the proportion of time a person spends investing, and to the rate of return on human capital. This interpretation gives reasonable results in practice. In particular we find a person just entering the workforce spends about half his time in self-investment, and earns a rate of return about 10%, which is plausible.

In addition to education and experience, earnings are affected by many other factors, including sex, colour, marital status, union membership, ability, and family background. In later chapters we explore most of these effects in more detail. A further interesting possibility, which we have yet to consider, is that employees earn little when they are young basically as a discipline device: in the event of their being dismissed for shirking they lose their earlier investment. This extra aspect of the earnings profile will be considered in chapter 9 on payment systems.

The theory has important policy implications. According to the theory, people forego earnings to buy training. When young, or new to a job, they ask for low rates of pay (indeed, in the old days, far from being paid, apprentices used to pay firms to be trained). Employers will pay a share of specific training costs. But attempts to raise this share by raising youth wages in the hope that young workers will be kept on in the same trainee-type jobs as before will be resisted by employers. In practice minimum wage legislation will reduce the extent to which young workers can find training slots in firms.

Further, laws forcing firms to allow workers to attend vocational training courses during working time are misconceived. Such attempts, if not accompanied by a fall in trainee wage rates, simply raise firms' costs. Instead of improving the volume of training, they have the opposite effect.

Appendix 4.1 Deriving the earnings function

Equation (4.2) in the text is:

$$\ln E_t = \ln E_0 + r_s S + r_p \sum_{i=1}^{t-1} s_i, \tag{A-1}$$

where E_t is capacity earnings in the t-th year, E_0 is 'original' capacity earnings, S is years of education, r_s, r_p are the rates of return to education and training, s_i is the fraction of earnings capacity foregone in year i to acquire human capital.

Let us now consider depreciation (see Mincer (1974) for a full discussion). Define net capital acquisition, C_{nt},

$$C_{nt} = C_{gt} - \delta PK_t,$$

where C_{gt} is gross capital acquisition (the dollar value of eds output every year, Q_t), δ is the depreciation rate, PK_t is the dollar value of human capital (remember $P = w/r = $ the capitalised value of an ed, where r is the discount rate). The capital stock grows through the additions of net investment, thus:

$$PK_{t+1} = PK_t + C_{nt}.$$

In other words, capital this year equals capital last year plus last year's net investment. Therefore:

$$PK_{t+1} = PK_t + C_{gt} - \delta PK_t.$$

Since $E_t = wK_t = rPK_t$, we then have an equation for E_t:

$$E_t = (1 - \delta)E_{t-1} + rC_{gt-1}$$
$$= E_{t-1}(1 - \delta - rs^*_{t-1}), \text{ defining } s^*_t = C_{gt}/E_t.$$

Building up the sequence of E_t, in year 1:

$$E_1 = E_0(1 - \delta - rs^*_0).$$

In year 2:

$$E_2 = E_1(1 - \delta - rs^*_1)$$
$$= E_0(1 - \delta - rs^*_1)(1 - \delta - rs^*_0).$$

In general:

$$E_t = E_0 \prod_{i=0}^{t-1} (1 - \delta - rs^*_i),$$

or:

$$\ln E_t = \ln E_0 + \Sigma_{i=0}^{t-1}\ln (1 - \delta - rs_i^*)$$

or:

$$\ln E_t = \ln E_0 + \Sigma (rs_i^* - \delta) \tag{A-2}$$

using the approximation:

$$\ln(1 - \delta + rs_i^*) \cong -\delta + rs_i^*.$$

Comparing (A-2) and (A-1), we see that (A-2) has δ explicitly included in the summation. Note that in later years of life δ will be greater than s_i^*, causing capacity earnings to tend downwards. In fact E_t peaks when $rs^* = \delta$, and the net investment fraction C_{nt}/E_t is zero. To see this, set $E_t = E_{t-1}$, as will be the case when E_t is peaking. Thus:

$$E_t - E_{t-1} = rs_{t-1}^* - \delta = 0.$$

Now:

$$\begin{aligned}s_t^* &= C_{gt}/E_t = (C_{nt} + \delta PK_t)/E_t \\ &= C_{nt}/E_t + \delta/r, \text{ since } E_t = rPK_t. \end{aligned} \tag{A-3}$$

If $s_t^* = \delta/r$, it can therefore be seen that C_{nt}/E_t, the net investment fraction, must be zero.

(A-3) gives the gross investment fraction in terms of the net investment fraction. Substituting this into (A-2) we find:

$$\begin{aligned}\ln E_t &= \ln E_0 + r \Sigma (s_i^* - \delta/r) \\ &= \ln E_0 + r \Sigma C_{nt}/E_t \\ &= \ln E_0 + r \Sigma s_i, \text{ since } s_t = C_{nt}/E_t. \end{aligned}$$

This equation is the same as (A-1), but we have now shown that the investment fraction in that equation is the *net* investment fraction. Notice how s_i becomes negative once s_i^* falls below δ/r. For example, if $\delta = 3\%$ and $r = 15\%$ (remember $r = i + \delta$, where i is the market interest rate), net investment becomes negative once s^* falls below $1/5$, i.e., once less than $1/5$ of one's time is spent investing.

The sequence of s's is assumed to take the value of unity in the school period. This gives the rS term in (A-1) above. After school it is simplest to assume that s_t declines linearly for those who never drop out of the workforce. (Married women will have a different pattern of investment – see chapter 6.) Since s_t is the net investment fraction, it must become zero when capacity earnings peak – say twenty-five years after leaving school. Thus:

$$\begin{aligned}s_t &= \alpha - \beta t \\ &= \alpha - \alpha t/25, \end{aligned} \tag{A-4}$$

where t is now post-school experience. α is the fraction of earnings capacity devoted to self-investment immediately on leaving school, and a reasonable figure has been found to be about 50%. (50% of earnings capacity is used for training purposes early in life – see Johnson (1978) for an explanation of why s_t does not smoothly decline from unity in terms of the fact that full-time school investment is subsidised, whereas part-time on-the-job training is not.)

Substituting (A-4) into (A-1) gives:

$$\ln E_t = \ln E_0 + r_s S + r_p \sum_{i=1}^{t-1} (\alpha - \alpha i/25),$$

where i ranges over the years between school and retirement. The sum is an arithmetic progression with value:

$$\alpha t - \alpha t(t-1)/2 \times 25 \cong \alpha t - \alpha t^2/50.$$

Thus

$$\ln E_t = \ln E_0 + rS + r\alpha t - r\alpha t^2/50. \tag{A-5}$$

In this way we derive equation (4.3) in the text, with the quadratic term in years in the workforce, t. Notice how knowledge of these terms will enable us to estimate α and r.

In fact we cannot perform the regression in (A-5) directly because it refers to capacity earnings, which we cannot observe. However, observed and capacity earnings are related:

$$E_t = Y_t + C_{gt},$$

or:

$$Y_t = E_t(1 - s_t^*) = E_t(1 - s_t - \delta/r). \tag{A-6}$$

In log terms:

$$\ln Y_t = \ln E_t - s_t - \delta/r,$$

using the approximation $\ln(1 - x) \cong x$.

Substituting into (A-5) gives the estimating equation (4.4) in the text:

$$\begin{aligned} \ln Y_t &= (\ln E_0 - \delta/r - \alpha) + rS + (r\alpha + \alpha/25)t - r\alpha t^2/50 \\ &= a_0 + rS + a_1 t - a_2 t^2. \end{aligned}$$

Taking the coefficients from equation (b) in table 4.1 we see that the coefficient on t is $a_1 = 0.081$ and on t^2 is $a_2 = -0.0012$. Thus:

$$0.081 = r\alpha + \alpha/25$$

and:

$$-0.0012 = -r\alpha/50.$$

We can therefore calculate r and α (r would here be the return to training, which we would hope is similar to the return to schooling). It turns out that $\alpha = 0.53$ and $r = 0.14$, which are reasonable figures.

5   Labour supply

5.1 Introduction

Up until now how much individuals work has been ignored. Instead we have concentrated on human capital accumulation assuming that individuals work full time over their life. However, clearly not everyone exhibits such work behaviour. As we shall see in chapter 6, assuming full work behaviour can lead us to overestimate expected human capital accumulation and earnings. To alleviate this problem we now study labourforce participation decisions.

Labourforce participation is harder to analyse than one might expect. Just as participation motivates human capital investment and hence wages (as will be discussed in the next chapter), so potential wages influence participation decisions. In fact, the influence of wages on work is the focus of this chapter. A further dimension of supply is the 'effort' which people put into their work. The issue of effort is related to supervision, and effort-related payment systems (piece rates), and will be considered in chapter 9.

Interesting questions arise in the participation/hours area. Married women's participation has increased considerably over time. For example in Britain in 1940 the participation rate of married women was only 10%, compared to about 50% in 1980. There has been a similar growth in the US as shown in table 5.1. Why has there been the increase? A further important question relates to the tax and welfare benefit system. Taxing people might make them work fewer hours, and – paradoxically – giving money to them via the benefit system can have the same effect (the 'poverty trap'). What are the sizes of these effects, and what are the implications for tax/transfer policy?

We will next consider models of participation and hours. Then in the following section we analyse the division of labour in the household and married women's labourforce participation. This is important because differences in labourforce participation due to the household division of labour might explain much of the gender gap in wages. After this the effects of the

Table 5.1. *Female participation as a proportion of population*

	Aged 15–64 (%)			
	1940/1	1960/1	1980/1	1986/7
US Married	17	32	51	56
Single	48	44	62	65
US 20–24	45	45	68	
25–44	30	39	65	
45–64	20	42	51	
UK Married	10	30	47:60	64
Single	74	69	61:74	73
UK 20–24	65	62	69	
25–44	36	41	60	
45–64	29	37	52	

Sources: US – Statistical Abstract, 1988, table 623; Killingsworth and Heckman, 1986, 104, 105, 108; UK – Labourforce Survey, 1986 (change of definition in 1981).

tax/benefit system on male labour supply will be discussed; this section also offers analysis of the retirement decision. We conclude with some observations on labourforce participation in a life-cycle context.

5.2 Models of participation and hours

The individual

In the first case we assume a two-fold division of time: market work and 'leisure', that is, all uses of time other than work. Later we will make the model more realistic, and separate out the 'home work' component of leisure. This latter form of work involves family rather than individual decision-making, and is most relevant for women.

The standard indifference curve diagram for analysing the choice between labour and 'leisure' is given in figure 5.1. The individual is assumed to have a family of indifference curves for goods and leisure shaped like II' in the diagram. The indifference curves are derived from a utility function:

$$U = U(G, H),$$

where G is money, or the value of goods bought, and H is hours of leisure; $T = H + N$, where T is total time, and N is market work. Along an indifference curve utility is constant:

$$dU = U_G dG + U_H dH = 0,$$

so the slope of an indifference curve is:

$$dG/dH = -U_H/U_G,$$

where $U_G = \partial U/\partial G$ is the marginal utility of money and $U_H = \partial U/\partial H$ is the marginal utility of leisure. Thus the slope is the ratio of the marginal utility of leisure to the marginal utility of money. This explains why the slope of indifference curves diminishes as more leisure is consumed – because the marginal utility of leisure declines as more leisure is consumed. It is also possible for indifference curves to slope upwards after a point, once 'satiety' is reached and the individual begins to dislike leisure (to enjoy work). The implications of such tastes will be illustrated later.

The individual's resource constraint or budget line is:

$$G = (1 - t)wN$$
$$= (1 - t)w(T - H) = (1 - t)wT - (1 - t)wH,$$

where w is the wage rate, and t is the tax rate, so $(1 - t)w$ is the after-tax wage. The resource constraint is thus a negatively sloped straight line with intercept $(1 - t)wT$ and slope $-(1 - t)w$. (w is an earnings stream, and depends on the individual's human capital.)

With the isoquant drawn as it is, the individual would maximise utility by moving to point A. Here the individual consumes goods worth M^*, consumes H^* hours of leisure, and works $T - H^*$ hours. At this point the slope of the constraint, the rate at which leisure is exchanged for goods on the market (the opportunity cost of leisure), equals the slope of the isoquant, the rate at which leisure is exchanged for goods 'in the mind' (the 'shadow' value of leisure).

If welfare benefits are available of value B when the individual does not work, this would be represented by point B in figure 5.1. A horizontal line from B would indicate that the benefits were 'means-tested', and withdrawn penny for penny as the individual earned more. Such a benefit system in effect implicitly subjects people to 100% rates of tax at low earnings levels. With the isoquant drawn as shown, the individual would move to point B, and not work at all. This illustrates a 'corner' solution, with the individual electing not to participate. At B the shadow value of time is greater than its market value (here zero).

The diagram can be used to illustrate several points about participation and hours:

1 An increase in the wage need not elicit an increase in hours worked. On the one hand the market price of home time has then gone up, so that less of it will be used – the substitution effect. On the other hand, the individual is better off. If hours at home are 'normal' goods, as is likely, the income effect

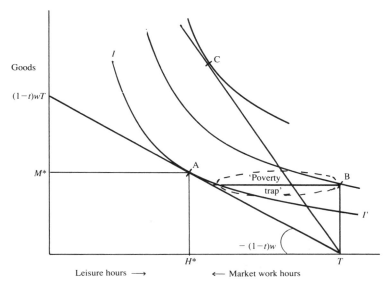

Figure 5.1 Labour–leisure choice

could overwhelm the substitution effect. This is shown in figure 5.2. The initial wage is $(1 - t)w$, the lower wage is $(1 - 2t)w$. The initial position is 3, and the final position is 1, with a substitution effect of 1 to 2, and an income effect of 2 to 3. The substitution effect is drawn in reference to a given indifference curve and shows how the goods and leisure combination would change if the (post-tax) wage alone changed, utility remaining constant. The income effect is likewise drawn in relation to a given indifference curve and shows how the goods and leisure combination would change if income alone changed, the wage remaining constant at its original level, $(1 - t)w$.

Supply curves can therefore be 'backward bending'. Figure 5.3 illustrates two such curves, for individuals A and B. Because of the substitution effect, however, if one could 'compensate' for wage increases (decreases) by taking away (giving) income from a person, a 'compensated' supply curve would always be upward sloping. Attempts have been made to estimate such compensated supply curves by taking situations where a wage increase does not have much of an income effect – for example the wage increase might only be a temporary one – see below.

Nevertheless, from the point of view of tax policy, since tax changes are rarely temporary, it is the uncompensated supply curve which is relevant. The fact that such supply curves are likely to be backward-bending has important implications for the tax policy: if the after-tax wage is reduced by a tax rise,

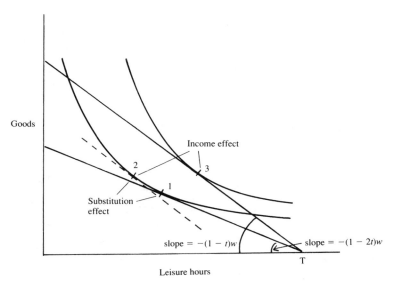

Figure 5.2 Income and substitution effects

there need be no reduction in hours worked. Higher taxes need not therefore be cancelled out by people working fewer hours, a result which is comforting for the tax collector.

2   Less comforting for the tax collector, a rise in taxes (fall in the after-tax wage) will always induce some not to participate – to drop out of the labour-force. Figure 5.1 shows the position. At a zero tax rate the individual would be at point C, say, working some hours in the market. If taxes at rate *t* were imposed, however, this person would go on welfare and stop participating (point B).

3   A rise in welfare benefits will always induce some workers not to participate. Again this can be seen in figure 5.1. Without welfare benefits, the worker would be at point A, for example. A rise in benefits to B would cause the worker illustrated to move to point B, and drop out. Welfare policy there-fore is inherently double-edged. Raising welfare helps the poor, but some of them will then 'live on welfare' which might be bad for them in the long run (causing work skills to deteriorate – 'welfare dependency'), and expensive for the taxpayer.

4   It is primarily the unskilled – those whose low productivity means they can only command low wages – whose incentives to drop out of the workforce are

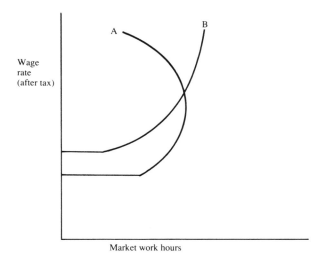

Figure 5.3 Labour supply curves

increased by tax and/or welfare increases. To illustrate, in figure 5.1 we can think of the lower budget line as representing a low wage worker's opportunities, and the steeply sloped budget line as representing a high wage worker. It can be seen that the budget line for the low wage worker is dominated by the horizontal welfare benefits section. It would take a large rise in taxes and/or welfare benefits to make the individual at C drop out, but not so for the individual whose choice is between point A and point B. For this latter person it is not worthwhile to work, so the horizontal section is labelled 'poverty trap' in the diagram.

Individuals who command low market wages are somewhat better off on welfare, and cannot improve their positions by working – they are trapped. The point to be emphasised is that both high benefits and *high taxes* – so long as welfare benefits are not taxed – worsen the poverty trap. If benefits are not taxed, and taxes increase, then the 'replacement ratio', that is, the ratio of benefits to post-tax wages, increases, and with it the poverty trap. This is the reason for measures to tax welfare benefits – to lower the replacement ratio.

5   The framework can illustrate the 'surplus' that workers get from their jobs, that is, the extent to which the wage a worker receives more than compensates for the disutility of working. Up to this point we have been assuming that people regard work as a 'bad'. This is why the indifference curves have been drawn as sloping downwards. However many people enjoy

at least some hours of their work. We can show that, because they enjoy it, they will work more hours (and bid down rates of pay) in a competitive economy. Consider figure 5.4. Panel A illustrates the usual case, in which work is a 'bad', and panel B illustrates an individual who 'loves his work' – a pop star for example. In the indifference curves in panel B, work becomes a good (or leisure a bad, which is the same thing) once the indifference curves begin to slope upwards.

Taking panel A first, we see that at wage w_1, the worker will locate at point 1. However, there will be some wage, w_{min}, at which he/she will stop working and move to point 4, on a lower indifference curve. The vertical difference between point 4, and point 3 (on the old indifference curve), is called the 'compensating variation', and represents the amount of money that would have to be given to this worker to compensate for such a fall in the wage. It is a measure of the 'surplus' the worker obtains from working. The surplus derives from the fact that this individual is paid w_1 for all hours worked, but in fact would work the first hours for less. Worker surplus can be represented on a conventional supply diagram as shown in the lower graph of panel A.

A different measure of surplus can be calculated by asking how much the worker would give to *avoid* being paid w_{min}. This is called the 'equivalent variation', and is calculated by drawing a tangent of slope w_1 to the zero work indifference curve. This gives point 2. Normally the two methods will give different answers. However where all indifference curves have the same slope for given leisure, as illustrated, they do not. Assuming the same slope means that U_H/U_G is the same at point 1, for example, as at point 2. Leisure is the same at both points 1 and 2, but the individual has more money at point 1 than at point 2, so assuming the slope does not change amounts to assuming the marginal utility of money is constant. This assumption will only be true for small changes in the wage – so our usual triangular measure of worker's surplus is just an approximation.

Turning to panel B and the person who loves work, we see that he/she obtains much bigger compensating and equivalent variations. This person would indeed *pay* to work the first few hours in the job in question, as shown by the fact that w_{min} is negative. Several hours work could be got for nothing. Note however that for this person as for the person in panel A, the marginal hour of work is unpleasant. This has to be the case, otherwise he/she would never stop working. Nevertheless such an individual would work for less than is available on welfare since welfare is conditional on no work being done, but this individual likes (some) work.

6   The model demonstrates the difference between permanent and transitory wage changes on labour supply, providing a bridge to the study of life-cycle effects. More educated individuals, for example, will have higher wages

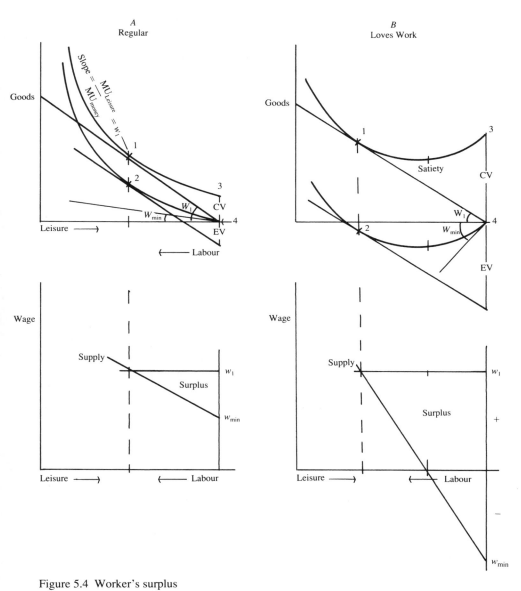

Figure 5.4 Worker's surplus

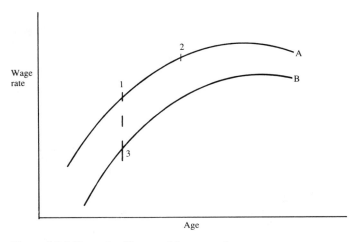

Figure 5.5 Life-cycle effects on labour supply

throughout their lives; they are wealthy. Contrasting such permanently high wage with permanently low wage individuals we expect to see an income effect. High wage earners will work shorter hours than low wage earners. An example of this is the fact that manual workers work longer hours and have lower wages at all ages than non-manual workers – because the non-manual workers have greater life-cycle wealth. In terms of figure 5.2, permanently high wage workers are at position 3, permanently low wage workers at position 2. A further example is the way in which black women, with lower lifetime earnings profiles (compared to white) participate more (Heckman and Killingsworth, 1986, 159).

However, a temporary wage increase will have mainly a substitution effect – a move from point 1 to point 2 in figure 5.2. In good times, for example, wages will increase, and workers can be expected to work for longer hours while this lasts – to 'make hay while the sun shines'.

In the life-cycle context, wages increase with age. The increase is anticipated and so as it occurs individuals do not feel wealthier. The increase therefore has no income effect, and so we would expect an increase in hours worked due simply to the substitution effect (Ghez and Becker, 1975, 12). Figure 5.5 illustrates the point with two earnings profiles, one for person A, the other for person B. Comparing points 1 and 2 for person A, as the wage increases we would expect an increase in hours worked. On the other hand, comparing person A with person B, who has lower wages throughout life and is therefore poorer, we can make no prediction as to who will work longer hours. Comparing points 1 and 3, for example, individual B might well work

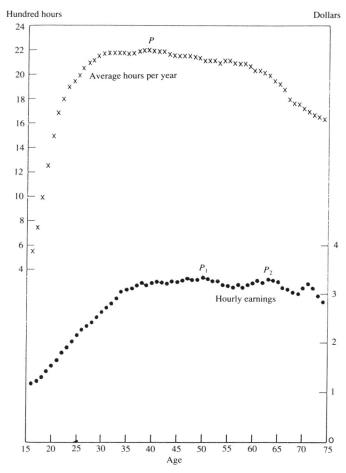

Figure 5.6 Hourly earnings and hours worked per year, US white males. *Source:* Ghez and Becker, 1973, 85

longer hours than individual A. The life-cycle elasticity of hours worked with respect to wages, wealth constant (comparing points 1 and 2) is called the 'intertemporal' elasticity (MacCurdy, 1981, 1060; see also Hotz *et al.*, 1988; Shaw, 1990; Jiang and Polachek, 1991; Adams, 1987; Ball, 1991), and is thus expected to be greater than the regular hours elasticity (a comparison of points 1 and 3).

The strong link between hours worked and earnings over the life cycle is illustrated in figure 5.6. As can be seen, yearly hours worked first increases and then decreases over the life cycle, just as does earnings. It is the high correlation between the two which gives the high value of the intertemporal hours elasticity.

The fact that hours worked follow the life-cycle profile of earnings has implications for the life-cycle pattern of consumption as well. When the price of leisure is high, people economise on leisure not only by working longer, but by substituting goods for leisure in consumption, e.g., they buy pre-cooked food so as to save time. Thus at ages where wages are high, people work more, earn more, and consume more.

7   Transitory changes in non-labour income (just as transitory changes in wages) can be expected to have more of an effect on hours worked than permanent changes (Mincer, 1962, 74ff). This is because people are expected to adjust their consumption to their permanent rather than their temporary income (the permanent income hypothesis). A temporary rise in income does not increase consumption – it just decreases labour hours. A permanent rise in income on the other hand would be accompanied by permanently higher consumption, and only a small hours decrease. It is as though it is more difficult to adjust consumption habits than hours of work, so that hours of work fluctuate to maintain consumption.

Refer again to figure 5.2. The parallel outward shift of the budget constraint represents an increase in income, and the movement from point 2 to point 3 is the individual's reaction – a decrease in market work hours. The argument is that this decrease will be less marked if the shift is permanent, than if it is temporary. The most natural examples occur in the case of married women (see next section). Suppose a woman is married to a rich man. She might not work much in the market. Suppose then that he suffers a reverse in his fortunes, causing an income effect for his wife. If this reverse is temporary, his wife will probably go out to work, or work longer hours so as to honour the family's fixed commitments such as interest on housing loans. But if the reverse is permanent the family will adjust by selling the house and the wife's working hours adjustment will be correspondingly smaller. Permanent income changes therefore have smaller labour supply effects than temporary changes.

The effects of permanent and transitory changes in husband's income on wife's participation is shown in table 5.2. Moving down the third column, we see how the average wife's participation changes only moderately from 31% to 38% as we move from wives with elementary schooled to wives with college educated husbands. This comparison corresponds to a comparison between wives with permanent differences in income. However if we look at the fourth column, the increase in participation when comparing wives with elementary to wives with college trained husbands is more marked – from 37% to 56%. This is because we are looking only at wives with low income husbands, but

Table 5.2. *Response of labourforce participation rates of wives to transitory changes in husband's income*

Husband's education	Husband's earnings	Wife's earnings	Wife's *LFP* when husband earns	
			Average	$2,000–$3,000
Elementary	$70 p.w.	$41 p.w.	31%	37%
High school	$80	$46	33%	45%
College	$115	$52	38%	56%

Note: Husband is 35–54 and family has no small children. Data are from the 1960 US Census.
Source: Mincer, 1962, table 3.

low income will be a transitory state for husbands with a college education. Because college trained husbands only temporarily earn less than $3,000, their wives help out with 56% participation rate.

The distinction between permanent and transitory income changes on labour supply underlies the 'added worker' effect. Thus wives might tend to search for work more intensively in a depression, so as to make up for their husband's temporary unemployment. The distinction also has implications for negative income tax experiments. US experiments (see below) have involved giving income guarantees to poor families. These families have responded by working fewer hours, and participating less (Robins, 1984, 580). However since these experiments only produced temporary income changes, their labour supply effects would probably be larger than for permanent programmes.

In sum, we have:
a) the permanently high wage individual (for example with a degree). This person is wealthy and hence experiences mainly an income effect compared with the low wage individual. Therefore the high wage has little effect on hours worked – such a person probably works somewhat fewer hours, if anything. Examples: manual workers work longer hours than non-manual; black women work longer hours than white; tax increases permanently reduce after-tax wages, and so people work the same or more hours (but remember some drop out of the workforce, so there is a decrease in the overall labour supply);
b) the individual with a permanent non-labour income change. This is similar to (a). For example, if a wife's husband fails his accountancy examination, the wife decreases her consumption permanently, for example by moving

into a smaller house (the husband's income being non-labour income for the wife), and does not change her hours worked much;

c) the transitorily high wage individual (for example receiving a special bonus). The extra wage does not affect income much, and so has mainly a substitution effect. There is thus a marked increase in hours worked – 'make hay while the sun shines';

d) the individual with a transitory non-labour income change. This is similar to (c). Thus if a woman's husband is laid off, the family maintains its consumption and the wife increases her work hours (the 'added worker' effect);

e) the life-cycle wage change, for example a young man earns less than he will when older. Such a wage increase is anticipated, and so the man does not feel 'poor' when young, or 'wealthy' when older. Since there is no wealth effect as wages increase, then hours increase with age due to the substitution effect.

Married women's labour supply

We have been speaking of a twofold division of hours, with leisure and market work. We now make a threefold division, splitting the 'leisure' category into hours actually worked at home, and true leisure (see Gronau, 1986, 282ff). Hours worked at home produce home goods, such as meals, child care, and health (even eight hours sleep is a form of homework in this sense – see Hamermesh and Biddle, 1990). Hours worked in the market bring in market goods. We can assume the total amount of goods available to the individual is the sum of these two – home goods and market goods. To enjoy either market or home goods requires the use of time as a consumption good, which we term 'leisure' time.

As before the individual is assumed to maximise utility requiring both goods (market or home produced) and time as inputs, subject to a budget constraint. But now the budget constraint explicitly distinguishes home work hours from leisure hours. This is useful when analysing married women, who work many hours in the home (see table 5.3 below).

The position is illustrated in figure 5.7. The 'household production function' summarises household production possibilities. The production function probably shifts upwards when the education of the wife increases, and with improvements in the household kitchen and cleaning equipment she works with. On the other hand a decrease in family size will move the function downwards. Over time, improvements in household technology will have shifted the function upwards while declining family size will have had the opposite effect – the net effect being uncertain. In fact, housewives appear to spend as much time on household work now as in the past (Vanek, 1974,

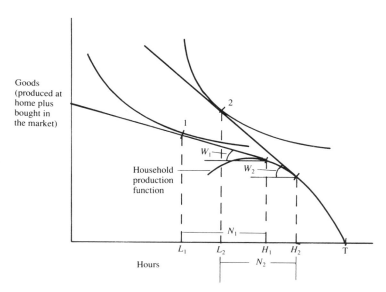

Figure 5.7 Household production and market work

116), so perhaps the household production function has not – on net – changed much.

The function would also vary with the activities of the husband. In particular if the husband becomes unemployed, and if his work can substitute for the wife's in the case of cleaning or working (but less easily in the care of younger children) the wife's home productivity would fall.

The full opportunity set is built up by combining household production opportunities with market opportunities. The latter are given by the usual budget line. For example, a low wage individual would have a budget line with slope w_1, and a high wage individual a line with slope w_2. To construct the full opportunity set, the budget line is shifted upwards until it is just tangent with the household production function. This gives the largest opportunity set, as can be seen.

Total time can now be divided into:

$$T = H + N + L,$$

where: L is consumption time or leisure; H and N are home work and market work respectively. With the given indifference curves, the low wage individual would locate at point 1, and the high wage individual at point 2 in the diagram. The indicated three-part division of hours results.

The diagram shows that an increase in wages definitely reduces home work hours (from H_1 to H_2). The reduction would be smaller the more curved the household production function, that is, the less substitutable market work is for home work in producing 'commodities' (for example, where there are young children in the home, H_1 to H_2 will be small). A wage increase will also tend to increase leisure hours from L_1 to L_2 – assuming leisure time is a normal good. The net effect on market hours depends on the resultant of these two effects: N_1 could be greater or smaller than N_2, depending on the changes in L and H. But notice that the reduction in H consequent upon a wage increase *always* helps counteract the increase in L, and helps make for an increase in market work hours, N.

The response of wives to wage increases therefore depends on two types of substitution effects (see Mincer, 1962, 70): the usual substitution effect as between leisure and work (giving L_1 to L_2), and the substitutability of market work for home work in the production of goods (giving H_1 to H_2). Men, in general, are only subject to the former type of substitution effect. However married women – to the extent they have household productivity – have an extra degree of freedom. Because of this extra margin of substitution, we would therefore expect the elasticity of married women's market work hours with respect to wages to be greater than the male elasticity.

Figure 5.8 illustrates the effects of changes in the household production function on a married woman's labour supply. Improved household cooking and cleaning technology can be illustrated as a move in home work hours from point A to point B. In this case fewer hours are spent in home work. Notice however that a different type of home productivity improvement would mean a move to C, with more hours spent at home. A less curved production function such as that passing through C would indicate that home time not only produced more home goods, but also that home time was more substitutable for market time in the production of goods.

However there is another force at work, as noted above: the decline in family size. Since a major component of household work is child care, a smaller family means household productivity is reduced – a downward movement in the function, for example a move from C to A (see Blau and Robins, 1991). Improved household technology and smaller family size thus pull the production function in opposite direction. Therefore we are inclined to believe that changes in the household production function over time have not been a major determinant of married women's increased market work.

Finally it is worth noting the effect of an increase in the husband's income on the wife's market work within this framework. An increase in husband's income simply moves the opportunity set in figure 5.8 upwards in a parallel way, so that it starts from point D. This leaves home work, H, unchanged (if the wife is working in the market before and after), increases leisure, L, and decreases market work, N. However the decrease in N is expected to be

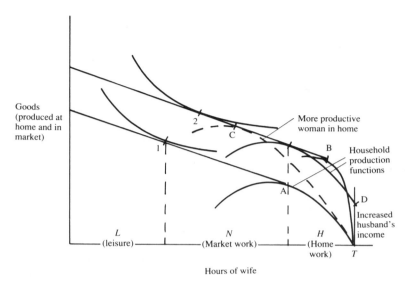

Figure 5.8 Household production – effects of changes in the household production function

more marked if the increase in husband's income is transitory, as discussed above.

It is interesting at this point to consider actual patterns of time use, as computed by the University of Michigan using time diaries. Some data are contained in table 5.3. Activities have been grouped into the three categories already discussed. Single men and women are distinguished from married men and women because of the greater division of labour in the married home, and the greater household productivity of the married woman (with children).

We would expect the two single groups to be similar, and they are – except for the surprisingly long time devoted by single women to house work. Married women not working devote most time to the home work category as expected, married and single men least time. Married men working full time devote most time to the market work category.

If we think of the married men working full time being paired with the married women not working – the 'traditional' family – table 5.3 brings out the great specialisation of tasks in such a family. The married woman who is not working spends forty-two hours a week on house work, child care, and shopping, compared to only thirteen hours for her spouse. The great importance of the household production option for married women is underlined by these data.

Table 5.3 can also be used to construct rough life-cycle patterns. Men start single, become married working full time, then retire and join the not working category. As can be seen, men's market work increases, then decreases with age. Women start single, then marry and for a time do not work in the market since they are looking after children – as shown in the last column. They afterwards return to the workforce full time. Women's market work decreases then increases with age.

In sum, from the economic point of view marriage can be thought of as two people pooling resources of time and market and home skills. Marriage also enlarges the household production set to include other 'outputs' such as children and companionship, which a single person household cannot produce. It is differences between the parties, permitting specialisation, which make the parties better off when married.

Both parties can work in the market, or work at home, or a mixture of the two. At home they produce home products such as companionship, childcare, home cooking. Both home products and market goods are needed by the household to produce final commodities. The two partners we assume allocate time between market work and home work so as to produce home products and market goods as cheaply as possible, given the wages facing the two parties, and their household productivities (see Cigno, 1989; for a game theory approach see McElroy and Horney, 1981; Mancer and Brown, 1980; and also McElroy, 1990). For married men, household production is relatively trivial – specialisation within the family requires this. However for married women it is important. Married women thus have an important extra margin of substitution, that is, they are able to substitute market work for home work. The implication is that married women's market labour supply will be more elastic with respect to the wage than married men's.

The argument that men mainly do market work and married women house work because of comparative advantage has been criticised because it ignores the 'power' of men over women. For example, Barbara Bergmann has compared the occupation of housewife to that of a 'caste' into which one is 'placed at birth' (1981, 84). The implication is that families could be organised differently in an ideal world. The difficulty with this point of view is to explain how millions of men can collude to enforce such a 'caste'. Nevertheless even if we were to consider the caste theory as a possibility, the analysis of figures 5.7 and 5.8 stands given that married women have higher household productivity than men (for whatever reason).

5.3 Empirical results – women's labourforce participation

Over the past century, the trend has been for the wage gap to narrow, and occupational structures to become somewhat more similar. At the same time,

Table 5.3. *Patterns of time use, by sex, and marital status (hours per week)*

	Activity	Males Single	Married Work FT	Married Not working	Females Single	Married Work FT	Married Not working
N	Market work	29 hrs	48	5	20	39	3
	Education	4	1	2	2	—	—
H	House/yard work	8	7	15	16	16	27
	Child care	—	2	1	2	3	7
	Shopping	4	4	5	5	6	8
L	Personal care, entertainment, leisure	123	106	140	123	104	123

Notes: Data are from time diaries for 971 adult men and women in 1975–6.

Market work: includes normal work, unemployment actions, non-work activities at the workplace (e.g., coffee breaks) and commuting.

House/yard work: 80% of the time is devoted to cooking and cleaning, including outdoor cleaning. Other activities are repairs, gardening, pet care.

Shopping: mainly shopping for everyday items such as food, drugs, clothing, small appliances. 40% of shopping time is travel.

Personal care, entertainment, leisure: sleep, washing, dressing, eating (10 hours per week), helping and caring for others, TV watching (14 hours), spectator activities, visiting, sport.

Source: Hill, 1985, 148; see also Juster and Stafford, 1991.

women's labourforce participation has increased markedly. The issue is whether the improvements are due to legislation (so more laws are called for), or to the operation of market forces, in particular a reduction in the advantages of the sexual division of labour within the family – itself a consequence of other factors such as improved birth control.

Trends in participation and associated variables

Table 5.1 shows the trends in participation. In both countries married women have shown a marked increase in participation, the 'revolution' in which we are interested. Single women have increased participation much more moderately. This is as one would expect, since changes in divorce and fertility affect the family, and thus primarily married women. Figures 5.9 and 5.10 illustrate the picture for different cohorts. The profiles have somewhat different shapes because the American graph relates only to married women. The British

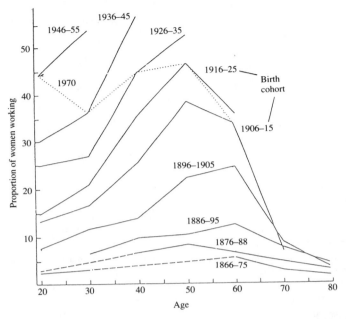

Figure 5.9 Participation rates of white married women, born 1866–1955, US. *Source:* Goldin, 1990, 22

profiles combine the effects of marriage as well as age which is more useful since a better picture results of the expected life-cycle participation of the average woman as she changes from single to married. In both countries the profiles move upwards over time.

Participation, wages, divorce, fertility, and education interact and cause each other (see also Nakamura and Nakamura, 1985). Tables 5.4 to 5.7 show trends over the post-war period in these variables for Britain and the US. Starting with the pay ratios, from table 5.4 we see that in the US the ratio has risen somewhat, as is the case in Britain as well. The increase in Britain is perhaps in response to the Equal Pay Act which was phased in during the 1970s. However Chiplin and Sloane (1988) point out that *male* skill differentials also decreased during the mid seventies. They suggest that government incomes policies addressed to raising unskilled pay levels are as important as the Equal Pay Act in raising female relative pay. It must also be remembered that a factor reducing average pay for women has been the drawing of less experienced and educated workers into the workforce as women's participation has increased. Making allowance for this, the pay ratio would have increased

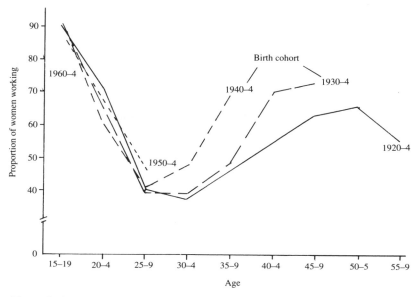

Figure 5.10 Participation rates of women by age and birth cohort, UK. *Source:* Martin and Roberts, 1984, 119

more than shown – in he US case, by about 3 percentage points for 1950 to 1980 (Smith and Ward, 1989, table 4 – the 3 point figure is an average across age groups).

Table 5.5 shows the corresponding revolution in divorce behaviour. In the US a marriage is more likely to break up than in Britain, but in both countries an average marriage now only lasts about six years. Britain has the highest divorce rate per 1,000 marriages of all countries in the European Community (Social Trends, 1989, table 2.20), and the increase has all occurred since 1960. Studies of participation are increasingly considering the effects of divorce, as noted below.

Table 5.6 shows fertility trends. These have been downward in both countries since 1960, following the post-war baby boom. Interestingly, not only has fertility declined, but there has also been a trend for fertility to have less of a negative impact on participation. This is shown in figure 5.11 which compares successive British cohorts. Recent cohorts are returning to work sooner (Klerman and Liebowitz, 1991).

Table 5.7 shows education trends. In the US males appear to have overtaken females, while in Britain, females are catching up with males. In both countries however there has been a considerable improvement in women's education and

Table 5.4. *Ratio of female to male earnings*

	1955	1961	1981	1986
US	0.60	0.59	0.65	0.69
UK	0.60	0.60	0.71	0.69

Sources: US Statistical Abstracts, various – the figure relates to annual earnings, full-time employees; Joshi *et al.*, 1986, S158; UK Annual Abstract, 1988, table 6.15 – figure relates to hourly earnings of full-time employees.

Table 5.5. *Divorce*

	1950	1960	1980	1986
US – per 1,000 population	2.0	2.2	5.2	4.8
per 1,000 marriages			22.6	21.5
UK – per 1,000 marriages	2.6	2.1	11.9	12.6

Sources: US Statistical Abstract, 1988, tables 81, 126; Social Trends, 1989, table 2.16.

Table 5.6. *Fertility: births per 1,000 population*

	1950/1	1960/1	1980/1	1986/7
US	19.4	23.7	15.9	15.5
UK	15.9	17.9	13.0	13.6

Sources: US Statistical Abstract, 1988, table 81; Social Trends, 1988, table 1.9.

Table 5.7. *Education*

	1960	1980	1986
US – Median school years completed,			
white females	11.2	12.6	12.6
white males	10.7	12.5	12.8
UK – qualified to 'A' level standard, cohorts reaching 25–9			
females	4.9%	9.3	16.2
males	6.9	13.0	17.8

Sources: US Statistical Abstract, 1988, table 202; UK Census, 1981, Qualified Manpower Report.

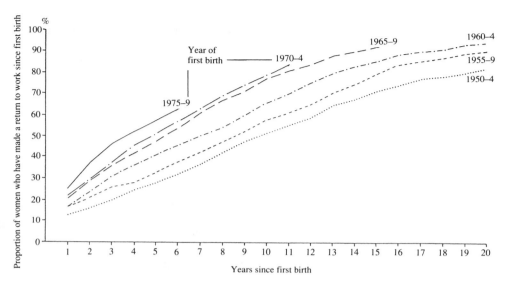

Figure 5.11 Proportion of women returning to work by interval since first birth, UK.
Source: Martin and Roberts, 1984, 127

we would expect this to have fertility, wage, and divorce consequences, as well as directly operating on labourforce participation.

The participation, wage, divorce, fertility system

Gary Becker has summarised the main linkages between participation and other variables as follows:

The major cause of the increased participation of married women during the twentieth century appears to be the increased earning power of married women as Western economies developed, including the rapid expansion of the service sector. The growth in their earning power raised the foregone value of their time spent at child care and other household activities, which reduced the demand for children and encouraged a substitution away from parental, especially mother's time . . . The gain from marriage is reduced, and hence the attractiveness of divorce raised, by higher earnings and labourforce participation of married women, because the sexual division of labour within households becomes less advantageous. Consequently this interpretation also implies the large growth in divorce rates over time . . . (1985, S34–5)

While the above argument summarises the linkages well, it is open to the charge of circularity. The prime driving force on which the argument relies, the increased 'earning power' of women, is itself at least partially caused by changes in participation, fertility and divorce. We have a system of four endogenous variables: wages, labourforce participation, divorce, and fertility. Education might well also be added since, as the quotation points out, the anticipation of higher labourforce participation means a greater incentive for education.

Such a system makes inference perilous. One cannot take a negative coefficient on labourforce participation in an earnings equation, for example, at its face value (career interruptions cause low wages), if low labourforce participation is in fact caused by low wages. Similarly, divorce is not exogenous either: expectations of divorce cause more human capital investment and thus cause increased wages and labourforce participation. On the other hand divorce is caused by high wages since high wage women have lower fertility due to higher opportunity costs of children. High wage women also gain less from marriage than other women. The two parties have less to exchange, since they are less specialised. Therefore, in addition to examining the strength of the forces linking the four or five main endogenous variables, we have to look beyond the system, to its determining exogenous variables.

In practice only parts of the full system have been studied. Part of the difficulty is that wages are not observed for those women not participating. One solution is to take a lifetime concept of participation – years worked as a fraction of potential years – and relate this to lifetime wages. Such an approach is taken by Mincer and Polachek in their original paper (1974, S99), proxying lifetime wages simply by education. Another solution is to predict wages for non-working women on the basis of a wage regression run for working women. It is then necessary to correct for 'selectivity effects' – the fact that working women are not representative of the population of women as a whole – and a large body of literature has developed on this problem (see Killingsworth and Heckman, 1986, table 2.26).

A major difficulty lies in specifying the exogenous variables to which the participation system variables respond. In the social science literature, the economic model has been criticised because it ignores 'technological and cultural changes', and 'discriminatory attitudes' (Duncan, 1974, S109). Some of these factors are exogenous, for example birth control technology, but 'culture' itself is often endogenous. For example a sample of British women were asked if they thought that young women with children 'ought to stay at home'. In 1965 75% said 'yes', compared to only 45% in 1987 (Social Trends, 1989, 21). However such a change in attitudes is itself a response to the increased earning power of women, and the increased probability of divorce, and so tells us nothing about causation. Only exogenous factors bearing on the need to stay at home, for example medical improvements which make young children less prone to illness, should be taken up – attitudes themselves are basically carriers, and take a secondary place.

Empirical studies

Single equation results

Most studies consider the effects of a given wage change on women's labour supply, without inquiring what caused the wage change in the first place. In Mincer's twelve country comparison (including the main European countries, the USA, Israel, and Japan), married women's participation elasticities range from 0.5 to 2.0, with an average of about 1.0 (Mincer, 1985, table 5). As for estimates of female hours elasticities, these vary widely: from slightly negative to plus 14, depending on how selectivity corrections for non-working women are made (Killingsworth and Heckman, 1986, table 2.25). Nevertheless the consensus is that women's – meaning married women's – labour supply is considerably more wage and property income elastic than men's (see Killingsworth, 1983, 432). The male own wage uncompensated hours elasticity appears to be negative, about -0.1 (see below).

The economic theory of the family, explained above, predicts larger participation and hours elasticities for married women than other groups. Men specialise in market work, while married women specialise in child care and household production. The reason for such a sexual division of labour depends on comparative advantage: the relatively higher home productivity of women and market productivity of men. Because many married women are on the threshold of market work, changes in the market wage have a bigger effect. According to this argument, whatever the econometric problems, we would be surprised if married women's labourforce participation, and market hours worked were not more elastic than men's.

The force of the family in shaping labour market behaviour can be tested by looking at single women. Because the family division of labour does not apply to single women, except to the extent that they expect to become married, a way of testing the power of the family division of labour is to see whether single women's labour market behaviour is similar to men's.

In fact, single women are like men in that the level of their participation rates are similar (though single women's participation is somewhat lower). However, little systematic analysis of single women's participation has been attempted. Participation studies have concentrated on married women, or else on single women heading families (and who therefore have family responsibilities). Joshi (1986, tables 11.1, 11.2) has a sample which includes married and single women, but she restricts the coefficient on wages in the participation equation to be the same for both. Wage elasticities, measured at the means, are in fact found to be considerably lower for single than married women, as the comparative advantage model predicts. O'Neill (1981, 79) also derives smaller coefficients for a sample including married and single women, than one for married women alone. It therefore seems that it is the family division of labour, rather than gender as such, which causes the different participation patterns of married women.

Changes in married women's wages, taken as exogenous, explain the evolution of their *LFP* over the post-war period quite well. In Mincer's twelve country study (mainly OECD countries), married women's *LFP* grew on average at 2.84% per year over 1960–80. Women's wages grew at 5.2% per year, men's wages at 4.4%. Participation elasticities were calculated for each country using the simple equation:

$$\ln LFP = a + b \ln(w_f) + c \ln(w_m),$$

where *LFP* = participation, w_f = wife's earnings, w_m = husband's earnings. Thus b = wage elasticity and c = income elasticity. Averaging b and c across countries gave $b = 1$ and $c = -0.4$.

Predicting the average married woman's participation increase by combining these elasticities with the actual changes in male and female wages over the period gives (1985, S11):

$$\begin{aligned} \Delta LFP &= b \, \Delta w_f + c \, \Delta w_m \\ &= 1 \times 5.2 - 0.4 \times 4.4 = 3.4\% \text{ per year.} \end{aligned}$$

The calculated growth of 3.4% can be seen to be quite close to the actual growth of 2.84%.

Adding further variables improves the explanation. Across countries, fertility rates are negatively correlated with married women's participation rates, and education levels and divorce rates positively correlated (Mincer, 1985, tables 9, 12, 13). The same holds true for time series analysis (see O'Neill, 1981, 79 for the US and Sprague, 1988, 692 for the UK). Since all these variables enter in the predicted way, Becker's family model seems to be borne out. But we might ask if the conclusions are changed if it is admitted that wages, fertility, and divorce are endogenous.

Multiple equation results

Several studies have analysed women's participation with wages and/ or divorce and fertility endogenous. R. Gronau takes participation and wages endogenous for a sample of women (married and single are not distinguished) who held jobs in 1976. His dependent variable is the probability of their leaving the labourforce in the 1976–9 period (28% of women left and 7% of the men – Gronau, 1988, 280).

Assuming wages exogenous, his findings are as for the usual *LFP* function, with the probability of leaving strongly negatively correlated with female wages and positively correlated with husband's income, holding education, experience, fertility, and divorce constant. Assuming women's wages endogenous, the findings remain, but the negative effect of women's wages becomes somewhat weaker. High fertility also continues to be associated with a higher probability of leaving, as does divorce – though education becomes positively associated with leaving, which is surprising. The results are built on strong identifying assumptions, in particular that divorce and fertility are exogenous. Nevertheless they generally support the usual picture of the determinants of women's *LFP*.

Cain and Dooley (1976) fit a three equation model, with married women's participation, wage, and fertility endogenous, to 124 US metropolitan areas. Divorce is ignored. Since the wage and participation data are averages for standard metropolitan statistical areas (SMSAs), the problem of missing wage and participation data for non-working women does not arise. Male wages, female education, religion, and industrial structure are among the variables assumed to be exogenous. The wife's wage is found to be strongly positively related to labourforce participation, and the husband's wage negatively related, in this system – with fertility surprisingly unimportant (1976, table 3). Here, the wage effect is strengthened if wages and fertility are assumed endogenous. Wife's education is found to increase participation for most age groups. However the fertility equation is not satisfactory: labourforce participation is negatively associated with fertility, which is appropriate, but neither the wife's wage nor her education are significant (1976, table 4).

Fertility is a difficult variable to make endogenous given that it tends to depend on the same factors as labourforce participation (see Mincer and Polachek, 1974, S99). However, Rosenzweig and Schultz (1986) develop an interesting method. They have data on month-by-month contraceptive use and birth rates for a sample of married women over the period 1975–85. By correlating birth rate and contraceptive use, as determined by exogenous variables, such as the couple's age, education, and religion, it is possible to compute how much each respondent's fertility differs from what she might have expected given her choice of contraceptive technique. The residual represents unplanned births, and is the exogenous aspect of fertility – or 'fecundity' (the ability to reproduce, rather than actual reproduction) as the authors call it. About 10% of the births in the sample are unplanned according to this methodology (1986, 1005). Exogenous 'fecundity' is what should properly appear in *LFP* and wage (and divorce) equations.

High 'fecundity' is shown to strongly reduce labourforce participation, other things equal. On the other hand, they show that use of children actually born in the participation equation has a weak effect – as Cain and Dooley found (see also Mincer and Polachek, 1974, tables 6, 7, and 9). Part of the explanation for the difference lies in the reaction of fertility to wages. In a wage regression the authors show that fecundity has a much bigger negative effect than children born. Children born reflect not only the opportunity costs of having children but also the competing desire of higher wage women for children. Unplanned births however are by definition not chosen. The fact that they negatively affect wages and participation shows that children and home time are complements. More fecund women therefore participate less, accumulate less work experience, and have lower wages.

Montgomery and Trussell note that in the social science literature the negative correlation between wages and children born (such as it is) is thought not necessarily to have an economic explanation, but rather an education explanation (1986, 264). High wage women are more educated and know more about birth control, so have fewer children. The argument does not stand up to the Rosenzweig/Schultz procedure. Fecundity is not chosen; it is the exogenous effect of fertility after countermeasures based on education have been netted out. The negative relation between fecundity and wages is caused by fecundity reducing investments in human capital.

In another paper Schultz (1985) obtains further results supporting the opportunity cost view of fertility. Here the case in point is Sweden in the nineteenth century where there was an exogenous rise in the female to male wage ratio due to a change in industrial structure from corn to dairy production, women being more productive in the latter industry. The rise in the ratio is found to be associated with smaller families, that is, reduced fertility.

Incorporating divorce into the system, the most interesting study is by Johnson and Skinner (1986) who compare a sample of families which experienced a divorce or separation in the period 1973–8 with a sample which did not. The wife's participation in 1972 and whether divorced in the subsequent five year period are taken as the endogenous variables. Exogenous variables include education, age, family income less wife's earnings, religious attendance, whether the family had close relatives living nearby, and – more controversially – past fertility (whether youngest child under three in 1968). Women's wages are assumed to be endogenous and are omitted.

In the sample the tendency for an increase in hours worked and in labourforce participation begins three years *before* the divorce. This is shown in figure 5.12. The eventual figure for hours worked is about 1,500 hours for women who divorce, compared to 800 hours for those who do not, with the increase setting in well before the divorce. This implies that labourforce participation causes divorce. However when the two equations are estimated simultaneously, in the divorce equation participation is positive but insignificant, other things equal. In the participation equation on the other hand, subsequent divorce has a significant positive effect (1986, 463). This implies that divorce causes participation rather than the other way around. It seems as though wives anticipate the divorce, and start gaining market experience before it happens. Notice also how husbands slacken off once single again. One social implication of the result is that the higher participation of black wives in the

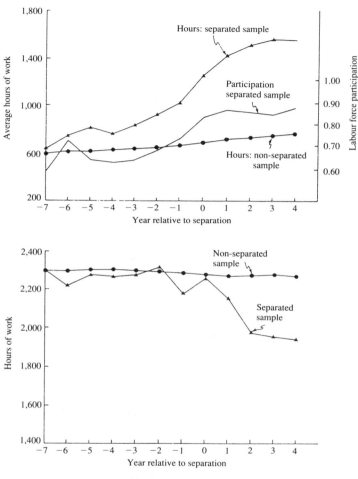

Figure 5.12 Male and female participation and hours of work relative to year of separation. *Source:* Johnson and Skinner, 1986, figures 1 and 2

United States is partly due to their higher marital instability (Reimers, 1985, 251).

A divorce directly raises the probability of participation from 0.68 to 0.88 according to these results. It also exerts indirect effects by causing education to have a bigger impact on participation and a child less negative impact. Taking all effects together, the authors estimate that over the 1960 to 1980 period in the US, higher divorce rates alone explain about one fifth of the increase in married women's participation (1986, 468).

To explain divorce rates themselves, the main exogenous variables suggested by the study are living in an urban area, not having close relatives nearby, and low religious attendance. Therefore to account for the rise in divorce rates, and thus partially the increase in participation rates, it seems we need to look at the 'anonymous cities and mobile populations' of modern society (Becker and Murphy, 1988, 8). Let us now consider such broader determining forces in more detail.

Exogenous variables
The following can be suggested:

1 *Religion.* Religious attendance has been found to be a significant determinant of divorce as noted above, and also of fertility (Rosenzweig and Schultz, 1986). However it could be that the 'decline of religion' has been exaggerated. Some trends are illustrated in table 5.8, and they are not particularly negative.

2 *Growth of white-collar work.* This is widely thought to be important (see for example Becker in the quotation above), and there has been a considerable change in industrial structure – see table 5.9. However, the variable does not seem to have much effect on labourforce participation in those studies in which it has been incorporated (O'Neill, 1981; Joshi *et al.*, 1986; Cain and Dooley, 1976). However industrial structure is generally entered in a participation equation which already includes divorce and women's wages, which are themselves partially a function of industrial structure, so this is probably not a fair test.

3 *Improved child health.* Schultz's Swedish study shows that reduced childhood mortality reduces fertility (1985, 1142). Improved child health could also have a direct effect on participation by releasing married women for work. There are no studies of the effect, but it could be quite large since improvements in child health have been so marked, even since 1960, as table 5.10 shows.

4 *Urbanisation.* Market opportunities for women are expanded by urbanisation (Mincer 1985, S15). So also is the probability of divorce (Johnson and Skinner, 1986; see also Sander, 1985, who shows farmers have half the divorce rate of other groups). Goldin (1983) includes urbanisation in her time series study of participation over the period 1900 to 1970, and it turns out to be not significant given women's wages and fertility. Nevertheless the trend in

Table 5.8. *Religious attendance*

	1950	1960	1980	1985
US – % of population	57%	64	59	60

		1975		1987
UK – % of adult pop.		21		18

Sources: US Statistical Abstract, 1988, table 76; Social Trends, 1988, table 11.8.

Table 5.9. *Industrial structure*

	Services as % of GNP			
	1950	1960	1980	1986
US	23	23	30	33
UK	35	30	39	49

Sources: US Statistical Abstract, 1988, table 1298, and 1965, table 1189, includes services plus distribution; UK Annual Abstract, 1988, table 14.7, includes distribution, education and health, banking and finance, and other services.

Table 5.10. *Child health: infant deaths (children < 1) per 1,000 live births*

	1930/2	1960/1	1980/1	1986/7
US	65	26	13	10
UK	70	22	11	9

Sources: US Statistical Abstract, 1988, table 81; Social Trends, 1981, table 1.11, 1988, table 1.13

urbanisation, as shown in table 5.11 for the US, can be seen to be considerable, even since 1960.

5 *Regional mobility*. This expands market opportunities, and also raises the probability of divorce (Johnson and Skinner, 1986). No participation research has specifically used the variable.

6 *Birth control*. According to Rosensweig and Schultz, the pill or IUD reduce fertility by 50% (1986, 1002). Thus the rise of modern methods of birth

Table 5.11. *Urbanisation*

	1940	1960	1980	1986
US Agric. emp. as % of total	20%	8.7	3.7	2.9
UK Agric. emp. as % of total	5.0%	1.8	1.7	1.3

Sources: US Statistical Abstract, various numbers; UK Annual Abstract of Statistics, various numbers.

control must have affected fertility, divorce, and *LFP*. However no time series evidence of the effects of birth control on participation yet exists.

7   *Household technology.* Vanek, comparing time budget studies over time, has shown that the introduction of labour-saving devices in the home has not reduced the home work time of women remaining in the home (1974, 116). However she does not consider women who have left the home – who could have been released for market work by the new machinery. Admittedly however the fact that there has been so little change in full-time housewives' behaviour implies that changes in household technology are not important. In any case, in our discussion of the household production function above, we noted that conflicting forces were pulling at the function. Sprague experiments with a variable based on the price of household durables relative to the consumer price index, but this is insignificant in her fertility regressions (1988, table 2).

8   *Increased wealth.* The rise of the welfare state makes children less necessary as a form of insurance, and so reduces fertility and increases divorce, and thereby participation. Greater stability, with no major war for fifty years and none in prospect, could have a similar effect. On the other hand children might be normal goods, and so the rise in wealth will encourage fertility. Increased wealth might be proxied by the male wage/husband's income variable which is incorporated in many participation studies. In fact however higher husband's income raises fertility, and lowers labourforce participation given fertility and divorce (divorce itself being unaffected (Johnson and Skinner, 1986)), so this factor might not be important.

9   *No-fault divorce.* Such laws could raise divorce rates and thus participation. Such laws might however be endogenous. Becker and Murphy for example believe that low birth rates and high women's participation stimulated no-fault divorce (1988, 14). In addition Peters does not find higher divorce rates in

states with no-fault divorce laws than in those without (1986, 447). She does find higher *LFP* in states with no-fault divorce but Johnson and Skinner (1986, 463) do not, which supports the view that these laws are not important causes.

10 *Equal opportunity laws.* Again such laws are likely to be endogenous. The question is whether we can ascribe much of the improvement in women's relative pay to these laws. In Britain it is thought that equal pay has something to do with the rise in relative pay in the seventies, though pay restraint policies angled against the high paid cloud the issue (Chiplin and Sloane, 1988). In the US, the rise in women's relative pay seems confined to younger cohorts, and cannot therefore be ascribed to equal pay policies (which are intended to be applied to all cohorts).

5.4 Male labour supply

Male labour supply trends have been different to female. While women have been tending to participate more, for men the tendency has been the reverse. Men are retiring earlier, and working fewer hours per year when they do work. One of the reasons for the reduced labour supply of men is presumably the changes in the family referred to in the previous section. As the family division of labour becomes less important, women's and men's labour market behaviour converges: women participate more, and men less. The other major reason is the expansion of the welfare state. Better retirement and unemployment incomes, coupled with higher marginal tax rates, discourage work.

Elasticity of supply

Empirical questions are whether the supply curve of hours is 'backward bending', and to what extent increased welfare benefits induce non-participation. Looking at these questions in turn, much effort has been expended in measuring the elasticity of labour supply. However it is necessary, as mentioned above, to remember that some wage changes are likely to have more marked substitution effects than others. Temporary wage changes and life-cycle wage changes (which are fully anticipated and thus have no income effect) are the cases to be borne in mind.

Pencavel summarises the results of fourteen studies of the elasticity of male labour supply. The uncompensated elasticity of hours supplied with respect to the wage is generally negative, but small, ranging from 0 to -0.7. The compensated elasticity (that is, adjusted to allow for income effects of wage changes), which should be positive, ranged from 0.8 to -0.2 (Pencavel, 1986, 69). To take a consensus single number, Pencavel suggests a figure of -0.1 for the uncompensated elasticity and 0.1 for the compensated (substitution) elasticity. These figures can be compared with uncompensated hours elasticities for married women which appear to be much higher, as we have seen above.

The above are regular hours elasticities, which, as noted, should be smaller than elasticities with respect to life-cycle wage changes. (Recall the strong association over the life cycle between hours worked per year and earnings, as shown in figure 5.6.) Interesting work on the latter has been performed by MacCurdy (1981). The author uses ten years of panel data from the Panel Survey of Income Dynamics so as to relate changes in wages to changes in hours for the same individual. Since we are considering only relationships for given individuals, we are keeping lifetime wealth constant (hence no income effects, according to the argument). The author estimates the life-cycle elasticity to be between 0.1 and 0.45 (1981, 1077).

Ghez and Becker (1975, table 3.7) obtain even larger estimates, by allowing for measurement error in earnings and in hours worked. Measurement error pulls the correlation between earnings and hours downwards. Their elasticity figures range from 0.3 to 0.7, suggesting high labour supply responses of men to life-cycle changes in wages. Thus life-cycle elasticities are positive, as expected, and seemingly several times larger than the regular compensated wage elasticity of about 0.1.

The relevance of life-cycle elasticities for policy is that government policy often affects incomes at particular stages of the life cycle. For example youth incomes are raised by higher welfare benefits, older people's incomes by subsidised health care, and married women's incomes by improvements in child care facilities such as paid maternity leave. However, changes in opportunities at one point of the life cycle affect choices at other points.

At any point in time, the hours individuals are working, and the goods they are buying can be seen as a result of working out a 'lifetime' plan. For example, anticipated paid maternity leave will influence women's early education plans, and cause them to participate more before and after childbirth. For older people, higher pensions will be foreseen: such pensions will raise lifetime wealth and to that extent reduce labour supply throughout life as well as bringing earlier retirement (see below). Reinforcing this – reducing hours supplied by older workers – we have the strong life-cycle substitution effect (wealth given) consequent on the fall in earnings power with age. On the other hand, the life-cycle substitution effect is a factor drawing young workers into the workforce, and working against higher incomes available out of work.

However the regular, smaller, hours elasticity is relevant for judging the effect of unanticipated permanent wage changes, such as those brought about by taxes, on labour supply. Since this elasticity is small, the implication remains that tax increases – since these are not anticipated – do not much affect labour hours supplied.

Table 5.12. *Probability of being unemployed in previous year, and replacement ratio, England 1980*
(Unskilled, low education heads of household) replacement ratio*

	Top third	Middle third	Lowest third
Single			
age < 26	21%	43	9
age > 26	33	37	5
Married			
age > 26			
No children	27	10	1
With children	29	7	2

Note: *Calculated as the ratio of the net income of the individual when unemployed to the maximum he could make, post tax, in a fifty-hour week. The ratio varies from around unity for low income individuals, to 1/4 or less for higher income individuals. *Source:* Minford and Ashton, 1988.

At the same time, it is possible that even though the regular hours elasticity is small for men overall, it is larger for particular groups facing high marginal rates of tax. Groups in this unfortunate position are low earners who are likely to be close to the poverty trap. We would expect their probability of unemployment to be sensitive to tax. Higher taxes reduce the post-tax income from being in work, but leave welfare income unaffected (usually), as noted in our discussion of figure 5.1. Higher taxes thus raise a person's replacement ratio, the ratio of net income when unemployed to net income when in work, and can be expected to cause unemployment.

We do indeed find that individuals with high replacement ratios are more likely to be unemployed. Contrasting individuals with ratios in the top one-third of the distribution of replacement ratios with those in the middle and bottom thirds gives the results for probability of unemployment shown in table 5.12. For example married individuals in the top third of the replacement ratio distribution have a 27% to 29% chance of being unemployed in the previous year, compared to 7% to 10% for those in the middle third, and even less for those in the bottom third. Note, this is not due to low education or skill of those in the bottom third, because we are holding education and skill level constant.

Interestingly, the same correlation between unemployment and the replacement ratio does not hold for the under twenty-six group. But there is a good human capital explanation for this. Measured pay understates 'full' pay by the value of the training that individuals are receiving. However young workers can be expected to be receiving more training than old. The result is a greater overstatement of the replacement ratio of the younger workers, with more of them wrongly assigned to the high replacement ratio category.

Negative income tax experiments

The negative income tax can be illustrated with figure 5.1. This type of tax aims to integrate the tax and benefit systems. For individuals with low earning power (wage $(1-t)w$), if their income falls below B, they are given money – a negative tax – to bring them up to an acceptable amount. If no work is done, they get the largest 'negative tax', or gift, of amount B. The segment of the budget constraint from B to the budget line illustrated in the diagram is horizontal implying 100% implicit marginal rates of tax. Normally it would be designed to have some positive slope, to avoid this problem.

The question with any supplementary income system is how much of a disincentive to work it is. The individual pictured in figure 5.1 would move from point A to point B once the option of a negative tax became available.

The US Government has sponsored several negative income tax experiments: in New Jersey (1968–72), rural Iowa and North Carolina (1969–73), Gary, Indiana (1971–4), and Seattle and Denver (1972–82). The last experiment had nearly 5,000 families involved. The experimental aspect involved randomly assigning different 'treatments' to the families. The treatments involved different implicit tax rates (generally between 0.5 and 0.7) and different minimum income guarantees (between 50% and 140% of the poverty level of $10,600 for a family of four in 1984).

In all the experiments the families reduced labour supply, whether measured in terms of hours or employment rates. The hours reductions ranged from 5% to 27%, and employment rate reductions ranged from 3% to 10% (Robins, 1984, table 6). Husbands exhibited the smallest reduction and wives the greatest, with single female heads in between – as would be predicted given the family model of labour supply.

However the permanent income hypothesis predicts that families on NIT experiments should experience a larger labour supply reduction than non-experimental families. The experimental NIT gives only a temporary rise in income, so it should not much affect consumption (which is adjusted to permanent income, according to the hypothesis), but should cause a correspondingly larger hours reduction. The effect appears small however, in that the compensated hours elasticity for men from the experimental studies is much the same as that from the non-experimental studies, i.e. about 0.1, with married women somewhat higher as usual at about 0.2 (Robins, 1984, table 7).

Though increases in welfare benefits must increase non-participation, there is some doubt as to the size of their impact on trend levels of unemployment. Over time, the replacement ratio has increased in real terms, more people have

Table 5.13. *Participation rates, older people*

	1960/1	1975/6	1985
	US		
Males: 55–64	75%	76	68
65+	32	22	16
	UK		
60–4	91	80	54
65+	25	15	8
	US		
Females: 55–65	27	41	42
65+	11	8	7
	UK		
55–9	—	54	52
60+	10	10	7

Sources: US Statistical Abstract, 1988, table 608; 1965, table 298; UK Social Trends, 1987, table 4.3; 1980, table 5.2.

become eligible for benefits, and the system has become administered less strictly. (In the UK, for example, the average replacement ratio increased from 40% in the 1960s to around 50% in the 1970s (Layard and Nickell, 1986, S369), and students became eligible to apply for welfare benefits.) Such forces could be in part responsible for the trend increase in unemployment in the UK from 3% to 7% in the 1960–85 period (and the somewhat smaller trend increase in the US – from 5% to 8%). Putting the replacement ratio in a time series the unemployment function gives varying results however, depending upon what other variables are included, and the time period studied (Johnson and Layard, 1986, 993).

Note that, over time, the real wage has been increasing as well, which raises the opportunity cost of non-participation and will tend to counteract rises in the replacement ratio. Johnson and Layard (1986) in their study of the natural rate of unemployment give the replacement ratio a subsidiary, though definite, role to play. They consider employment protection legislation, structural mismatch, trade unions (which increase wages), and the productivity slowdown (to which wage bargainers must have taken some time to adjust) as more important determinants of unemployment (1986, 994ff).

Retirement

Retirement is another interesting life-cycle decision. As table 5.13 shows, there has been a marked tendency for men to retire at ever earlier ages. Women on

Table 5.14. *Influence of pension plan on retirement decision*
Pension rule: pension = \$500 per year × years service. Assume interest rate = 3%, age start work = 40, expected age death = 80

Age of retirement	Pension per year	Present value of pension at age 55
55	\$7500 = 15 × 500	\$130,000 $= \dfrac{7500}{.03} \left[1 - \dfrac{1}{1.03^{25}} \right]$
57	8500	\$132,000 $= \dfrac{8500}{.03} \left[1 - \dfrac{1}{1.03^{25}} - (1 - \dfrac{1}{1.03^2}) \right]$ *
65	12500	\$111,000 $= \dfrac{12500}{.03} \left[1 - \dfrac{1}{1.03^{25}} - (1 - \dfrac{1}{1.03^{10}}) \right]$

Note: *The present value of the pension at age 55, if one retires at age 57, is the present value of \$12,500 a year received for 23 years, starting in 2 years' time.

the other hand show a tendency to increase participation, though from a much lower base. Again there seems to be a tendency for convergence of the sexes.

When people are asked why they retire, the main reason they give is health (Quinn, 1977, 331). We have difficulty in interpreting individuals' responses to questionnaires. Poor health might act as an inducement to retire, but it can only do so if there is sufficient money to live on. In any case, poor health cannot account for male retirement time trends, because health has been improving. For example, the life expectancy at birth of US men was sixty-seven years in 1970, and seventy-one years in 1985 (see Chuman and Erlich, 1990).

An alternative hypothesis is that changes in the opportunity set facing men have been causing their earlier retirement. Better private and public pension provisions raise incomes in retirement. Such provisions will have wealth effects, as noted above, which will encourage retirement or part-time work. In both America and Britain state pensions are payable in full, even if the individual is earning, so long as earnings fall below a certain level. Hence the stimulus to move to part-time work – though for many no doubt part-time pay opportunities are too unrewarding, and full retirement results.

Private pension schemes might act as a particular incentive to retirement. Pension plans are often constructed so that the pension has a higher value if there is early rather than late retirement. The reason is that early retirement means a longer period over which to enjoy the pension. Tying the pension to finishing salary does give a counteracting force – since pay increases with age

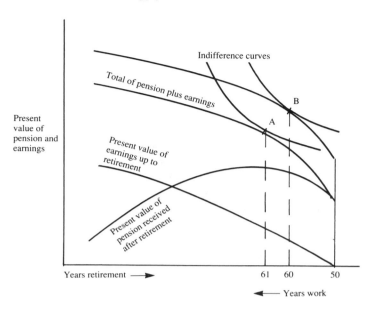

Figure 5.13 The retirement decision

up to a point, and so later retirement means a higher yearly payment. The flatter the earnings profile, the weaker this force.

The reason for the encouragement to early retirement could have to do with the internal labour market. In such a market firms want a long-term commitment, and one way of engendering this is to pay long-serving workers more than alternative wages, and more than current marginal product. In such a case, however, there needs to be a definite incentive to retire so as to limit the period of high wages (see chapter 9 on payment systems for more detail).

An example of a simple pension scheme giving an incentive to early retirement is shown in table 5.14. Here the pension rule is that the person receives $500 for every year of service. As can be seen, the present value of the pension benefits would be highest if the retirement age was fifty-seven, viewed from the perspective of age fifty-five (we assume that this is the earliest date that retirement would be contemplated). While the illustrated pension scheme is simple it does in fact capture the time path of actual schemes – as can be seen from the study of ten pension plans by Mitchell and Fields (1984, table 2).

The retirement decision is analysed in figure 5.13. The budget constraint has two parts: the present value of the pension(s) expected after retirement, and the present value of the wages earned up to retirement. The former tends to have a declining value the later one retires (the longer one works), as already discussed. The present value of wages curve generally increases the longer one works. The sum has a curved shape, indicating that one's wealth (the present value of one's pension plus wage income) increases with retirement age, but the increase occurs at a decreasing rate. A higher pension moves the constraint outwards in a parallel way. A higher wage would increase the slope.

To decide on the age of retirement requires combining the budget constraint with a set of indifference curves. The indifference curves are drawn in figure 5.13 on the assumption that higher wealth value of income, and longer years of retirement are both desired. As drawn, the person retires at age sixty-one. If the pension entitlement increased, and years of retirement was a normal good, then the income effect would prompt earlier retirement, e.g., to point B, age sixty.

Private and public pension schemes have increased considerably over the past decades. In both the US and the UK the real value of assets of pension funds has tripled between 1970 and 1985. About 25% of retired workers are currently covered by private pension arrangements in the US (Lazear, 1988, 2). An equivalent figure for men in Britain is about 20% (Zabalza *et al.*, 1980, table A1). (Women have, however, historically been less likely to be employed in large firms with internal labour markets, and thus are not so well covered by private pensions.) As for public pensions, in the United States social security benefits were raised by about 20% in real terms in the early 1970s (Burtless, 1986, 802) – though they have not increased by nearly so much in the UK. Thus the pension factor could be an important determinant of male retirement trends.

Empirical research has indicated that indeed improved pensions have affected retirement decisions, in addition to health. However there is some controversy over the size of the pension effect. One difficulty is that the large increase in US public pensions, for example, could not have been anticipated, so naturally would not much affect retirement decisions of current older workers. One US study (Quinn, 1977, 342) indicates that men up to the age of sixty-five, *without* health limitations, who are eligible for both Social Security and private pensions, have 22% lower participation than if they were not eligible. If they have health limitations, the figure is doubled. However higher wage workers do not appear to retire later (though in the study by Burtless they do (1986, 798)). British research has suggested that retirement decisions are moderately pension elastic: a 20% pension increase only increasing retirement probability for a man of sixty-eight from 0.81 to 0.84 (for a woman the effect is seemingly much more marked – from 0.76 to 0.83; so also is the wage effect) (Zabalza *et al.*, 1980, tables 6 and 7; see also Warburton, 1987, 193).

It is interesting to make a back of the envelope calculation of the impact of better pensions on retirement by considering the effect of increased US Social Security coverage. Coverage has increased from 78% in 1970 to 87% in 1985 (US Statistical Abstract, 1988, 561). Labourforce participation of the male fifty-five to sixty-four age group in 1970 was 76%. Denote the participation of the uncovered as x, and assume the participation of the covered is 20% lower, that is $0.8x$. The 0.76 overall labourforce participation figure is a weighted average of the covered and uncovered, that is:

$$0.76 = x\,(0.22) + 0.8x\,(0.78),$$

implying that x, the participation of the uncovered, was 0.90. This gives the participation of the covered as $0.8x = 0.72$. If these participation rates remained the same, but coverage increased, then in 1985 the average participation of this age group would be:

$$0.90\,(0.13) + 0.72\,(0.87) = 0.74.$$

In fact in 1985 participation for the fifty-five to sixty-four group was 68% (table 5.13). So increased coverage alone might explain 2 points ($= 0.76 - 0.74$) out of the 8 point ($= 0.76 - 0.68$) US fall – about a quarter.

5.5 Conclusions

Women: It seems that the increase in married women's participation in the labourforce is not due to legislative action, but rather to a complicated set of market responses to urbanisation, secularisation, and birth control improvements. Increased education is also important, and, to the extent that this is a result of wider education subsidies (rather than itself being a consequence of higher participation), this can be taken as a policy success.

On the research agenda, a more thorough-going use of simultaneous equations approaches to the question of female labourforce participation is called for. Just as important, single women and married women should be compared so that, holding gender constant, the force of changes happening within the family can be demonstrated. In any case it is evident that men and women have very different lifetime labour supply behaviour, partly due to the division of labour within the family, and partly perhaps to labour market discrimination (to be dealt with in the next chapter).

Men: Male labour supply is quite inelastic when we consider unanticipated changes in wages, such as might be caused by tax changes. However it is important to remember some groups are more elastic in supply – particularly the highly taxed. Very low earners in particular are highly taxed, the implication being that they will be responsive to tax reductions. Reduced taxes both increase the national income by stimulating the productive high earners, and lower poverty by encouraging the less skilled out of the poverty trap.

The response of labour hours to changes in wages that are fully foreseen (and thus do not affect wealth), can be termed the life-cycle supply elasticity. This elasticity seems considerably higher than the regular hours elasticity. The life-cycle elasticity is relevant for those policies that affect groups at particular points in their life cycles: the old, the young, the pregnant. The young, for example, anticipate an increase in wages with age, and this will cause an hours increase which will tend to counteract more generous unemployment benefits. For older workers, the evidence suggests that more generous pension provisions have been an important factor in encouraging them to retire earlier.

From the above it is apparent that men and women have very different lifetime labour supply behaviour. In part these differences are dependent on exogenously given differences in tastes (some data are given in the next chapter) and in part on differences in wages. At least in the past, husbands on average have tended to have a higher earnings potential. Both factors lead to specialisation and to a division of labour within the family. Market discrimination (to be dealt with in the next chapter) exacerbates this pay gap, further accentuating husband–wife differences in specialisation. In what follows we take these husband–wife life-cycle labour market participation differences as given, and try to ascertain their impact on labour market earnings.

6 Gender in the labour market

6.1 Introduction

Women's economic position is not comparable to that of men's. Data on both earnings and occupational achievement leave no doubt that women have a secondary economic position. This is true not only in the United States and England, but in all countries for which data exist (see Blau *et al.*, 1986).

Women are segregated into what some have called 'women's jobs'. Table 6.1 depicts the relatively unequal occupational distributions for 1960–81. But even this table cannot detail the more subtle sex differences omitted by broad occupational categories. Whereas women seem to be sufficiently represented in prestigious occupations such as the professional category, this statistic is somewhat misleading. Professional employment includes teachers, nurses, and other relatively low-paying jobs within the professional category. Thus looking at broad occupations is not always a satisfactory way of measuring female economic success. For this reason earnings data are often used to obtain more information on the relative position of women.

Table 6.2 contains earnings data. Gender differences in economic well-being are clear. Pay of women averages 65% to 90% that of men. The gap has been relatively constant (Beller *et al.*, 1988), but here is some evidence of a narrowing in recent years (see table 5.4 above, and O'Neill *et al*, forthcoming.)

However marital status, life-cycle and family characteristics also affect the size of male–female differentials. As an illustration, consider table 6.3. It contains income ratios by sex and marital status for the United States in 1975 and 1985. Comparisons between singles groups are less likely to be marred by unmeasured motivational factors (for example, married women are more oriented towards home work, rather than market work, as shown in table 5.3 in the previous chapter). The single male to female comparison should therefore be most reliable with regard to discrimination. As can be seen, the single female–male ratio is around 84% to 87%, much higher than the 56% to 63% ratio for all women relative to all men. Nevertheless, before concluding that the

Table 6.1. *Occupational distributions of women and men (USA)*

Mainly women			Few women		
Dental hygienists		99.5%	Loggers		1.0%
Preschool teachers		98.8	Auto mechanics		1.7
Secretaries		98.4	Tool and die makers		2.0
Receptionists		97.6	Skilled building trades		2.1
Practical nurses		96.9	Millwrights		2.7
Day-care centre workers		96.1	Stationary engineers		2.7
Typists		95.6	Mechanical engineers		3.7
Dressmakers		95.5	Aircraft mechanics		4.2
Where women have gained	1970	1985	Professional degrees	1963	1985
Typesetters	17%	71%	Advertising	31%	63%
Bartenders	21	48	Journalism	44	61
Sales supervisors	17	31	Pharmacy	24	48
Farmers	5	14	Personnel	9	48
Telephone installers	3	13	Accounting	11	45
Sheet metal workers	2	5	Business	10	39
			Law	8	36
			Computer science	14	35
			Banking/finance	4	32
			Medicine	9	27

Source: Hacker, 1986.

remaining difference between the singles groups is the result of discrimination, we must be sure we are comparing like with like – which requires adjustment for productivity differences, as explained below.

Other interesting demographic patterns have also been found. For example, number and spacing of children affect the size of the gender wage differential. Men with large families tend to earn more than men with small families, and women with large families earn less than those with small families. The life cycle, too, is important. While small gender wage differentials occur in the early work phases, these expand over the working life until about age forty, then decline. For men and women between eighteen and twenty-five the wage ratio is about 80%. For thirty to forty year olds, this ratio decreases to less than 50%, and eventually rises to about 65%, for the fifty-five to sixty-four year olds. Theories about gender differences in wages must be able to explain such life-cycle and marital status patterns.

Explaining why women seem relegated to an inferior economic position is important. If these patterns emerge because of unequal opportunities caused by

Table 6.2. *Female earnings as a percentage of male*

UK 1991			USA 1990	
Managerial	66%	(64)	Executive, administrative, and managerial	66%
Professional	79	(90)	Professional	74
Associated professional and technical	74	(80)	Technical, sales and administrative support	67
Sales	63	(65)		
Clerical and secretarial	83	(89)		
Personal and protective service	65	(70)	Service occupations	72
Craft and related	58	(66)	Precision production craft and repair	65
Plant and machine operatives	65	(73)	Operators, fabricators, and labourers	69
Labourers and other occupations	68	(78)	Farming, forestry, and fishing	82

Sources: UK – New Earnings Survey, 1991 – the bracketed figure refers to hourly earnings, excluding overtime; US – unpublished data from US Bureau of Labor Statistics, supplied by E. Mellor, 1991.

Table 6.3. *Comparisons of pay by sex and marital status (USA)*

	1975	1985
All women/all men	$\frac{8273}{14733} = 0.56$	$\frac{18092}{28764} = 0.63$
Single women/single men	$\frac{8289}{9926} = 0.84$	$\frac{18659}{21338} = 0.87$
Single men/married men	$\frac{9926}{15591} = 0.64$	$\frac{21338}{34460} = 0.62$

Source: Current Population Survey. Data relate to full-time workers over 18.

unfair hiring practices, then the economy is failing to fully and appropriately utilise highly productive employees. Economic inefficiencies thereby come about, providing a justification for government intervention. On the other hand, if unequal economic outcomes result from differing individual choices despite equal opportunity, then government intervention to force 'equal pay' would lead to a distorted allocation of resources and inefficiencies within the economy. In this case, rather than helping disadvantaged groups, productive efficiency is hampered so that in the long run all end up suffering. Thus, the comprehension of the causes of gender differences in economic success is important.

In assessing the reasons for differences in pay between men and women it is useful to consider first the possibility of bias or discrimination *within* the labour market. 'Discrimination' can reasonably be defined as 'unlike treatment of likes'. In a labour market context, discrimination then occurs when men are paid more than women of the same productivity. Since the firm is the locus of such discrimination we can also call this 'demand-side' discrimination.

There is also the possibility of bias or discrimination *prior to* the labour market, in the education system, or in the family. Such bias affects the productivity characteristics (e.g., education, or motivation) which workers bring with them to the market. The family forms tastes and treats girl children differently from boy children. Many feel such different treatment to be a form of discrimination 'in the childhood formation of preferences' (Cain, 1976, 1236). Because tastes are difficult to measure economists have traditionally preferred to regard taste formation as a black box, and explain behaviour in terms of reactions to prices with tastes given (West and McKee, 1983, 1110). However, some studies exist of pre-labour market discrimination, and we will consider these. Since such discrimination affects the characteristics of the worker, and has nothing to do with the employer, we can call it 'supply-side' discrimination.

The supply and demand sides are inter-related, because expected demand discrimination will affect worker supply. For example, if women expect poor promotion prospects they will elect to have less education. However, the distinction is still useful for analytical purposes. We will consider these two sides in turn, then discuss policy issues.

6.2 Demand-side discrimination

Prejudice models

If there is a prejudice against women on the part of employers or other male workers, then women will receive lower pay than men with the same productivity. In a competitive labour market however this explanation cannot hold

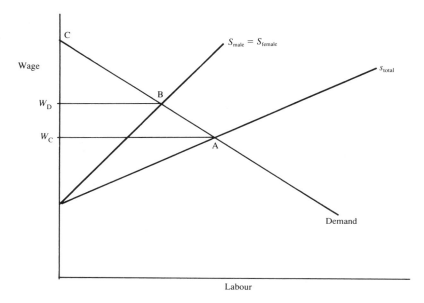

Figure 6.1 Discrimination and the firm's opportunity set

water. In a competitive market, if men were paid more than similarly productive women, some firms would be able to lower their costs by hiring women
instead of men. These firms would expand their market share, bidding up
the pay of women. Men's and women's wages would thus be brought into
equality.

The position is illustrated in figure 6.1, showing a firm with male and female
applicants, both of whom have the same supply curve, for simplicity. The total
supply of labour available to the firm is given by S_{total}, which is the summation
of the male and female supply curves. Men and women are assumed to be
equally productive, so there is a single labour demand (MRP) curve. Equilibrium without discrimination occurs at point A. The profit triangle is given by
triangle CAW_c.

Now suppose that the firm begins to discriminate against women, for some
reason. Discrimination in this example could be characterised as the firm
refusing to hire women. If it limits itself only to males, then its opportunity set
is reduced, and labour will be more expensive. The resulting equilibrium will
be at point B, with a smaller profit triangle CBW_D. Discriminators therefore
'pay' for their discrimination, and consequently profit maximisation will drive
out discrimination.

A further problem with discrimination as prejudice is that of motive: why should discriminatory prejudices exist? Becker's original 1957 formulation by-passed the question of motivation and simply attributed discrimination to a 'taste' for it. But it is difficult to justify such a 'taste'. It is more likely that some groups of men discriminate against women, if they do, because these groups *make money* in some way from it. But then some mechanism whereby men can collude against women has to be brought forward. Unionisation provides a possible vehicle here. British printing unions, for example, have a long history of preventing entry by women – presumably so as to restrict supply (EOC, 1984, 9). Unions have also been a widespread source of discrimination against black workers (see Marshall, 1965). Another possibility is that firms respond to the desires of their customers to discriminate against women (Ashenfelter and Hannan, 1986; Borjas and Bronars, 1989; Nardinelli and Simon, 1990).

One could go further, as radical economists do, and claim that employers have an ability to 'segment' the labour market so as to promote the 'disunity of the working class' (Gordon *et al.*, 1982, 213). In the radical view, indeed, workers are seen as quite powerless in the face of a manipulative employer or big-business class. Thus: 'Employers recognised that the segmentation of white-collar work would be facilitated by channelling women into the lower level clerical occupations. Large numbers of female workers were shunted into the emerging secondary white-collar occupations . . . ' (Gordon *et al.*, 1982, 205). If this occurred, profits would be available for firms that did not shunt women into secondary occupations. The difficulty is to show how millions of employers can collude to prevent firms making profits by not discriminating.

Discrimination can also result if labour is immobile. Workers are sometimes seen as 'tied' to firms by lack of knowledge, by specific capital investments, by internal labour markets, and by lack of alternative employers (e.g., nurses tend to face monopsony). For example according to Gregory and Duncan, 'Employment is allocated by creation and destruction of job opportunities and not by changes in relative wages. Wages are determined largely by social custom and institutional factors . . . ' (1981, 403).

Admittedly with worker immobility there is scope for capricious wage differentials. The internal labour market, and the institution of long-term contracts, is analysed in detail in chapter 9. We question there whether these institutions do interrupt the proper functioning of labour markets and reduce labour mobility. Internal labour markets often seem constructed so both parties to the bargain are protected – these are more situations of bilateral monopoly than monopsony, and it is not obvious whether this works to the disadvantage of the worker side.

However even where a firm is earning above-normal profits, and so can therefore afford to indulge a 'taste' for discrimination against women, there need not be discrimination in the long run. Such a firm would be more profitable for a non-discriminating management, and so would be bought out

(Becker, 1957). Admittedly the transactions costs of take-over are large enough to prolong this process – such costs average over 10% of post-take-over share value (MacIntosh, 1987, 302). Even so, transferable private property and the profit motive will continually be eroding discrimination.

Statistical discrimination

Within the competitive framework a further source of discrimination can be identified. This is statistical discrimination. Statistical discrimination can be said to occur when individuals are judged not as individuals, but on the basis of their group (see Phelps, 1972; Lundberg and Startz, 1983). For example, women live longer than men, and so women have generally been required to make higher pension contributions than men. However it is often argued that this is unfair since individuals not representative of their group will be disadvantaged/advantaged. Consequently statistical discrimination on the basis of gender is sometimes outlawed. In the case of pension plans for example, discrimination by gender in the setting of premiums has been illegal since 1978 due to a Supreme Court judgement. The British Equal Opportunities Commission also wants 'gender based insurance premium differentials based on historical differences between the sexes' to go. Company pension schemes are now being based on unisex mortality tables, ignoring the shorter expected life span of men.

Let us consider the pension example in more detail, since the 'efficiency' aspect of statistical discrimination – and how it is not true discrimination – can best be described with a concrete example. The first question to be asked is whether the insurance companies are correct, even on average, about women living longer than men. Sometimes these, and other, statistical judgements about groups (for example, young drivers are less safe than old, women are more likely to leave the workforce than men) are questioned as being unjustified 'stereotypes'. However, after the age of sixty, the male mortality rate is twice that of the female, which is certainly a large difference. Nevertheless, it is often argued that there is generally a large overlap between the distribution, so that to attribute to an individual the characteristics of his/her group must result in large random errors (statistical 'noise').

In principle we would expect competition to drive out unjustified stereotypes. If some firms have the wrong stereotype, or place too little weight on individual performance, or use overly 'noisy' tests, then firms with better methods will generate more profits and oust the mistaken firms. We do not have to say that knowledge is perfect, only that systematic, repeated mistakes are not made.

In our example, the basic question is whether there is a cheaper way to acquire reliable knowledge about longevity than considering gender. There are admittedly other individual-oriented ways, such as interviews, or special tests – and these are used – but the extra benefits have to be judged against the extra costs (see chapter 8 on the economics of information acquisition). The firms concerned are in the best position to judge these costs and benefits (who is in a better position?), and given competition, there is every reason to expect them to exercise their knowledge.

This brings us to the second question: the possible gains and losses of disallowing statistical discrimination. The considerations involved can best be shown with the help of a simplified model. For the population over sixty-five, suppose that we know that 40% will die at seventy, and that the remaining 60% will not. Breaking the picture down by gender however, suppose there are the following mortality proportions (numbers in brackets):

	Dies before 70	Dies after 70	Total
Male	90% (36)	20 (12)	(48)
Female	10 (4)	80 (48)	(52)
	100 (40)	100 (60)	(100)

Note there is overlap between the distributions, as is realistic.

If the insurance company had the above information, by discriminating statistically by gender it could make a better estimate of the likelihood of a particular person dying before seventy than simply taking a 60/40 split. The actual longevity table would look as follows:

	Dies before 70	Dies after 70	Total
Male	75% (= 36/48)	25 (= 12/48)	100
Female	8 (= 4/52)	92 (= 48/52)	100

Suppose that pensions are x per year (a 'standard pension' – in a full analysis x would also be selected) and that dying before seventy means a pension for five years, a total of $5x$, while dying after seventy means a pension for ten years, a total of $10x$. A man must then pay in premiums at least:

$$C_m = 0.75(\$5x) + 0.25(\$10x) = \$6.25x,$$

and a woman must pay:

$$C_f = 0.08(\$5x) + 0.92(\$10x) = \$9.6x.$$

On the other hand, without discrimination, contributions will be the same:

$$C = 0.4(\$5x) + 0.6(\$10x) = \$8x.$$

We thus see men paying $8x$ for insurance costing on average $6.25x$, while women pay $8x$ for insurance costing on average 9.6.

Let us follow through the consequences of charging a common price for a

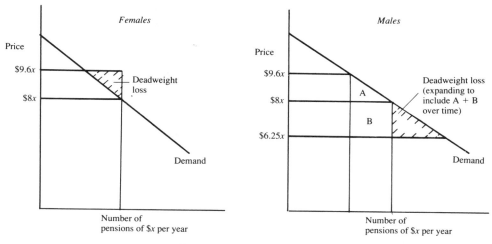

Figure 6.2 Statistical discrimination in pensions

different service. Some men, the less risk averse, will be driven to reduce their
retirement coverage, perhaps hoping to make up the difference out of savings.
Their sacrifice however will constitute a deadweight loss – see the supply and
demand diagram figure 6.2. Insurance companies will earn higher profits on
the remainder – but the gain in profits will be less than the loss in male
consumer surplus – hence the deadweight loss.

More women on the other hand will initially take out retirement pensions
(and increase the value of their pensions – x in practice will be variable), since
these are now priced below cost. Insurance companies will be making a loss on
such business. The extra losses will outweigh the extra benefits to women,
causing a deadweight loss in the female market as well – see diagram.

Over time advantages to women are likely to decline. Deadweight losses will
tend to further increase due to continuing adverse selection. As more (long-
lived) women enter, and (short-lived) men leave, the longevity of the insured
population will tend to increase. Insurance company losses on female business
will therefore increase, and premium rates will have to go up, driving male
coverage further down, and compounding the problem. There will therefore be
a tendency for costs to approach their original female level ($9.6x$), with even
women little better off, and *all* men worse off (deadweight losses in the male
diagram expand to include areas A and B).

This example illustrates that, while information will be imperfect, so that
random errors will be made, the position is worse still if the available information is not utilised. The point is relevant in many other contexts. In

particular some people will be highly motivated market workers, and others are not so highly motivated, and the firm must sort the two groups out with only limited information on motivation including the knowledge that women are less market work oriented than men. If the government then bans the use of gender information, and compels firms to gain more individual information about their new hires, or their promotions, then, according to the above argument, it would be second-guessing firms and raising costs. Outlawing statistical discrimination presumably, reflects a belief that the competitive assumptions stressed above do not hold in practice, or that the gains to particular groups outweigh lower efficiency. Our example nevertheless illustrates the possibility that there may be very real net losses.

To summarise, the discussion has shown the importance to the economy of mobility among workers, and independent profit-seeking among firms. Where there is competition then discrimination based on prejudice or tastes is unlikely to be important, and statistical discrimination will be efficient (cost-minimising). The converse holds for sectors of the economy where competition is lacking. Empirical work therefore requires tests of the competitive assumption: measurement of the pay gap between men and women adjusting for productivity so as to assess the extent of discrimination, assessment of whether discrimination is in fact lower where there is competition, and measurement of the size of substitution effects when relative pay is changed.

6.3 Empirical findings on market discrimination

To assess the importance of discrimination ideally would require, as we have seen, an evaluation of how competitive the economy is. This is not easy, so various tests have been devised. The pay gap between men and women is measured, adjusting for personal characteristics; the wage gap (and employment opportunities) is assessed to see if it is lower in competitive circumstances; employment effects consequent on relative wage changes are checked to see if the labour market is working to allocate labour (see, e.g., Oaxaca, 1973, as well as modifications of this approach by Polachek, 1975b; Butler, 1982; Jones, 1983; Neumark, 1988).

Wage discrimination

We might first ask whether discriminatory pay differences have been measured. If there is no market, or demand-side, discrimination, then the pay gap between men and women of the same productivity should be zero. The difficulty is to operationalise the concept of the 'same productivity'. Sometimes productivity can be directly measured – as when workers are paid directly for output (e.g., harvesting). Women's output has been found to be

20% to 30% less than men's in these cases (Phelps Brown, 1977, 155–6). More often productivity is not observed and so proxies such as years of education, labourforce experience, tenure with the firm have to be used. These are clearly imperfect – how does one measure motivation for example? Nevertheless the approach is all that is available, and this has been accepted by the courts.

For example in 1983 the female faculty of the City University of New York sued the University on the grounds that they had been discriminated against in payment of salary (Melani, 1983, 655). They won the case on the basis of salary regressions with independent variables including age, years of service, academic degrees, quality of degree, and certificates. Holding these variables constant, women earned less then men. Notice how marital status was not held constant, presumably on the grounds that the advantage this represented for men and disadvantage for women would represent 'illegitimate' statistical discrimination.

Even when data on preferences are included, the wage difference does not shrink to zero, though preferences make a healthy contribution (Daymont and Andrisani, 1984, 419). Since men and women with the same measured characteristics are earning different hourly rates, some are prepared to conclude that the residual difference is 'discrimination'.

Others would say that the residual is a measure of our ignorance – it would only be evidence of discrimination if supply-side differences were truly being kept constant. Married women might have a lower increase of earnings with experience for example, and consequently lower pay than men with the same experience. If married women have chosen jobs with flatter earnings profiles for the 'atrophy' reasons mentioned below (such jobs offer higher starting wages, and also it matters less if one drops out of the workforce), this is hardly evidence of discrimination on the part of the employer.

In addition, for married women, the labour market experience variable tends to be mismeasured. Experience is typically proxied as the time period elapsed since a person has left school – but this is a bad proxy in the case of married women, since some of their time since leaving school will have been spent in home rather than in market work. In one sample of British women, it has been estimated that actual labour market experience is only sixteen years, compared to the twenty-three year time period since leaving school (Zabalza and Arrufat, 1985, 82). Moreover, mismeasuring married women's labour market experience will cause the regression coefficient on experience to go towards zero (see figure 7.5 in the next chapter for a diagrammatic explanation of why this happens). We will think people are not being paid for experience, but in fact they will be – it is just our measure of experience which is wrong.

One way round the problems of omitting motivation and mismeasuring experience is to compare only the single groups. The supply-side differences in

Table 6.4. *Comparisons of earnings by sex and marital status, librarians in England*

	Actual ratio	Ratio holding earnings function constant*	Points unexplained	Interpretation of points unexplained
MW/SW	0.91	0.93	2	Family role of wife + marital status discrimination against MW
SW/SM	0.99	1.00	1	Sex discrimination not significant
SM/MM	0.77	0.91	14	Family role of husband + marital status discrimination against SM

Note: *There are two possible earnings functions – the result illustrated uses the numerator group's function in each case. Included in the function was education, experience, tenure, children, years looking after family, size of library, size of town.
Source: Siebert and Young, 1983, table 6.

single men's and women's participation rates are smaller. Also, single women will have spent most of their time since leaving school in the workforce. Sure enough, the adjusted difference in the pay of single men and women is much smaller than that between men and women in general. Often in fact their adjusted pay is found to be the same.

An example of adjusting for productivity differences, and allowing for marital status as well as sex when making earnings comparisons, is given in table 6.4. The table relates to a sample of 2,500 librarians, this occupation being chosen because it is one of the few which is relatively evenly divided between men and women. (Years of labour market experience is actually known for the women in this sample, and does not have to be proxied by elapsed time since leaving school.) Reading across the top line, 0.91 is the actual married to single women pay ratio, and 0.93 is the ratio that would be expected given the differences in education and experience and other variables as between the two groups. Thus 0.93 is the ratio that would be expected without discrimination – it would not be unity because married women are less productive than single, but it would be higher than the actual ratio. The 2 point (= 0.93 − 0.91) difference between the actual and hypothetical ratios demonstrates that married women are paid less than single women for reasons other than differences in productivity. The reasons could be unmeasured supply-side differences (married women being more home work oriented than single), or discrimination against married women.

Looking at the other groups, single women and single men in this sample have almost the same actual and adjusted ratios. This indicates no sex discrimination. Finally, comparing single and married men, we see the actual ratio is 0.77, but the ratio that would be expected on the basis of differences in measured productivity characteristics alone is 0.91. Single men are paid less than expected either because we have omitted some variables such as the extra motivation of married men, or because there is real discrimination against single men. Since it is unlikely that firms discriminate against single men, this last row shows the importance of omitted motivation variables when adjusting pay for differences in productivity.

It is also interesting to note the effect of family size on earnings. Married men with children earn more than married men without (other things equal), while married women with children earn less than married women without. It is therefore marital status, and the presence of children, which appears to cause differences in pay between the sexes, not sex per se. Again the implication is that it is not demand-side discrimination, but supply-side factors which are responsible for the pay gap.

The crowding hypothesis

A popular hypothesis is that women earn less because they are in 'women's jobs'. This theory has come to be known as the occupational segregation or 'crowding' hypothesis. The claim is that certain jobs are 'set aside' for women, though men are allowed to choose any occupation. The result is that women are 'crowded' into a small number of occupations, lowering wages there.

One procedure to test the crowding hypothesis is to compute the extent to which differences in occupational distributions can explain wage differentials. This entails assessing how average male and female wages would react if occupational distributions were reversed. To illustrate the procedure, let us assume only two occupations, skilled (S) and unskilled (U), say. Average male pay is then a weighted average of male pay in the two occupations:

$$\bar{w}_m = w_m^s p_m^s + w_m^u (1 - p_m^s),$$

where w_m^s, w_m^u are male skilled and unskilled rates of pay, and p_m^s is the fraction of males doing skilled work. Similarly for women:

$$\bar{w}_f = w_f^s p_f^s + w_f^u (1 - p_f^s),$$

where the subscript, f, denotes female wages and proportions. Hypothetical female pay assuming women have equal (male) pay in each occupation is:

$$\bar{w}_f^H = w_m^s p_f^s + w_m^u (1 - p_f^s).$$

We now compare $\bar{w}_f^H$ with $\bar{w}_m$ and $\bar{w}_f$. For example:

$$\bar{w}_m - \bar{w}_f^H = w_m^s (p_m^s - p_f^s) + w_m^u (p_f^s - p_m^s).$$

Thus if $\bar{w}_m = \bar{w}_f^H$, then $p_m^s = p_f^s$, and the only reason that $\bar{w}_m$ could differ from $\bar{w}_f$ is that $w_m^s > w_f^s$, and $w_m^u > w_f^u$, that is, there is wage discrimination. Conversely, the larger is the difference between $\bar{w}_m$ and $\bar{w}_f^H$, the bigger must be the difference between p_m^s and p_f^s, and the more important is occupational 'crowding'. Also:

$$\bar{w}_f^H - \bar{w}_f = (w_m^s - w_f^s)p_f^s + (w_m^u - w_f^u)(1 - p_f^s).$$

This shows that if $\bar{w}_f = \bar{w}_f^H$, then wages given occupation must be the same, and the reason that $\bar{w}_m$ is higher than $\bar{w}_f$ must be because women are 'crowded' into the unskilled occupations.

In practice what is found is that the difference $\bar{w}_f - \bar{w}_f^H$ is quite large relative to the difference $\bar{w}_m - \bar{w}_f^H$, indicating that it is differences in pay given the job, not differences in the kinds of jobs done that mainly causes female average earnings to be lower than male. Taking $\bar{w}_m = 100$, one American study using 222 occupational categories (only occupations employing at least 100 women and at least 100 men being included) finds $\bar{w}_f = 64$ and $\bar{w}_f^H = 93$. Thus average earnings of women would rise by 29 ($= 93 - 64$) points if they had the same pay as men given the job, and by only 7 ($= 100 - 93$) points if they had the same occupational distribution as men (Treiman and Hartmann, 1981, 34–5). A UK study with over 1,500 occupations finds that 80% of the pay gap is due to differences in pay given the job, and only 20% to different jobs (Sloane, 1990, table 5.8). Another US study shows that, confining the comparison to the single-never-been-married groups only, making occupational distributions alike would not change the male–female pay ratio at all (Chiswick *et al.*, 1975). This technique suggests it is differences in pay given the job that matter, and not the crowding of women into different jobs.

However the technique of comparing hypothetical occupational distributions is flawed because the importance of occupational composition increases the more narrowly occupation is defined. In the limit there would be as many occupations as there were people, so that differences in occupational composition would explain all of the gender wage gap. For example when one compares pay given the job between males and females in the *same* firm, the difference is minor compared to when one does not control for firm. What is happening is that women are ending up in the lower paying firms – the smaller, non-union firms. Crudely comparing occupational distributions therefore is not satisfactory because it depends too much on how one defines an occupation.

An alternative procedure is to see whether occupations employing a greater

Table 6.5 *Regression results on occupational segregation and earnings*

Dependent variable: female to male hourly earnings ratio, 46 industries

Variable	Coefficient
Expected earnings*	1.63[a]
Per cent in government	0.145[a]
Per cent female	−0.052
Per cent unionised	0.023
Employment growth rate	4.82[a]
Establishment size	−0.012
Age profile†	−14.1[a]
Mean female earnings = $1.66 per hour; male = $2.84	

Notes:

[a]Denotes significance at the 5% level or more.

*Expected earnings allow for each industry's female/male age, colour, and education composition.

$$\dagger\text{Age profile} = \frac{\text{Expected earnings, white males aged 45–54}}{\text{Expected earnings, white males aged 20–34}}$$

Source: Fuchs, 1971.

proportion of females (PF) pay lower wages, holding personal productivity attributes constant. In a wage regression a large PF coefficient would imply that an occupation's gender composition *as such* explained a large portion of the gender wage differential, supporting the hypothesis that 'women's jobs' paid less not because of lower productivity, but because of crowding.

Perhaps the first to apply such a framework was Victor Fuchs. For this reason we present Fuchs' results in table 6.5. The female to male earnings ratio is the dependent variable. The variable, 'expected' female earnings relative to male, holds constant the effect on the earnings ratio of sex differences in age, colour, and education. The government variable allows for the possibility that the public sector is more favourable to women. In fact we see that female earnings in an industry composed entirely of government employees would be 14.5% higher than in an industry which is completely private, other things equal. Whether this means that private industry discriminates against women or that the government favours women is not certain.

Most interesting from our point of view is the inclusion of the age profile variable. In chapter 4 we noted that the slope of the earnings profile can be interpreted as indicating the extent of investment in on-the-job training – with a flat profile meaning zero self-investment. The equation shows that women do relatively worse in industries in which there is much on-the-job training. This finding might be explained in terms of the fact that women are less likely to undertake such training, because of a shorter expected period in the workforce (see below). Consequently they are at a disadvantage in circumstances where much training is expected.

As for the per cent female variable (PF), this does not seem very important. The female–male pay ratio in an industry goes down as PF goes up, but the decline is not statistically significant. Other studies have found significant effects however. For example. Aldrich and Buchele find that the difference in pay in an occupation which has no women, and one which has 100% implies a decline in the male–female gap of about 3% (1986, 123). In any case it is possible that the per cent female variable is picking up other, unmeasured, productivity differences, or perhaps tastes. The suggestion is therefore that while occupational segregation (measured by per cent female in the occupation or industry) does have an impact on female wages, allowing for productivity differences, the impact is not major.

Discrimination and competition

There is also the question of whether discrimination has been found to be less in competitive circumstances (see Dex *et al.*, 1989, 86 ff). Is the residual wage gap between men and women higher, or women's employment opportunities lower in monopolistic than competitive firms?

In fact it is difficult to assess discrimination because wage discrimination tends to vary in the opposite way to employment discrimination. Consider figure 6.3, which pictures women as having lower marginal product – perhaps because of intermittency – than men in a given job. Then if men and women are to have equal chances of employment in the job, L_1 each for example, women's pay would have to be w_1, less than men's, w_2. Thus for employment discrimination to be zero, 'wage discrimination' is required. Indeed, in South Africa, the way in which white craft unions historically implemented employment discrimination against blacks, was by insisting that whites and blacks be paid the same – the 'rate for the job' (Van der Horst, 1942). Similarly, if wage discrimination (or, more strictly, wage difference) is outlawed, then women lose employment opportunities, and a form of employment discrimination results.

Becker (1957) first analysed the link between wage discrimination and monopoly, and found some evidence that discrimination was more likely in monopolistic industries. Sloane has summarised the results of several studies on this issue (1985, 100; see also Addison and Siebert, 1979, 219). In the studies involving race there does seem less wage discrimination and better black employment opportunities where market structure appears more competitive – six out of eight studies give results consistent with competitive

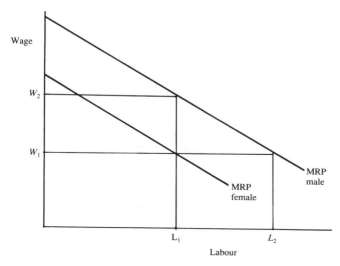

Figure 6.3 Wage discrimination and employment discrimination

theory. However for women, the picture is less clear. Only two out of five studies examined give a clear-cut relationship in the right direction (higher female wages and/or employment in competitive industries), two are inconclusive, and one gives a perverse relationship. Nevertheless a recent study of the US banking industry has shown that women are more likely to be bank managers where there is a low concentration ratio for banks in the local labour market than where there is a high concentration ratio (Ashenfelter and Hannan, 1986, 162). Since a low concentration ratio suggests more competition, the implication is that competition improves women's employment opportunities.

A difficulty of studying the impact of competition on discrimination is that – if some firms discriminate by paying women less than men of the same productivity – a competitive process will be set in motion which eliminates both wage and employment differences between men and women. This is because women will tend to move away from the more discriminatory firms. Women's wages will then tend to be bid up relative to men's, and women will find employment opportunities (at all levels, presumably) in non-discriminatory firms. The end result will simply be male-dominated and female-dominated firms, that is, segregation. However it is true that this process of segregation will tend to be easier in some markets than others. For example in large towns there is a bigger selection of firms, and thus more opportunity for women and non-discriminatory firms to match up. This suggests an empirical test: if some firms really do dislike women for some reason, we should therefore find a greater tendency towards segregated firms in large towns. When the test is performed, however, it points against discrimination. If anything, there seems to be *less* segregation amongst firms in large towns than in small (Lindsay and Maloney, 1988, table 1). Thus it seems that women's employment patterns cannot easily be explained by their attempting to avoid discrimination when choosing among firms.

Further evidence backing up the hypothesis that competition erodes discrimination is the fact that women are more likely to be employed in small firms than men. Small firms are probably more competitive, and are certainly less unionised (see chapter 10). Small firms are also likely to be more adroit in judging the quality of applicants since the owner is closer to the point of hiring, and there is less 'control loss' than in the larger firm (Stigler, 1962, 103). Garen (1985) for example has found that small firms put more weight on ability than large firms, while large firms stress qualifications. The logic that competition, and consequent tight management, helps women is borne out by these results.

Finally, there is the study by Moore (1983). He compares the self-employed with the employed, the rationale being that discrimination in employment will only, by definition, be manifested against women in the latter field. However, he does not find the female/male pay ratio to be higher for the self-employed group, nor greater female than male participation in self-employment. Thus, whatever the disadvantages women experience, they experience them equally in self-employment, implying that it is not employee status as such which is the cause of women's relatively low pay.

6.4 The supply side

Differences in tastes

We can generalise the definition of discrimination to mean 'unlike treatment of likes' in any field, including within the family. However to say that different treatment of boys and girls within the family – 'playing doctor or playing nurse' – is discriminatory is then to imply that the sex of children does not or should not matter. There is no way of proving this. Psychological studies of parents indicate they have deeply held conceptions that their girls and boys are different: for example, parents rate girl babies as smaller than boy babies even when they are the same weight (Shepela and Viviano, 1984, 48). Parents, it seems, see what they want to see in this respect. This could be indicative of a deep biological and cultural necessity to have sexual differentiation – rather than some erroneous 'stereotyping' on the parents' part.

In any case, women's involvement in child rearing might be felt by the family to be good for the children. In Japan, where women have a more family-oriented role, they are strongly involved in pre-school education

(Edwards, 1988, 245) – and Japanese children's educational performance is good by comparison with other countries. The mean mathematics score for thirteen year olds in Anderson's international study was 31.2 for Japan, 20.2 for Australia, 19.3 for England and 16.2 for the USA (Anderson, 1967, 191).

Whether the reasons be good or bad, men and women do appear to have different tastes and this affects occupational choice. Daymont and Andrisani (1984) analysed high school pupils' responses to questions about the importance of various job rewards when choosing a career. Women were found to be significantly more likely to be interested in a career with opportunities for helping others, and for working with people, and less likely to want a career with the emphasis on making money and being a leader. Proportions answering 'Yes' to questions about tastes were as follows (Daymont and Andrisani, 1984, 412):

	Male	Female
Very interested in a career with opportunities to help others	47%	72%
Very interested in working with people	40	68
Very interested in leading	22	11
Very interested in making money	22	13

Later, in college, the same sample of men and women were found to have different majors, with the men favouring business, engineering, and the professions, and the women health or biology, the humanities, and education (1984, 414). Tastes thus affect motivation and the type of education which an individual chooses, and these factors will then affect earnings.

Intermittent participation and reduced human capital

Women differ from men in their expectations of lifetime labourforce participation. Women, especially married women, tend to participate in the labourforce more intermittently than men. Using the 1967 National Longitudinal Survey, figures for years out of the workforce for married women at work in 1966 vary by age and education. For those aged thirty to thirty-four the figure is 9.9 years (4.2 years) for women with less than twelve (more than sixteen) years of education. Equivalent figures for the forty to forty-four age group are 15.7 (9.7) (see Mincer and Polachek, 1974; Mincer and Ofek, 1982). For those who had not worked since the birth of their first child (about 1/3 of the sample of 3,000) the period out of the workforce is about 50% higher. Those not at work in 1966, but who had ever worked, give an intermediate figure. Thus, to take a round figure, we might assume that ten years, on average, are spent out of the labourforce to bear and raise children. Still more

Table 6.6. *Gains from human capital investments for continuous and intermittent workers*

Age	Continuous worker: Partici- pation	MG_t	Intermittent worker: gain from 1 ed Partici- pation	FMG_t
20	1	10 × 0.986*	1	10 × (0.379 + 0.986 − 0.782) = 5.81†
25	1	10 × 0.978	1	10 × (0 + 0.978 − 0.650) = 3.28
30	1	10 × 0.964	0	10 × (0 + 0.964 − 0.436) = 5.25
35	1	10 × 0.943	0	10 × (0 + 0.943 − 0.091) = 8.52
40	1	10 × 0.908	1	10 × 0.908
45	1	10 × 0.851	1	10 × 0.851
50	1	10 × 0.761	1	10 × 0.761
55	1	10 × 0.614	1	10 × 0.614
60	1	10 × 0.379	1	10 × 0.379
65	1	0	1	0

Notes:

*Assume the value, w, of an ed is $1 a year, i.e., buying 1 ed raises potential earnings, E, by $1 a year for the rest of one's working life. Assume the discount rate is 10% (so buying 1 ed raises the value of the capital stock by $w/0.1 = \$10$), and people retire at age 65. If the ed is invested in at age 20, then the extra $1 received for 45 years has a present value of

$$\frac{\$1}{0.1} \left[1 - \frac{1}{(1.1)^{45}} \right] = \$9.86.$$

†Assume the period out of the labour force lasts from age 26 to 35. Then the returns from an investment of 1 ed made at age 20 are gained for five years initially:

$$\frac{\$1}{0.1} \left[1 - \frac{1}{(1.1)^5} \right] = \$3.79$$

and then for 29 years in 16 years' time:

$$\frac{\$1}{0.1} \left[1 - \frac{1}{(1.1)^{45}} \right] - \frac{\$1}{0.1} \left[1 - \frac{1}{(1.1)^{16}} \right] = \$10 (0.986 - 0.782).$$

The total present value is therefore $5.81.

time (about four years) is spent in intermittentparticipation as children are growing up. In the case of Britain, Joshi assumes eight years for 'Mrs. Typical' with two children (1987, 13).

Figure 6.4 depicts sex and marital status labourforce participation patterns for the United States. Married men have by far the highest labourforce

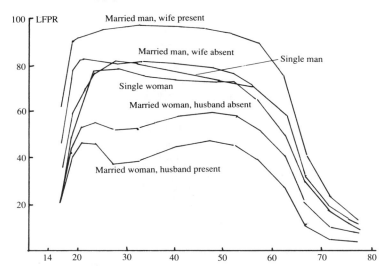

Figure 6.4 Labourforce participation by marital status, US 1970. *Source:* Robert Fearn, *Labor Economics, The Emerging Synthesis*, Cambridge, MA: Winthrop Publishers, 1981

participation. Married women have the lowest, peaking at about 43% at age twenty-three, and then again at forty-eight. The trough at around age thirty reflects labourforce intermittency related to child bearing. The gap between single men and single women is the narrowest. Single-never-married males and females have roughly similar lifetime work behaviour patterns. Over time, to be sure, the dip in participation for women in the twenty-five to thirty-seven age group has become much less marked (see chapter 5). Nevertheless women's labourforce participation remains much less than men's.

Human capital theory links occupations and wages to lifetime labourforce participation and the division of labour within the family. Because monetary gains from investment cannot be reaped when not at work, the average woman's returns from investment are reduced by the present value of the extra earnings from investment she would have earned had she continued to work instead of staying at home. Thus the effect of lower lifetime labourforce participation and intermittency is to lower gains from human capital investment.

Table 6.6 illustrates the position by contrasting two individuals one of whom works continuously until age sixty-five, while the other leaves the workforce between ages twenty-six and thirty-five. The left-hand column shows that the present value of an 'ed' assumed to raise wages by $1 a year falls smoothly with advancing age; the 'marginal gain' from investing in an 'ed' is almost $10 at age twenty, and falls to zero by age sixty-five. The right-hand column shows quite a different pattern. Due to the expected break in labourforce participation (when nothing is earned), the present value of an 'ed' is much less at age twenty. The table shows the present value to be $5.81, falling to $3.28 at age twenty-five. Then for the next ten years the marginal gain to investment is increasing. But whether any investment is made is another matter. If post-school investment consists strictly of on-the-job training, then none can be made. The person's capital stock and capacity earnings will fall accordingly. Upon reentry at age thirty-six marginal gain from investment follows the same path for both continuous and intermittent workers.

Figure 6.5 graphs the consequences of intermittent participation for a woman's capital stock. The top left quadrant shows the marginal cost and gain curves. However, the MG curve does not slide smoothly down the MC curve (compare figure 2.6 in chapter 2), but goes down, then up, then down again – as in table 6.6. Consequently investment falls then rises, then falls as shown in the bottom right quadrant. As noted, if there is no opportunity for training during the period out of the labourforce ($LFP = 0$) then investment could be zero during this period. More likely there will be some investment, but not enough to offset depreciation, so the capital stock will tend to fall slowly during this period.

The path of capital stock is shown in the top right quadrant. The capacity earnings path will have the same shape, on the assumption that each ed composing the capital stock brings an income of $1 a year. The capital stock starts at value, PK_0 determined in the main by education (the more educated a person, the higher is K_0). Then the stock increases quite quickly initially due to the initial marginal gain of $5.80 (as shown in table 6.6), and then more slowly. During the home period the value of the stock will decline at the rate of depreciation if there is no investment. Then upon reentry the capital stock will increase sharply for a while, before declining in the normal way. Thus one consequence of women's intermittent participation is that they can be expected to have lower and flatter, and more 'bumpy', earnings profiles – just as we see.

Intermittent participation and occupational choice

Further, individuals expecting labourforce intermittency will choose occupations in which the penalty for intermittency – the 'atrophy' or depreciation or human capital – is lowest. Such occupations will have high starting wages and thus flat earnings (a job cannot have both a high starting wage and a high rate of increase of pay with experience, because everyone would go for that job – see the discussion of figure 4.1). It would not make sense for someone who was expecting to leave the workforce to become a trainee manager, for example. Men who are not expecting to leave pull the starting wage of such jobs down. A worker who does leave will thus have incurred the penalty of a

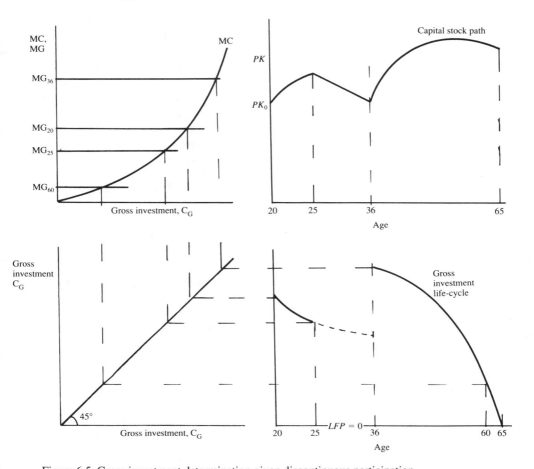

Figure 6.5 Gross investment determination given discontinuous participation

low trainee wage, and will not be around to enjoy the later higher wages (see chapter 7's discussion of compensating wage differentials).

One implication is that women will be less well represented in professional and managerial jobs for reasons of income-maximising choice (given competition from men) – quite apart from demand-side discrimination in hiring or promotion. Indeed we do find in practice that occupations with the highest depreciation during periods of hometime tend to have female workers with the fewest years out of the workforce. Professional and management jobs for example have high depreciation compared to the service job category, and the proportion of years spent as 'hometime' is about 30% for women in the former, compared to 60% in the latter (see chapter 7, table 7.4 below).

Another implication of the hypothesis is that the jobs taken by single women will differ from those of married women, given the latter's family care commitments, and be similar to those of single men. The empirical evidence here appears to support the proposition. Roos (1981) illustrates occupational patterns for employed women for twelve countries (mainly OECD). For each country except Israel and Sweden, a greater proportion of never married women are in professional, technical and administrative jobs. This contrasts with the large proportion of married women in more menial service and agricultural jobs. In addition there is a reasonably good correlation between occupations which have high percentage female, and which employ women with high intermittency (and have low atrophy rates – see table 7.4 below). England however does not find a correlation between percent female and intermittency (per cent hometime) using detailed occupations (1982, table 4). But it is more appropriate to proxy intermittency with per cent home time than per cent female. Also, since the human capital model is designed to represent lifetime occupational choice, broad occupational categories are more appropriate than detailed (current) occupations.

Following up the point about expectations, a further implication of labour-force intermittency is that women who expect to remain in the workforce should choose jobs with lower starting salaries and steeper age–earnings profiles than those who did not. This has indeed been demonstrated empiri-cally. A sample of young women (average age nineteen) were questioned as to whether they planned to be in the workforce at age thirty-five. Analysing their pay five years later, those who did have such plans were found to be earning 10% *less* than the others, but had much faster earnings growth (Sandell and Shapiro, 1980, 342). Individuals aiming to remain in the workforce thus appear to invest more in themselves, as we would expect.

Intermittent participation and the wage gap

The effect of intermittency on the wage gap is illustrated in figure 6.6. $0''H$ represents an age–earnings profile for a typical individual with full lifetime labourforce participation, ignoring curvature for simplicity. It reflects earnings capacity at each level of experience, and thus rises with age.

Those labour market participants with intermittency have a different profile. First of all, initial labour market earnings (the vertical intercept) is smaller (point 0) because of the smaller investment in education. Second, the slope with respect to initial experience (e_1) is smaller (rising to level A). Third, earnings are essentially zero during the period (H) when one is out of the labourforce. And fourth, and perhaps most interesting, the reentry wage (B),

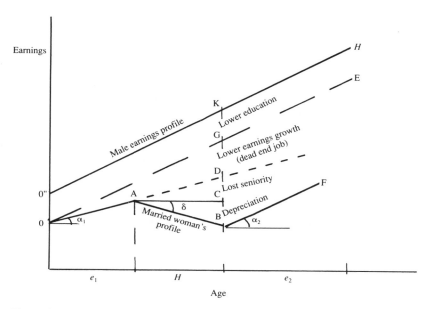

Figure 6.6 The effect on earnings of labourforce intermittency

after a period of intermittency, is lower in real terms than the wage at the point just prior to leaving the labour market (A).

The total loss in wages caused by intermittency can be expressed as segment (BK), the difference between reentry wage (B) and the wage the individual would have received had she been in the labourforce fully. This gap can be divided into three segments: (1) BC represents the direct depreciation of skills due to atrophy, (2) CD reflects the lost wages due to lost seniority, and (3) DK reflects the extra wage one would have obtained with initially high expectations of labourforce participation. This latter gap DK is composed of two parts, DG and GK. The gap DG reflects the additional earnings attributable to extra on-the-job training that would be obtained by those with expectations of complete labourforce continuity. Similarly, the gap GK reflects the additional earnings attributable to extra schooling (including the study of more market oriented fields) for those who plan to specialise more in a career than home activities.

These ideas of labour market segments composed of work and non-work periods, can be used to modify the earnings function derived in chapter 4 (equation (4.1)) so that the magnitudes of these effects can be obtained. Recall that earnings can be specified as the accumulated return to life-cycle investment (see chapter 4, equation (4.2)), so that:

$$\ln E_t = \ln E_0 + rS + r\sum_{i=1}^{s-1} s_i,$$

where s_i represents the amount of time-equivalent investment for each year of post-school experience, r is the rate of return, S is schooling, and E is potential earnings. It is reasonable to assume s_i declines monotonically when one works continuously. On the other hand, investment need not decline continuously when one's work history is divided into work and non-work segments.

To modify the above equation one must divide the t-S potential work years into segments, so that each segment's investment can be parameterised and incorporated. Assume three life-cycle segments, e_1 the period before the first child, H the period at home, and e_2 the period when the labourforce is re-entered. It is not so necessary to assume a linear decline of investment given the shorter duration of the segments, so we take investment in each segment to be constant:

$$\ln E_t = \ln E_0 + rS + r(a_1 e_1 + a_2 H + a_3 e_2).$$

In terms of observable earnings, Y_t, we have:

$$\ln Y_t = a_0 + rS + \alpha_1 e_1 + \delta H + \alpha_2 e_2.$$

The coefficients α_1 and α_2 reflect real growth in wages during the work segments e_1 and e_2 – and correspond to the angles graphed in figure 6.6. The angle δ reflects the depreciation in earnings power related to intermittency. Typically the α coefficients vary from about 1.2% to 4.0%, depending upon the population subgroup under study. The δ coefficient ranged from about -0.5% to -2.0%. These figures imply that the human capital stock depreciates at between 0.5% and 2% per year when a person leaves the labourforce, while it grows during work segments at between 1.2% and 4.0%. In general, the higher one's education and the more skilled one's job the greater the magnitude of these coefficients.

The typical woman (from the National Longitudinal Survey data) can be assumed to drop out of the labour market about ten years. Taking $H = 10$ we can compute the distance BD, a lower bound estimate of the difference in earnings between the intermittent and continuous worker. Taking typical α_1 and δ estimates of 0.015 and -0.005 respectively, one can compute the difference between B and D to be 20%; B–D = $10 \times 0.015 - 10 \times (-0.005)$ = 0.20. Recalling that the gender wage gap averages about 40%, we find that dropping out of the workforce alone explains about 50% (the 20% explained wage gap divided by the 40% total wage gap) of the male/female wage differential.

Table 6.7. *Earnings equations for married males and females, allowing for differences in human capital*

Dependent variable: dollar earnings (*t* values in parentheses)

	(1)	(2)	(3)
Coefficient on gender dummy (1 = F)	−3032 (54.9)	−80.3 (1.07)	−2533 (40.4)
Coefficient on expected capital*	not included	0.076	not included
Other variables	Education, experience, hours worked/yr, years married	Hours worked/yr, number of children under 6, 6–11, 12-17, over 18, 9 occupations, 12 industries	As for (2)

Notes and *Source*: as for table 6.8.

Estimating male and female capital stocks

A way of incorporating intermittency into analysis of the wage gap is to estimate male and female capital stocks, and relate capital stock to wages. The details of the calculations are given in the appendix, and results are given in table 6.7. Three columns are shown, giving the value of the coefficient obtained for 'sex', a dummy gender variable, under different circumstances. The coefficient −3032 represents the dollar difference in earnings using the 1960 US Census one-in-a-thousand sample, holding constant education and experience (and experience squared), hours worked, and years married. This is the usual simple human capital model, and as can be seen it leaves a large amount unexplained, i.e., a $3,000 difference between individuals ostensibly with the same human capital.

The best approach is to use in the earnings regression a measure of an individual's human capital stock – which depends on education, age, and expected labourforce participation. The consequence of this for the coefficient on 'sex' is shown in columns (2) and (3) of table 6.7. Column (2) includes as a regressor the expected human capital of the individuals in the sample. It can be seen that this variable is highly significant. Its coefficient measures the relation between earnings and human capital, 7.6%, which should approximately equal the return on human capital ('approximately', because the dependent variable is observed, not capacity earnings).

Most interesting, we see that in column (2) – using expected human capital – the coefficient on the sex dummy drops to $80.3, a negligible amount. The implication is that most of the difference in earnings between the sexes is due to differences in human capital accumulation due to differences in life-cycle labourforce participation. Note that this regression does not include education and experience variables because these were used to compute the human capital variable. Occupation and industry dummies are included, however, as well as numbers of children. That it is not these variables that account for the fall in the sex coefficient is shown in the last column. The regression run here includes all the new variables, but drops the human capital variable. In this case the sex coefficient rises again to -2533, showing it is the human capital variable which is doing the work.

To lend credence to these results, a similar computation is performed looking not at gender differences, but at marital status differences given gender. These results are contained in table 6.8. Here 82% of the $3,000 earnings premium married males receive over single males can be explained by married/single differences in life-cycle participation. Likewise, about 75% of the $625 premium single women obtain over married women can be explained by lifetime labourforce participation differences.

Monopsony and absenteeism

Two further supply-side differences between men and women are worth mentioning. Firstly women with children tend to have a more geographically limited area of job search. Data on travel to work distances are contained in table 6.9. It can be seen that the singles live quite close to work, about seven to eight miles, and marrieds without children live further, about ten to eleven miles – but with both husband and wife commuting about the same distance. The interesting column is the last, which shows that those working married women with children commute only 7.7 miles on average, while their husbands commute 12.5 miles. Notice as well that the single woman heading a family also only commutes 7.7 miles to work, the same distance as the working married woman with a family. Children are therefore associated with a marked decrease in a working woman's mobility.

Presumably the fact that married women with children work closer to home reflects the family division of labour. Family income maximisation requires that wives make a larger 'compromise' by working close to home, while their husbands are free to search further afield. Single women with children do not have this constraint, but still presumably have to compromise their locational choices so as to look after the children (for example, be near relatives). Having a smaller travel to work distance therefore means that fewer alternatives are open to working women with children. Such women will find it more difficult to match their talents to an appropriate job.

Smaller travel to work areas means that the pay of women with children will be lower than that of other individuals with the same personal characteristics.

Table 6.8. *Earnings equations by sex and marital status, allowing for differences in human capital*

Dependent variable: wage, salary, and self-employment income

	Male regression coefficients		
Constant	3068[a]	387[a]	156[a]
Marital status	3002[a]		535[a]
Expected capital*		0.110[a]	0.106[a]
R^2	0.064	0.250	0.252
	Female regression coefficients		
Constant	1797[a]	1957[a]	3142[a]
Marital status	−625		−148
Expected capital*		0.039[a]	0.036[a]
R^2	0.063	0.076	0.077

Notes:
*Expected capital stock – see appendix for method of calculation; marital status is a dummy (1 = married)
[a] Denotes significance at the 5% level or more.
Source: Polachek, 1975a.

Table 6.9. *Travel to work distances*

	Single	Married, no children		Married, with children	
		Husband working	Both working	Husband working	Both working
Male	8.2 miles	10.4	11.1	11.8	12.5
Female	7.5 miles	—	10.1	—	7.7

Single woman with children: 7.7 miles

Source: Madden, 1981, 185, from the 1976 Panel Survey of Income Dynamics.

It will look as though the market is discriminating against such women, but in fact it is compromising locational choices which are the cause. On this argument the diminution of the opportunity set should matter less if the family locates in a big town than a small. This is indeed the case as shown by the fact that male wages increase less than female wages as size of town increases, which is to be expected if males have more mobility. Holding region, education, and labourforce experience constant, it has been found that married women in towns with under 250,000 population earn 35% less than those in towns of over 750,000. The corresponding figure for males is only 20% (Frank, 1978, table 4). Lower mobility might also be the reason why married women tend to be found in smaller establishments than other groups, since these are more dispersed (Siebert and Young, 1983).

Secondly, women tend to have somewhat higher quit and absenteeism rates than men. For example, regarding absenteeism, as measured by the proportion of days absent in the last ten working days, Leigh gives a figure of 4% for men, and 5.5% for women (1983, 355). Most of the difference seems to be attributable to the greater response of female absenteeism to the presence of children under six in the family. As for quit rates, Shorey's British data give an average of 3.8 (2%) quits per hundred workers per quarter for women (men) (1983, 220). However, much of the difference, Shorey finds, can be ascribed to the lower wages of women; for a given wage, male and female quit rates are similar. Models of the relationship between quit rates and wage differentials also show that the small quit rate difference cannot explain much of the male–female wage differential so we should not stress this factor (see Sloane, 1985, 108–10, for a review).

To summarise the supply side, men and women enter the labour market with differing characteristics, in particular a lower attachment to market work on the part of women. These differences could be a consequence of:
a) tastes;
b) a rational (family wealth maximising) division of labour in the home due to women's comparative advantage in child-bearing and rearing; and
c) expectations of future labour market discrimination.

We have seen that tastes do differ, and this is likely to explain in part the family division of labour. However women's role in bringing up children is also a major factor. Changes in household technology, fewer children, and easier pregnancies are reducing the advantages of specialisation in household production, and consequently women's labourforce participation patterns are becoming more like men's (see chapter 5). As for reverse causation, factor (c), this will have a role to play due to statistical discrimination – but only for exceptional women. However policies to overcome reverse causation, for example 'eliminating' gender wage differences via a comparable worth programme, are difficult to devise, as we shall now see.

6.5 Policy issues

Current policy

The wage gap has been a political issue at least since the early 1970s. Government policy promoting sexual equality in the market place has been oriented almost solely towards business. Firms are sued because they allegedly have unfair hiring practices and because they allegedly pay unequal wages for equal work. Britain has an Equal Pay Act, and a Sex Discrimination Act. The United States has Title VII of the Civil Rights Act of 1964, which prohibits discrimination on grounds of sex, religion, or national origin, and other legislation (for example, federal contractors must comply with affirmative action guidelines). In America, the government as well as individuals have brought class action suits at unprecedented levels.

Despite such legal activity, wage differentials have only narrowed slowly, and occupational distributions remain very different. This slow progress has most likely resulted because government legislation treats corporations as the primary culprit of most sex differences within the labour market.

As demonstrated above, such an approach is seriously limited in perspective because it neglects social factors. Whereas it may be true that some of the sex differences in labourforce participation are caused by women being discouraged from working continuously, we have argued that little of the differences are caused by firms. Rather it is the more subtle forms of social conditioning taking place directly within the family, and the power of gender specialisation within the household which are important. The specialisation factor is shown by the fact that single-never-been-married women have greater lifetime labourforce commitment than their married counterparts, as well as a higher level of earnings and better jobs. Specialisation within the household is also the reason that we observe that the gender wage gap is smaller for singles than marrieds, smaller at younger ages, and larger for those with children.

Despite the apparent failure of governmental equal employment opportunity type policies, greater sexual equality is coming about. It is not noticeable among all women, but is widely observed among the younger cohorts. Young women are entering the labour market in unprecedented numbers. They are doing so with expectations of greater labour market continuity brought about by postponing marriage, bearing fewer children, and having almost epidemic divorce rates. These expectations are causing the younger cohorts to increasingly invest in human capital skills. School attendance by women is becoming larger than that of men, and women are now entering what used to be occupations in the male domain. Law school, business school, and medical school enrolments which only a decade ago were at meagre levels for women are now approaching 40% (see table 6.1). For these groups there is rough parity with men.

While the older cohorts are also increasing their role in the economy, they are at a great disadvantage. They are reentering the labour market after spending an average of about ten years out for child rearing responsibilities. Because of this time out, many of their skills have atrophied, resulting in an earnings power lower than it otherwise would have been. It is the inclusion of these reentrants that tend to bias downward the aggregate statistics measuring equality between the sexes.

Comparable worth

Comparable worth is being considered widely as a means to reduce the gender wage gap. Such a programme involves allocating points to jobs for 'skill, effort, and responsibility', and then paying according to point scores of the various jobs. Such a 'job evaluation' is a widely respected management tool for preserving pay equity within a company, and the points scores are normally explicitly linked to market wages at various points. Comparable worth diverges from the normal job evaluation however in that the market reference point is not to be used, because market wages are said to reflect 'discrimination'.

The attraction of the job evaluation method of bringing about equal pay is that it can be much more far-reaching than the simple requirement of equal pay for equal work; we now have equal pay for work of 'equal value', where 'equal value' is decided by the job evaluation committee. The door to comparable worth was opened in the US by the Supreme Court in 1981, with the ruling that female prison wardens be paid according to their employer's job evaluation scheme (women prison warders had been evaluated at 95% of the points of men, but were paid only 70% as much). The European Community is also looking with enthusiasm at the concept, and required Britain to incorporate it into the Equal Pay Act in 1983. Comparable worth is now in the process of expansion in Europe, with the possibility that women will be compared with men doing 'comparable' jobs not only in their organisation, but also in other organisations.

The major difficulty about relying on job evaluation is conflict with supply and demand. The orthodox economic analysis is shown in figure 6.7 with nurses and computer analysts as examples. These two occupations have been regarded as 'comparable' in past comparable worth exercises. Nursing is pictured as female dominated for reasons of preference, and/or 'societal conditioning', and/or because it might offer less of a penalty for labourforce intermittency than being a computer analyst which is male dominated. Female and male supply curves are summed to give total supply S_{Total} to each occupation. Demand curves have been drawn in to give a higher equilibrium wage for analysts, W_c, than nurses, W_n, as is realistic.

Suppose comparable worth established the same wage, w^*, in both occupations. As drawn, the nurses' wage would rise, and that for analysts fall. (Though equal pay laws say that no-one's pay is to be reduced, in practice, to finance the programme, male jobs' pay is likely to increase more slowly.) Employment in both occupations would fall from point 1 to point 2. There

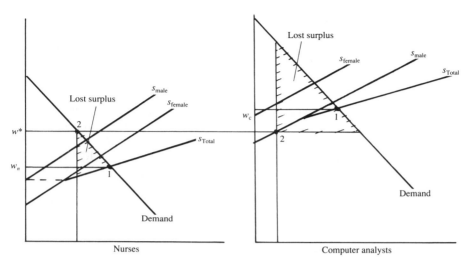

Figure 6.7 The losses caused by comparable worth

would be excess supply of nurses, with both more men and more women applying to enter but nurses being laid off because there would not be the money to pay all of them the higher rates. There would also be an excess demand for computer analysts.

The cross-hatched triangles show the 'dead weight' losses resulting from the policy – the fact that the gains of the gainers are less than the losses of the losers. To put this in another way, the triangle in the left-hand panel, for example, bounded by the demand and S_{Total} curves, gives the sum of consumer and producer surplus arising from nursing. The cross-hatched tip of this triangle is lost when employment falls to point 2. In the case of nurses, while the pay for some will go up (a transfer from the profit of the employer), this will be more than outweighed by the lost surplus of nurses who are laid off and the lost surplus of patients who cannot afford nursing.

An additional important effect, not shown in figure 6.7, is that pay in women's jobs not covered by comparable worth will go down. This is because small, non-union, firms are less likely to have job evaluations. The nurses who have become unemployed in the covered sector will have to seek jobs in these firms. This will put downward pressure on wages in the uncovered sector, making workers there worse off, but firms better off.

A further effect, again not shown on the diagram, is that comparable worth will cause less on-the-job training in the female-dominated jobs. Training is a fringe benefit on which firms will try to economise when wages are raised. This effect is akin to the effect of minimum wages in discouraging training, discussed in chapter 4. Comparable worth is analogous to minimum wage legislation in that it puts a floor under some wages. Indeed, comparable worth is more far-reaching than minimum wage legislation because by controlling wage relativities, it implies wage maxima (for male-dominated jobs) as well as minima.

Sometimes it is contended that the analysis of figure 6.7 is static in that it ignores the possibility that the supply curves to the two occupations will change as a result of comparable worth. Thus the higher wage in nursing might attract more men there (even though there are fewer job opportunities); and the excess demand for computer analysts might attract more female applicants (even though wages and employment have gone down). In this way sex segregation could be broken down (Becker, 1986, 939). It must surely be admitted however that the incentives do seem wrong – more women are likely to be attracted to nursing once its pay is increased.

We have the results of one case study of employment effects, relating to the comparable worth programme in Washington State. A clear fall in the employment of those whose pay was raised the most is found (Brien et al., 1989). The low paid gained the largest percentage pay increase – an increase from $5.90 to $7.47 – but their share of employment fell the most – from 12.6 to 9.6% (see also Orazem et al., 1990; Pike, 1985).

If a policy has adverse effects on the national income, as comparable worth is likely to have, then at least it should have beneficial distributional effects – make low paid workers better off. But it is not obvious that comparable worth has this effect. Evidence bearing on the distributional question has been assembled by Smith, who argues that comparable worth will apply primarily to women in government and large firms (1988, 235). It is only in large organisations that job evaluations can be performed, and – just as important – it requires a union to press for and monitor the evaluation. Part-timers are also likely not to be helped by comparable worth, since they are poorly unionised. In fact part-timers and uncovered workers in smaller firms are likely to experience the effects of crowding, as large firms economise on labour once comparable worth is instituted. Thus comparable worth will help the 'haves' in large unionised organisations, and reduce the wages of other, uncovered, groups.

It must be emphasised that even if one takes the view that there are significant market imperfections, it does not follow that comparable worth is the best way to proceed. Other policies, designed to decentralise wage setting, or improve women's labour market opportunities (affirmative action), or to reduce their family role constraints (subsidised day-care facilities) could be more appropriate. If the market is imperfect, it does not follow that making it more imperfect by the setting of wage relativities (as comparable worth

implies) is the solution. As Fischel and Lazear (1986) have pointed out, comparable worth amounts to penalising firms which employ many women. Their
costs will be raised, but the firms not employing many women, and who might
be discriminating, will be unaffected. An analogy would be if a cartel of oil
producers were raising the price of oil – the price of coal then rising in parallel
as people switch into the cheaper fuel. One policy would be to impose a
ceiling on coal prices, a better alternative would be to tackle the problem at its
root – the barriers raised by the cartel. A comparable worth programme is an
example of the former type of policy, which leaves aside the question of
barriers to women's employment, and instead attacks the wage structure which
is doing a perfectly good job.

Appropriate policies to combat sex discrimination

There are two issues governing the legal aspects of anti-discrimination policy.
One has to do with opportunity and the other with outcome. Equal opportunity
implies that such characteristics as race, sex, and religion cannot be used as
a determining factor prohibiting a person from any job. Also these factors
cannot be used to govern the pay a person receives.

For an economy devoted to free enterprise the problem of unequal opportunity cannot exist. Long-run competitive forces will drive out of business any
firm that engages in discrimination. If only high profit firms can exist in the
long run then those firms that discriminate will be at a competitive disadvantage. Their lives will be short. Thus competition is the greatest tool for
fighting unequal opportunity.

Not all economic sectors are competitive. Governments, not-for-profit
institutions, and regulated monopolies do not compete strongly in the market
place. As such they need not minimise costs nor maximise profits, and
consequently are capable of discriminating. In addition unions can be a force
reducing the power of competition. Indeed, it is the public sector unions which
have been foremost in promoting the policy of comparable worth, which, as we
have seen, will benefit only their members. Anti-discrimination policies
should be targeted towards these sectors.

Government policy concentrates on bringing the firm to trial if wages, job
level, and promotions are lower for any minority group. Such action focuses
only on outcome and not on opportunity. Such action is often misdirected and
costly because it does not get at the true causes of unequal gender well-being.
As indicated, such inequality is caused not by unequal opportunity but by
unequal incentives embedded in the family structure. It is the wife who bears
the primary family responsibility, and it is the wife who foregoes wages and job
opportunities to take on these responsibilities.

Whereas it is not up to the state to legislate how many children families should have or whether the husband or wife must take responsibility in raising children, the state does in part set the costs. High marginal tax rates on wives' earnings decrease their labour market incentives. Low availability of low cost day care does the same – though is it not obvious that the state (and thus the taxpayer) should subsidise day care.

Equality of outcome is hard to achieve. But even when achieved it is difficult to measure because everyone is not at the same point in their life-cycle investment process, even for those of the same age. Only with changes in the family, and in the resulting division of labour patterns, would we observe similar sexual outcomes in the labour market. To the extent that division of labour remains, true economic parity in wages or occupational structure will not be achieved. However, with current demographic trends a more rapid convergence is coming about. As the new cohorts age, these trends should be more easily discernible in the data.

Appendix 6.1 Calculations of human capital stock for continuous and intermittent workers

This appendix shows how human capital stock can be estimated at each age, and for continuous and intermittent workers. The example is simplified – for more complete calculations see Polachek (1975a).

We start with a person of given education, twelve years, and with assumed complete labourforce participation (*LFP*) in each year twenty to sixty-five. Such a person is contrasted with one who leaves the workforce for ten years, from ages twenty-six to thirty-five. In a more realistic calculation *LFP* rates in each year of the life cycle would be actual averages for particular population groups. Since married women have *LFP* considerably less than unity even when they have returned to the workforce (see figure 6.4) this would lower their (expected) returns to human capital investment, and consequently cause the amount of investment to be below that estimated.

A similar procedure would be followed for each education group. For example, individuals with sixteen years' education enter the workforce with more capital than those with twelve.

The steps in the calculations are as follows. For the continuous worker we can compute net investment, C_{nt}, using the equation (see appendix 4.1):

$$C_{nt} = s_t E_t = s_t Y_t / (1 - s_t - \delta/r),$$

where s_t is the net investment fraction (C_{nt}/E_t), δ is the depreciation rate, and r is the discount rate. We assume certain values for δ and r, for example $\delta = 1\%$

a year and $r = 10\%$ a year, and also that s_t is given as the linear function (equation A-4 of appendix 4.1):

$$s_t = \alpha - \alpha t/25$$
$$= 0.5 - 0.5t/25.$$

Thus taking someone just entering the labour market ($t = 0$), for example, net investment would be $C_{n0} = 0.5Y_0/0.4$. If observed earnings, Y_0, were $5,000, then net investment would be about $6,250.

To derive the capital stock for each year of the life cycle, we cumulate the net investments, assuming the individual enters the labourforce with an initial capital stock of PK_0. The top right quadrant of figure 6.5 illustrates the process. To derive PK_0 we make use of the equation (see A-3 and A-6 in appendix 4.1):

$$C_{gt} = (s_t + \delta/r)Y_t/(1 - s_t - \delta/r),$$

where C_{gt} is the value of gross investment. In the first year, in our example, when $s_0 = 0.5$, and $Y_0 = 5,000, $C_{g0} = 1.5Y_0 = 7,500. Therefore potential earnings, E_0, must equal $12,500 ($= 5,000 + 7,500$), and the value of the initial capital stock – which is the capitalised value of potential earnings – is $125,000 ($= 12,500/0.1$).

We know the worker's marginal gains from investment in each year, MG_t. These are calculated and displayed in table 6.6. Thus at age twenty the capital value of an extra ed is $9.860. According to human capital theory, gross investment is determined where the marginal cost and marginal gain curves intersect, so $MG_t = MC_t$ – see figure 6.5. At age twenty, for example, $MG_0 = MC_0 = 9.860, and this gives rise to $C_{g0} = 12,500.

For the intermittent worker we can also calculate MG_t in each year at work (table 6.6). We now assume that a given MG_t causes as much investment for intermittent as for continuous workers (that their marginal cost curves are the same). We therefore use the known relation between MG_t and C_{gt} for continuous workers to estimate a series on C_{gt} for intermittent workers. Given C_{gt} we can derive C_{nt} with a depreciation assumption, and by cumulating C_{nt} develop a series on the value of the intermittent worker's life cycle capital stock.

For example, at age twenty the intermittent worker's marginal gain from investment is only $FMG_0 = 5.81$. For continuous workers, such a low value of MG is only reached after the age of fifty-five (see table 6.6). We therefore attribute the fifty-five year old continuous worker's level of gross investment to the twenty year old intermittent worker. This gives the slow rate of increase of the intermittent worker's capital stock pictured in figure 6.5. Only after the age of thirty-six do the two groups invest the same, because after that age they have the same marginal gains from investment.

7 Compensating wage differentials and heterogeneous human capital

The whole of the advantages and disadvantages of the different employments of labour and stock must, in the same neighbourhood, be either perfectly equal, or continually tending to equality . . . Actual differences of pecuniary wages and profits are due partly to counter-balancing circumstances, and partly to want of perfect liberty. (Adam Smith, 1976)

Until a man has had experience of a certain kind of work, he is unlikely to know it is dangerous and then the damage is often done. And even when the danger is known, most people are inclined to suppose they can escape dangers which overcome others. (Hicks, 1963)

7.1 Introduction

In a competitive market, workers whose jobs have undesirable aspects must be paid more if firms are to attract labour to these jobs. The classic discussion of such compensating differentials is by Adam Smith, who identified five job characteristics which would require compensating changes in pay (1976, 112ff):

a) the 'agreeableness or disagreeableness' of the job;
b) the 'difficulty and expense' of learning the job;
c) the 'constancy or inconstancy' of employment in the job;
d) the 'small or great trust' required of the person doing the job;
e) the 'probability or improbability of success' in the job.

The idea that wage rates adjust to compensate for differences in the characteristics of the job is fundamental in the analysis of labour markets. We have already used the idea extensively in discussing investments in education and training. Thus the wage differences between more and less educated people, analysed above, are simply compensating wage differentials, the compensation being required to adjust for the extra costs incurred in becoming educated. The 'net advantage' of the jobs of educated and less educated people, taken over their life cycles, are meant to be equal. In this chapter we probe further into the compensating wage differentials idea, and provide further tests of its predictive reach by analysing two further sets of problems: workplace accidents and occupational choice.

The area of workplace health and safety immediately calls to mind the issue of compensating wage differentials. Smith himself used the 'hardship, disagreeableness and dirtiness' of the work of colliers in Newcastle to explain why they earned two or three times more than common labourers in Scotland (1976, 132). The process of equalisation of net advantages of jobs can however be hampered if workers do not know about the characteristics of their job (as maintained by Hicks in the opening quotation). Given the many possible obstacles to mobility and acquisition of correct information, there has always been a lively controversy as to whether there are compensating differentials for the kind of job characteristics noted by Smith.

The analysis has important policy implications. If workers in dangerous jobs are paid more than those in safe jobs, then the market itself penalises unsafe workplaces. Accordingly the rationale for government industrial safety policy is limited – and some forms of state intervention might even be counter-productive, as we will see.

Compensating differentials are also bound up with the sort of jobs that people choose over their life cycle. In previous chapters we adopted a life-cycle model in which the individual determined his or her earnings solely by adjusting the amount of time devoted to enhancing future human capital stock. This chapter argues that such a view is too simplified. It assumes human capital to be *homogeneous*, so that all variation in wages comes about only because of individual differences in *amounts* of human capital. There are no implications concerning *kinds* of human capital.

However occupations are so varied, and men and women in particular have such different occupational distributions, that it is useful to think of the different occupations as requiring investments in different *kinds* of human capital. For example a person would invest in developing mathematical rather than verbal ability if the aim was to become an engineer. Part of the pay of an engineer is then a compensating differential for the extra effort, and scarce talents, required to become good at mathematics. Again, occupations differ in the extent to which labourforce intermittency is penalised – in the extent to which skills 'atrophy'. Those jobs, such as management, in which there is a large earnings loss in the event of a career interruption should therefore pay more than other jobs, *ceteris paribus*. At the same time, despite the compensating wage differential, workers who foresee career interruptions, such as women planning to bring up families, should avoid this type of occupation. People choose occupation, and thus atrophy rate, as well as amount of human capital.

7.2 Theory

A simple model

A simple model of compensating differentials can be constructed which shows what they are, and why they are an important aspect of the labour market. Suppose we are analysing jobs in which there is a chance of dying in an accident at work. Then there should be some upward sloping wage-risk-of-accident opportunity locus as in figure 7.1. The opportunity locus starts at the risk-free wage, w_0, and increases as the chance of accident increases. For any particular accident risk, say R^*, the wage demanded by workers, w^*, is higher than the risk-free wage and the compensating wage differential is $w^* - w_0$, as shown.

On the employer side there are certain costs of accident prevention. Costs of accident prevention per worker are shown as the C/L line in the diagram. (A per-worker formulation is used for comparability with the wage line, which is also per-worker.) The line is shown downward sloping because, as less is spent on prevention, accident risk rises.

The C/L line will be determined by management skill – it shows the best that can be done for given safety expenditures. 'Slack' management will allow the C/L line to drift upwards. The C/L line will also be technologically determined: a dangerous industry such as construction, for example, would have a C/L line displaced to the right of a 'safe' industry such as selling groceries.

The analysis can be applied to job risks other than physical injuries. For example, investment banking is physically safe, but it is risky in the sense of providing insecure jobs. Firms in the industry will have to compensate employees for bads, such as job loss. Measuring risk of job loss along the horizontal axis, the C/L curve of investment banking would be high relative to secure industries such as teaching. 'Safety expenditures' here would be contractual provisions to protect workers' jobs, rather than safety railings around machines. The C/L line would have the same downward sloping shape because the more protected workers' jobs are, the more risky it will be for investors to invest in that firm, and the higher the cost of capital will be. While wages go down as risk of job loss falls, the cost of capital rises and the firm trades the two off (see appendix 7.1).

We can picture the firm as wishing to minimise the sum of wages and costs of safety measures. The sum of the two costs are drawn in, with a minimum at R^*. At the minimum the slope of the wage locus equals the negative of the slope of the safety equipment line. At this point the employer is equating the marginal dollar spent on safety measures with the marginal dollar saved on wage compensation for dangerous work.

The model demonstrates several points.

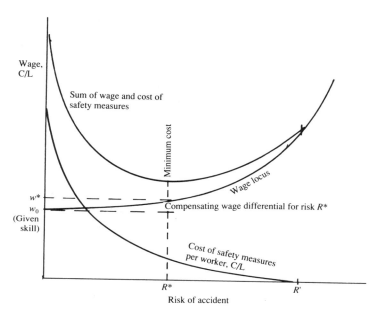

Figure 7.1 Determination of accident rate in factory

1   It is the demand by workers for wage premia for danger which deters accidents. Another way of looking at this is that workers are bearing the risk of an accident, and the firm is paying them an insurance premium for doing so. If workers underestimated the chances of an accident, the wage locus line would be too flat, the compensating wage differential too low, and the accident rate would rise towards R'. The same would happen if, for some reason, workers were immobile, and could not move to the job which suited their preferences as between money and safety. Knowledge and mobility mean that the compensating wage differential $w^* - w_0$ exactly measures expected accident costs as evaluated by the marginal worker hired.

2   At point R^*, about as much is being spent on avoiding accidents as the accidents would damage the workers involved in their own estimation (the compensating differential). This is prudent. It avoids the charge of 'negligence', which has been defined as taking precautions whose cost is less than the value of the injuries the precautions are designed to avoid (Judge Learned Hand, cited in Chelius, 1974, 705). In other words, given C = cost of precautions, p = probability of injury, I = loss consequent upon injury, then $C < pI$ means negligence. In fact at R^*, the cost of safety equipment per worker C/L, need not be the same as the compensating wage differential, but

they will not diverge widely. It can be seen that at half R^*, for example, much more would be spent on preventing accidents than was justified by the harm caused by accidents. Thus reducing accidents below R^* would not make sense.

3   Making firms strictly liable for damages resulting from accidents involving their workers could have the same effect as an upward sloping wage locus line in preventing accidents. For example, suppose firms have to buy workers' compensation insurance costing £y a year per worker. The probability of a fatal accident is p each year, and the payout in the event of an accident is £I. Fair insurance requires approximately $y \cong p (1 + a) I$, where a, the insurance 'loading', is small. In other words, with $p = 0.0001$, $I = £1$ million, and $a \cong 0$, the premium would be about £100 a year. With rational workers knowing p and I, once there is a workers' compensation scheme, the compensating wage differential will fall by £100. In terms of figure 7.1, the wage locus line would become flatter if workers were reimbursed out of the insurance fund. However, employer insurance costs would rise with the accident rate, so prompting firms to take precautions against accidents. With fair insurance, there thus seems little to choose between the free market and workers' compensation.

A supply and demand diagram of the situation is shown in figure 7.2. A set of demand curves can be drawn, one for each level of accident prevention expenses, and thus for each level of workplace risk. The highest demand curve, $D|_{r=\max}$, shows the wage the firm could pay if it made no safety expenditures, so that the risk of death or injury was at its greatest. There is a family of demand curves, one for each level of safety expenditures. The lowest curve, $D|_{r=0}$, shows demand if a large amount is being spent on safety, so that risk of injury is zero. Corresponding to these demand curves will be a set of supply curves. The risk-free supply curve is shown on the diagram as $S|_{r=0}$, and supply curves get successively higher as risk increases, ending at $S|_{r=\max}$. The parties will *trade*, and choose that level of risk, say $r = r_1$, which maximises the sum of consumer and producer surplus – the triangle between the demand and supply curves. At the surplus maximising point, employment is also maximised. This provides an easy real-life test of how well the markets for safety and jobs are working: is employment as large as possible?

As can be seen, when risk is at its maximum or minimum, the triangle of surplus is small (or non-existent, if the demand and supply curves fail to cross). As drawn, the surplus-maximising level of risk is $r = r_1$, the equilibrium point is at B, and employment is at its maximum L_1. Here, workers are receiving a compensating wage differential BD, and this is approximately equal to the firm's accident prevention costs AB.

If firms are required to pay a workers' compensation insurance premium the demand curve will shift further to the left, to $D(WC)$. Distance BC measures the extra cost of this insurance. However if workers' valuation of the expected

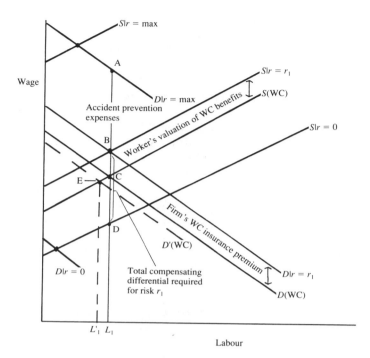

Figure 7.2 Workers' compensation wage differentials

benefits of workers' compensation equals firm costs (if insurance is fair), then the labour supply curve will also shift down by distance BC to $S(WC)$, and nothing will have changed – as can be seen, since employment has not changed. Note however that it is possible that the two shifts are not the same. Firms might pay out more in insurance premia than the workers value the benefits (so as to cover the profits of the insurance companies for example) – shown as a shift to $D'(WC)$. Equilibrium would then be at point E, and employment would fall to L'_1, which is less than employment without workers' compensation. In that case, both parties would be better off without workers' compensation. On the other hand, there might be economies of scale for a firm when it insures its workforce against accidents, economies not available to individuals when they take out insurance on their own. Both parties will then be better off if the firm assumes the risk. But, if this is the case, the question then arises why legislative compulsion is required. We take up this question in the section on 'externalities' below.

   In practice insurance is not fair, and this enables a test to be developed of the model in figures 7.1 and 7.2. A rise in insurance premia in accordance with accident experience is called 'experience rating'. In the UK the Employers' Liability (Compulsory Insurance) Act of 1969 makes firms carry approved policies covering injury and disease of employees. But premia are usually based on average experience in the particular line of business, and are not experience rated (Bartrip, 1987, 73). In the US only 15% of firms are experience rated; the rest are placed in one of 600 occupation-industry classifications by the National Council on Compensation Insurance (Ruser, 1985, 488).

Making firms liable for their workers' accidents via workers' compensation schemes will reduce compensating wage differentials demanded by workers – if worker rationality, knowledge, and mobility prevail. A workers' compensation scheme promising £l will reduce compensating wage differentials by about £pl, as noted above. At the same time firms' costs will be raised. But the rise in costs will not be related to accident experience. Consequently accidents should increase – and employment should fall. The effect should be stronger the more generous workers' compensation is. A natural experiment arises in the US where some states have more generous workers' compensation rules than others. We would expect the generous states to have (a) higher accident rates, (b) lower compensating wage differentials for industrial accidents, and (c) less employment, if workers are knowledgeable and mobile, other things being equal.

4   There is a final point in connection with the model in figure 7.1: injury rate R^* minimises accidents plus accident prevention costs. Therefore forcing a reduction in R by centrally imposing safety standards (noise standards, dust, toxic chemicals) raises costs. The higher cost firms, for example small firms, have to exit the industry, and the dangerous sectors, such as construction, contract relative to the safer sectors. The Chief Inspector of Factories in Britain has said that 'small companies are gaining an unfair advantage over their competitors' by failing to meet health and safety requirements (TUC, 1985, 132). Higher standards might thus have the effect of shutting down the small non-union firms. According to public choice analysis this could be why higher standards are proposed.

The diagram illustrates some of the issues. If the wage locus is 'wrong' because workers are poorly informed, or immobile, then the state might well wish to prevent accidents – though this is not easy, as will be seen. Let us now consider the wage locus in more detail.

The wage–job risk locus

The wage locus is determined by the coming together of workers on the one side and firms on the other. This was first shown by Rosen (see Rosen, 1986), and we will not go into the technicalities.

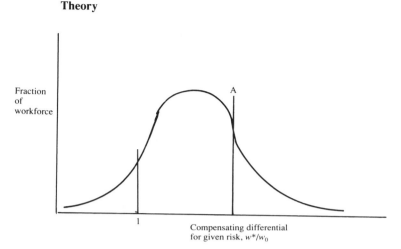

Figure 7.3 Density of worker tastes for injury risk

Much research effort has been expended on calculating the slope of the wage opportunity locus. The slope is essentially caused by the differential attitudes to risk that people have – either due to their tastes or to their economic circumstances. We will see below that poor people can less afford to be choosey, and will ask for lower compensating wage differentials for given risk than rich. Thus poorer people will tend to take the riskier jobs.

Because people are different, while we can compute an average compensating differential for some probability of injury, say R^*, from the wage demands of individuals risking that level of injury, we cannot say that this compensating differential will be required by other workers. More risk-averse workers for example would require a greater differential. Workers are 'sorted' into the jobs they like the best, and what the incumbent of a given job will accept will generally be lower than what others not in the occupation can be prevailed upon to accept. This is sometimes called the problem of 'selectivity' (our samples are not random).

For example, we might find that a compensating wage differential for a given dangerous job is low or even zero. This could mean market failure – lack of worker knowledge or mobility. But it could also mean that there are not many risky jobs relative to the size of the workforce. Figure 7.3 illustrates a distribution of worker tastes for a given risk of injury, as shown by the compensating differential (actual wage divided by risk-free wage) required. As drawn, some workers are risk lovers, and do not require any differential, but most are risk averse. If there is a high demand by firms for workers in risky jobs then a large fraction of the workforce will need to be induced to take up such jobs. The compensating differential would then be high – in a position such as A. If the demand fir risky jobs fell, A would move leftwards, perhaps even to where no differential were offered. But this would not mean that the average person would not require a compensating differential. The important measurement point is that measured compensating wage differentials will only provide a *lower bound* to the true population compensating wage differential.

Wealth and risk

We noted above the role of poverty in driving people to take risks. On the basis of simple models of consumer behaviour, it seems that wealthier individuals will demand less risky jobs – or a higher premium for undertaking a job of given risk, which is the same thing. In other words it appears that safety is a 'normal' good (see Thaler and Rosen, 1976, 276). In Jones-Lee's question-naire study of the price people would pay for transport safety improvements, he found the price closely related to respondents' incomes (1989, 84). For example a 10% increase in the respondent's income implied a 3% increase in the amount he would pay for a car safety feature that would reduce his chance of dying in a car accident from 1/10,000 to 1/20,000. Wealthier individuals can afford to forego earnings in return for a safer job, but poor individuals cannot afford to do so – they need the money.

There is likely to be a difference between wealth which accrues from non-labour sources and that accruing from labour sources. Non-labour sources are less likely to be affected by a work accident than are labour sources. It seems therefore that an individual with little human capital relative to his physical capital will be less risk averse (see Li, 1986, for a model). In fact individuals with high levels of non-labour income might tend to be quite carefree since the job risks they take have little effect on their incomes.

The implications of the above seem to be somewhat inegalitarian. In addition to their other burdens the poor take the dangerous jobs, while the rich take the safe jobs (though some of the very rich might be an exception). This at least is the empirical prediction. Policies to limit job risk could then have their basis in wealth inequalities. But it is difficult to think of a good policy. Higher safety standards for example would not help the poor, since such standards simply reduce their opportunity set – the highly paid, unskilled, risky jobs (e.g., steel erector) would go, and what would unskilled, strong, men do? Some sort of supply-side measures, to attack lack of skills at the root, would probably be best. Compensating wage differentials would then be pulled up (as people became better off and turned away from dangerous jobs), and injury rates would automatically fall.

Knowledge and risk

The burning question is whether wages are based on informed worker choice. The answer given is often 'no', as shown by the quotation by Sir John Hicks at the beginning of the chapter. It has even been said that 'people prefer to believe that their work is safe', even if it is not (Akerlof and Dickens, 1982, 308). However it is hard to believe that such wishful thinking – called 'cognitive dissonance' – is widely prevalent.

Nevertheless the informational task is certainly daunting: individuals must assess non-pecuniary aspects either through reports from fellow workers, or by directly experiencing the job. There is no recognised index for measuring non-pecuniary aspects such as dangers to health. Moreover many accidents occur so infrequently that the small samples available to workers tell little. Steel erectors in Britain have a 1/2,000 annual chance of a fatal accident, as do shunters; for coal miners the risk is 1/4,500, similarly for fishermen; fire brigade officers have a 1/7,000 chance. These are the biggest numbers – other occupations have much lower death probabilities, and the mean figure is 2/100,000 (Marin and Psacharopoulos, 1982). Then there are the occupational diseases which take many years to become manifest. There is thus ample room for mistakes in risk assessment.

However we do not need to assert that workers know everything. They can have imperfect information, learn about job conditions while on the job, and quit if they do not like it. In fact, as Viscusi and O'Connor (1984) have argued, it is sensible in certain conditions for workers to enter jobs about which they have little information, because there is then a payoff to learning. It is generally possible to leave, but if the experience is favourable one can stay and gain a higher wage. Workers' choice among hazardous jobs is thus 'part of an on-going adaptive process' (1984, 948). In experiments with a sample of chemical workers, when workers were told that the hazards of their job had gone up due to working with new substances (asbestos, TNT), they demanded higher wage premia, and were more likely to quit (955). People learn about jobs, and change when it suits them.

Viscusi has also used a learning framework to explain Lichtenstein *et al.*'s (1978) interesting study showing people's lack of knowledge about death risks. The study for example showed the average person thinks tornadoes are bigger killers than asthma, even though the latter is 20 times more probable (though still very infrequent at 1/100,000) (1978, 555). More generally it was found that people systematically *overestimated* small risks. (Note how this finding contradicts the 'cognitive dissonance' view, and carries the implication that people demand *higher* risk premia than are warranted.) According to Viscusi it is as though people assess infrequent events by starting with a prior assessment based on 'average' risk – which tends to be large. They average this with an assessment of the given event, coming up with a resultant which is above the true risk (1985, 383).

Worker knowledge can be assessed in two ways. The first is direct: ask the people concerned. The problem with the direct approach lies in interpreting the answers – people might not take the questions in the same way, they might not try (questionnaire decision-making is costless), and they will not know much about injury risks. The last disadvantage can however be an advantage in that it enables statements about what the 'average' member of the public thinks. If a selected, knowledgeable sample were used there would always be the problem that this sample was unrepresentative – steel erectors, for example, are knowledgeable about the risks of their trade, but are presumably less risk averse than average. Thus there is a place for carefully constructed questionnaire studies (for example Jones-Lee *et al.*, 1985). But, given the diffi- culties, economists have traditionally preferred to look at what people *do* rather than what they *say*.

The alternative way in which knowledge can be assessed is therefore based on what people do. It is termed the method of 'revealed preference', because the compensating wage differentials that people actually demand for different levels of risk reveal their valuations of risk in practice. The question is whether the pattern of compensating wage differentials squares up with what is to be expected if workers are knowledgeable. Thus we assess whether there are 'reasonable' compensating differentials, whether these differentials shrink as predicted when workers' compensation is increased, and whether the differentials are smaller for poor than wealthy workers. Such an assessment is carried out below. To preview the findings, the evidence bears out the view that workers are knowledgeable. In particular, the implied values of a 'statistical life' are high, in the millions according to both US and British results.

The role of trade unions

We have been assuming that individuals are free to make individual bargains. However large firms have internal labour markets so that employees can only quit at a cost: they are 'tied' to the firm. It is necessary to be careful here: both parties will foresee the tie, which will give rise to its own compensating dif- ferentials – so employees need not be disadvantaged (see chapter 9 below). Nevertheless enterprise unions might help in this context by revealing to man- agement worker preferences – unions have been said to have an 'internal demand revealing function'(Duncan and Stafford, 1980, 357). In a large fac- tory safety is to some extent a public good: all are affected by a given safety policy, and unless there is a collective voice not enough will be done to repre- sent workers' points of view since workers will free-ride on each others' efforts. In addition unions, because of their permanency, might know more about risks than workers (Dorsey and Walzer, 1983, 647).

No one knows how important the above considerations are in practice. We would expect a well-managed firm to be able to set up its own consultative safety committee without the help of a union if this lowered accidents and thus wages enough to make it cost effective.

It is true that unions are in the forefront of moves for legislation on workplace safety. But there could be several reasons for this apart from concern for worker safety *per se*. A safety programme for an industry could be supported because:

  it would have the effect of driving out the smaller non-union firms (as already noted);

  it could be a way of increasing full pay (the same pay packet, but less risk than when one first took the job is an increase in full pay);

  it could be a way of gaining unions more power (in Britain only a union representative can sit on a company Safety Committee set up in terms of the Health and Safety at Work Act of 1974).

Perhaps if compensating wage differentials are larger for union members than others, *ceteris paribus,* it would indicate that unions are better informed about risks than individual workers (Marin and Psacharopoulos, 1982, 834). We shall look for this in the empirical section.

In sum, the problem is to assess whether accidents and other bad job characteristics have costs which are 'internalised' – which workers and employers foresee, and for which they contract. The alternative is that bad job characteristics are like pollution – negative externalities imposed on non-consenting parties. Polluters do not have to pay. The question at bottom is whether firms using dangerous industrial processes have to pay.

Externalities

Sometimes a case based on 'market failure' is put forward to justify compelling firms to join a workers' compensation scheme, or to observe certain safety regulations. The source of market failure that is relevant is 'adverse selection'. It is argued that if only one company institutes special safety rules there will be adverse selection: that company will attract mainly the accident prone. Consequently the company's costs will go up, and the policy will not be viable. Only if all companies have the same policies will adverse selection be avoided and costs contained.

L. H. Summers has put forward the following numbers to illustrate the issues (1989): suppose that for unhealthy workers health insurance is worth £300 a year (the price they pay on the private market), but it would only cost £270 for their company to provide it. For the healthy workers health insurance is worth £100, and it would cost the company £90 to provide. Suppose also that there are currently 10% unhealthy workers in the workforce. Finally, suppose that the company cannot tell in advance which workers are healthy and which are not. Providing health insurance for its workers would therefore cost the company:

$$£108 = 0.9 \times £90 + 0.1 \times £270.$$

In other words if pay levels were reduced by £108 the company would be no worse off, healthy workers would be somewhat worse off (their pay would have fallen by £108, in return for insurance worth only £100 to them), and unhealthy workers considerably better off (their pay falls by £108, but they receive insurance worth £300 to them). The above solution would however only be possible if *all* companies provided insurance, so that pay everywhere fell by £108. If only one company provided the insurance there would be adverse selection: healthy workers would avoid that company (since their pay is £8 less there) and the company would find itself flooded with unhealthy workers (since their pay is £192 higher there). The final equilibrium would be with pay £270 or more lower in the company, and all its workers unhealthy.

In this example there is an efficiency case for over-ruling freedom of contract. There is a transfer from the healthy which, while not strictly Pareto improving (someone is made worse off), is nevertheless potentially Pareto improving (the gainers could compensate the losers, and still remain better off). Compulsion makes the generality of workers better off, in this sense. In addition, common-sense notions of equity are satisfied: it seems patently fair that the unhealthy should receive a transfer from the healthy. A similar argument can be made for other mandated benefits which are often proposed such as more extensive dismissals protection (see chapter 10). However, three possible weaknesses in the example should be noted.

In the first place the example assumes that the firm can provide health insurance more cheaply than the insurance market. This could be due to transactions costs: it is cheaper for a company to take out one policy covering many workers, than for individuals to take out their own. This assumption would have to be examined on a case by case basis. In the second place, the assumed 10% component of unhealthy in the workforce will not remain constant once company health insurance is mandated. Since the unhealthy are now better off, there will be an increase in their supply, and more will enter the labourforce. The opposite will happen for the healthy; they will retire earlier, or find uncovered employment. Such adverse selection operating at the level of the workforce will push all firms' insurance costs up, so that wages will have to fall by more than £108. Such second round effects depend on the elasticity of labour supply to the market of the two groups – but they diminish the force of the efficiency argument and push us back on to equity. Finally, if wages do not, or cannot, fall once company insurance plans are mandated, unemployment will ensue. This effect is more likely for unskilled workers, whose wages are closer to the minimum wage (or unemployment benefit) level – and therefore cannot fall. Yet it is precisely this group which are being targeted on equity grounds.

The wage–job atrophy locus

Risk of death or injury is only one job attribute. There are many other job characteristics, such as whether the job requires special mathematics skills, whether it requires overtime work, whether one must supervise other employees, whether it has a grievance procedure (see chapter 10), and so on. Also affecting pay are long-run considerations: whether the job requires continual training, and whether accumulating seniority is important.

We now take up some of the long-run considerations, in particular the implications for pay and occupational choice of skill depreciation or atrophy. The last chapter developed the segmented earnings function, and showed that intermittency was penalised. However the penalty is likely to be greater for some occupations, such as the crafts, than for others. In the crafts continuity is essential since dropping out even for a short time makes one's skills rusty. Other jobs, say for example clerical work, will be less demanding, since a definite skill is not involved (Polachek, 1981).

High atrophy rates are a bad, so the market should compensate with higher earnings. However high atrophy rates are worse for women than men, in general, because women's chances of labourforce intermittency are higher. Their expected atrophy costs are higher. Therefore we would expect women to select the occupations with lower atrophy. The very fact that women tend to select the lower atrophy jobs while men select the higher atrophy jobs will reduce the slope of the wage–atrophy locus. The actual market slope will be determined by the economy's need for high atrophy relative to low atrophy jobs. If many high atrophy jobs are required, so women as well as men are recruited, then the atrophy premium will increase.

More formally, suppose an individual has a lifetime of T years, and of these T years, S are spent at school and H are spent at home out of the workforce. Then lifetime income, Y, can be expressed as the product of $(T - H - S)$, the human capital rental rate $w(\delta, I)$, where I indexes personal characteristics and δ indexes the job, and the lifetime quantity of human capital stock, $K(S, H, \delta)$:

$$Y = (T - H - S) \, w(\delta, I) \, K(S, H, \delta).$$

We assume that the person chooses δ and S to maximise Y.

The $w(\delta, I)$ function is the wage–atrophy locus already described. Wages must increase as atrophy possibilities increase – however for any individual there will eventually be diminishing returns (so the function bends downwards). As for the $K(S,H,\delta)$ function, this should depend positively on δ and on hometime. A function which has these properties is:

$$K(S,H,\delta) = (1 - \delta)^H k(S).$$

This specification implies a constant percentage depreciation of human capital for each year out of the labourforce, but not at such a high rate that human capital stock completely depreciates, even if one never works. Capital stock varies directly with S (assuming $k' > 0$), inversely with time out of the workforce H (remember that since $1 - \delta < 1$, $d(1 - \delta)^H/dH < 0$), and inversely with δ. When full lifetime labourforce participation occurs, $H = 0$, the $(1 - \delta)^H$ term equals one, and the model returns to the classic depiction of human capital in terms of schooling alone (on the above see Polachek, 1981).

First-order conditions for maximising Y are obtained by setting the partial derivatives $\partial Y/\partial S$ and $\partial Y/\partial \delta$ equal to zero. The condition for δ is:

$$\partial Y/\partial \delta = K(S,H,\delta)\partial w/\partial \delta - w(\delta,I)k(S)H(1 - \delta)^{H-1} = 0,$$

and

$$\frac{\partial w}{\partial \delta} = w\frac{H}{1-\delta}.$$

Here the first term on the left-hand side is the marginal gain from choosing an occupation with a higher δ (the fact that wages will be higher up to a point), and the term on the right is the marginal cost (higher δ means a smaller capital stock). Notice how marginal cost decreases as H decreases, and is in fact zero when $H = 0$. In this case, a high δ will be chosen, so $\partial w/\partial \delta = 0$. The important point is that for men, who generally have lower H than women, the marginal cost of selecting a high atrophy job is lower than for women, so δ is likely to be higher.

In sum, those individuals expecting to withdraw from the labourforce would face relatively large wage losses in the high atrophy occupations. Thus theory predicts that high labourforce intermittency means choice of jobs with lower occupational atrophy rates.

7.3 The facts on compensating differentials

In the previous discussion we showed that, if workers were knowledgeable and mobile, the following predictions could be made:
a) there should be compensating differentials for 'bad' job characteristics;
b) compensating differentials for a given risk should be lower where workers' compensation is higher;
c) accidents should increase as workers' compensation increases;
d) poorer workers should be in the riskier jobs (safety is a normal good);

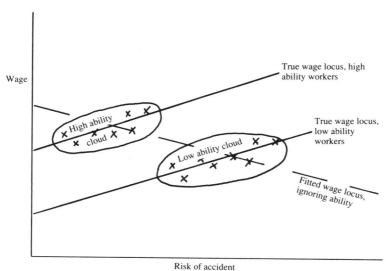

Figure 7.4 Effect of omitted variables on estimation of wage locus

e) young workers might demand smaller compensating differentials (evidence of misperception?) and unionised workers larger differentials (collective voice?);
f) jobs with large penalties for labourforce intermittency (atrophy) should exhibit high wage levels, and workers with higher intermittency, such as women, should be in the lower atrophy jobs.

Measurement difficulties

Several measurement problems have to be confronted when testing the predictions. All lead to underestimation of the compensating wage differential. So we must be wary of studies claiming to have found 'no differential'.

In the first place, *omitted variables*: other things must be held equal when fitting the wage locus. If there are omitted variables, such as ability, which are correlated with risk of death – as when more able individuals take safer jobs – then measurement of the effect of risk on wages will be biased downwards. The position is illustrated in figure 7.4. Suppose there are two wage loci, as shown, going through the two clouds of observations. If the split between the two clouds is ignored, then the fitted line will not have the same slope as the two true lines, but will be biased downwards, following the dashed path as indicated. (This is an example of the omitted variable formula – see appendix 7.2). A way of overcoming omitted variables is to follow individuals over time.

Changes in wages, for a given individual, consequent upon changes in accident risk cannot be due to omitted factors such as ability, so long as these themselves are not changing. A differencing technique is thus called for.

A second problem concerns *measurement error*: error in the measurement of accident risk (or other job characteristics) will also make the slope of the wage locus seem flatter than it is. The position is shown in figure 7.5. Four people are taken as an example, two with a true injury risk of 2/1,000, and two with a true risk of 4/1,000. However, because of measurement error, suppose we measure risks of 1/1,000 and 3/1,000 for the first pair, and 3/1,000 and 5/1,000 for the second, as shown. Fitting a line through the observations by the method of least squares entails minimising the sum of (squared) vertical deviations between the line and the observations. The dashed line in figure 7.5 does this, for there are then only two vertical deviations such as ab to contend with. Any other line, for example the true line, would give a bigger sum of deviations (deviations such as cd would have to be added on). The important point is that the mismeasured, dashed, line is flatter than the true line – we underestimate the true compensating differential.

There are likely to be large errors in measurement of the non-pecuniary aspects of jobs. Typically we do not know the actual risks people face, but have to assign them a risk based on their occupation or industry. However the individuals concerned might not face the average risk in their industry – for example surface workers in mining are safer than underground workers. One solution is to use only blue-collar workers, the assumption being that industry accident rates are more typical of manual worker experience. Another approach is to use workers' self-assessment of their working conditions. However because there is no way of comparing such self-assessments with each other the technique also requires a longitudinal approach, following individuals over time and looking at changes in self-assessed working conditions and corresponding changes in wages.

A third problem is that of *selectivity bias*. As noted above, we can only measure a compensating wage differential based on the experience of people actually doing the job. But people doing the job will have selected themselves – they will be the ones who like doing it (or least dislike doing it). Measured compensating differentials will thus mark a lower bound to the premium that people in other jobs would require to induce them to move.

A way around the selectivity problem is to incorporate the selection process into the estimation of the wage locus. Statistical procedures have been developed (see Rosen, 1986, 656) which basically revolve around the idea that the smaller the fraction of the population doing a job with particular characteristics, the less representative must be the current compensating differential for the characteristic. The measured differential is then adjusted upwards to show how much people in the population as a whole would need to do that job.

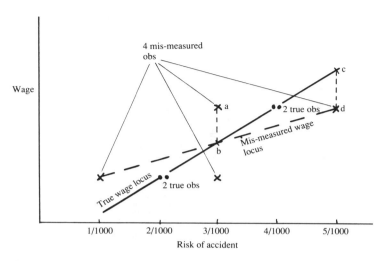

Figure 7.5 Effect of measurement error on estimation of wage locus

Examples of the above problems and the techniques used to overcome them are shown in the studies in tables 7.1, 7.2, 7.3, and 7.4 to which we now turn. Allowing for measurement and other error, do the results bear out the logic of the market outlined earlier?

The evidence

The wage–job risk locus

Table 7.1 gives some of the main research results on compensating wage differentials for risk of death and injury. Looking at the studies in turn, that of Brown (1980), line 1, is well known because it finds no premium for death risk. This is worrying because the author has the advantage of special longitudinal data, enabling him to relate the change in wage of given individuals to the changes in occupation of those same individuals, so by-passing the omitted variables problem. A possible reason is the youth of the sample; wages of young workers are not representative of lifetime wages. The study also excludes college graduates, and is thus confined to poorer individuals. Such individuals can be expected to demand lower differentials, as noted above, so the sample is not representative. In addition the author had to assume that individuals faced accident risks based on the average risk in their industry, and so his accident measure is likely to have problems of mismeasurement.

At any rate the rest of the research finds large compensating wage

Table 7.1. *Fatal accidents: compensating differentials*
Dependent variable: log wage

Study	Risk data	Sample, country year	Coefficient on deaths p.a. per 1,000†	Statistical value of a life*	Remarks
1 Brown, 1980	Fatal accident rate in respondent's occupation (zero assumed if occ. not hazardous)	Young male excluding college graduates, longitudinal US	Insign.	zero	No death risk premium
2 Olsen, 1981	Deaths per 100,000 workers – matched by 3 digit industry	Full time workers private sector US 1973	0.360	$3.2 to 3.4m ($8m for union $1.5 for non-union)	Expected cost of workdays lost is $19 per annum; risk premium is $850 per annum
3 Veljanovski, 1981	Fatalities per 100,000 workers by industry	53 manufacturing industries UK 1971		£0.8 to 1.1 m (1971 prices) (£4.5m, in 1990 prices)	Industry injury rate variable has perverse effect
4 Marin and Psacharopoulos, 1982	Fatal accident rate in respondent's occupation (200 occupations)	Male employees UK 1975	0.229	£0.6 to £0.7m	Union premia lower

Study	Risk measure	Sample	Result	Value of life	Comments
5 Dorsey and Walzer, 1983	Non-fatal accident rate in respondent's industry	Blue collar employees US 1978	Positive for non-union workers, larger when firm liability controlled	n.a.	Obtains insig. results for union workers
6 Duncan and Holmlund, 1983	Dangerous work self-assessed	Male employees, longitudinal Sweden, 1968–74	Positive, signif. at 1% level	n.a.	When data not entered in change form, result insignif.
7 Moore and Viscusi, 1988	Fatal accident rate in respondent's 2 digit industry	Non-farm employees, US 1976	n.a.	$6 m (1986 prices)	Young workers demand higher premia
8 Garen, 1988	Deaths per 100,000 workers, matched to respondent's 3 digit industry	Blue collar males US 1981/2	0.239 (OLS) 0.547 (2 stage)	£4 m $9.2 m	2 stage procedure makes choice of death depend on income

Notes:

*Calculated as how much 1,000 people would pay, per year, for a 1/1,000 reduction in the probability of dying.

†Gives % increase in wage for increase in death risk from 0 to 1/1,000.

differentials, so the bulk of the evidence favours Adam Smith. Olson (1981), on line 2, finds the 'implicit value of a life' to be over $3 million. In other words, the risk premium a worker requires is 0.36 of $9,200 (the annual wage) = $3,000 for a 1/1,000 increase in death risk. The implication is that 1,000 people would pay $3.3 million to save one life a year. To look at it in another way, a firm employing 1,000 workers has to pay $3 million extra a year if it increases fatal risks in the factory from 0 to 1/1,000. This is termed the 'statistical value of a life'.

The study indicates a higher differential for unionised workers (the implied statistical value of a life is $8 million for union members, $1.5 million for non-union), but this is not a universal finding (see lines 4 and 5 which find lower union differentials). This study also considers wage premia for days lost in non-fatal accidents. In this sample, about half a day is lost per person per year in such accidents, corresponding to a cash loss of about $19 (half a day's work at $37 a day). However the premium actually demanded for this risk averages $850 a year, implying that earnings loss is only a small part of the cost to people of accidents, and that the 'pain and suffering' cost is much greater.

The next two lines give the only British results yet available. Veljanovski (1981), on line 3, was the first study, using fifty-three industries as the unit of observation. Average male manual workers' wages were positively correlated with industry fatality rates, holding constant such factors as were measurable at the industry level, such as the average age of the industry's workforce. The implicit value of a life using 1971 data was found to be around £1 million, which is large (over £4 million in today's money). But the coefficient on the industry's non-fatal injury rate was positive, which does not make sense. Interestingly, there were signs that industry wages were lower the higher were state industrial injury benefit payouts (1981, 74, equation 2), which is as expected. However correlations at the industry level have too many omitted variables to enable a fine test of our market hypotheses.

Line 4, Marin and Psacharopoulos (1982), is more satisfactory in that they use data on individuals. A value of a life of £600,000 to £700,000 is found using 1974 data (£2 million in today's money). Note that the study finds that compensating wage differentials are apparently *lower* in unionised industries. However the authors did not have individual level data on unionisation, and had to attribute to the individual the unionisation rate in his industry. Therefore perhaps the union result cannot be taken seriously – though it is repeated in the next study.

Line 5, Dorsey and Walzer (1983), is chiefly significant because it shows how workers demand lower compensating wage differentials for jobs of given risk in states with more generous workers' compensation laws than in states with less generous laws. It will be recalled that a workers' compensation scheme promising £*l* will cost about £*pl* in liability insurance premiums where *p* is the annual chance of injury. It should also reduce the compensating wage differential by about £*pl*, if workers are knowledgeable and mobile. The authors find that workers in states with insurance premiums 1% higher do indeed have compensations wage differentials for given injury risk about 1% lower (1983, 648). In terms of figure 7.2, as curve *D*(WC) moves down, so curve *S*(WC) moves down.

This dollar for dollar substitution of workers' compensation for compensating wage differentials only holds for non-union workers. However the study has to attribute liability insurance premiums to each worker using the average for his occupation in the given state. In another study using data from 3,000 firms, where liability insurance premiums for each firm were known, the result also holds for union workers (Dorsey, 1983, 94).

The prediction that compensating wage differentials decline as workers' compensation increases is thus borne out. The remarkable result is not a flash in the pan. Viscusi and Moore (1987) have a similar result, using a different dataset. In their sample the average injury risk was 3.8 cases per year per 100 workers, i.e. approximately a 0.04 annual risk. For every $1 increase in workers' compensation, wages should therefore decline by 4¢ (= 0.04 × $1). The authors found in practice that increasing workers' compensation by $1 implied a wage decrease of between 9¢ and 18¢ for given injury risk (1987, 258). This is again the negative expected relation, but it is too sharp, given the risk rate of 0.04. It seems as though employees want more workers' compensation – since they are prepared to give up more in wages than the expected benefits of the compensation. In terms of figure 7.2, the *S*(WC) curve moves down more than the *D*(WC) curve. Perhaps the reason more workers' compensation is not provided is the link noted above between compensation and accidents. Higher insurance might mean more accidents, so insurance needs to be underprovided.

Notice how allowing for workers' compensation affects the value of a 'statistical life' as calculated by the revealed preference method. Where there is workers' compensation the compensating wage differential demanded by workers will be lower, as we have seen. One cannot therefore infer the value of a life simply from the compensating wage differential in these circumstances. Arnould and Nichols find that the value of a statistical life is 12% greater once workers' compensation is properly accounted for (1983, 337).

Line 6, Duncan and Holmlund (1983), for Sweden, is another interesting piece of work. The data here are longitudinal, with individuals followed over time, so omitted variables such as ability do not matter. In addition, the accident risk measure is self-assessed, which gets around the risk measurement problem (i.e., assigning to people an accident risk solely based on their industry). A significant earnings premium in risky jobs is found. The premium disappears if longitudinal data are not used, which shows the importance of such data in minimising measurement and omitted variable errors.

Line 7, Moore and Viscusi (1988), use detailed accident and workers' compensation variables. They not only find wages respond positively to expected life years lost (probability of death multiplied by respondent's remaining work years), but also negatively to the capital value of the annuity the respondents' dependants would expect to receive in the event of death. Note also that the study gives a *higher* risk premium as being demanded by younger workers. This goes against the accepted wisdom that the young need to be 'protected from themselves'.

Finally, line 8, Garen (1988) is the only study which does not take death risk as exogenous, but attempts to model it as a choice variable. Basically he takes into account the fact that poorer people – those with less schooling, and less non-labour income – will take the riskier jobs (see also table 7.2 below). As can be seen, when allowance is made for the selectivity effect, the statistical value of life is more than doubled from $4.0 to $9.2 million. The $9.2 million figure corresponds to the conceptual experiment of assessing how much the average person *not* doing the risky job would require to be compensated for the risk of it. This figure is naturally higher than the $4 million required by the individuals actually employed on the job, since they will be the ones who least dislike doing it. Clearly allowance for such selectivity effects is important and should really be included in all compensating differential studies. At any rate, if the imputed value of a life is of the order of $9 million, it can hardly be contended that the market does not generate pretty powerful incentives for workplaces to be safe.

Table 7.2 summarises some results which bear on the predictions regarding accident rates. The Garen study has already been mentioned as supporting one aspect of market logic: that wealthier people are more likely to choose safer jobs. This is also borne out using another dataset – see line 1. The same effect is suggested using British data by Marin and Psacharopoulos, who find a negative correlation between earnings and accident risk (1982, 833).

Table 7.2 is also relevant to the question of whether better workers' compensation for accidents means more accidents. Are firms (and workers) more careless when their accidents are paid for? The famous study by Chelius has found that states with higher workers' compensation do indeed have higher injury rates, other things equal, as shown in line 2. There is also an indication that the same thing happens in Britain – see the Veljanovski results in line 3. Admittedly, reporting effects cast a cloud over these results. In other words, people must report more accidents when it pays them to do so. In a simulation exercise, Kneisner and Leeth (1989, 292) find that increasing workers' compensation benefit levels raises reported injuries while actually *reducing* true injury rate (which seems to prove too much).

Table 7.2. *Dependence of accident rates on workers' compensation*
Dependent variable: accident rate

Study	Sample	Remarks
1 Viscusi, 1978	Disabling injuries per million hours by respondents 3 digit industry, 1969	Significant negative relation with respondents' net assets, given education and colour
2 Chelius, 1982 "	Accident frequency rate, 2 digit industry, 36 states, 1972–5. Days lost per accident, same sample	Positive coefficient on workers' compensation by state. Negative coefficient on workers' compensation by state
3 Veljanovski, 1981	Deaths per 100,000 workers per quarter time series for manu-facturing, quarterly, 1959–76	Industrial Injury payments positive, but not significant. Dummy for HSWA significantly negative. Fines increase accident rate
4 Ruser, 1985	Injuries per 100 workers per year, 41 states, 1972–9	Positive coefficient on workers' compensation by state, coefficient larger for small firms (whose insurance premiums are not experience rated)
5 Lyttkens, 1988	Accident per hour, employees compared with self-employed, agriculture, Sweden	Employees have much higher accident rate than self-employed

Two research results question the importance of overreporting. Firstly, the study by Ruser in line 4 finds that generous workers' compensation raises small firms' accident rates more markedly than large. Both types of firm will be subject to reporting effects; the difference between the firms is that large firms are more likely to have insurance premiums that are experience rated. This suggests that it is the rise in workers' compensation unaccompanied by a rise in insurance premia that matters, not simply reporting effects. Secondly the Lyttkens study of Swedish farm workers, line 5, is hard to explain in terms of overreporting. In Sweden, employed farm workers are almost fully compen-sated for earnings losses due to injuries, but the self-employed are not. Both face the same working conditions and occupational hazards. Yet employees suffer a much higher accident rate. Only if the self-employed reported 60% less accidents would the significant difference between the accident rates disappear (1988, 184). It seems therefore that reporting effects cannot entirely obscure the effect of market incentives.

Table 7.3 collects together research results on further types of compensating

Table 7.3. *Studies of various types of compensating differential*

	Sample	Nature of differential	Remarks
1 King, 1974	Professional workers, 1960	Dispersion of income in respondent's occupation	Wages rise with dispersion; wealthier family background associated with riskier occupation
2 Hamermesh, 1977	White collar employees, 1973	Job satisfaction	Satisfaction higher for older workers, *cet. par.*
3 Duncan and Stafford, 1980	Blue collar employees	Poor work conditions	Wages rise with poor conditions; union wage advantage diminished when work conditions included
4 Feinberg, 1981	Manufacturing employees, longitudinal 1971–6	Income	Wages higher for respondents with more variable incomes
5 McNabb, 1989	Manual workers, male, UK 1975	Poor work conditions	Wages rise with poor conditions; no higher for workers in industries with high unionism

wage differential. Line 1, King (1973/4) shows that wealthier people choose occupations with more variable incomes. This is a puzzle because it contradicts the findings in table 7.2, showing safety is a normal good. It could be that both the rich and the poor act as risk lovers, and it is the people in the middle who are risk averse (this is the Friedman–Savage (1948) utility function).

The Hamermesh (1977) study, in line 2, is interesting because it takes job satisfaction as the dependent variable. If we accept Adam Smith's theorem about the equalisation of the whole of the advantages and disadvantages of jobs, then there should be no systematic differences in job satisfaction. However Hamermesh's analysis finds that older workers seem more satisfied. Essentially his explanation is that older workers know more about their jobs, while being paid at rates which have to be high to attract in the younger, uncertain workers. Adam Smith's proposition holds an entry into the workplace, but holds less exactly as individuals age.

Next consider line 3, the Duncan and Stafford study. The study is well known because it seems to suggest that part of the union pay differential is in fact a premium for the poor working conditions, in particular repetitive, machine-paced work, which union workers face. Not all the union pay

Table 7.4. *Earnings and atrophy rates by occupation*

Occupation	Earnings[a]	Atrophy rates[b] (per year out of workforce)	Per cent hometime[b]	Per cent female[c]
Professional	$420 per week	−$0.45	33%	65
Managerial	460	−0.30	37	17
Clerical	260	−0.22	39	80
Sales	300	−0.13	53	47
Craft	380	−0.45	50	19
Operative	280	−0.08	46	52
Household work	120	−0.06	58	97
Service	190	−0.15	56	80

Notes:

[a] Median weekly earnings, 1983 (US Statistical Abstract).

[b] Calculated using National Longitudinal Survey data for women aged 30–44 (Polachek, 1980, table 2).

[c] Average % female of detailed occupations in group (England, 1982, 362)

Correlations between atrophy rates and:

earnings	0.655
per cent hometime	−0.600
per cent female	−0.521

differential is a rent therefore, but part seems to be a compensating differential for 'alienating' work conditions.

Finally consider line 5, the only modern British study of compensating wage differentials for poor working conditions. McNabb (1989) uses the 1975 General Household Survey, which gives him a large sample of 5,000 men. He finds workers with self-assessed poor working conditions earn 3% to 4% more per hour, holding constant education, experience, trade union coverage, race, marital status, and broad occupational category. The study thus indicates that the market compensates poor working conditions.

Wages and job atrophy – findings

We can apply the wage regression models of the last chapters to test whether there are compensating wage differentials for high atrophy conditions. Table 7.4 presents estimates of atrophy rates by occupation using equations of the form:

$$\Delta w = a_0 + a_1 S + a_2 H + a_3 X,$$

where Δw = wage(1972) − wage(1967) from the National Longitudinal

Survey panel of women aged thirty to forty-four, $S =$ years of schooling, $H =$ number of years out of the labourforce since eighteen; $X =$ other controls. Thus the 0.45 figure for professions means that for each year out of the labourforce, wage growth between 1967 and 1972 was 45 cents lower. For managers the atrophy rate is about 30 cents per year.

The first column of table 7.4 lists average wages in the occupations. Given that atrophy is a bad, there should be a positive correlation between wages and atrophy rate in an occupation. There is indeed such a positive correlation: $r = 0.655$. This is consistent with the theory of compensating wage differentials.

The last column of table 7.4 shows the link between atrophy rates and labourforce intermittency, here measured by the percentage of years out of the workforce of an occupation's female incumbents. Since leaving the labourforce is more costly in high atrophy rate occupations, we would expect low labourforce intermittency in such occupations. As can be seen there is the expected negative correlation: $r = -0.600$. Only the craft occupational category is an outlier, with an unexpectedly high amount of intermittency among female craft workers, given the occupation's high atrophy rate. (Note also the expected negative correlation between atrophy and per cent female.)

It is possible to link women's occupational distribution empirically to marital status, education, experience, and years out of the labourforce. We can then predict what occupations women would have if their per cent hometime were zero. The results of this exercise are given in table 7.5. From the table it can be seen that differences in life-cycle labourforce participation alone account for much of the disparity in professional and menial employment. If women were to work continuously, the number of women professionals would increase 35% (from 14% to 19%), the number of women in managerial occupations would more than double, and women in all the unskilled occupations in the last three rows would decline. The overrepresentation of women in clerical occupations, and their underrepresentation in the crafts would remain however.

Atrophy is only one aspect of a job. Another aspect which has been recently studied is the mathematical requirements of a job. Paglin and Rufolo (1990) have used data on scores in Graduate Record Examination mathematics (GRE-M) and verbal ability (GRE-V), to demonstrate that occupations such as scientist and engineer have higher GRE-M scores than occupations such as teacher and social scientist. In addition occupations with higher GRE-M scores pay more to graduates than those with lower scores (1990, 139). This finding is consistent with the view that pay by occupation acts to compensate for the difficulty of learning mathematics, and the scarcity of mathematical talent in the population.

GRE-M scores are lower on average for women (488) than men (569). The difference is presumably due to the different 'socialisation' of women, which

Table 7.5. *Occupational distributions of women adjusted and unadjusted for labourforce intermittency, females 30–44*

	Actual female	Adjusted female[a]	Actual male[b]
Professional	15%	19	17
Managerial	3	7	17
Clerical	46	49	7
Sales	7	3	6
Craft	0.9	0.8	26
Operative	15	13	22
Household	1	0.5	0
Service	13	9	5

Notes:

[a] Adjusted assuming zero hometime – see text.

[b] The male (30–44) distribution is taken from the 1967 Survey of Economic Opportunity.

Source: Polachek, 1981, table 3.

causes different tastes, as discussed in chapter 6. Whatever the cause, given the male comparative advantage in jobs requiring mathematical skills, production is cheaper if the sexes sort themselves into the appropriate occupations. If many women had to be attracted to the mathematically oriented occupations, pay in those occupations would have to be higher. Thus it need not be because of 'discrimination' that women are underrepresented as scientists or engineers, and overrepresented as teachers (and clerical workers), but because it is efficient.

To summarise the empirical side:

a) There do seem to be compensating differentials for bad job characteristics. When measured correctly the implicit value of a life could be as high as $9 million (in 1986 prices) (Jones-Lee gives a figure of £2.2 million in 1987 prices – 1989, 96). This means that a firm employing 1,000 average workers would have to pay $9 million extra to increase the probability of a fatal accident by 1/1,000. (Firms in fact pay about half of this because the first to be employed in risky jobs are those who like – or least dislike – such jobs.)

b) Compensating wage differentials appear to decline as workers' compensation is increased. This is shown by the fact that compensating differentials for a given accident risk are lower in states with more generous workers' compensation. There are even signs that the compensating wage differential decreases by as much as the employer's liability insurance premium increases.

c) Accidents do seem to increase as accident compensation increases. This could be just a reporting effect, but the indications are that it is more than that.
d) People with less income are in the riskier jobs.
e) Evidence on whether young workers, or unionised workers obtain higher or lower compensating wage differentials is mixed.
f) Occupations with high atrophy rates appear to have high wages. Also groups with high labourforce intermittency, such as women, appear to avoid occupations with high atrophy rates.

7.4 Policy issues

Let us look first at policy issues concerning workplace safety and then turn to gender occupational segregation.

Workplace safety

In all industrialised countries there is extensive state regulation of workplace safety. No country admits to looking to market-established compensation differentials to deter accidents and compensate workers. To the man in the street the very idea of an 'optimal injury rate' would seem to be heinous. The emphasis is on regulation. In fact, however, we will see that the market is much more important than it seems.

Safety standards
In England the first Factory Act, laying down safety standards, dates from 1838. This was also the time when prohibitions on child labour were introduced. (Interestingly, child labour was banned, it seems, as a result of a successful campaign by steam mill owners to advantage themselves against their competitors, the water mills, which were labour intensive. The prime aim was not protection of children – see Marvell (1977).) Since then the standards have become steadily more elaborate, with an Occupational Safety and Health Administration (dating from 1968) on one side of the Atlantic, and a Health and Safety Executive (dating from 1974) on the other. Both administer an inspectorate to enforce standards with respect to clean air, noise, and poisons.

There are various difficulties associated with the setting of standards. In the first place standards can be expensive to comply with, and disproportionate to the quantity of the danger. For example, the British blue asbestos standard is so rigid that the use of such asbestos is effectively ruled out. Legislated safety measures following the 1988 Piper Alpha oil rig disaster in the North Sea, in which 167 people were killed, might add 10% to 15% to the cost of oil rig operations (*Financial Times*, 28 April 1989). US Deep Sea Diving standards are so expensive that they are calculated to imply that a life is worth $15 to $39 million (Smith, 1979, 351). The OSHA arsenic standard costs perhaps $70 million a life saved (Viscusi, 1986, 129). This is far higher than the values calculated in table 7.1. In terms of figure 7.1, regulations can push us below point R^*, so that more is spent on preventing accidents than is justified by the harm caused by them.

Secondly, standards are difficult to enforce, and not much help for workers in small companies. An inspector is needed – and a union as well – to monitor company compliance with official directives. Small firms are less 'visible' to the inspectorate, and are also much less likely to be unionised (see chapter 10). Workers in small companies therefore cannot much rely on regulation to help them – they have to rely on the market.

Thirdly, penalties levied are small. A fine of only £1,000 is used by Fenn and Veljanovski in their study, and the expected fine (= actual fine × probability of conviction) is much smaller (1988, 1068). Only so many firms can be visited per year by the inspectors who in any case do not know of the new dangers (standards tend to be out of date). In addition, inspectors might well be 'captured' by the firms they are designated to police.

Fenn and Veljanovski (1988) have put forward a model which disputes the 'capture' view. They note that fines could be low because negotiation rather than prosecution is a cheaper way of bringing about compliance. A fine requires prosecution, which takes up more days of an inspector's time than does negotiation. Also costs of compliance with an 'overinclusive' law might be thought to be too high by inspectors, who will want to use their discretion. The authors show that disciplinary action is indeed less likely in high unemployment areas, where the employment consequences of strictly enforcing the law would be high (1988, 1068). Inspectors are not 'captured', but are rather behaving in a way akin to the market, recognising that poor areas, like poor people, can less afford to be choosy. Inspectors are on a knife edge, it seems, fearing to be too easy on firms, while at the same time mindful of bankrupting them.

Contrast the necessarily crude regulatory effects with the precisely targeted incentives generated by the market's compensating differentials. If market incentives are working well, every dangerous workplace has to pay more, whether or not an inspector knows of the workplace and the danger. According to the research results, markets do work well. Olsen calculated that blue-collar workers are paid 14% more per week as a result of the average chances of death and of losing days in an injury (1981, 180). The average expected penalty for violating a safety standard is by comparison small.

Whether it be because inspectors are tentative, or fines small, or – most likely – market forces are overwhelmingly strong, American results indicate that official inspections make little difference to safety (see McCaffrey, 1983,

137). We can compare the annualised injury rate of firms which were inspected a certain time ago, six months say, with that of firms currently being inspected. (It is not correct simply to compare inspected with non-inspected firms because the latter will be less hazardous – inspections are triggered by complaints.) If inspections make an impact, those firms which were inspected six months ago should have lower injury rates. But they do not. The implication is that inspections have little effect.

Finally, standards are the outcome of a political lobbying process. Industries often themselves initiate requests for regulation. US standards for bottles, lawn mowers, fire extinguishers are examples (Cornell *et al.*, 1976, 493). Safety standards could thus be a way of restricting entry. We have already seen how British trade unions see the small firm as the safety 'culprit' – but it is the small firm which provides non-union competition. Safety might be a 'cover story' for limiting competition.

Workers' compensation

Around the turn of the century, the movement towards workers' compensation began. Britain led the way in 1897 with the first Workman's Compensation Act which provided 'no fault' compensation for employees, at the same time as limiting employer liability. The Act became a model for US practice (Bartrip, 1987, xi). In both countries the common law doctrines of contributory negligence, and 'willing assumption of risk' had made it difficult for workers successfully to sue firms in the courts. It might be noted as well that the causes of occupational diseases are more difficult to pin down than those of industrial accidents, due to the long latency period of disease. Thus the drawing up of a schedule of recognised industrial diseases such as lead poisoning – but excluding lung cancer or heart disease which are not clearly industry related – simplified proof.

The question arises as to whether compulsory workers' compensation should replace market-generated compensating differentials as a means of compensating for (and reducing) accidents. In a way, as we have seen, they come to the same thing. If there were zero transaction costs, the parties would decide whether employees should bear the risk of accidents at the cost of a compensating wage differential, or whether an insurance company should bear the risk via an employer-funded scheme of workers' compensation. The outcome would be that the party who could most cheaply insure would do so – whether or not the courts placed legal liability for accidents on one side or the other. This is the Coase theorem.

The Coase theorem can be illustrated with figure 7.2. The position where workers 'freely assume risk' is point B, with employment L_1. Now assume that legislation making firms strictly liable via a workers' compensation scheme is not Pareto optimal, and causes a shift to a point such as E, with lower employment L'_1. In this case, if transactions costs of negotiating permit, the two parties would want to negotiate their way back to B and by-pass the workers' compensation scheme. On the other hand, if the new equilibrium were at C, the parties would be indifferent, and if it were to the right of C (Pareto optimal) both parties would be in favour of workers' compensation.

In practice, as we have seen, each dollar in increased workers' compensation is balanced by approximately a dollar fall in the compensating wage differential. On this evidence we seem to have a movement similar to that from B to C, and workers' compensation does not make much difference. On the other hand we have also seen that workers' compensation seems to be associated with more accidents. This is because the lack of experience-rating of the schemes breaks the link between compensation for an accident, and the workplace in which that accident occurs, and actually encourages accidents. This would suggest that workers' compensation, as it has evolved, has not been Pareto improving (a move more like B to E).

In their implications for accidents, the British and American systems are somewhat different. In Britain, the coming of the welfare state after the second world war called into question the philosophy of paying injured workers on a different basis from other people on low incomes. Why specially compensate those who had been injured more than those who are unemployed, or those who are sick? In fact a specific 'injury benefit' was retained at a higher level than state grants for unemployment or sickness, but in 1967 this difference was frozen in monetary terms, and consequently has faded away. Accompanying the change in philosophy, a worker's injury compensation came to be paid out of taxes, like any other state benefit. It is no longer related to the firm's accident experience. The fact that accidents, unlike sickness, are a consequence of *choice* is ignored.

In America on the other hand the various state systems function more like proper insurance schemes, with firms paying insurance premia averaging about 3% of payroll (Dorsey and Walzer, 1983, table 1), according to their risk rating. These risk ratings are imperfect as noted above (see table 7.2, line 4), but it can be seen that the American system should act as more of a deterrent to accidents than the British. British firms do in fact buy a little insurance against being sued by their workers. But workers do not sue much because of the great expense and difficulty. British firms' insurance against court claims only comes to about 0.3% or 0.4% of their payroll (Department of Employment, 1990, 432). The low level of British premiums indicates that firms do not in practice face much chance of being successfully sued by accident victims.

So why have workers' compensation laws been such a popular policy? The answer could be the greater apparent certainty of workers' compensation. Public opinion does not seem to believe in the practical existence of compensating wage differentials, and can only see the very real difficulty that workers face in proving injury in the courts. A typical statement is that by Brown: 'if no fault could be proved, if the injury appeared to be the result of a pure accident or of some action taken by the worker himself, then the victim had to bear his own losses' (1982, 1). Public opinion emphasises explicit contracts. But this ignores the advantage of the market-determined risk premium – that it is not dependent on an inspectorate or the courts for enforcement.

The British Industrial Injuries scheme breaks the link between compensation for an accident, and the workplace in which that accident occurs. Such a scheme does not merely replace *ex ante* compensating wage differentials with *ex post* state compensation. Because the firm does not pay more if it has more accidents, more accidents will occur. This is so particularly since workers are compensated (to some extent) for accidents. The scheme encourages accidents. This shows the dangers of ignoring the essential framework of choice within which accidents are determined as shown in figures 7.1 and 7.2.

Research and information

Information about safety has public good aspects. Since the information is a 'non-excludable', no profit is made from providing it. This means that private markets will produce too little safety information. There will be a role for government here, assisting research into hazardous processes, and research into the operation of the industrial compensation system.

'Caring' and comparable worth

Our view of occupational choice is based on compensating wage differentials and comparative advantage. Women will supply their labour more cheaply than men to nursing occupations, for example, but more expensively to engineering occupations. In engineering, atrophy rates are higher and also mathematics training is required, both of which are more of an obstacle to women on average than to men. Essentially since nursing does not reward 'male' qualities, there will be a lower supply of men to nursing.

Acknowledging there are other relevant qualities in which men and women differ, in particular the more 'caring' attitudes of women which empirical studies have revealed as noted in chapter 6, will make the gender difference in terms of supply larger (see Filer, 1986). However 'caring', unlike mathematical skill, for example, does not require an investment on the part of the worker which has to be recouped in the form of higher wages. The opportunity to 'care' seems to be a good attribute of a job and hence brings with it a negative compensating pay differential. This is a further reason for the female nurses' supply curve to be below the males'.

Market equilibrium will be where total supply equals demand in the two occupations. Average pay in the engineer-type occupation will be higher than in the nurse type because of the need to offer compensating wage differentials. Engineering is associated with bads such as mathematics, nursing with goods such as caring. Occupational composition thus differs. There are many fewer men than women in engineering, and the reverse in nursing.

Two types of policy are put forward to eliminate these disparities: comparable worth on the wages side, and affirmative action on the employment side. Comparable worth policies propose that women be paid the same as men not only in the same jobs but in 'comparable' jobs, where comparable is to be assessed on some job evaluation scheme. Comparable worth as a policy is easier to institute than affirmative action with its connotations of labour direction. Wages are easier to set and monitor than employment. We have already discussed comparable worth policies in chapter 6, and concluded that they would reduce employment and adversely affect women in small non-union firms. The discussion here indicates an additional reason to reject such policies, since they attempt to override compensating differentials, and will therefore result in labour misallocation (see also Beider *et al.*, 1989).

7.5 Conclusions

In this chapter it has been argued that labour markets are capable of being self-regulating. The evidence from a number of statistical studies indicates that wages reflect risk and other 'bads' such as atrophy of job skills.

If one examines tables 7.1, 7.2, 7.3, and 7.4 one cannot help being impressed at the weight of the evidence. It is not so much the mere fact that compensating differentials for industrial accidents exist, as that they change in the expected direction when workers' compensation laws become more generous. Moreover, once we make more careful measurements – controlling for an individual's ability, allowing for sample selectivity bias – the compensating wage differential becomes substantial. A sum of several millions as the statistical value of a life is hardly insignificant.

Compensating wage differentials for industrial accidents are important because they are the way in which the market itself deters accidents and rewards risk bearing. Such differentials are precisely targeted. They are policed by the worker concerned, and by the firm (and the firm's insurance company). This form of deterrence does not depend upon an outside agency which might not know of the risk. It applies in small firms without union safety representatives as well as large firms. Moreover the deterrent effect is large – hundreds of time greater than the expected penalty for violating a safety standard.

What the research therefore suggests is that market incentives to safety are so strong that we do not depend much upon government regulation for deterring accidents. This is why regulations, for example noise at work, or poisons cause little difficulty in industry. But it need not be like this, and overly expensive safety regulations are always possible.

As for occupational choice, much of the differences between men and women can be explained as a rational response to differences in labourforce intermittency, in mathematical abilities, and in tastes. The alternative explanation is discrimination, but, as we saw in the last chapter, such an explanation needs to rely on a motive for discrimination – and no strong motive has been found. Labour mobility and competition among firms will eradicate discrimination, and allocate labour to its most productive uses so minimising costs.

Appendix 7.1 How 'job protection' lowers wages, but raises the cost of capital

When a firm is breaking even, (net) revenues equal factor payments:

$$pQ = rK + wL,$$

where pQ = value of firm's output, r = return on capital, K = capital stock, w = wage, L = labour.

Let us now analyse the firm's behaviour over the business cycle. The correlation between the firm's output, and national output, GNP, is $\text{cov}(pQ, \text{GNP})/\sigma_{pQ}\,\sigma_{\text{GNP}} = \text{cov}(pQ, \text{GNP})$ if we assume that pQ and GNP are measured in units such that they both have mean zero and standard deviation equal unity.

We can write $\text{cov}(pQ, \text{GNP}) = r\,\text{cov}(K, \text{GNP}) + w\,\text{cov}(L, \text{GNP})$, where $\text{cov}(K, \text{GNP})$ is the covariance between the firm's capital and national output; and $\text{cov}(L, \text{GNP})$ is the covariance between the firm's labourforce and national output. This covariance relation follows from the rule:

$$\text{cov}(x, pQ) = \text{E}(x - \bar{x})(pQ - \bar{p}\bar{Q}) = \text{E}(x, pQ),$$

letting $\bar{x} = \bar{p}\bar{Q} = 0$ for simplicity (x is any variable – e.g. GNP in our case). Since $pQ = rK + wL$, where K and L are random variables, then:

$$\begin{aligned} \text{cov}(x, pQ) &= \text{E}(x(rK + wL)) = r\,\text{E}(x,K) + w\,\text{E}(x,L) \\ &= r\,\text{cov}(x, K) + w\,\text{cov}(x,L) \end{aligned}$$

since $\text{E}(x,K) = \text{cov}(x,K)$ given that $\bar{x} = \bar{K} = 0$, and similarly $\text{E}(x,L) = \text{cov}(x,L)$. Thus the covariance (or correlation) between pQ and any variable, x, depends upon the covariances between that variable and capital and labour inputs.

Now suppose that $\text{cov}(pQ, \text{GNP})$, the correlation between the firm's fortunes and economy-wide conditions, is given. Then if $\text{cov}(L, \text{GNP})$ goes down because of '*job protection*', the burden of adjustment will fall on w, r, and cov(K, GNP). But less labour adjustment means more capital adjustment; in other words a fall in cov(L, GNP) must mean a rise in cov(K, GNP). w will fall since jobs are protected, but r will rise to cover the extra risk on the capital side (see Li, 1986, for a full analysis).

Appendix 7.2 Omitted and mis-measured variables

The omitted variable formula
The omitted variable formula is as follows. If the true regression is

$$y = a + bx + cz,$$

and z (ability) is omitted, so we measure:

$$y = a' + b'x,$$

then:

$$b' = b + cp_{z.x},$$

where $p_{z.x}$ is the coefficient on x in a regression of z on x. If c is positive (ability increases y) and $p_{z.x}$ is negative (risk and ability negatively related, as shown), then b' will be less than b.

Measurement error
Suppose $y = a + bx^T$, but we measure $y = a' + b'x^0$, where $x^0 = x^T + v$, $v =$ random measurement error. Then:

$$b' = \frac{\text{cov}(y,x^0)}{var(x^0)} = \frac{\text{cov}(y,x^0)}{\text{var}(x^T + v)} = \frac{\text{cov}(y,x^0)}{\text{var}(x^T) + \text{var}(v)}$$

$$= \frac{\text{cov}(y,x^T + v)}{\text{var}(x^T) + \text{var}(v)} = \frac{\text{cov}(y,x^T)}{\text{var}(x^T) + \text{var}(v)}$$

since we assume y and v are unrelated.
Now, true b is:

$$b = \frac{\text{cov}(y,x^T)}{\text{var}(x^T)},$$

so $b' = b/(1 + \text{var}(v)/\text{var}(x^T))$.
Thus $b' < b$, and the divergence is greater the larger is the error, $\text{var}(v)$, in relation to the true value, $\text{var}(x^T)$.

8   Information and wages

8.1 Introduction

An important assumption underlying the competitive market model is that of 'full information', whereby buyers know all sellers' selling prices. Because all buyers strive to obtain the lowest price, a unique market clearing equilibrium price emerges. In addition, resources are fully utilised: buyers demand exactly the number of commodities that sellers are willing to sell. In a labour market this amounts to 'full employment'.

In practice, 'unique' market clearing prices are rare. This is true for markets in general, but is probably particularly true for labour markets, where price dispersion abounds. Thus, the highest paid worker in an occupation in a given town often earns twice as much as the lowest paid, and even within a given firm there is wage dispersion, with a spread apparently of up to 40% for the same job (Buckley, 1985, 12). For example, for switchboard operators within the same establishment, the highest paid worker exceeds the lowest paid worker by 22%, and for janitors the figure is 42% (Buckley, 1985, table 1). Nor do labour markets clear – there are often large pools of unemployed workers eager to find jobs. Of course some unemployment will occur in smoothly functioning labour markets as workers move between jobs. This is called 'frictional' unemployment. However, the rate of unemployment varies dramatically. In the 1960s 4% unemployment was considered 'full employment'. In the 1970s this figure had risen to 8%. If frictional unemployment is 'natural' as is sometimes argued, why is 'natural' unemployment often so high?

That there should be wage variation and unemployment in a competitive economy need not be a mystery. George Stigler in the early 1960s proposed a model to explain the paradox. This model has become the foundation of a new body of literature known as search theory. It centres around the costs and benefits of searching for information, and explains the necessarily incomplete information that searchers acquire.

Stigler's logic goes like this: to a job seeker (consumer), finding a higher wage (lower price) provides greater earnings (saves money). This leads job seekers (consumers) to search. The greater the price dispersion the greater the gains from search. However, after a point diminishing returns sets in, so that the gains decline with the number of searches. If search is costly one can determine optimal search by equating at the margin the costs and benefits of search.

Firms can take advantage of workers (consumers) who fail to adequately search. For example, if job seekers (consumers) know little about wages (prices), then firms can underpay (overcharge) the less knowledgeable employees (consumers) – in the sense that such employees earn less (and consumers pay more) than their best alternative. Lack of knowledge or 'ignorance' leads to wage (price) dispersion, meaning that employees can earn different amounts for the same job, just as consumers can pay different prices for the same commodity.

An equilibrium situation can evolve (Rothschild, 1973; Sattinger, 1991). Incomplete information leads to wage (price) dispersion, but wage (price) dispersion leads to search thereby diminishing market 'ignorance'. Since search is costly, it is not optimal to search for an infinite length of time. Consequently an equilibrium wage (price) dispersion results. In short, given that information is costly to procure, unique wages (prices) are an 'ideal' that we would not expect to observe even in a competitive world.

In previous chapters we considered earnings differences that could be attributed to different human capital investments. We also considered the effects on earnings of differences in labourforce participation, as well as other variables such as gender and the non-pecuniary advantages and disadvantages of jobs. However, these factors fail to explain all earnings variations. What remains could be pure noise caused by mismeasuring earnings – or it could be the effect of other forces omitted from the analysis.

Information is one such factor: even holding worker quality (e.g., education and experience) constant, firms find it costly to evaluate worker reservation wages. By the same token, given an evaluation of working conditions, it is difficult for workers to know maximum wages firms are willing to pay for a given job (jobs have to be taken before they are experienced, and there is little 'repeat' buying). For this reason the labour market gives rise to information gaps, to different wages for the same job, and to unemployment.

This chapter concentrates on the implications of incomplete information for wage dispersion. We also analyse unemployment duration since this is a natural adjunct to worker search. It must be remembered however that search theory can only explain supply-side reactions of people to unemployment; it is at its best in explaining unemployment duration. The other aspect of unemployment, the flows into unemployment, are much more a matter of layoffs and dismissals over the business cycle than a matter of individual choice (though a sizeable fraction of the unemployed have quit in order to search). The higher flows of some groups into unemployment in business contraction, for example unskilled workers, are better explained by firms' policies with respect to specific training. This is covered in the next chapter. Macroeconomic policies to alleviate business contraction via government monetary and fiscal policy however we do not treat (for surveys emphasising this aspect see Knight, 1987 and Nickell, 1990).

8.2 Search in the labour market

A simple model

When analysing how workers search for jobs, and choose among job offers, we picture them as attempting to choose the best (highest income, for simplicity) job offers given the costs of finding out about jobs. The job searcher will continue to search for new offers so long as the benefits of an extra search exceed the costs. It must however be assumed that the searcher has some advance knowledge about the labour market. Generally it is assumed that the searcher knows the mean and variance of the distribution of wage offers he or she is likely to encounter. What is not known prior to searching is which firms will make the good offers. Were the high paying firms known in advance there would be no search problem.

The worker has to act as a statistician, essentially, and calculate the payoff to searching further, given some knowledge of the distribution of wage offers he or she faces. We can show that the more dispersed is this wage offer distribution the more worthwhile it is for the worker to continue to search. It is also possible to show how reducing the 'costs of search' increases the duration of search – and thus of search unemployment.

The model also applies to search during employment as well as unemployment. Some modifications are required – costs are lower, possibly, for someone who is employed because he/she does not have to forego earnings while searching. Acting against this is the fact that it is more difficult to take time off to search when employed. Returns to search will also be lower since the individual has already found an acceptable job, and will not be able much to improve on it because of diminishing returns to search. Employed search is important, as shown by the fact that about 80% of quits are to take another job, and only 20% are into unemployment (Barron and McCafferty, 1977, 689). The young however are particularly likely to quit to search while unemployed (ibid., 688). Thus the same ideas of balancing costs of and returns to search can be applied to both employed and unemployed search.

Let us take a simple case first. Assume there are only two types of firm: those paying annual wages of $10,000, and those paying $11,000. Assume that the labour market is made up of 50% of one type of firm, and 50% of the other.

Table 8.1 *Benefits and costs of search – two types of firm model*

Number searches	Probability of highest wage being[a]		Expected wage	Marg. benefit	Marg. cost
	$10,000	$11,000			
1	1/2	1/2	$10,500	—	—
2	1/4[b]	3/4	10,750	$250	$90
3	1/8	7/8	10,875	125	90
4	1/16	15/16	10,938	63	90

Notes:

[a] Market comprises 50% of firms paying $10,000, and 50% paying $11,000.

[b] There are 4 possible sequences in 2 searches: 11, 11; 11, 10; 10, 11; 10, 10. Only one contains no $11,000 offer, giving probability = 1/4.

This is the wage distribution, which is known to the worker. Firms are outwardly indistinguishable. The searchers face a foregone earnings cost for each search in terms of lost income from not taking a low wage job immediately – say three days at a wage of $30, minus any welfare benefits or home income.

We ignore for the moment the fact that there will also be travel costs and preparation costs associated with each search. There is also the fact that the number of days required to generate an offer (and thus search costs per offer) will be higher in bad times, and for inefficient searchers, because the 'offer arrival rate' is lower. We take up this problem later.

How many searches will the average worker undertake? The calculations are set out in table 8.1. On his/her first 'drawing' from the population of firms, that is, on his/her first search, the decision-maker has a 50:50 probability of turning up a good offer. His/her expected wage is therefore $10,500 (= 0.5 × 10,000 + 0.5 × 11,000). On the second search, the probability of getting a $10,000 offer both times is 0.5 × 0.5 = 0.25, and of getting an $11,000 offer at least once is 0.75. The expected wage at this stage is therefore $10,750, and the increase in the expected wage as a result of the search is $250. The 'payoff' is $250, which should ideally be capitalised over the length of time the worker expects to remain in that job (for example, if interest rates are 10%, and the horizon is long, say twenty years, then the capital value of $250 a year is approximately $2,500 = 250/0.1) – however this is a detail we will ignore for the moment. If the worker searches again he/she can expect to make an unlucky draw all three times with a 0.125 (= 0.5 × 0.5 × 0.5) probability, and to contact a high paying firm with a 0.875 probability. The payoff is $125, compared to further search costs of $90. On the basis of these data therefore the average worker can be expected to undertake between three and four job searches.

This simplified model is graphed in figure 8.1, and demonstrates several aspects of the search process:

1   There are diminishing returns to search, as can be seen from the table, and as is shown by the curvature of the expected wage, $E(w)$, curve. Given a maximum wage, b, and a minimum, a, the $E(w)$ curve starts at the average of the distribution, $(a + b)/2$, and asymptotically approaches b. It rarely pays to search so much that the chance of getting a low job offer is zero – to become 'fully informed'. Some ignorance is rational. In figure 8.1, ignorance is measured by the actual wage achieved, X, compared to the maximum that individual could achieve, b. Estimates of ignorance, calculated in this way, are discussed in a later section.

2   An increase in wage dispersion will raise the optimal number of searches. This can be seen by positing a mean-preserving increase in dispersion, so that the top-paying firms pay $15,000 rather than $11,000, and the low-paying firms pay $5,000. The sequence of expected wages then becomes $10,000, $12,500, $13,750, and so on. The marginal benefit from search increases tenfold. Alternatively, as shown in figure 8.1, if there is no wage dispersion, the $E(w)$ line becomes flat (shown dashed). Since the marginal benefit to search is then zero, there will then be no search – as is sensible, since, if the 'law of one price' holds, why search for a better deal?

3   The role of the costs of search is demonstrated. The higher the cost per search, the steeper is the TC curve, and the fewer searches. We have been taking costs mainly as lost working time valued at the going rate. But if a searcher becomes eligible for welfare benefits, then the foregone income costs of search (remaining unemployed) will be lowered by the amount of the benefits. The TC curve will decline to TC', for example, and the person will move from X to Y. Holding other things equal unemployed workers receiving welfare benefits should therefore not only reject more job offers (search more) than those without benefits, but should also achieve better job matches and higher wages – since Y is greater than X.

4   The model demonstrates the consequences of obstacles to search. If there is minimum wage legislation, or union rules setting high wages, workers will again reject job offers (however the rejections will be coerced, not the result of some optimisation). Eventually they will achieve better jobs and higher wages than without the law. But in the process they will have been unemployed for longer. Again, if there is unexpected inflation, so that more firms are offering high wages, but the worker does not know this (the mean of the nominal wage offer distribution has shifted upwards, though the real wage offer distribution

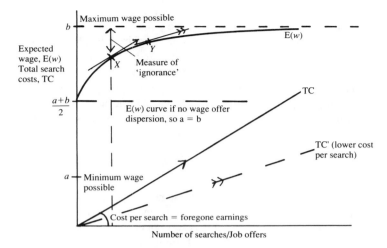

Figure 8.1 Costs and benefits from search

is unchanged), workers will accept jobs they otherwise would have rejected. Real wages will fall, and unemployment duration will fall, for a while, until the new distribution is recognised. This is essentially the reason that Friedman gives for why Keynesian-type inflationary monetary policies reduce unemployment – but the reduction is only temporary (Friedman, 1968).

5   The model illustrates the implications of search for the dispersion of wages. In our example, 50% of the firms were offering $10,000 a year, and 50% offering $11,000. Thus 50% of the workers were earning $1,000 less than the other 50%, for the same work – violating 'the law of one price'. If this dispersion were to be an equilibrium, that is, be maintained through time, it would have to be compatible with the amount of search undertaken by workers in that market. The more search that is undertaken the lower will be the supply of labour to low paying firms, and the more pressure on them to raise their wages. By the same token, since more workers will find the high paying firms, such firms will be able to lower their wages. Suppose, in our example, that the result of this process is to cause low-paying and high-paying firms to offer $10,250 and $10,750. The expected value of the first job offer will still be $10,500, but of the second only $10,625. It will hardly be worth searching further than the first job (given the assumed search costs), and the wage distribution will be stable so long as the amount of searching is compatible with firms' vacancy rates.

Pay dispersion therefore depends on search. Taking a given type of work, pay dispersion should be greater when comparing states than within a state because of the greater costs of search across states. Again, educated workers are likely to have lower pay dispersion than uneducated workers, other things equal, because the educated are better informed about search methods so searching is cheaper. Older workers can be expected to have more pay dispersion, other things equal, because they have shorter horizons, so the (present value of the) payoff to search is lower, causing them to search less; they might also have higher search costs, reinforcing this effect.

The Stigler search model

The earliest formal model is that of Stigler. It is 'non-sequential', as was the simple model above, in that buyers decide how much to search before a purchase is actually made. Again, the aim is to explain how a dispersion of wages for a given skill can exist, given that information collection has costs as well as benefits.

In the more formal model, we suppose wages are not divided into two job categories, but follow a particular distribution. In the simplest case wages are taken to be uniformly distributed, for example:

$$f(w) = 1/(b - a), a \leqslant w \leqslant b,$$

where $f(w)$ is the distribution of offer wages, and a and b are upper and lower limits to the wage distribution – see figure 8.2. For this distribution, the distribution of maximum wage offers, y, can be shown to be (see appendix 8.1):

$$g(y) = \frac{n(y - a)^{n-1}}{(b - a)^n},$$

where n is the number of searches.

More simply, if $b = 1$ and $a = 0$, $g(y) = ny^{n-1}$. Thus for one search ($n = 1$), the distribution of y is the same as the distribution of w, for 2 searches the distribution is $g(y) = 2y$, for three searches $g(y) = 3y^2$, and so on. These distributions are illustrated in figure 8.2.

The maximum wage offer, y, can be thought of as the actual wage people receive. Thus *offer* wages, w, differ from *actual* wages observed, y. To rationalise the difference in the distributions (assuming it continues over time), we must assume – for example – that some firms continue to offer low wages, close to a, perhaps because they can afford to wait longer than other firms for labour. For a fully satisfactory theory, we would thus have to model firm search as well, but this would take us too far afield.

Nevertheless it can be seen that the observed wage distribution will differ from the underlying offer distribution. And this difference will be greater the

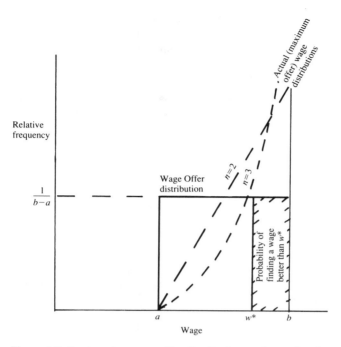

Figure 8.2 Rectangular wage offer distribution, and associated actual wage distributions, for different amounts of search

more 'choosey' workers are (the higher is the number of searches, n). This observation is the basis for Reuben Gronau's famous paper (1974) on 'selectivity bias' (this bias has already been encountered in chapter 7 in connection with estimating compensating wage differentials). For example, if white women place a higher value on their home time than black women (perhaps because the latter have less well off husbands), and so are more choosey about getting jobs than black women, then white women will have higher wages than black women, and participate less, even though they might face the same wage offer distributions. It might be thought that there was discrimination in favour of white women, even though there was not (in the sense of them facing the same wage offer distributions).

Equally for male–female comparisons: the offered and observed distributions are likely to be more similar for males than females. Married women in particular tend to be more choosey about market work since they have a high value in home production compared to their offered wages – the opportunity cost of searching and not earning money in the market will be lower for them.

(Admittedly married women's shorter expected job tenure will work against this, by reducing the returns to search and making married women less choosey.) Actual average wages for married women, $\bar{w}^F_A$, could consequently be much higher than the (unobserved) average wages that firms offer, $\bar{w}^F_O$ (Gronau, 1974, 1128). This is shown in figure 8.3. The difference for men however is small, $\bar{w}^M_O \cong \bar{w}^M_A$. Therefore differences in actual wages as between men and women could be smaller than differences in underlying offer wages. (Dispersion of actual wages could also be lower for women – see below.)

The expected (or average) actual wage accepted is the mean of the maximum wage distribution. This can be shown to be (appendix 8.1):

$$E(y) = (a + nb)/(n + 1).$$

As can be seen, there are again diminishing returns to search, that is, the maximum wage found rises with search at a diminishing rate. For example, it is $(b + a)/2$ for one search, $(a + 2b)/3$ for two searches, and approaches b, the maximum possible wage, as search goes to infinity.

This formula can be used to draw up a schedule of expected actual wages by number of searches as we have already done for the simple case of table 8.1. The marginal gain from search is:

$$mg = \partial((a + nb)/(n + 1))/\partial n$$
$$= (b - a)/(n + 1)^2.$$

If one wished to be more accurate, and introduce the future by taking present values, a better estimate of the marginal gain from search would be:

$$G = PV(H \times mg),$$

where PV is the present value operator, and H is the expected total duration of the job in hours.

How much does the job seeker search to obtain the highest wage? The economic approach is to equate search benefits and costs at the margin, and solve for the optimal number of inquiries, n. If we assume that the cost of an extra search (marginal search cost) is the number of hours required by a search, S, times the average wage, $(a + nb)/(n + 1)$, then:

$$MC = S(a + nb)/(n + 1).$$

Equating this with the value of the marginal wage gain over the H expected hours of the job (and ignoring discounting) gives:

$$H(b - a)/(n + 1)^2 = S(a + nb)/(n + 1).$$

Solving for n using the quadratic formula and setting $a = 0$ for simplicity gives:

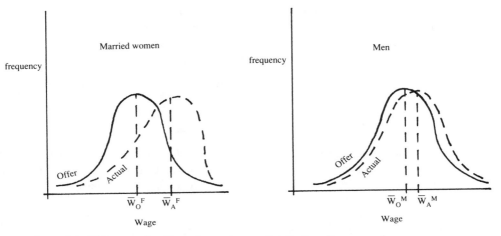

Figure 8.3 Differences in offer and actual wage distributions for men and women

$$n* = \frac{-b \pm \sqrt{b^2 + 4Hb^2/S}}{2b} = -1/2 + 1/2\sqrt{1 + 4H/S} \cong \sqrt{H/S}.$$

For example if a job is expected to last three years ($H = 6,000$ hours), and takes $S = 50$ hours to find, then it will be worth searching $n* =$ eleven times. It can be seen that the optimal number of searches, $n*$, increases with the expected length of the job, H, and decreases with the number of days a search requires, S.

The optimal number of searches will also increase with offer wage dispersion, $b - a$. This is not apparent from the formula in the previous paragraph, because we set $a = 0$, so that b also dropped out of the formula. The simplest way to show that the number of searches increases with wage dispersion is to appeal to figure 8.1. The expected wage curve, $E(w)$, reaches a higher asymptote when $b - a$ increases, encouraging more searches.

Table 8.2 gives a numerical example of optimal search. Here the assumed wage distribution has $a = \$0$, and $b = \$1$ per hour. It is also assumed that it takes fifty hours work to generate a wage offer, there is no home income (unemployment benefit or home production), and that a job will last for $H = 6,000$ hours. These assumptions lead to the optimal number of searches $n* = 11$, the average wage $n/(n + 1) = 11/12 = \$0.92$ per hour, and the cost of a search, MC $= \$46$ per search. Notice how if a worker was not allowed to accept $\$0.92$ per hour because of minimum wage legislation, he or she would have to search more. If only wages of at least $\$0.95$ were lawful then workers would have to make nineteen searches, and would be unemployed for longer.

It is also important to consider the resulting dispersion in wages, since this, too, will depend upon search. The variance σ_y^2 of the actual wage distribution, y, for the case where $b = 1$ and $a = 0$ is given by (see appendix 8.1):

$$\sigma_y^2 = n/(n + 1)^2(n + 2)$$

and the coefficient of variation (standard deviation as a percentage of the mean) is:

$$cv = 1/\sqrt{n(n + 2)}$$
$$\cong 1/n^* = \sqrt{S/H}.$$

We see how wage dispersion as a percentage of the mean declines as search increases – and increases as costs of search S increase. This is also apparent from figure 8.2, where the observed wage distribution, y, tends to a spike at b as the number of searches increase.

An implication of the link between dispersion and search is that those groups which have lower search costs should search more and hence have lower wage dispersion. Women, for example, should have a lower wage dispersion than men with similar skills, to the extent that women search for longer time than men (as implied by Gronau above). Looking at the pay of UK academics (and thus holding other things equal in that sense) we find that women academics however have a *higher* wage dispersion than men: the interquartile range of female pay as a percentage of the median is 0.62 compared to only 0.54 for males (Metcalf, 1973, 500). This result suggests we are wrong to equate being choosey about jobs with necessarily knowing much about the labour market – women's non-participation does not imply real search as unemployment would. Pay dispersion nevertheless appears to be lower for younger academics, which would accord with young workers searching harder than old because the young have a longer period over which the search pays off.

Sequential search – the optimal stopping rule

In the Stigler search model the job seeker knows not only the wage offer distribution, but also is able to search and accumulate job offers. He (or she) takes only the very best one after n^* inquiries – non-sequential search. Essentially the search problem is one of deciding on the optimal sample size. In fact, however, non-sequential search can be shown to be inefficient (Nelson, 1970).

The argument for sequential search goes like this. If an individual receives an extraordinarily high wage offer relative to the wage offer distribution, why should he/she continue his searching? Would it not simply be more efficient to accept the good offer without incurring additional search costs? Clearly this is the case if the individual finds the highest wage (wage b) early in the search process. But almost equally clearly there must be some wage somewhat below b for which it pays to cease searching as well. In sequential search models

Table 8.2. *Cost and benefits of job search – non-sequential model*

Number	Maximum wage[a]	Marg. benefit[b] per hour	Marg. benefit[b] over 3 years	Marg. cost[c]
1	1/2	0.25	$1,500	$46
2	2/3	0.11	660	46
3	3/4	0.06	360	46
—	—	—	—	—
10	10/11	0.008	50	46
11	11/12	0.007	42	46

Notes:

[a] Calculated assuming a rectangular wage distribution with the wage uniformly distributed between 0 and 1. In terms of figure 8.2, $b = \$1.00$ and $a = 0$. Thinking in terms of cents, the intercept is $1/b - a = 1/100$. The expected maximum wage is then $n/(n + 1)$ dollars (per hour, say).

[b] Calculated from the marginal gain formula $mg = 1/(n + 1)^2 \times 6,000$ hours.

[c] Calculated as follows: assume the cost of a search is 50 working hours at the average wage, $n/(n + 1)$. Thus $mc = n/(n + 1) \times 50$. Equating with mg and solving for n gives $n \cong \sqrt{6,000/50} = 11$, therefore $mc \cong 50 \times 11/12 = \$46$.

subsequent to Stigler this wage is called the '*reservation*' wage. The searcher's problem according to these sequential models is to determine the optimal reservation wage – an optimal stopping rule. This in turn defines the duration of search because the higher the reservation wage the longer it takes to find a job. The implication for unemployment is that the higher are unemployed individuals' reservation wages, the longer they will be unemployed. The sequential search model offers insights into the determinants of the reservation wage, a variable which does not explicitly enter the non-sequential model.

In sequential search models the job seeker must decide after each offer whether to accept the offer, or instead search further. At least intuitively the problem is easy. Upon receiving an offer one needs to decide if the (present value of) expected gains from searching for a better offer – minus the costs of searching for the offer – exceed the (present value of) income from the current offer. The problem defines a reservation wage against which offers are judged. If the offer distribution does not change over time, and the worker's evaluation of the distribution does not change, and if we assume an infinite horizon, then the reservation wage – and implied duration of future search – is itself unchanging period after period.

The probability per week (say) of receiving an offer $w > w^*$ is the area under the density function between w^* and b, as shown in figure 8.2, i.e.:

$$\begin{aligned}
\text{prob}(w \geqslant w^*) &= \int_{w^*}^b f(w)\, dw \\
&= \int_{w^*}^b 1/(b-a)\, dw \\
&= \left. \frac{w}{b-a} \right| \begin{matrix} w = b \\ w = w^* \end{matrix} \\
&= (b - w^*)/(b - a) = p^*.
\end{aligned} \tag{8.1}$$

Now, choice of a reservation wage w^* implies an offer probability p^*, which in turn implies a certain expected search duration D^*. In fact, D^* is simply:

$$D^* = 1/p^*. \tag{8.2}$$

For example if w^* is such that offer probability $p^* = 10\%$ per week, then $D^* = $ ten weeks on average. Expected total search costs of finding w^* are then:

$$(C - w_h)D^*,$$

where $C = $ value of foregone earnings and $w_h = $ income while not working (unemployment benefit, or – in the case of women especially – home production).

Expected benefits from further search, given w^*, are the expected higher wage, i.e.:

$$E(w|\, w \geqslant w^*) = \frac{\int_{w^*}^b w\, f(w)\, dw}{\int_{w^*}^b f(w)\, dw},$$

by a rule for taking conditional expected values. In terms of our uniform distribution, as can be seen from figure 8.2, this just equals (see appendix 8.2):

$$(b + w^*)/2,$$

the average of b and w^*.

The optimal stopping rule can now be stated for the case where w^* does not change from one period to another: choose w^* so that w^* equals the income from searching for another offered wage between w^* and b minus the cost of searching an extra D^* weeks for that wage. In other words (ignoring discounting for simplicity):

$$w^* = E(w|\, w \geqslant w^*) - (C - w_h)D^*. \tag{8.3}$$

Notice how this reservation wage, w^*, must be less than the wage people expect to earn when a new job is found, $E(w|\, w \geqslant w^*)$. Moreover w^* goes up as the expected wage increases, and as unemployment benefits, w_h, increase.

Rearranging equation (8.3) we can obtain expressions for the marginal costs and benefits of search:

$$w^* = \frac{\int_{w^*}^b w\, f(w)\, dw}{p^*} - \frac{C - w_h}{p^*},$$

which becomes:

$$\int_{w*}^{b} w f(w) \, dw - w^*p^* = \int_{w*}^{b}(w - w^*) f(w) \, dw = C - w_h.$$

In terms of the uniform distribution we have:

$$\int_{w*}^{b}(w - w^*) f(w) \, dw = \frac{(w - w^*)^2}{2(b - a)} \bigg|_{w = w^*}^{w = b}$$

$$= \frac{(b - w^*)^2}{2(b - a)} = C - w_h.$$

The term on the left-hand side can be interpreted as the marginal benefit from choosing a longer expected search period D^* (and thus a higher w^*), while the right-hand side is the marginal cost of D^*. Where the two are equated gives the best w^*:

$$w^* = b - \sqrt{2(C - w_h)(b - a)}. \tag{8.4}$$

To elucidate the concepts of marginal benefit and marginal cost in this context, it is instructive to construct the total benefit and total cost curves corresponding to the marginal curves. The total cost curve is simply:

$$TC = (C - w_h)D^*.$$

As for the total benefit (TB) curve, note first that:

$$TB = \int_{D = 1}^{D = D^*} MB \, dD.$$

Secondly:

$$MB = \frac{(b - w^*)^2}{2(b - a)}$$

$$= \frac{b - a}{2} \cdot \frac{1}{D^{*2}}, \text{ since } D^* = \frac{b - a}{b - w^*}.$$

Therefore:

$$TB = -\frac{b - a}{2} \cdot \frac{1}{D} \bigg|_{D = 1}^{D = D^*}$$

$$= \frac{b - a}{2}(1 - 1/D^*) + \text{constant of integration}.$$

Notice how the TB curve begins at point $(a + b)/2$, the mean of the distribution, since the very first wage offer – if one decides on a reservation wage implying one week's search – is expected to be that. This is the constant of integration. The curve then approaches b, the maximum wage, asymptotically, just as in the simpler Stigler model.

For some purposes the reader might wish to express marginal costs and benefits in terms of the reservation wage. This is no problem since by equations

(8.1) and (8.2) above, the reservation wage and the implied reservation search period are related:

$$w^* = b - (b - a)/D^*.$$

Search duration increases the wage, but at a decreasing rate – and infinite search is implied by selecting w^* equal to the highest possible wage, b. Therefore:

$$\frac{\partial TC}{\partial w^*} = (C - w_h)\frac{dD^*}{dw^*} = \frac{(C - w_h)(b - a)}{(b - w^*)^2},$$

which shows marginal cost increasing, and becoming infinite, as w^* approaches b. This curve is graphed in figure 8.4. Notice also how the marginal cost of search declines as unemployment benefit, w_h, increases.

By contrast, the marginal benefit curve, expressed in terms of the wage is simply a horizontal line, with intercept = $1/2$:

$$\frac{\partial TB}{\partial w^*} = \frac{\partial TB}{\partial D^*}\frac{dD^*}{dw^*} = \frac{1}{2}.$$

Increase your reservation wage by one penny, and you increase your expected wage by half a penny. This can actually be seen by varying w^* in figure 8.2. When w^* is as low as it can be (a), the expected wage is $(a + b)/2$, and raising w^* by a given amount raises the expected wage by half that amount.

The model shows how search duration depends inversely on search costs, $C - w_h$, and positively on the benefits to search – which are related to the wage offer dispersion $(b - a)$ (and also to the expected length of a job, H, though we have not considered this explicitly in this section). In these respects the model is similar to that of Stigler. The reservation wage selected, w^*, also depends inversely on search costs, and positively on the benefits to search, as figure 8.4 illustrates. Notice how if $(b - a)$ were very small (a competitive market), the marginal cost of choosing a higher w^* would tend to zero, and w^* would tend to equal b, the maximum and only wage in the market. With wage offer dispersion, w^* falls below b.

Consider the implications for unemployment. The probability of leaving unemployment to take a job is technically defined as a 'hazard' – the changing of one's labour market 'state'. Define $h(t)$ to be the hazard in time period t. If the probability of obtaining a job offer during a given search is one, then $\Pr(w > w^*)$ is the probability of accepting an offer w, given w^* – that is, it is the hazard of getting a job and leaving unemployment. As we have already noted, this probability equals the shaded area in figure 8.2, and equals, from (8.1) and (8.4):

$$(b - w^*)/(b - a) = \sqrt{2(C - w_h)/(b - a)}.$$

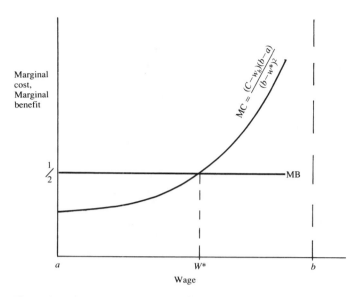

Figure 8.4 Determining the reservation wage

This is the 'hazard' of leaving the unemployed state, and becoming employed.

The equation shows that the chance of becoming employed increases – and hence unemployment duration decreases – the higher are foregone earnings, C, the lower is unemployment compensation, w_h, and the lower is wage dispersion $(b - a)$. The sequential model involving the reservation wage thus has the same predictions as the non-sequential model. However because C, w_h, and $(b - a)$ also influence the reservation wage (equation (8.4)), the sequential search model therefore generates additional predictions involving this variable.

Nevertheless these simple models can still lead to peculiar results. Unemployment duration increases in depression, yet the expected wage resulting from search is presumably lower then. Unless costs of search are reduced in depression – perhaps because wages and thus foregone earnings are lower then – we would therefore expect unemployment duration to decline rather than increase. A similar problem arises when explaining the longer unemployment duration of older workers. Since their foregone earnings while searching are higher than for young people, we would expect older workers to search less than younger, not more. To clarify these problems it is useful to introduce the idea of a 'job offer production function'.

The job offer production function

Up to this point we have been thinking of time, that is, weeks of search, as the only input into the process of obtaining job offers. But a person can obtain more offers also by varying search intensity, that is, travelling further, making more phone calls, and mailing more letters. In addition some people might be better at searching than other (Vishwanath, 1988). A person with specific knowledge of a particular job who is unexpectedly dismissed will not have much labour market knowledge, and can be expected to search less efficiently than a person who is more current. Search is also more productive in good times, when job vacancies are abundant. Again, the long-term unemployed might simply not be effective at producing job offers. Cutting their unemployment insurance as a means to reduce unemployment duration, as implied by the simple model, would therefore be shooting at the wrong target (Nickell, 1979, 38).

The concept of a job offer production function allows us to incorporate these possibilities into the analysis. It is easiest to make job offers, F, a function only of two variables, search time, S, and search 'intensity', z. Search intensity could be indexed as total miles travelled, or letters mailed and so on, or simply the number of days per week that a person will search each week of search. To fix ideas we will concentrate on miles travelled. The individual can then be pictured as choosing a total search budget (TC), and deciding as well on how to apportion this budget into the total number of weeks he/she intends to search, and the total number of miles to travel. The problem is analogous to that faced by a firm which chooses a budget (total costs), at the same time apportioning this budget among capital and labour inputs so as to minimise costs. The choice problem depends on the production function, and the prices of inputs.

A production function is illustrated in figure 8.5. There is a family of curves relating job offers to search time, one for each level of miles travelled. A person who travels fewer miles, z_1 (perhaps without access to a car), will be able to search less intensely and obtain fewer offers for a given amount of search time than someone travelling many miles, z_2. Keeping job offers at F_0, for example, the individual travelling z_1 miles would require S_2 weeks, compared to only S_1 for the individual travelling z_2 miles.

Individuals will choose between search time and search intensity in accordance with the costs of these inputs. The process of choice is illustrated in figure 8.6. The production function gives the isoquants which have the usual shape, and F_0, F_1, and F_2 signify successively higher levels of offers. The budget line is made up of search time and search intensity costs. The cost of search time is foregone earnings, as usual, which we measure as the actual or potential wage rate minus unemployment pay. The cost of search intensity is the cost of transportation. The total search budget, TC, is therefore:

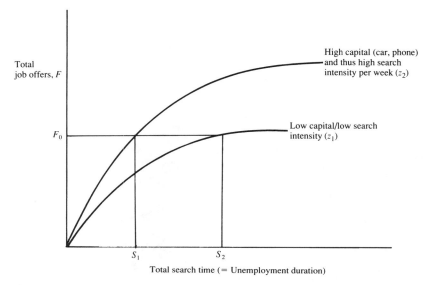

Figure 8.5 The job offer production function

$$TC = (w - w_h)S + kz,$$

where S is total weeks searched, $w - w_h$ is weekly net wages, z is total miles travelled, and k is cost per mile. A person with a low (marginal) travel cost, for example owning a car, will locate at C. A worse off individual would locate at B. Similarly, a person with high foregone earnings – a high wage or low unemployment insurance – would locate at A with less search time and more search intensity than a low wage individual.

The implication for unemployment duration is that high costs of search intensity will mean less search intensity, more weeks of search, and hence longer unemployment (taking unemployment duration to be the same as weeks of search). Previously we had reasoned that high search costs would *shorten* unemployment (rotate the TC line in figure 8.1 upward). However we were then only considering the foregone earnings search costs. This is still true – a rise in foregone earnings will move a person from B to A in figure 8.6, shortening the search time chosen from S_2 to S_1, and reducing offers from F_1 to F_0 (and consequently also reducing the expected wage). But high costs of travel could have the opposite effect and increase unemployment duration as a person substitutes time for goods in the search process. In the case graphed, a rise in travel costs would move the person from C to B and slightly reduce

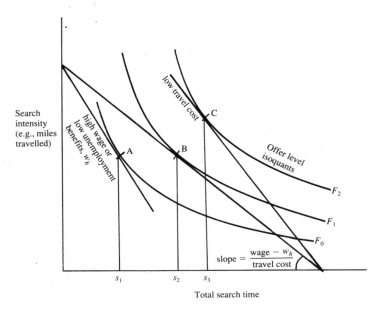

Figure 8.6 Choosing search intensity and search time

unemployment duration because of the adverse income effect – but it could easily have gone the other way.

The relevance of search time and search intensity for policy is that it might be possible to make search intensity effectively cheaper via, for example, counselling and 'job clubs' which provide free telephones, photocopying equipment, and advice. Such a course of action means a move from B to C, and would lead to a higher level of offers (a movement from F_1 to F_2), and thus a better post-unemployment job match. The alternative policy is to reduce (or tax) unemployment assistance, which will lower unemployment duration, but will also reduce the individual's opportunity set.

A further way to use the production function is to picture the effects of exogenous shifts in the offer arrival rate on unemployment duration. Consider figure 8.7 which analyses the connection between the business cycle and unemployment duration. Quadrant (1) shows two job offer production functions, one for good and one for bad times. Quadrant (2) then gives the associated total search cost function, and quadrant (3) maps total cost around to quadrant (4) which brings together total costs and expected wages as a function of offers. In bad times the offer arrival rate will fall for a given search effort, as indicated in quadrant (1). This will be reflected as a rise in total costs

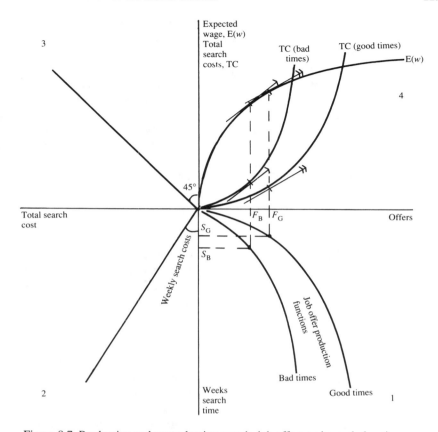

Figure 8.7 Productive and unproductive search, job offers and search duration

of TC (bad times) in quadrant (4). There will be a fall in the number of offers the individual decides to process (or, equivalently, a fall in the reservation wage) from F_G to F_B, and probably a rise in unemployment duration from S_G to S_B. There need not be a rise in unemployment duration, it is true (it depends on the curves chosen). But in practice we do see a rise in unemployment duration in bad times, and this would be the way to picture it.

It is tempting to argue that in times of high unemployment the foregone earnings cost of search falls because expected wages fall. In such a case the movement from F_G to F_B will not be so great, and longer unemployment duration is guaranteed. However we must be careful, because in such circumstances wage dispersion could decline. Wage dispersion would decline if the maximum wage people could expect fell more in bad times than the minimum wage, which is reasonable. A decline in dispersion would reduce the slope of the $E(w)$ curve, reduce the returns to search, and so act to counteract possible changes in search costs.

A similar analysis can be applied when contrasting able searchers with the less able, for example, the prime age versus the old, the more educated versus the less educated, and perhaps also white youths versus black. In particular, black youths have much longer unemployment duration than white. This could be explained in terms of the job offer production of black youths being below that for white youths. A possible reason is that the black youths' network of labour market contacts is smaller than that of the whites (whites use friends and direct contacts, blacks use state agencies which are less effective (Holzer, 1987, 447) – see below).

Demand-side influences

There is also the demand side, that is, decisions taken by firms, to be considered however. Search theory shows us only worker responses – supply-side responses – to costs and benefits of search. The demand side can be thought of as chiefly influencing involuntary flows into unemployment via dismissals and layoffs. It is chiefly young workers and unskilled workers – who have not established long-term contracts and made specific investments – who suffer from involuntary terminations.

The picture is given in table 8.3. There it can be seen that a group's unemployment rate is the product of its flow into unemployment, and the duration of its unemployment. When considering unemployment flows and duration over the life cycle, inflow rates decline with age, but duration increases. Older workers are less likely to lose their jobs, but when they do the resulting unemployment lasts for a long time. In general, more skilled workers are less likely to become unemployed, but face severer consequences when they do. This can be seen by comparing workers in the professional category with other groups.

Flows into unemployment are partly voluntary (quits to search), and partly involuntary (dismissals, and layoffs). Voluntary flows into unemployment can be explained by the same search models we have already discussed. Thus when times are good and vacancy rates rise, the returns to search might be so great that it pays to quit in order to search full time. We do find that quits into unemployment (presumably to search) are higher when vacancy rates are high (Kahn and Low, 1984, 111).

However involuntary flows into unemployment can best be explained by the nature of the jobs done. Unskilled workers will have higher employment variability because of lower specific capital investments in hiring and training (Oi, 1962). The theory of specific training is outlined in more detail in the next

Table 8.3. *Unemployment duration and inflows, by age and occupation*

	Britain 1984			US 1987		
	Inflow rate, S/N	Average duration	Unemp. rate, U/N	Inflow rate, S/N	Average duration	Unemp. rate, U/N
Age						
16–24	3.3%/mon.	8.5 mons	22.1%	10.2%/mon	2.0 mons	16.9%
20–4	1.3	15.3	16.9	4.5	2.4	9.7
25–54	0.7	13.1	8.8	1.8	3.0	5.0
55–64	0.5	19.2	8.3	1.0	3.7	3.5
Occupation						
Professional and managerial						
	0.5	11.2	5.3	0.7	3.0	2.3
Clerical	0.9	10.1	8.0 ⎫			
Other non-manual			⎬	1.7	2.6	4.3
	1.1	11.8	12.2 ⎭			
Skilled manual						
	1.0	14.2	12.6	2.0	2.9	6.1
Personal services						
	1.3	14.1	15.5	3.0	2.4	7.7
Other manual						
	(included in personal services)			2.8	3.0	9.4
Total	0.9	12.8	10.8	2.2	2.6	6.2

Proportion of long-term (over one year) unemployment in total group unemployment, 1985

	Britain	United States
Youths	28.5%	5.1%
Prime age workers	44.3	11.0
Older workers	55.9	15.3

Notes: Occupation of the unemployed is their previous occupation. U = number unemployed; S = monthly inflow into unemployment, and N = employment. If inflows Y equal outflows, $U/N \cong S/N \cdot U/S$, where U/S is average months duration.
Sources: Jackman, Layard, and Savouri, 1991, 50, 58; OECD, 1986, 34.

chapter. It provides a logical explanation for the greater tendency for some jobs and some worker groups, young workers in particular, to experience variable unemployment. The influence of specific capital on unemployment rates is graphically shown in figure 1.1, in chapter 1, where black workers in England are seen to have much wider unemployment rate fluctuations than white workers. This is partly explained by the greater concentration of black workers in unskilled jobs. Gilman (1965) calculated in the US case that about half of the difference between black and white unemployment rates is due to the less favourable occupational distribution of black workers. The remainder could be due to the supply-side search reasons – for example, lower education, worse transportation – which we have discussed.

8.3 Empirical results

Thus there is 'rational ignorance'. It takes time to become informed and it is rarely worthwhile to be fully informed. Some search unemployment is inevitable and a consequence of optimal allocation of time. The more costly is search time (high foregone earnings or low welfare benefits when unemployed), and the less costly is search intensity, the shorter will be search unemployment. At the same time if search costs are high, wage dispersion will increase. Also greater benefits to search – longer expected jobs, or higher wage dispersion – will increase search unemployment, given search costs.

Studies of reservation wages and unemployment

Regardless of whether one uses a sequential or non-sequential search model, what emerges is a link between a set of fundamental variables: reservation wages, duration of search, search costs, wage dispersion, expected hours of work, and expected job duration. Of these some are known, predetermined, exogenous variables, while the rest are unknown. Solutions for the unknown variables can only be obtained by solving for these in terms of the known exogenous factors. In fact this is the principle upon which much of the current empirical search theory research is based (see Devine and Kiefer, 1991, for a survey).

Two strands exist. One is to test whether unemployment (and wage gain) is lower the lower is wage dispersion and the higher search costs (see Ehrenberg and Oaxaca (1976), Classen (1977), as well as Katz (1977)). The other approach focuses on the determinants of the reservation wage. We have been assuming that individuals know the wage distribution that they face. However if they learn about it while searching, the reservation wage will decline the longer the unemployment spell (Kiefer and Neumann, 1979, 91). Reservation wages could also decline with unemployment because, as the potential employment period shortens, the level of savings declines, and the marginal utility of leisure decreases (Sandel, 1980, 342).

The Ehrenberg–Oaxaca study is a good example since it deals with measuring whether compensation from unemployment insurance (UI), which lowers foregone earnings due to search, affects not only the duration of unemployment, but also wage gains upon obtaining employment. Essentially

Table 8.4. *The effects of unemployment insurance on unemployment duration and wage gain, US 1967/8*

The impact of increasing replacement fraction by 10%

	Strata			
	Males 45–59	Females 30–44	Boys 14–24	Girls 14–24
Change in unemployment duration	1.5 weeks	0.3 weeks	0.2 weeks	0.5 weeks
Annual percentage wage change	9.0%	1.5%	Not significant	Not significant

Source: Ehrenberg and Oaxaca, 1976, table 5.

this study is composed of two sets of regressions: one where unemployment duration is treated as a dependent variable, and the other where wage gain subsequent to unemployment is the dependent variable. Both are regressed against the UI 'replacement ratio' denoting the proportion of one's previous (after tax) salary covered by unemployment insurance.

The computations are broken up into four gender and age groups as shown in table 8.4. The crucial independent variable is the replacement ratio. Adjustments are made for 'standardising' variables including colour, marital status, education, and previous wages. What is striking is that in all cases UI benefits increase unemployment duration. For adult men a 10% increase in the replacement ratio would increase unemployment duration by nearly two weeks. In the British case the corresponding figure is about one week – declining to zero, however, for older workers, and the long-term unemployed (Narendrenathan *et al.*, 1985, 321). Such workers can be thought of as having a very low job offer production function (figure 8.5), and will have long unemployment duration whatever the costs of search.

It is important to note as well however that in most cases wages also increase significantly when unemployment compensation is high. This implies productive search – more time to accumulate job offers (shown by the movement from A to B in figure 8.6). Thus there are perhaps economic efficiency reasons, that is, national income increasing reasons, as well as equity reasons for unemployment insurance. In judging the efficiency of increased unemployment compensation, however, we need to assess whether the increased burden on tax payers is outweighed by the more productive search of the unemployed. A possible argument is that the unemployed help others by becoming unemployed and re-allocating themselves to more productive jobs. In the presence of such an externality there could be *too little* unemployment (labour re-allocation) without unemployment compensation.

The effects of other variables on unemployment duration are given in table 8.5. Some results might seem paradoxical. One would think that 'knowledge of work' increases one's search efficiency, as does education – yet the table suggests that neither knowledge of work nor education reduce unemployment duration. However, as noted in connection with figure 8.5, we would expect high wage individuals to substitute search intensity (e.g., miles travelled) for time in the search process. Their job offer production function will be higher due to the higher search intensity. However, as noted in relation to figure 8.7, this need not decrease *total* search time. In figure 8.7 total search time does decrease with higher search productivity (the higher production function), but a different shaped $E(w)$ curve could reverse this result. Barron and Mellow in fact show that search intensity (days searched per week) increases with an individual's education (1979, 402), which is as expected.

It can be seen that both a high past wage and being married are associated with lower unemployment duration. Both these variables could indicate a higher mean to the wage offer distribution, and thus higher foregone earnings when searching. In such circumstances individuals should then search more intensely, that is, substitute goods for time in the search process. Supporting this view, Barron and Mellow find that unemployed workers with high past wages search more days per week (1979, 399).

It can also be seen that black workers have longer unemployment duration than white. It is difficult to account for this. A related aspect is that the reservation wages of unemployed black youths appear to be unrealistically high. Thus Holzer reports black youths' reservation wages to be 8% higher than their previous received wage; white youths' reservation wages were 7% lower than their previous received wage, by contrast (Holzer, 1986b, 164; see also Stephenson, 1976). These reservation wages, $4.20 on average, were considerably above the minimum wage (about $3 at the time), so minimum wage laws apparently are not the cause. The network of labour market connections of black youths could be smaller than that for white youths, as noted above. It is also true that they have less easy access to cars and telephones (in another sample, 66% of white youths owned cars compared to 42% of blacks (Stephenson, 1976, 107)). Both these factors will reduce the pro-ductivity of search and lead to a 'discouraged worker' effect. The difficulty with this explanation, however, is that, as figure 8.7 shows, while less efficient search leads to longer search, S_B, it also leads to fewer offers, F_B, and should therefore lead to a lower expected (and consequently reservation) wage – yet the black youth reservation wage seems too high. A possible further factor could be the higher non-market income of black youths, including income from crime (one study gives 25% of black youths' non-wage income

Table 8.5. *Qualitative determinants of unemployment duration*

	Ehrenberg and Oaxaca US 1967/8				Holen US 1970 Males and females	Narendrenathan et al. UK 1978 males
	Male	Female	Male youth	Female youth		
Race (1 = black)	NS	+	+	+	+	
Married	+NS	−NS	−	NS		−
Home owner	−NS					−[a]
Local unemp. rate	+	+NS	+	NS		+
Past wage	−NS	NS	NS		−	−
Bad health		+NS	NS	NS		+
Education	NS	−NS	−	NS	−	−
UI benefits	+	+	+	+	+	+[b]
Knowledge of work test			NS	NS		
Husband's income				−		
Sex (1 = male)					−	
Age					+	+

Notes:

NS: not statistically significant at the 0.10 level.

[a] 1 = home owner, 0 = renting privately or from the state.

[b] UI effect insignificant for older workers, and those unemployed longer than 6 months.

Sources: Ehrenberg and Oaxaca, 1976; Holen, 1977; Narendrenathan, Nickell, and Stern, 1985.

as coming from illegal activities (Holzer, 1986a, 780)), which could increase search time.

Turning to the life cycle, we see that the young have shorter unemployment duration than the old. Young workers generally have higher unemployment rates, but these are caused more by their high inflows into unemployment (that is, by high turnover) due to lack of specific skills, as noted above, than by long duration of unemployment. When an older worker becomes unemployed the unemployment lasts for a long time presumably both because of less efficient search due to long absence from competition in external labour markets, and because of greater returns to search due to a dispersed wage offer distribution. Greater dispersion arises because older workers are possibly less homogeneous, both from their own point of view and from that of prospective employers, than young workers. Mincer shows that the variance of earnings, given education, increases with age (1974, chart 6.1), which supports the view

Table 8.6. *The effects of housing market distortions on mobility, UK 1973*

Household type	Proportion	New address in past year and:	
		no regional movement*	regional movement*
Owner	49%	328 per 10,000 households	2,685
Renting:			
privately	18	1,208	1,374
from state	33	501	178

Note: this table is for households living in the south-east of England, with a head of household aged 35 to 54 years in a junior non-manual occupation and who has completed high school with an 'O' or 'A' level qualification.
*a 'region' is one of 11 statistical regions.
Source: Hughes and McCormick, 1981, 935.

that older workers have a more dispersed wage offer distribution, and thus greater returns to search.

At the same time, the long duration of unemployment spells, particularly for older workers in Britain, hardly seems compatible with a picture of search unemployment (Johnson and Layard, 1986, 940). But we must remember that unemployment assistance is provided for an indefinite period in the UK. Also the national system of collective wage setting prevents many people from setting a low reservation wage.

In addition, the policy of state subsidised housing lowers regional mobility because movers to a new area give up the subsidy in their old area and take time to qualify in the new area – particularly if there are many movers to that area (Minford *et al.*, 1987, 114). Tenants in state housing can thus only move with difficulty to areas with high vacancy rates. Consequently their search productivity is lowered, and search duration increased. This is demonstrated in the final column of table 8.5, which indicates that those who own their own house have shorter unemployment duration than those living in state-owned housing. This is likely to be an important factor, because about one third of the population live in state-owned housing.

Table 8.6 shows that the mobility rates for those renting from the state in Britain are only 178 per 10,000 families, compared to 2,685 for owners, holding age, education, and occupation constant. That it is not some unmeasured factor which stops the state tenants from migrating is shown by their high tendency to move between addresses within a given area (second column). In the US, where these inflexibilities are lacking, search by older workers is more effective: only 15.3% of unemployed workers were unemployed for over a year in 1985, compared with the 55.9% UK figure.

Table 8.7. *Qualitative determinants of reservation wages: evidence from past studies*

	Kiefer–[a] Neumann	Sandell[b] (women)	Stephenson[c] (youths)	Lancaster[d] Chesher
Unemployment insurance	+	+	+	+
Race (1 = black)		−	+[e]	
Education	+			+
Children	NS	−NS		+
Marital status	−			+
Age	−			+
Age squared	+			−
Direct costs			+NS	
Local unemployment rate	+	+	+	−NS
Husband's income		+		
Unemployment duration	−	−		

Notes:

[a] This study uses a sample of 517 workers in 14 states who had been permanently separated from their job.

[b] This study is based on asking wage data from National Longitudinal Survey of Mature Women 30–44 Years Old in 1967 for years 1967, 1969, 1971, and 1972.

[c] This study is based on asking wage data from a survey of 300 unemployed male youths.

[d] This study uses a random sample of 642 unemployed men, questioned about their reservation wage in 1974.

[e] See Holzer's study of the National Longitudinal Survey youth cohort (1987, 164).

NS: not statistically significant at the 0.10 level or better.

Sources: Kiefer–Neumann, 1979; Sandell, 1980; Stephenson, 1976; Lancaster and Chesher, 1983; Holzer, 1987.

Moreover regional differences in unemployment persist in the UK, whereas they tend to be eliminated quickly in the US (Jackman *et al.*, 1991, 55). Persistent regional unemployment differences in the UK are thus evidence both of impediments to labour mobility, and a wage structure that does not vary enough by region, due perhaps to national wage bargaining.

Reservation wage studies also appear consistent with search theory – see table 8.7. Unemployment insurance strongly increases reservation wages, as predicted. Education also tends to increase reservation wages, presumably because it indicates a higher mean wage offer distribution for the more educated. For the British data both marital status and age – up to a point – increase the reservation wage as well. This again presumably marks the higher wage offer distributions for these individuals.

However a higher local unemployment rate increases reservation wages, which is puzzling – but there is a possible explanation. Hall has found signs that wages are higher in cities with higher unemployment, holding human capital factors and regional cost of living constant (1972, 734). He reasons that this is an equilibrium phenomenon, with high wages needed to attract workers to cities with high unemployment (a compensating wage differential as studied in chapter 7), and high unemployment needed to promote worker efficiency so as to enable firms to pay high wages. He reasons that high local unemployment increases labour productivity because firms then need to train less, and do not need to hoard labour (this is an early example of the 'efficiency wage' argument, see chapter 9). If this reasoning is to be believed, then high reservation wages in high unemployment areas simply mark the higher mean of the wage offer distribution in these areas.

There are further interesting aspects of the table: married women have higher reservation wages the higher their husband's income. Such high reservation wages link in with the tendency we have observed (chapter 5) for lower participation rates among women with high non-labour (including husband's) income. Also reservation wages decline with unemployment duration. This is probably a selectivity effect because those workers with low reservation wages are employed first, leaving the sample containing only those with high reservation wages. Finally, we have already noted the problem of accounting for the high reservation wages of black youths.

Table 8.8 shows some actual reservation wages, as given by a sample of unemployed men, correlated with the men's assessment of their expected wage. It will be recalled from equation (8.3), that the reservation wage should always be less than the expected wage. Table 8.8 shows that in only three cases out of the 642 was the reservation wage higher than the expected wage. A similar joint frequency distribution as between the reservation wage and the unemployment income level the individual was receiving can be drawn up. According to equation (8.3) the reservation wage should always be at least as great as unemployment income. In fact, for this sample, in only five cases is equation (8.3) violated (Lancaster and Chesher, 1983, appendix). A similar finding is also available for a sample of black American youths. The reservation wage was $3.39, considerably lower than the individuals' (self assessed) expected wage of $4.66 (Holzer, 1986a, 780).

A model of ignorance in the labour market

It is possible to cast further light on the role of search in the labour market by considering the residuals from earnings functions. People who earn less than would be expected given their education and experience are presumably not

Table 8.8. *Frequency distribution of reservation wages and expected wages, UK 1974*

Reservation wage, w^*	Expected wage (midpoint of income category)										
	14	17.5	22.5	27.5	32.5	37.5	42.5	47.5	55	65	75
14	24	11	6	1							
17.5	1	60	79	5	2						
22.5	1		78	71	11	2	2				
27.5				81	69	11	8	2	1		
32.5		1			30	27	5	2	4		
37.5						14	7	2	1	3	
42.5							4	6	2	1	
47.5								2	2	1	1
55								1			

Note: The measure of the expected wage was taken from the question: How much take home pay would you expect to earn in a new job? The measure of the reservation wage was taken from the question: Would you tell me the lowest possible amount you would be prepared to accept after deductions?
Source: Lancaster and Chesher, 1983, appendix.

well informed. The approach can be used to show which type of worker is not well informed.

Assume that worker i finds a job with firm j, and receives wage w_{ij}^0. Wage w_{ij}^0 must exceed, or equal, the worker's reservation wage w^*. However, had worker i more information, he/she could have received a wage even higher than w_{ij}^0. Denote w_m to be the maximum wage offer (capacity wages) a worker of i's quality could have obtained had he/she full knowledge of each firm's pay scale.

The gap between w_{ij}^0 and w_m will vary across individuals, depending upon relative success in the job search. The gap is shown in figure 8.1 as the distance between the actual wage, $E(w)$, line and the maximum wage line, b. Barring the impact of luck which will be discussed later, the greater one's knowledge of the labour market, the greater the chance of achieving one's potential wage (w_m). Thus, we define the gap between w_{ij}^0 and w_m to be an index of individual i's ignorance.

By the same token firm j pays more than necessary to hire the i-th worker, since it pays w_{ij}^0 when the worker is willing to work at his/her reservation wage w^*. The gap $(w_{ij}^0 - w^*) \geq 0$ represents firm ignorance concerning worker i. But, in addition, worker i need not be the lowest reservation waged worker, so that firm ignorance is really $w_{ij}^0 - w_{min}$, where w_{min} is the minimum reservation wage of all workers who could do the job of worker i. The average $w_m - w_{ij}^0$

across all individuals in a market can then be defined as mean worker ignorance, and the average $w_{ij}^0 - w_{min}$ across all firms as mean firm ignorance.

The approach is to estimate average employee ignorance, $\bar{u}$, for various groups. This yields a set of different $\bar{u}$ values, one for each group. Interpreting $\bar{u}$ as employee ignorance is reasonable if these values compare favourably to search theory predictions. For example, if unemployment insurance is generous, search should be extensive and $\bar{u}$ should be low, *ceteris paribus*. This is what we find.

To give a flavour of the research we concentrate here on worker ignorance (consideration of firm ignorance does not much modify the results –see Polachek and Yoon, 1987). To specify worker ignorance empirically, rewrite observed market wages as:

$$w_i^0 = w_m + u_i,$$

where $u_i \leq 0$ is a 'one-sided' error term and the firm index j is dropped for simplicity. If $u_i = 0$, then person i has attained his or her maximum wage w_m, whereas if $u_i < 0$, then person i has accepted a wage below his/her maximum. The case where u_i is taken to be a half normal distribution is shown in the top panel of figure 8.8.

Human capital considerations posit that the logarithm of capacity wage, w_m, is expressed as a function of education, experience, tenure, age, and other productivity determining exogenous variables:

$$w_m = \Sigma_{k=1}^k x_k \beta_k + v_i,$$

where the k x's are observable determinants of w_m (now expressed as a logarithm), and v_i is a disturbance term assumed to be distributed normally as $N(O, \sigma_v^2)$.

Combining the equations gives the equation for the observed wage:

$$w_i^0 = \Sigma_{k=1}^k x_k \beta_k + \epsilon_i,$$

where $\epsilon_i = v_i + u_i$ represents the composite error. The one-sided error u_i quantifies the role of the labour market ignorance. The v_i component reflects statistical noise in the data, and individuals' good or bad luck.

The equation for w^0 is estimated by maximum likelihood. Basically we take the distribution of residuals from the wage equation shown in the lower part of figure 8.8. This distribution has a fat lower tail. Assuming a half-normal distribution for the employee ignorance error term enables us to use this shape to identify the two component parts of the error term.

The next step in the analysis is to compute $\bar{u}$ for different groups, holding constant productivity characteristics. The results of the exercise are given in table 8.9. The entries in the table are to be interpreted as the percentage extent

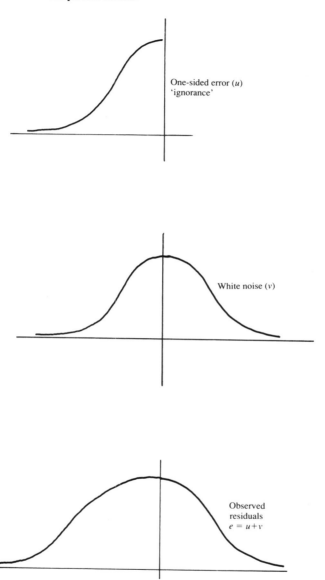

Figure 8.8. Residuals from the worker 'ignorance' wage equation

by which wages are reduced due to worker ignorance. Thus white male workers have wages 31% lower than their potential, on average. Black workers fall short by 44%. These residuals are no doubt too large, because it is impossible fully to control for quality (Gaynor and Polachek, 1991. Nevertheless the differences between groups are likely to be in the right direction, and give measures of relative ignorance.

The ignorance differences between each group seem consistent with a priori expectations concerning the costs and benefits of search. Blacks possess less information than whites, college educated more information than non-college educated, the unhealthy less information than the healthy, and the recipients of unemployment insurance possess more information than non-recipients. This result ties in with the search literature which implies that since unemployment insurance recipients search for longer they obtain a wage which is closer to their maximum wage, that is, obtain a better match. Finally, union members seem to possess more information than non-union members. Perhaps unions therefore help their members in the process of search.

In addition, a comparison of ignorance levels by marital status, gender, and colour is interesting. For example, note that black female heads of household are estimated to be less ignorant than white female heads. Given the higher lifetime labourforce participation rates of black women compared to white women, it makes intuitive sense for them to have more information than white women. Similarly the higher lifetime labourforce participation of married men is consistent with them having more information than single men – which we find. On the other hand, the level of ignorance of single men is estimated to be higher than for married women, which is hard to explain – except that these two groups are very different in other, unmeasured ways.

The approach can be extended to encompass employer ignorance as well (Polachek and Yoon, 1987). It turns out that employers, too, pay more for labour of given quality than they would if well informed. Figures for about 40% overpayment are derived. In addition, it seems that employers are better informed about reservation wages of union than non-union workers, which is reasonable (1987, table 2).

Search and mobility over the life cycle

Not all search takes place at a moment in time. In most instances search continues throughout one's life. Both job mobility and geographic mobility are examples, as people often view their job or location as a stepping stone for further advancement. Searchers can thus be viewed as 'perspicacious peregrinators' because they seek and weigh information on locational and occupational choices in each time period. Here mobility becomes an on-going rational process in which individuals continually gather information. However,

Table 8.9. *Estimates of employee ignorance*

Demographic groups	Males		Female heads of household		Female spouse and cohabitants	
	N	i	N	i	N	i
White	1828	−0.31	352	−0.42	987	−0.39
Black	860	−0.44	413	−0.27	427	−0.41
		(13.95)[a]		(−9.96)		(1.79)
Less than college	1808	−0.36	572	−0.41	944	−0.42
College	979	−0.35	218	−0.33	433	−0.15
		(−2.43)		(−3.67)		(−23.63)
Health limits work	251	−0.37	91	−0.47		*b*
No limitation	2536	−0.35	699	−0.34		
		(−1.96)		(−4.02)		
Married	2300	−0.27		*b*	1431	−0.32
Not married	486	−0.54				*b*
		(16.37)				
Union job	869	−0.27	166	−0.25	219	−0.24
Non-union job	1801	−0.35	618	−0.39	1138	−0.32
		(15.35)		(11.44)		(10.56)
No unemployment insurance received	2586	−0.36	746	−0.38	*b*	*b*
Unemployment insurance received	201	−0.15	44	−0.21		
		(−42.92)		(−8.81)		

Notes:

[a] The t-statistics testing the null hypothesis that the two means are equal are in parentheses.

[b] Too small a number of observations in one category precludes computation of mean ignorance level.

Source: Polachek and Hofler, 1991, table 4.

individuals act on this information with a move or job change only when a move is economically efficient.

In the traditional framework individuals are assumed to find their best 'match' and stay there forever. More realistically there is repeated mobility, with actual moves occurring periodically, though with declining frequency, throughout one's life. The recurrent nature of job change is well illustrated in table 9.2 in the next chapter, which shows the cumulated job changes of individuals over the life cycle. In the US the average male has about ten jobs in a lifetime, and in the UK about seven. Job changing slows down with age however: the final job is taken in one's forties, and lasts to retirement. Matching models have been applied to many markets. There have been applications to marriage (Becker, 1974; Mortensen, 1988a) and occupational choice (see the discussion of estimating tenure wage gradients in chapter 9, also Mortensen, 1988b), as well as locational choice.

Within the human capital investment model, in each time period individuals purchase capital up to the point that the present value of the gain from marginal investment equals the marginal investment costs. This leads to a declining investment time path as investment present values diminish over the life cycle.

Similarly we can analyse information within a life-cycle framework. Investment in information provides knowledge of available wages: how much more can we earn if we switch jobs or move to a better location? There are life-cycle implications not only because older workers have a shorter time period to reap returns from information, but also because each successive move will become more difficult to improve upon as we approach our capacity wage more closely.

To be more specific, let us view a person's stock of labour market information (I) as knowledge of what other jobs pay relative to one's current job. There is no direct monetary gain, however, until knowledge is used to move to the highest paying job about which the searcher has acquired information. At the time the worker actually switches jobs a wage gain is achieved, but the value of the worker's information stock also drops to zero, since he/she then knows of no better job. Once in the new job the worker begins searching afresh and again, when a sufficiently good job is found, a switch occurs. However as one gets older the gains from mobility decrease due to the shorter horizon. Therefore people do not stay in one job all their lives; they have a succession of moves, but the chance of leaving a job, holding tenure constant, decreases with each successive job, as shown in table 9.2 below.

All this can be illustrated graphically. Denote the costs of moving as C. These costs probably vary over the life cycle, but for our purpose we assume C constant. Costs represent down time – the lost work days from changing a job – and the direct moving costs to change one's geographic location often associated with a move. As such C can be graphed as a horizontal constant cost curve (C) in figure 8.9.

On the other hand the benefits from moving will vary over time. The benefits are the present value of the gains from the move. Initially these are zero since one has no information about other jobs relative to one's own job. However, over time with search, information increases, enabling the worker to achieve a positive potential wage gain. Thus the marginal gain of moving curve (G) is positively sloped from the origin point 0. At each time period up

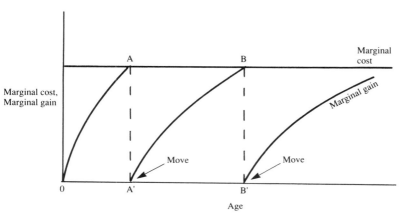

Figure 8.9 Migration as a life-cycle investment process

until A, the marginal cost exceeds the gains of a move, thereby implying no mobility. However, at age A, the gain exceeds the cost leading the worker to move. Information about new jobs then falls to zero. Nevertheless search continues, and mobility benefits rise, however, at a slower rate since it becomes more difficult to find a better match, and in any case the present value of any gain diminishes as one ages. Thus the MG curve shifts and becomes flatter (A'B). This means a longer duration until the next job change. This process repeats itself, but eventually one no longer changes jobs.

We can test the above model, using data on geographic migration. Two equations need to be estimated: one equation for the probability of a move and the other for the expected wage gain consequent upon a move (also see Stern, 1989, for a simultaneous equations model). The equation representing the probability of moving can be written:

$$\text{prob (migration)} = f(\Delta Y, C),$$

where ΔY is the change in income expected if a move is made, and C denotes migration costs. The probability of moving can be measured just as a dummy variable taking the value of 1 (mover) and 0 (non-mover). The probability of moving should increase with ΔY, increase the longer one has been in a job (given age), and decrease with age.

To measure potential migration gains, ΔY, requires an estimate of the earnings a person would receive if a move occurred. For a mover the hypothetical earnings he/she would have without moving, Y'_m, is calculated by substituting his characteristics, X_m, into the equation for the stayer group:

$$Y'_m = X_m \beta_s,$$

where β_s are the stayer group coefficients. Similarly hypothetical earnings for the stayer, Y'_s, if he/she moved are:

$$Y'_s = X_s \beta_m,$$

where X_s are stayer characteristics and β_m are mover coefficients. Thus $\Delta Y = Y'_m - Y$ for movers and $\Delta Y = Y'_s - Y$ for stayers, where Y is actual earnings.

Table 8.10 contains an estimate of an equation system for earnings and migration. The second equation gives estimates of the factors determining the probability of moving. However the important factor, the estimated present value of the gain to moving, is determined by the first equation. Looking at this first equation, we see that migration brings a large gain of $5.6 an hour, other things equal, for those that embark on it. At the same time we see from the interaction terms that more tenured workers, and those with higher earnings in the origin achieve smaller benefits of migration. Professional workers however appear to achieve higher wage gains.

The predicted wage gain for each individual, as calculated using the first equation, is then substituted as an independent regressor into the second equation. This is the ΔY variable in the migration equation above. (Note that ΔY is calculated from a panel, so correcting for unmeasured individual heterogeneity.) Its positive coefficient demonstrates that migration increases as expected migration benefits rise, which is as predicted by the search model. Age lowers the chances of moving, as expected. However individuals who had moved in the previous year are *more* likely to move the next year. They should be less likely to move if they had been successful in their prior move, as required by the theory. The fact that some people are 'movers' has also been found in other studies (for example Cymrot *et al.*, 1987, 58). Further research probably needs lifetime job histories of individuals to capture the declining periodicity of moves over the life cycle.

Average values of ΔY for movers and stayers, as calculated above, are interesting. Male movers actually gained a wage increase of $3.30 an hour over the period 1971–5, but would have gained only $2.13 per hour if they had stayed. Non-movers would face a 65 cent loss had they moved, compared to a 55 cent gain in fact. Wives in families that moved face a loss of $1.63 per hour while wives in families that did not move would have had a loss of $1.21 had they moved. These results have implications with regard to family mobility. The rationale of family migration presumably depends upon the sum of the husband's and wife's expected gains. It is therefore reassuring to find that expected total family gains for movers are in general positive while being strongly negative for non-movers.

Table 8.10. *The determinants of geographic mobility*

$Y = 5.5 - 1.2\,Y\text{ origin} - 0.02\text{ Age} - 2.0\text{ Tenure} + 1.1\text{ Prof} + 5.6\text{ M}$
    (21.9)   (1.8)   (3.3)   (3.4)   (2.1)
    $- 2.0\text{ M*Y origin} - 0.2\text{ M*Tenure} + 14.9\text{ M*Prof,}$
    (3.3)   (1.7)   (7.8)

Prob $(M = 1) = -1.4 + 1.7\text{ Past migration} - 1.5\text{ Relatives} - 0.5\text{ OCW} - 0.03\text{ Age}$
                (1.4)   (3.3)   (1.5)   (1.2)
            $- 0.13\text{ EDW} + 0.05\,\Delta Y$
            (2.2)   (2.1)

Variable definitions
Y = present value of wage increases 1971–5, discounted at 6%
ΔY = hypothetical wage change as predicted from the wage equation
Past migration = moved in previous year, 1970–1
Relatives = relative in origin location
OCW = wife in non-menial job
Age = age of head
EDW = education of wife
Y origin = earnings in origin location in 1971
Tenure = tenure in job at origin
Prof = professional occupation
M = 1 denotes migration between states, 1971–2, 0 otherwise
M*Y = interaction between M and earnings at origin
M*Tenure = interaction between M and tenure on job at origin
M*Prof = interaction between M and whether one is in a professional occupation

---

Notes: The sample is 1,500 families remaining intact 1971–5. Migrants are those who crossed state lines in 1971–2. The migration regression is calculated as a logistic regression, so that an approximate measure of the impact of an independent variable on the probability of moving can be derived by dividing the coefficient by 4.
Source: Polachek and Horvath, 1977, 139.

8.4 Conclusions

Simple economic theory predicts a unique equilibrium in competitive markets. However, in the real world such equilibria are elusive. Labour markets typically contain considerable wage variation even when controlling for worker human capital differences.

This chapter argues that incomplete information explains at least part of these wage variations. Sequential and non-sequential search models were explored, both illustrating how efficient behaviour leads to incomplete information and hence rational ignorance. Factors affecting search costs and benefits were explored yielding theorems on search.

Incomplete information also has a bearing on frictional unemployment. Unemployment insurance can be seen as a way of subsidising search. States with the highest unemployment insurance subsidies tend to have the greatest unemployment. However, this does not necessarily mean that subsidising search is inefficient. For most groups it can be shown that more generous unemployment insurance and consequent greater unemployment duration leads to higher wages, implying more productive search.

The extent to which wages in a labour market vary is a gauge of the amount of information possessed by workers and firms. We were able to estimate the degrees of worker ignorance in various labour markets, and to show it varies in predictable ways given the costs and benefits of search for the various groups. We were also able to show how job changing has a life cycle aspect, with gains to movement declining with age and job tenure.

Appendix 8.1. Calculating the average maximum wage offer for the uniform distribution

The derivation goes as follows:
Assume that X_i is uniformly distributed on (a, b). Then the probability that a random drawing, X_i, is less than a given value, y, is:

$$\Pr(X_i < y) = (y - a)/(b - a).$$

The probability that the maximum of n drawings of X_i is less than y is the probability that all n of the X_i's are less than y, that is:

$$\Pr(X_1, X_2, \ldots, X_n < y) = \left(\frac{y - a}{b - a}\right)^n = F(y).$$

Here F is a cumulative density, that is it shows the probability of getting y or less. The probability of getting exactly y, the probability density of y, is:

$$g(y) = dF/dy = n(y - a)^{n-1}/(b - a)^n.$$

This is the distribution of maximum wage offers.
    The mean of y is:

$$E(y) = \int_a^b y\, g(y)\, dy.$$

This is best evaluated by transforming y such that:

$$y = a + (b - a)t \text{ (thus } y = b \text{ when } t = 1, \text{ and } y = a \text{ when } t = 0),$$

and integrating with respect to t, thus:

$$E(y) = \int_0^1 ((a + (b - a)t)n \frac{(a + (b - a)t)^{n-1}}{(b - a)^n} \, d(a + (b - a)t)$$

$$= (a + nb)/(n + 1).$$

The variance of y is calculated in a similar way. By the formula for the variance:

$$\sigma_y^2 = E(y^2) - (E(y))^2.$$

We have already calculated $E(y)$, so it remains to calculate $E(y^2)$:

$$E(y^2) = \int_a^b y^2 \, g(y) \, dy$$

$$= n\left[\frac{a^2}{n} + \frac{2a(b - a)}{n + 1} + \frac{(b - a)^2}{n + 2}\right].$$

It is instructive to simply set $b = 1$, and $a = 0$, so then:

$$\sigma_y^2 = n/(n + 2) - n^2/(n + 1)^2$$

$$= n/(n + 1)^2(n + 2).$$

This shows how the dispersion of observed wages, y, declines with increasing search.

Appendix 8.2 Evaluation of E(w| w ⩾ w*) for a uniform distribution

$$E(w| \geqslant w*) = \frac{\int_{w*}^b w \, f(w) \, dw}{\int_{w*}^b f(w) \, dw}$$

$$= \frac{\int_{w*}^b \dfrac{w}{b - a} \, dw}{\int_{w*}^b \dfrac{1}{b - a} \, dw}$$

$$= \frac{w^2}{2(b - a)} \left|\begin{array}{l} w = b \\ w = w* \end{array}\right. \div \frac{b - w*}{b - a}$$

$$= (b + w*)/2.$$

Thus for a given $w*$, the expected value of a random drawing of w is the average of b and $w*$.

9 Payment systems and internal labour markets

9.1 Introduction

Within the human capital framework studied so far, workers are paid according to their marginal product. Being paid according to productivity gives workers an incentive to invest in training, since training increases marginal product which in turn increases wages. The general training human capital model considered until now thus assumes individuals have a measure of control over their earnings. Armed with knowledge of interest rates and the wages associated with different jobs and career paths, individuals invest in schooling, on-the-job training, and information to maximise the present value of their earnings. Within this framework workers bear investment costs, but are able to reap all accrued benefits.

In many jobs, however, employers have considerable difficulty in assessing marginal product. Such conditions arise in at least three situations: (1) when the job entails team production so that the output of individual workers is not discernible; (2) when there are long delays in observing output, as for example in the case of research scientists; or (3) when the job entails numerous and varied tasks so that creating an output index is difficult, as is often the case for mid-level corporate managers.

In these instances, because worker output is difficult to measure, employees have an incentive to shirk. They fail to put forth as much effort as possible. After all, why work hard if you are not appreciated! It is in the employer's and the worker's interests to guard against such situations, because, if productivity is not observed then the best job matches are not made, firm output fails, and pay for all groups (high and low ability) falls.

Since it is in both the worker's and the firm's interest to maximise each worker's productivity, both parties will benefit from creating an environment with disincentives for shirking. Creating such an environment entails augmenting the human capital model to allow for a life-cycle contract, defining a wage payment scheme between workers and firms. The nature of such long-term contracts, and their consequences for the operation of labour markets, are the subject of this chapter.

9.2 The labour contract

Labour contracts differ from commodity contracts in at least two ways. Firstly, employment contracts involve workers being 'ordered about'. That is, in return for a wage and a necessarily implicit (i.e., not written down and enforceable in court) understanding of what will be required of him/her, the worker agrees to allow management to 'manage'. Labour contracts tend to have implicit terms because jobs are 'idiosyncratic' – only at high cost can many job details be fully described and effectively communicated – and the number of possible contract contingencies is large (Williamson, Wachter, and Harris, 1975, 261). Commodity contracts, by contrast, are specific: you buy this in return for that. Because labour contracts are necessarily less precise, 'agency' problems arise.

An agency relation is where the 'principal' engages another person, the 'agent', to perform some service on the principal's behalf which involves delegating some decision-making authority to the agent (Jensen and Meckling, 1976, 308). The principal has to limit divergence from his/her interest by establishing certain incentives, and by monitoring: measuring and observing the agent, and devising budgetary restrictions and operating rules. Agents, for their part, have to try and show they will not harm the principal. Agents thus attempt to 'invest' in the relationship, for example by training in skills only useful to the principal, so as to exhibit a desire for cooperation – indeed, 'consummate cooperation' (Williamson et al., 1975, 266).

The agency problem is quite pervasive; it could even be the rationale for the capitalistic business firm (Alchian and Demsetz, 1972). Here the owner is himself 'monitored' – prevented from shirking – by being the residual income claimant in the firm. The owner in turn devises ways to monitor his employees. According to Alchian and Demsetz the owner in fact earns his rewards principally by controlling shirking in team production, so raising marginal product and thus earnings for all in the team. Other examples of the agency relation are separation of ownership from control in the firm (how do the shareholders control their agents, the managers?), and the relation between the professional (doctor, lawyer, plumber) and his or her client.

The second way in which labour contracts differ from commodity contracts is that labour contracts tend to be of long duration. Commodity contracts generally give rise to 'spot' or 'auction' market prices. Such transactions are generally completed quickly, given fair dealing. But most people are in jobs which last for years. In Britain the length of job of the average person is 20.7 years for males, and 12.2 years for women. This is shown in table 9.1. A similar figure obtains for America, and for Japan, as can be seen.

Table 9.1. *Eventual tenure in Britain, the United States, and Japan*

Group	Tenure
UK, All industries: males	20.7 years
females	12.2 years
US, Private sector industry:	
males	15.6 (9.6) years
Japan, Private sector industry:	
males	25.0 (23.6) years

Notes: Figures in parenthesis give estimated eventual tenure in small firms with 1–10 workers.
Sources: UK – Main, 1981, 158; US and Japan – Hashimoto and Raisian, 1985, 726.

The pattern of job changing over the life cycle is given in table 9.2, using the 1983 General Household Survey, and the methodology developed by R. E. Hall (1982). Hall's results show that the average US worker (male or female) has only about ten jobs in a lifetime, the last one being found by about age forty-five (Hall, 1982, 723). Analysis of the British data indicates even less job changing: about seven (eight) jobs are held in the life of the average male (female), the last one being found by the age of about forty. The typical labour contract lasts as long as the typical marriage.

Turnover statistics admittedly usually indicate short jobs. For example turnover rates in British manufacturing are about 30% a year, implying that the average job only lasts about three years. But the length of an *average job* is a misleading statistic. The average is brought down by the mobile sector of the workforce having many short jobs. Thus while the *average job* might be of short duration, the job of the *average person* lasts a long time. For example, suppose the workforce consisted of ten people, each working for forty years. Suppose five have twenty jobs each, all lasting two years (0.5 job changes a year), while five have one job each, lasting forty years (0.025 changes a year). The average length of a job is:

$$\frac{5 \times 20 \text{ jobs} \times 2 \text{ years} + 5 \times 1 \text{ job} \times 40 \text{ years}}{105 \text{ jobs}} = 3.8 \text{ years.}$$

(Average turnover is $0.5 \times 0.5 + 0.5 \times 0.025 = 0.265 = 1/3.8$ jobs a year.) The job of the average person lasts:

$$\frac{5 \text{ people} \times 2 \text{ years} + 5 \text{ people} \times 40 \text{ years}}{10 \text{ people}} = 21 \text{ years.}$$

Table 9.2. *Estimates of the number of jobs in a lifetime, males, UK and US*

| Age group | % in new job[a] | New jobs over age interval[b] | Cumulated number of jobs | |
			UK	US[c]
16–19	70%	2.1 jobs	2.1 jobs	2.7 jobs
20–4	29	1.2	3.4	4.1
25–9	15	0.6	4.0	5.8
30–4	14	0.6	4.6	7.0
35–9	14	0.6	5.2	7.9
40–4	14	0.6	5.8	8.7
45–9	5	0.2	6.0	9.3
50–4	10	0.4	6.4	9.8
55–9	5	0.2	6.6	10.2
60–4	7	0.3	6.9	10.5

Notes:
[a] This column gives the fraction of the age group with a job lasting a year or less. It is estimated as twice the fraction of those with tenure under 6 months (the assumption being that on average these will be observed halfway through their jobs).
[b] This column multiplies the first column by the age range. Thus on average those 16–19 have 0.7 jobs a year, or 2.1 jobs over the 3 years between 16 and 19.
[c] This column gives corresponding figures from Hall, 1982, 723.
Sources: UK – General Household Survey, 1983, unpublished data; US – Hall, 1982.

The reason for this peculiar result is that some people move a lot, others hardly at all. If all workers were identical, the two measures would coincide.

The preponderance of lengthy jobs underlines the importance of the 'internal labour market', that is labour market rules favouring long tenure, promotion from within, seniority, pensions, and 'due process' in dismissals. With such long-term relationships, the parties have to forecast the future (make 'contingent' contracts). Thus wages will generally not be set with current conditions in mind. This gives rise to 'sticky' wages, and violates the equality of spot wages with spot marginal product.

Some idea of the extent of internal labour markets can be gauged by the distribution of employment by firm size. Only the larger firms can (or need) develop their own enterprise markets. For example, a firm has to be above a certain size before it can establish a job evaluation system; about 500 has been taken to be the employment cut-off point here (Smith, 1988), though admittedly many firms as small as 100 have forms of job evaluation. In addition, contract theories, as we will see, require that a firm be sufficiently long-lived and 'visible' to have a credible reputation. Such firms have to be 'very large', with over 1,000 workers according to Walter Oi (1983, 64). Since firm size is a continuum, however, there can be no definite dividing line.

Not all workers in large firms will be members of internal labour markets. We can reasonably eliminate the seasonal, casual and temporary workers. We can probably also ignore most part-timers, since their tenure is too uncertain to allow of specific training. In fact large firms make little use of part-timers (perhaps for this reason). The public–private sector distinction is also helpful: it can be assumed that most full-time public sector employees are in an internal labour market of some sort. Using this methodology, a rough approximation of the size of internal labour markets in Britain is about half of the workforce (Siebert and Addison, 1991, 77); a comparable estimate for the US is 40 per cent (Oi, 1983, 105).

As we will show, the different types of wage payment system, and other features of the labour market such as long-term jobs and pensions, can be viewed as attempts to solve the problem of monitoring worker effort. Firms devise payment systems and 'governance structures' so that workers have an incentive to work hard without being explicitly supervised.

The governance structure in the long-term contract is designed to forestall individual 'opportunism' (Williamson *et al.*, 1975). Opportunism arises because of the problem of small numbers: in situations where workers acquire job specific skills, they come to enjoy an advantage over outsiders. They can hoard that knowledge to their personal advantage because the self-policing benefits of competition, or *large numbers exchange*, are lacking. A governance structure is required to ensure cooperation between groups within the firm.

The governance structure could have many of the features of a stylised internal labour market. In order to reward cooperative behaviour, access to higher level positions is not open, but restricted to those already working for the firm. Grievance procedures are set up to cover gaps in the incomplete contract, so that individuals' claims are not allowed to endanger group interests. In such a structured internal labour market, the repeated nature of transactions discourages opportunistic behaviour by either party (Wachter and Wright, 1990, 251–2).

In addition, given lack of competition within the internal labour market, unions could have a part to play as a 'contract cost reducing' institution (Klein *et al.*, 1978, 315). Unions might monitor the sharing of rents from specific capital investment, and are also part of the grievance procedure which subordinates individual to group interests (Williamson *et al.*, 1975, 277). It is important to note however that the unions envisaged here are independent enterprise unions such as in Japan (which has about 30,000 enterprise unions), and not industrial-type, multi-firm unions. Multi-firm bargaining and concomitant industry-wide strike threats are not needed for monitoring within-firm agreements.

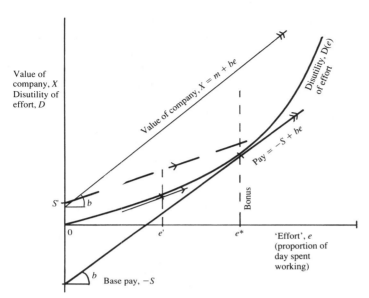

Figure 9.1 Bonus payments

9.3 Piece rates and the principal agent problem

Piece rates, or bonus schemes, are the most obvious way to raise worker effort, so long as output can be measured. Piece rates simply relate pay to output, so the question of monitoring is less important. However if output cannot be measured, then a salary must be paid – that is, pay will be according to input (time) – but monitoring will then be required to ensure that work is done.

Piece rate pay for a given job is likely to be higher than time rates of pay for the same job. There are two reasons: (a) paying by the piece will induce greater effort, and this effort must be paid for if workers are to consent to be paid by the piece; and (b) paying by the piece gives rise to a more variable income than paying by time, and this extra variability should give rise to a compensating differential.

A diagram applicable to piece rates is given in figure 9.1. Assume the individual's contribution to the value of the company, X, depends upon his/her effort, e, thus:

$$X = m + be,$$

where b is a parameter signifying the person's impact on the value of the company, and m is a constant. Presumably b will be a small positive number for most people. Now draw in a disutility of effort line, $D(e)$. A person has to be paid at least D if it is to be worthwhile for him/her to work. What the firm should do is pay the worker D, and maximise profit per worker, $X - D$, that is, move to point e^*. Supposing effort can be measured, for example by number of pieces made, point e^* can be attained by paying the worker a piece rate based on their contribution to the company, be^*, coupled with a negative basic pay amount, $-S$, as shown. At e^* the worker is doing the best he/she can, and the firm is also doing the best it can. In the case of company chief executives, e might be proxied by movement in the share price, in which case a bonus based on this would be the most cost effective way to elicit effort.

The diagram shows how linking pay to output will result in extra effort, and also how this extra effort requires a compensating extra payment. In practice admittedly we do not see a very close connection between a person's pay and the value of the firm even where this would seem to be natural as in the case of senior management (see next section). Nor do we see individuals accepting sizeable negative basic salaries. In practice we are more likely to see positive base salaries such as S', and a flatter bonus line (shown dashed). This will give rise to a lower effort level, e', and lower profits per worker. Presumably a strict pay schedule like $-S + be$ is not applicable because of the difficulty of measuring b, and the fact that the value of the company, X, depends on much besides the effort of the employees. If X is low in one period, through no fault of the worker(s) in question, bonuses will be low. To limit the 'down-side risk', associated with the variability of bonuses, a positive basic salary is required.

The extra effort associated with piece rate pay and the extra variability has been analysed by Eric Seiler using US data for production workers in the footwear and men's suits and coats industries, both of which use piece rates for about 75% of their production workforce (Seiler, 1984, 367). The distributions of earnings in the two industries by method of wage payment are shown in figure 9.2. In both industries incentive workers' average pay is somewhat higher – in fact, about 14% higher holding constant occupation, region, firm size, sex, and unionisation, *inter alia* (Seiler, 1984, 375). (Phelps Brown notes that in Soviet-type economies, as well, piece rate workers are paid more for the same job – a figure of 16% is quoted for Soviet engineering (1977, 50).) Pay is also more variable for the piece raters, as is shown by the wider dispersion of their earnings distribution. However it is not *much* more variable. The implication is that most of the difference in income as between piece and time rates is a compensating differential for extra effort rather than for extra income variability.

Piece rate payment schemes cover a substantial proportion of the production worker workforce, though the proportion has been declining – and white-

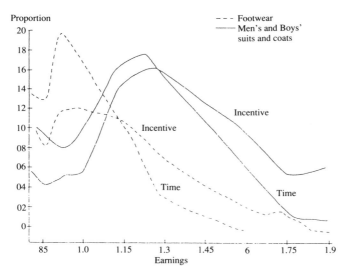

Figure 9.2 Frequency distributions of earnings by method of wage payment. *Source:* Seiler, 1984, 368

collar workers are much less likely to be paid by the piece. Among production workers in US manufacturing, about 20% were on incentive schemes in the 1970s, compared with 25% in the previous decade (Carlson, 1982, 17). In Britain in the 1980s, about 40% of manual males and 30% of manual females received some of their pay on a payments by results basis. The fraction of white-collar workers paid by results was less than a half of this. For most groups of workers on piece rates it is unusual for the bonus element to amount to more than 10% to 15% of pay (Department of Employment, New Earnings Survey).

Important factors influencing choice of piece rate payment schemes include capital intensity and firm size. In a capital-intensive production process (vehicles, chemicals) workers are likely to have less control over the pace of production. Workers can also damage machinery by working too fast. Therefore in a capital-intensive environment piece rates are likely to give the wrong incentives.

At the same time, large firms are more likely to have piece rates (Parsons, 1986, 805). In a large firm, direct supervision will be less effective than in a small firm in which management is closer to the workforce. Consequently it pays to redesign jobs in large firms in order to make output more measurable, and so payable by the piece.

9.4 Promotion as an incentive – the 'tournament'

Instead of relating pay to performance with a piece rate payment scheme, the link can be made via a promotion system: the better performers are promoted, and this up-grading carries with it an increase in pay. Promotion in fact seems more popular than piece rates as a way of rewarding – and thus encouraging – performance. In fact even in the case of Chief Executive Officers, where a good measure of performance is available in the form of the movement of the company's stock price, the link between performance (stock price) and pay seems to be weak. Rather, CEOs' pay seems based primarily on the size of their firm. CEOs receive a large increase in pay when promoted, and it has been hypothesised (Lazear and Rosen, 1981, 847) that it is the competition for promotion – the 'tournament' – which generates incentives among the middle managers to work hard. We might still ask, however, why there is little emphasis on pay-for-performance compensation policies, and more emphasis on promotion.

The salary of CEOs should be related to the profits they generate (to overcome the agency problem). This would be a form of payment by results. An investment project should be undertaken whenever expected returns are greater than costs. If a manager bears the costs in terms of effort, but does not benefit, he/she will not undertake the project, so some profitable projects will be bypassed. Moreover tying pay to performance would have beneficial self-selection effects since only those people will become managers who can perform (those who cannot perform would receive low pay).

A relation between executive compensation and share price certainly exists, though there is controversy over whether it is strong enough. American results show that the average chief executive officer (CEO) in major manufacturing companies receives a rise of about 3 cents in salary and bonuses for every $1,000 of increased shareholder wealth (Jensen and Murphy, 1986, 13). UK results are similar, with an 8p rise in CEO pay (not including the value of share options) for an increase of £1,000 in company value, holding company size constant (Main, 1991, 223). Including the value of the CEO's stockholding in his firm, the relation naturally becomes stronger. The wealth of the average CEO in this sample increases by $6 for every $1,000 increase in shareholder wealth (the median CEO owned $1.4 million of stock, measured in 1985 $s). Thus CEO holdings in their own companies are likely to provide important additional incentive effects. It is interesting to note however that companies in which the CEO has a small stockholding do not seem to 'make up' for this by tying his pay more closely to company performance. The question therefore arises in these companies as to why the executive pay–performance link is not stronger.

There also seems to be a clear relationship between executive salary and firm size. This can be given a performance interpretation in that size of firm might index the complexity of the management job, and also its responsibilities. The executive pay–firm size relationship has even been crystallised into a rule by compensation consultants: 'As sales volume doubles, executive pay increases by one third' (cited in Baker *et al.*, 1988, 610). The rule is in fact borne out in both American and British data. The elasticity of executive salary plus bonus with respect to firm sales is approximately 0.3 for a wide range of US industries, and for several time periods (Baker *et al.*, 1988, 609). Thus a firm which is 100% bigger than another firm has a CEO who is 30% better paid. The British figure seems of a similar magnitude. Looking at the 192 largest British firms in 1989 (1990 Korn Ferry International compensation survey), for example, median earnings for the top executive were £120 thousand in companies with sales around £300 million, and about 90% larger than this (£226 thousand) in companies with sales three times larger (around £1,000 million). Main's recent British study finds a similar size effect, but it is worth noting that size becomes much less important when company profitability is allowed for (1991, table 2).

For executives, in fact, salary prospects depend primarily upon promotion, rather than company performance. In a sample of 105 large US firms average pay of the CEO was $800 thousand, and of the top Vice Presidents only $372 thousand (O'Reilly *et al.*, 1988, 264). Indeed, as noted above, for most people piece rate pay is only a small fraction of total pay, say 10%, and promotion makes much more of an impact on pay. Hence the question posed above, of why there is the emphasis on promotion rather than merit pay or piece rates as a means of generating incentives.

A model of how promotion increases effort is as follows (see Lazear and Rosen, 1981). We can imagine two middle managers, say, vying for promotion. Neither they nor the firm knows in advance who is best – managers' output is determined by effort plus a random 'ability' factor, and both have the same expected effort. If the one with the highest output is promoted and rewarded with a high wage, then both will have an incentive to work hard so as to increase the probability of winning. The manager's expected wage is:

$$E(W) = PW_1 + (1 - P)W_2 - D(e)$$

where W_1 is the wage received on promotion, W_2 is the base wage, P is the probability of winning, and $D(e)$ is the disutility of effort function. If we make the probability of winning depend on effort, say $P = ae$ where a is a factor showing how much impact effort has on promotion, then $E(W)$ becomes:

$$E(W) = W_2 + (W_1 - W_2)ae - D(e).$$

Choosing e to maximise $E(W)$ gives:

$$d\mathrm{E}(W)/de = (W_1 - W_2)a - D'(e) = 0, \text{ or } (W_1 - W_2)a = D'(e),$$

which shows that the spread in prizes $W_1 - W_2$ increases effort, *ceteris paribus*. In this simple model, a positive spread is required to bring about any effort.

The eventual size of the promotion 'first prize', W_1, that comes about will be determined by the effect of pay on the competitors' effort. We might assume, as is natural, that effort increases with the prize, but at a decreasing rate. Then it can be seen that, after a point, as W_1 rises effort will rise less than proportionately, so that managerial labour costs per efficiency unit will begin to rise. This will put a limit on W_1. (In golf, the winner takes about 18% of the purse, second place 10%, down to 20th with 1% – Ehrenberg *et al.*, 1990.)

The tournament promotion scheme might offer several advantages over piece rate systems. In the first place information requirements are smaller. Instead of having to measure output as such, only *relative* performance – order within the grade – is required. Relatedly, measuring performance at a few discrete promotion points in a person's career could be easier than attempting to measure performance all the time. Secondly, risk from the worker's point of view is smaller. A contest reduces all possibilities to simply gaining or not gaining a prize. Were pay more closely related to output, as in an ordinary piece rate system, the 'down-side risk' – the chance of gaining a very small wage – might be judged too high. Thirdly, a promotion based system only identifies 'winners' without explicitly identifying 'losers'. People can feel they were passed over for promotion without feeling too badly about it, which makes the system easier to bear both for the judgers and the judged.

There are several difficulties with promotion as an incentive device, too. Firstly, once promoted, individuals might rest on their laurels. This is particularly true at the top of the hierarchy: promotion by definition cannot motivate the CEO. This makes more necessary the development of a performance pay relationship for the CEO. Secondly, promotion incentives will not work for those who have been repeatedly passed over, and who have given up hope of ever having a placing in the promotion tournament. In golf or yachting tournaments, for example, the device of handicapping is used to overcome this problem. In the labour market, promotion according to seniority (a head start for older workers even though they might be less productive) could be an example of efficient handicapping. Another solution is to require the person who has failed to gain promotion to leave. This is observed in professional partnerships, and research universities. Thirdly, promotion requires organisational growth to feed the system. A firm might therefore be tempted to engage in unprofitable growth so as to feed its promotion-based incentive system (Baker *et al.*, 1988, 600). Finally, where the best performers at one level are not the best performers at another, promotion will lower efficiency by not matching individuals to jobs. For example, where the best sales person is not good at management, promotion out of sales will weaken both the sales and management teams.

9.5 Efficiency wages

The model

The discussion above has shown some of the problems in linking pay to performance, whether via piece rates, or via promotion tournaments. The problems are particularly acute in large firms where the 'arms length' relationship between management and workers prevents managers accurately assessing worker performance. Indeed it is generally found that large firms pay more for observationally equivalent workers than do small firms. Thus, using British data we find that plants employing 1,000 or more pay 8% more than small plants (employing 100 or less), holding constant the usual human capital variables plus occupation and industry (Siebert and Addison, 1991, 81). Similar results are found using US data (Mellow, 1982; Idson and Feaster, 1990).

Admittedly it is not certain that large firms pay more for labour than small, because we can never measure ability. The cause of the differential could be the higher (unmeasured) ability of workers in large firms. Nevertheless, Stigler (1962, 102) has hypothesised that smaller firms will suffer less 'control loss' and consequently be better managed than large. Consequently small firms are likely more easily to recognise and reward ability. This does appear to be the case – IQ, a measure of ability, has more impact on pay in small firms than large (Garen, 1985, 731). Hence workers in large firms should be less rather than more able, other things being equal, which implies that large firms must be genuinely overpaying their workers. Large firms tend to hire the more educated worker, particularly for white-collar jobs – presumably because their greater monitoring problems require the hiring of more productive (educated) managerial workers (Oi, 1983, 90).

However it is possible that it is efficient (cost-minimising) for large firms to pay more for given skills than smaller firms. One line of argument is that a firm will decide to pay more than the worker's alternative wage so as to generate a 'penalty' arising from dismissal. The implication is that high wages increase worker effort, and allow the firm therefore to economise on supervisor time. This has been called the 'efficiency wage' model. If the model is correct then unemployment also increases worker effort (because it reduces the alternative wage), so firms in a sense need – or at least make use of – unemployment.

A diagram illustrating how high wages increase effort is given in figure 9.3. Assume that a person has the option of shirking which is measured by $1 - e$, where e is between 0 and 1 (e can be thought of as the fraction of a day spent working, so $1 - e$ is the fraction of a day spent not working, that is, shirking). Let $D(e)$ be the disutility of effort function already encountered in figure 9.2.

Suppose that the firm pays foremen to detect shirking, and consequently there is some probability, C, of being detected in shirking. The probability, P, of being dismissed is the probability of shirking times the probability of being detected, that is:

$$P = (1 - e)C.$$

Assume the person earns W in the firm and B outside the firm (B is the alternative wage or unemployment pay). Then the person's expected utility from income, $E(U(Y))$ is:

$$E(U(Y)) = (1 - P)U(W) + P\,U(B),$$

where U denotes the utility function. The equation gives the average of $U(W)$ and $U(B)$, with weights being the probability of being dismissed and of remaining – the weights must add up to one. Rewriting:

$$E(U(Y)) = \underbrace{CU(B) + (1 - C)U(W)}_{\text{intercept}} + \underbrace{C(U(W) - U(B))}_{\text{slope}}\, e.$$

This is a straight line showing how expected utility of income varies with effort, with intercept and slope as shown. It is graphed in figure 9.3. Faced with W, C, and B, the worker can be thought of as selecting effort, e, so as to maximise the expected utility from income minus the disutility of effort.

As can be seen, e^* will be chosen so that the slopes of the two curves are the same. This means that the marginal disutility of effort will equal its marginal utility in increasing pay. Increasing the wage the firm pays, W, will increase the slope of the $E(U(Y))$ curve, and result in a higher e. Higher wages thus increase effort. Similarly, increasing the amount of supervision C will increase effort. Notice how, due to the increasing slope of the $D(e)$ curve, a given increase in pay elicits less extra effort, the higher effort is. Also note how if $W = B$, $e = 0$, that is, wages have to be higher than the worker's alternative to induce any effort at all. If $W = B$, then the dismissal threat is empty, and in this simple model workers do not then put forth any effort.

From a 'sociological' viewpoint, it has also been argued that paying wages above what is strictly necessary increases worker effort – because a 'gift' from the firm elicits a 'gift' from the work group in the form of extra effort. As an example of the gift idea, in a piece rate system poor performers are often not penalised by their employer, because this would disturb fellow workers: workers 'gain utility if the firm relaxes pressure on workers who are hard pressed; in return for reducing such pressure, better workers are often willing to work harder' (Akerlof, 1982, 550). Thus there are various ways of explaining how increased pay can increase effort.

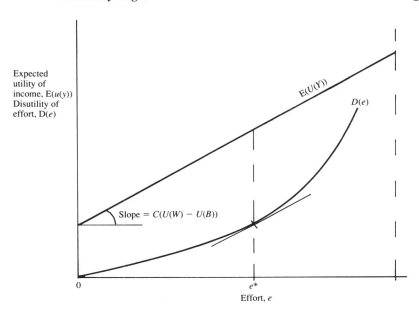

Figure 9.3 Selecting effort, given W, B, C and preferences

Just because wages increase effort, wages will not necessarily be sky-high. What wage the firm will set (and what will be spent on supervision), will be given by the link between wages and effort, and the contribution of effort to profits. We can think of the firm as selecting W so as to minimise labour costs per efficiency unit. Labour costs per efficiency unit can be written as $h = W/e(W)$ where W is the wage, and $e(W)$ signifies that effort is a function of the wage as we have shown (for simplicity take C, the probability of being detected shirking, and B, the unemployment benefit level as unchanging). A unit of effort can be thought of as the amount that can be done in a day when $e = 1$. To minimise h the firm chooses W so that $dh/dW = 0$, giving:

$$(e - Wde/dW) = 0, \text{ and so } dW/W = de/e.$$

Thus at the minimum, the firm chooses W so that the percentage change in the wage equals the percentage change in effort.

Implications

The first implication of the efficiency wage model is that, in hard to monitor situations (large firms), workers will be paid more than the minimum they will work for. Consequently a queue of workers at the factory gate will not pull wages down. The queue is necessary for the employed to be motivated to work. According to this model, unemployment is part of the system of 'worker discipline' (Shapiro and Stiglitz, 1984).

Secondly, unemployment benefits will raise the natural rate of unemployment not by reducing incentives to search (the usual reason), but by lowering the 'penalty' from being fired. To compensate for higher unemployment benefits, firms have to raise their wages, which reduces their labour demand.

Thirdly, it is said that employer discrimination will become easier, because discrimination might not have such a negative effect on profits (Malcolmson, 1981). This follows because firms have queues of workers wanting to become employees, so there might be several equally well qualified male and female candidates for the job. The firm's managers can then afford to indulge their preferences for male employees, for example, without much penalty.

Backing up the model, it has been claimed that, when unemployment is high, people do indeed work harder. A 'cost of job loss' index has been calculated (Weisskopf, Gordon, and Bowles, 1983, 404):

$$\text{'Cost of job loss'} = \text{Unemp} \times (W - B)/W,$$

where Unemp is the fraction of a year the average unemployed person is unemployed, and W and B are average wages and average unemployment benefits respectively. The bigger the index, the bigger is the earnings cost if a job is lost. This index seems to be positively related to changes in aggregate labour productivity, other things equal, suggesting that when unemployment goes up, people work harder – supporting the efficiency wage theory.

Note how, according to specific capital theory (see below), we expect labour productivity to go *down* when unemployment is high, because firms 'hoard' workers with specific training at such times. Thus the positive relation between the 'cost of job loss' index and labour productivity goes against human capital theory. However, Weisskopf *et al.* need to hold 'capacity utilisation' constant to obtain their positive relation between the cost of job loss index (unemployment) and labour productivity. Capacity utilisation in fact moves closely in line with labour productivity. This backs up human capital theory: when capacity utilisation is low and machines are idled, trained men are also idled so they can be used later in the upturn, and labour productivity is consequently low. So the relationship between 'cost of job loss', unemployment and labour productivity is a complicated one, which could well admit of other explanations than efficiency wages.

The fact that large firms pay more for observationally equivalent labour than do small has also been said to support the efficiency wage idea, as we have seen. The argument is that it is the large firms which have the 'arms length' relationship with their workers – making supervision difficult – and they thus require an efficiency wage policy (Kreuger and Summers, 1988). Accompanying the tendency for large firms to overpay is the fact that large firms – whether union or non-union – are less likely than small to stress individual 'merit' when setting pay. Large firms tend to use seniority-based systems (and sometimes piece rates, as noted above). Thus in a study of about 1,500 union and 1,700 non-union firms, Brown (1990, 178-S) finds that the percentage of a firm's workforce on seniority pay arrangements decreases by 4 points for every 10% decrease in establishment size in the non-union sample. (In the union sample there is little variation by firm size, with seniority important even in small firms.) The tendency to overpay workers in large firms – as is implied by the stress on seniority pay – could be given an efficiency wage justification if the overpayment increases effort.

An objection to the argument immediately arises, however, in that job tenure in the large firm is usually so long that it is difficult to argue that the dismissal threat on which the efficiency wage model is based has much credibility. Some believe that it is rather in the *secondary*, small firm, sector that dismissal is an important employee motivator (Rebitzer, 1989, 28). Perhaps however the efficiency wage theorist could bolster the model by saying that promotion/ demotion acts in lieu of the dismissal threat in the large firm.

The major objection to the efficiency wage hypothesis however is that it ignores life-cycle considerations. It is possible to construct a pay scheme where a worker receives more than his/her alternative wage later in the life cycle, but less earlier. In this case the present value of the earnings are not worth more than the present value of alternative earnings, so markets clear. At the same time the motivating power of the dismissal threat is retained, because for much of the time wages are above alternative wages. This is now shown.

9.6 Deferred compensation

A payment scheme in which a person was initially paid lower than his/her alternative wage, and only later, after having proven to be hard-working was paid more, would motivate workers (Becker and Stigler, 1974). The initial low earning period is sometimes called the period when the worker 'posts a bond'. This bond is paid back later in the form of high wages and a pension. In addition it can be seen that it would be more worthwhile for stable individuals to post such a bond. Such workers would 'self-select', i.e., be more likely to present themselves to the firm than below average individuals.

Notice that for such payment schemes to work it is necessary for the worker involved to be assured of stable employment (otherwise the bond would not be repaid). Hence a long-term contract must be guaranteed, as least implicitly. Moreover once we have long-term relationships, workers and employers are tied together, insulated, as it were, from the external labour market. An 'internal labour market' arises. Hence there is an element of bargaining even in situations without unions. Competition does not decide at all.

An illustration of an earnings profile which would discourage shirking is given in figure 9.4. The alternative wage line BF is shown horizontal for simplicity. It is easiest to assume it also equals marginal product. Then if in the first year the worker is only paid OA, a loan of AB is effectively made to the firm. In succeeding years the worker can be paid the interest, BC, on the bond. Then in the worker's final year the bond is returned as a pension DE. The effort problem is solved since a worker will not wish to shirk for fear of being dismissed and of losing the bond and associated interest. Earnings path ABCDE will be made to have the same present value as the alternative earnings and marginal productivity path, BF. This is necessary if the firm and the worker are to be indifferent between the two paths. Thus in this case the worker is not paid more than his/her alternative wage, taking account of the worker's tenure with the firm as a whole.

Note how the pension is a necessary part of the incentive scheme. Without it, the threat of dismissal would become increasingly less painful as the worker neared retirement. Various other paths are possible (see Lazear, 1981, 611) – for example the worker could be paid less than MP all his/her life, and compensated by having an extra large pension. This would also obviate shirking.

Note also how the date of retirement, T, has to be agreed upon in advance in this model. Retirement is required because older workers will generally be earning more than their marginal product, and alternative wage, and so will not want to leave (Lazear, 1979b).

It is necessary however to consider the possibility of firm default. The firm may try and cheat by declaring that the workers have shirked (and who will know they have not?) and thereby collect their performance bonds (Shapiro and Stiglitz, 1984, 442). A fair termination would require severance pay. Against this it has been argued that, if firms cheat they will lose 'reputation', and workers will not post bonds. The W line will be less steep (see figure 9.5), the present value of lifetime MP will be lower, contracts will be shorter (T will be smaller), and the firm less profitable. This should be a deterrent at least for the large 'visible' firm. Nevertheless it has been surmised (Lazear and Moore, 1984) that the possibility of a firm dishonestly laying a worker off early stops the wage line becoming very steep (as will borrowing constraints for the worker). There is a happy medium between flat and steep wage lines.

According to the model, the slope of earnings profiles originates in part from the need to provide incentives to work in circumstances where output is hard to measure. If the theory is true we would expect earnings to increase less over the life cycle for the self-employed, who do not have the monitoring problem (they monitor themselves). It has been argued that this is the case (Lazear and Moore, 1984, 278). Doctors, for example, have high present values of earnings,

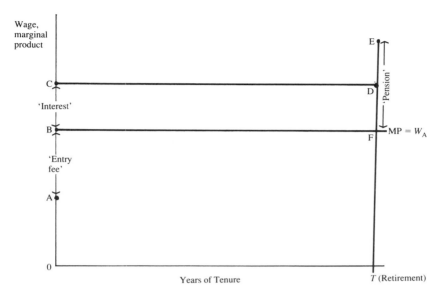

Figure 9.4 Deferred compensation pay scheme

yet the slope of their earnings profiles is small. Piece rate workers also have flatter earnings profiles. This can be explained in terms of the fact that their output is by definition easy to measure, so the incentive structure of a deferred pay scheme is not required.

There is other evidence consistent with the deferred compensation model. The fact that some labour contracts place mandatory retirement ages on employees is consistent with older workers being paid more than their marginal product. There is also the fact that pension schemes are often constructed so as to encourage early retirement (see chapter 5). Furthermore, it is common for firms in Britain to provide additional severance or redundancy pay over and above statutory provisions (Booth, 1987). Such payments can be rationalised as repaying a worker's investment where the long-term contract has come to a premature end, and are part of the 'due process' in dismissals characteristic of internal labour markets. Again, we find (non-vested) pensions to be an important part of large firms' payment policies. For example in Britain only about half the full-time male workers in small (less than 100 employees) firms have a company pension, compared to nearly all the workers in large (over 1,000 employees) firms (Siebert and Addison, 1991, table 4). In the US highly repetitive jobs have a lower likelihood of a pension, and also less likelihood of mandatory retirement (Hutchens, 1987). This backs up the view that pensions are an aspect of the deferred pay incentive scheme, since such a scheme is more necessary in the large firm with its arms length relationship with the workforce.

Finally, the prediction of the deferred pay model, that wages rise faster with tenure than does productivity, in fact seems to be borne out in some cases. Medoff and Abraham's (1981) analysis of several large firms found that, while workers' pay rises the longer they remain within a grade, their productivity within that grade – as measured by their supervisor's performance evaluation – hardly rises at all. It must be said however that supervisors' ratings are not very reliable indicators of productivity. Thus different supervisors rating the same worker give ratings which correlate only 0.6, and supervisor ratings correlate poorly, 0.27 to 0.42, with actual performance in experiments in which this is carefully measured (Bishop, 1987, S38). Moreover supervisor ratings cannot address the productivity of those who move between grades, which is also an important aspect of productivity.

9.7 Specific training

The theory of specific human capital can also provide an explanation of many of the features of labour contracts in large firms. In the specific human capital model, employment has fixed costs: the worker and the firm invest in hiring and screening (Oi, 1962), and then in knowledge specific to the firm – the 'firm's particular circumstances of time and place' (Williamson *et al.*, 1975, 251). As we noted above (chapter 4), it is necessary for the firm and worker to share in both costs and returns in order to engender the correct incentives for neither party to interrupt the investment process with a premature quit or dismissal (see Becker, 1975).

The specific human capital model requires long-term (implicit) contracts, and self-selection of stable employees. It differs from the deferred compensation model however in requiring that a worker's marginal product rises faster with tenure than does his/her wage. This is illustrated in figure 9.5. Panel A gives simplified linear earnings profiles for the specific training model (for a fuller explanation see figure 4.2 in chapter 4 above). Panel B is a variant of figure 9.4, and illustrates how wages rise more (not less) steeply than marginal product in the deferred compensation case.

The tenure implications differ between the specific training and the deferred pay models. In the specific training contract both quit and layoff probabilities should diminish as tenure increases. Post-training wages are above the wage available in other firms thus reducing quits, and worker productivity exceeds worker wages thus reducing layoffs. Hence we would expect to see both quit and layoff rates diminish with tenure, which we do (Parsons, 1986, 828). This is not necessarily the case for the deferred pay model. Here in the post-bond period, since wages exceed marginal product, workers have no incentive to

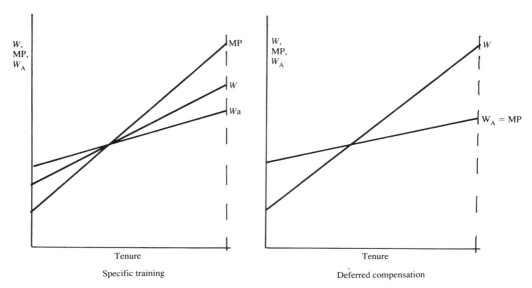

Figure 9.5 Specific training and deferred compensation compared

quit. However, layoff probabilities are enhanced as the wedge between wage and marginal product grows – even requiring, as noted, mandatory retirement. The only force preventing premature layoff in the deferred compensation model is firms' fear of tarnishing their reputation. The incentive structure of the specific human capital model seems more plausible.

Against the human capital model, as an alternative explanation for why wages increase on the job, selectivity and 'matching' arguments have been raised (Altonji and Shakotko (1987), and Abraham and Farber (1987)). The selectivity argument is that the higher ability workers will be promoted and stay with the firm, implying that the more tenured workers are the more able. Thus longer tenure workers are better paid not because their productivity rises with time on the job, but because they are of higher quality than the less tenured. A similar problem arises when some workers, by luck or judgement, make better 'job matches' than others. A good job match is likely to last longer than a bad one. Thus by comparing high with low tenured workers one might be comparing high ability or good job match workers to their lower ability or poor match counterparts. For this reason it is argued that cross-sectional studies overstate the tenure–wage gradient (see also Addison et al., 1989).

The appropriate strategy to hold constant unmeasured individual character-istics such as ability is by utilising panel data. Here the same individuals are followed over several time periods, and the change in wage related to the change in tenure for the given individual. The main US panel dataset is the Panel Survey of Income Dynamics (PSID), which has been following some 6,000 families since 1968.

Using PSID data for white males for 1968–83, Robert Topel estimates the combined effect of tenure and experience, eliminating special job effects (good matches) and individual effects (ability), by relating changes in earnings to changes in tenure for those *not* changing jobs. He finds that such within-job wage growth is about 12% for the first year of tenure for the new entrant (zero experience), falling for those with more experience (it is about 6.5% in the first year of tenure for those with ten years of experience) (Topel, 1991, table 2). He then estimates the effects of experience alone on earnings by regressing earnings on experience for those starting new jobs (and for whom tenure is thus zero). Since the return to experience alone is about 7%, the implication is that the return to tenure starts at about 5% ($= 12 - 7$) for the first year on the job for the new entrant, though falling for those with more experience. Nevertheless the effects of ten years' increased tenure for the typical worker with twenty years' experience are large: about 30% (Topel, 1991, 159). In fact the adjusted panel estimate of earning increase with tenure is little different to the cross-sectional ordinary least squares estimate.

Apparently the dramatic results of Altonji and Shakotko are in part due to mismeasuring tenure – in the PSID, tenure is given in intervals, so measured tenure need not change even when actual tenure does (Topel, 1991, 155, 167). It must be remembered that the technique of regressing changes in wages on changes in tenure is more prone to measurement error – resulting in a downward bias to the coefficient on the mismeasured variable, in this case change in tenure (see chapter 7 for an example of measurement error in the context of industrial accidents, and chapter 10 in the context of union/non-union wage differentials). Thus the specific capital model appears to survive the challenge.

In addition, there is every indication that considerable on-the-job training occurs. Using a survey of hours devoted to training (including hours spent by co-workers and trainers) in the first three months of the job, Barron *et al.* estimate about 30% of the new employee's time is devoted to training (1989, 15). Furthermore, the amount of training is closely related to pay, and to a productivity 'score'. In fact the authors find a 10% increase in training leads to a 3% increase in productivity growth, but only a 1.5% increase in wage growth (1989, fn 17), suggesting about half the training is specific. British data from the 1986 Survey of Graduates show that fourteen days are spent on *formal* training courses (unfortunately there is no measure of informal training) during the first year on the job. An extra day of such training is associated with a 1% increase in pay, and more training is received the longer the individual's tenure (Booth, 1989, 22).

Further evidence on training comes from the Panel Survey of Income Dynamics, in which workers were asked about 'the time it takes for an average person to become fully trained' in their job. Considering workers whose tenure with their firm was less than this, and who were still being trained therefore, considerable wage growth was found: 10% over the average 1.1 years of training, and about 20% over a four year training spell (Brown, 1989, 981). After the training period was over wage growth was found to be much smaller. These results support the view that training within the firm is occurring, and causing wages to increase (see also Mincer, 1989, 21).

Finally, while the suggestion that pay–tenure slopes are low reduces the importance of worker financed specific training, it does not bear on whether or not there is employer financed specific training. After all, if there is employer financed training, productivity will increase with tenure, but wages will not. In sum, while both the deferred compensation and specific human capital models have advantages and disadvantages, the specific human capital model applies both to worker monitoring and to training problems; also it depends on firms' self interest rather than 'reputation', which is more plausible.

9.8 Contracts and wage rigidity

One of the earliest modern theoretical developments pointing to long-term attachments between workers and their firms emphasises risk aversion on the part of workers (Baily, 1974). The basic argument is that workers receive lower pay (lower than their marginal product) in good times, in return for receiving higher pay in bad. Because employment contracts 'allocate risk' we have, it is argued, an explanation for the stability of wages over the business cycle, and for the fact that people are laid off (with the option to return when business expands) rather than fired in bad times. Given the assumption that workers are more risk averse than employers are (see appendix), the long-term employment contract thus permits gains from trade. Note that from the workers' viewpoint a third party cannot supply insurance against bad times because of a moral hazard – people fully insured against bad times do not work. This is why private unemployment insurance is not feasible. Because the firm is in a position to monitor effort the moral hazard argument does not apply with such force, and insurance becomes feasible.

As for the assumption that the firm is less averse than its employees, this can be justified on the grounds that firms' capital portfolios are more diversified than workers'. It is true that even big firms might be risk averse to some extent. This is because, as noted above, it makes sense for shareholders to try and make managers accountable, e.g., by having them own some of the firm's stock. Managers are not therefore allowed to diversify away all risk – so they will be risk averse about variation in the firm's profit stream. There will be consequently less scope for insurance, though it seems reasonable to assume still that firms are less risk averse than workers.

A difficulty with the model concerns enforcement. What is to prevent the worker quitting in good states of nature, or the firm from sacking the worker in adverse states, having already secured a lower wage? Mobility costs or the stigma of being regarded as an unreliable worker may deter the worker. Loss of reputation may deter the firm. In the latter context, the model can again best be applied to large firms which are visible and long lived.

There is also the difficulty that information is likely to be 'asymmetric'. In particular, the firm will have better information about the demand for labour. It might deliberately cheat and misrepresent the state of nature to its own advantage by saying that times are worse than they actually are, so as to secure a lower wage. A possible solution to this problem is a contract which lays down that employment is to be reduced (so penalising the firm) when a low state of demand is declared. However the idea of workers negotiating to be laid off when times are hard certainly seems artificial – though rules like 'last in first out' might make this easier. For this reason many regard the differential risk aversion model as not particularly helpful in explaining long-term contractual arrangements – though it might explain the mechanism behind smoothing once a relationship is established.

9.9 The role of trade unions

We have been considering the different types of wage payment system and other features of the internal labour market, such as long-term jobs and pensions, as 'efficient', that is, as reducing the cost of monitoring worker effort. However there is an argument for the internal labour market being based not on efficiency considerations but, rather, on equity – and requiring unions for its enforcement. According to Jacoby, for example, 'When employment practices first achieved a semblance of rational organisation, stability and equity, these features were not a managerial innovation but were imposed from below' (1984, 28), and 'the unions' allocative, wage, and dismissal practices embedded the employment relationship in a web of impersonal, equitable rules . . . an internal labor market' (1984, 29). To account for internal labour markets in non-union firms we have 'the threat of unionisation' (Rebitzer, 1989, 26), together with the 'personnel management system', itself partly a consequence of increased government labour market regulation.

The main historical evidence for the link between unions and internal labour markets is the decline in quit rates (see Ross, 1958, table 1), which is coupled with the rise in trade unionism. We might note however that Ross himself thought the decline in quit rates slight. He attributed it to lower turnover among junior employees only, not the workforce as a whole. In 1917–18, as in 1956, 90% of separations were among those with less than two years' tenure (Ross, 1958, 914).

Nevertheless, though the historical connection between unions and internal labour markets is arguable, the literature emphasising transactions costs as the basis for the internal labour market sees a role for enterprise unions, as we have noted. Thus there might be an economic efficiency, as well as an equity, link between enterprise unions and internal labour markets.

On the face of it, if unions can help develop and monitor the internal labour market's (implicit) contracts, they might also be expected to raise labour productivity. This is a question upon which much research effort has been expended, as we will see in chapter 10. In fact there it will be shown that the effect of unions on labour productivity seems, if anything, negative. Unions also appear to have adverse effects on company profits, employment, and perhaps investment. These probable negative effects must caution us against accepting an efficiency basis for any link between unions and internal labour markets.

Part of the problem might be unions extending internal labour market type rules into small firms. If the monitoring cost arguments are correct, internal labour market rules are only cost minimising in 'large' firms. In fact we have already seen that small *union* firms are quite like large *union* firms as regards emphasis on seniority rather than merit in the determination of pay (small non-union firms are more likely to stress merit). It turns out that small union firms are also like large union firms in respect of factors such as long tenure of workers, wide pension coverage, and low usage of part-time staff (see Siebert and Addison, 1991, table 4). Taking male manual workers for example, average tenure is eleven to twelve years in firms (union or non-union) employing 1,000 or more, and almost the same in small union firms with 100 or fewer workers. Yet average tenure is only about five years in small non-union firms. It might be that introducing inflexibilities into small firm contexts where it is inappropriate is the root of the real union productivity problem.

9.10 Policy

This chapter has been analysing primarily the within-firm 'enterprise' market rather than the open market. Such a market substitutes within-firm rules generating long tenure, promotion from within, pay by seniority, pensions, and 'due process' in dismissals for the basic supply and demand forces that govern an open market. Internal labour markets modify, and might even interrupt, the process of labour mobility which establishes the 'law of one price' for given grades of labour, and which matches workers to the jobs in which they will be most productive.

Some have interpreted the primary effect of the internal labour market as being to reduce the importance of competitive economic forces (Ryan, 1981, 16). The 'insiders' within the internal labour market are said to be able to secure better conditions for themselves than comparable 'outsiders' employed by the small, unstable firms in the rest of the market. Wage differentials become capricious: 'Government and large organisations have internal labour markets which are impervious to the fluctuations of the external labour market' (Remick and Steinberg, 1984, 292). A more active role for government wage setting and job regulation follows. If wage differentials do not correspond to supply and demand and the net advantages of jobs, why not establish new differentials via, for example, a comparable worth pay programme? Or again, if the market fails to establish a pay premium for dangerous jobs, should there not be much stricter safety standards and closer supervision imposed from without, via government regulation of workplaces? The question of the extent and consequences of internal labour markets and associated segmentation therefore has an important bearing on whether there should be government labour market intervention.

What our analysis has suggested is that some internal labour markets do not merely 'substitute rules for markets'. Rather, the rules themselves often reflect competitive pressures to minimise costs. On the competitive view, such internal labour markets develop in part because of the agency problem – the necessity for team production and consequent difficulties in worker monitoring. In part they also develop because of specific investment and the need to protect both worker and firm during the investment process. Other internal labour markets, however, are not cost-minimising but are instead the result of strong industrial unions, or poor management ('X-inefficiency').

It appears likely that in large private firms the internal labour market is an efficient response to specific training and problems of worker monitoring. This is most clearly suggested when we rule trade unions out of the picture, and simply compare non-union workers in large firms with non-union workers in small firms. The non-union worker in the large firm has longer tenure, is more educated, has more pension rights, is more likely to be full-time, and is more likely to be paid by seniority than by merit than his counterpart in the small firm. The pattern can be explained in terms of the arms-length relationship which requires worker bonding to the firm, and the substitution of indirect sanctions (such as the loss of specific training investments) on poor performance for direct supervision. In addition there is the necessary bureaucracy of the large firm: the various divisions in such a firm are further removed from the discipline of a close connection between revenue and expenditure. The centre must therefore impose thrift by regimentation, that is, bureaucratic rules.

Another explanation for internal labour market type rules is that they are the result of pressure from insider groups, the strongest of which are the unionised groups. The potency of unions in causing internal labour markets is suggested when we consider only small firms – in which monitoring costs and bureaucracy arguments cannot hold by definition. The labour markets in which workers in union and non-union small firms operate are generally different. Unionised workers in small firms enjoy internal labour market conditions. This is presumably a consequence of their unions' efforts to improve wages and conditions, a factor which has nothing to do with the efficiency of the firm.

Policy questions hinge on an alleged shortage of 'good jobs'. The older segmentation literature argued for an expansion of public sector jobs. The newer variant mandates firms to provide better working conditions – to encourage internal labour markets via, for example, laws making dismissal more difficult or part-time work less attractive. This is envisaged under the European Community Social Charter of workers' rights (Addison and Siebert, 1991). However according to the analysis in this chapter, where there is competition internal labour markets need no encouragement since they are the reasonable outcome of needs for specific training, and costs of information. Extension of internal labour market conditions to areas where, for example, specific training is inappropriate (part-time workers) would cause unemployment and lower labour mobility.

Since many secondary workers do not have the skill endowments suitable for primary sector employment, there is scope for policy intervention in the area of targeted training policies. Such policies could broaden the opportunities for some workers to move into internal labour markets. Some workers will, by exposure to this process, take on attributes which make them worth employing in high-paying jobs. Gradually they will move up and on. By contrast, a programme to mandate 'best practice' conditions will cut jobs, and so frustrate the process. Therefore there is little scope for attempting to generalise the 'best practice' conditions sometimes observed in large firms, where they are likely to be appropriate, to all firms.

Appendix 9.1 Contracts and wage rigidity

Suppose that a worker would have a wage and marginal product of Y_1 in bad state and Y_2 in good state. Suppose there is a given chance, P, of a good state and chance $1 - P$ of a bad state. Then the actuarial value of the worker's income is:

$$E(Y) = PY_2 + (1 - P)Y_1.$$

Using $X = Y_2 - Y_1$, i.e., X is the loss that would be suffered in the event of the bad state occurring, we can write:

$$E(Y) = Y_1 + PX.$$

$(1 - P)X$ would be the actuarial value of the loss for the worker in the event of a bad state. For example, if Y_2 was 9 and Y_1 was 4, and there was a 60% chance of the good state, $PX = 3$ and $E(Y) = 7$. This function is graphed in the lower panel of figure 9.6, with intercept Y_1 and slope X.

If a person is risk neutral, he/she is indifferent as between a given, certain, income of value $E(Y)$, and a gamble of the same expected value. The expected utility from a gamble is defined as the weighted average of the utilities in the two states:

$$E(U(Y)) = PU(Y_2) + (1 - P)U(Y_1).$$

For the risk-neutral person the expected utility from a gamble equals the utility from a sum with the same value as that given in the gamble, that is:

$$E(U(Y)) = U(E(Y)),$$

where $U(E(Y)) = U(PY_2 + (1 - P)Y_1)$. But generally, individuals can be thought of as risk-averse, so:

$$E(U(Y)) < U(E(Y)).$$

For example take the utility function $U = \sqrt{Y}$, and let $Y_1 = 4$, $Y_2 = 9$. Then the expected utility of the gamble is:

$$E(U(Y)) = 3P + 2(1 - P) = 2 + P.$$

The utility of a sum with expected value equal to the gamble is:

$$\begin{aligned} U(E(Y)) &= (PY_1 + (1 - P)Y_2)^{1/2} \\ &= (9P + 4(1 - P))^{1/2} \\ &= (4 + 5P)^{1/2}. \end{aligned}$$

The situation is as in figure 9.6. $E(U(Y))$ and $U(E(Y)$ coincide at points F and E, when there is certainty ($P = 1$ or 0). But when there is uncertainty $U(E(Y))$ is greater than $E(U(Y))$. For example if $P = 0.6$, $E(U(Y)) = 2.6$ and $U(E(Y)) = (7)^{1/2} = 2.65$. So a certain sum of 7 has a greater utility (point C) than expected utility from a gamble valued at 7 (point B). Another way of looking at it is to say that a certain level of income, 6.76, would give the individual the same utility A as a higher actuarial income, 7. Thus $2 (= (1 - P)X = BD)$ is the actuarial value of the loss the person faces, but he or she would be prepared to pay up to 2.24 ($= AD$) to avoid this loss. If there were 'fair insurance' (premium $=$ expected loss, BD) then the person pays 2 to receive certain 7, and moves up to utility point C. Even if there were unfair insurance (premium $>$ expected loss), this individual would still be better off so long as the premium was less than 2.24.

If the firm is risk neutral then the (utility of) profits will only depend on the expected value of wages, i.e., utility of profits will not be lower because wages are uncertain. Hence the firm would be prepared to guarantee $E(Y)$ (assuming

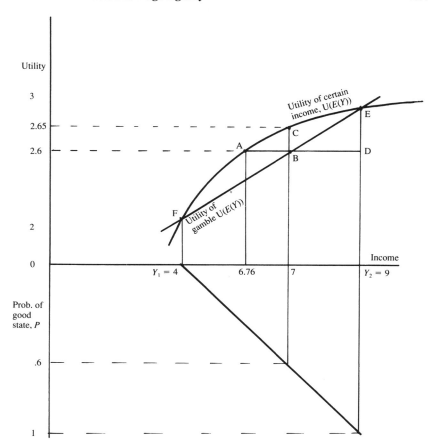

Figure 9.6 Contracts and wage rigidity

fair insurance). If the good state eventuates then the worker has a marginal product of Y_2, but only receives $E(Y)$, i.e., pays premium PX. If the bad state eventuates, marginal product is only Y_1, but the worker collects $E(Y)$. In fact, as noted above, such complete insurance would not occur (income would have to be somewhat lower in the bad periods than in the good), but this is the basic idea.

10 Unionisation

10.1 Introduction

Labour contracts can be of two types: contracts whose main terms are decided by collective bargaining, and contracts determined via individual bargaining. Collective bargaining essentially is a procedure for joint determination of labour contracts, that is, the union side has joint power with management in determining wages and working conditions, and – possibly – employment. Collective bargaining is thus an important component of industrial democracy. Individual bargaining on the other hand corresponds to the competitive model. Here the worker's power lies not in the trade union – the power of 'voice' – but in his or her ability to move among firms – the power of 'exit'. The debate has always been whether the power of exit is sufficient. State legislatures have generally concluded it is not, and have encouraged unions.

In America today the proportion of workers who are trade union members is about 15%. In Britain it is much higher, about 45%. In both countries, however, the importance of unions is greater than the membership figure indicates, partly because collective agreements also cover non-union workers. In America the proportion of workers represented by a union, including non-members, is approximately 20%. Unions also form organised political lobby groups which give them a power disproportionate to their numbers. The 'union vote' is important for law-makers. This point is underlined by the fact that such a high proportion of government workers are unionised in both countries – 36% even in the US in 1986 (Statistical Abstract, 1988). Thus collective bargaining has widespread effects.

In addition to having numerous union members, both countries have an old union 'movement'. Britain's trade unions probably have the longest continuous history of any in the world. There is a record of a combination of Journeymen Feltmakers as far back as 1696. The record might even go further back, to the medieval guilds – though some dispute the connection, arguing the guilds were primarily associations of independent producers, not workers

278

(Webb, 1919, 12). In America as well, in the late 1700s after the War of Independence, we see the emergence of unions. Shoemakers organised in Philadelphia in 1792, carpenters in Boston in 1793, printers in New York in 1794. Though unions are currently in decline, the long history of collective bargaining implies that unions will always be a power to be reckoned with.

Topics that will be covered in this chapter are:

1) union membership: who joins unions and why?
2) models of union wage and employment objectives;
3) empirical research on union wage and employment effects, including effects on non-union workers;
4) unions and industrial democracy;
5) the professions – these form union-like bodies governing entry and earnings.

10.2 Union membership

Time trends

Before 1800 both Britain and America were mainly agricultural countries without the factories within which collective bargaining could take place. Then with the industrial revolution in the late eighteenth century came the growth of factories, the increase in the scale of industry owing to transport improvements, and increased unionisation. Stable groups of workers began to develop, and with them the Friendly Societies – mutual help organisations. In Britain an Act regulating these societies dates from 1793. From these societies pressure often came for 'combinations' by men with similar interests to raise wages – the beginning of trade unionism (Webb, 1919, 26). In both Britain and America, however, combinations were treated as criminal conspiracies in the beginning. It was not until 1842 in America, with the Supreme Court ruling in the case of Commonwealth v. Hunt, that it was decided that combinations as such were not illegal (Cohen, 1975, 336). In Britain a similar position was reached in 1871 with the Trade Union Act. By 1900 therefore, both countries had a small but significant union movement – see table 10.1.

In Britain, as can be seen, union membership has always been a larger fraction of the workforce, even in 1900, before modern pro-union legislation. The answer probably lies in political changes in the nineteenth century. Britain had a restricted franchise until the 1832 and 1868 Reform Acts widened the franchise to include urban workmen. They used their power to elect union sponsored members of Parliament. There were eleven such MPs by 1885, and they were responsible for setting up the Independent Labour Party in 1893 – the forerunner of today's Labour Party, established in 1906. Today, about half the Labour Party's candidates are union sponsored, and unions provide 80% of the party's funds, giving unions an important political role. In America, however, the Democrats have never been simply a labour party. Thus only about 40% of Democratic Party congressional campaign funds are raised via union-sponsored political action committees. Unions thus appear to have had a more important political role in Britain, which is perhaps the cause of greater union density. Given the legal framework, however, unions behave in similar ways in both countries, as we shall demonstrate.

Table 10.1 shows that the main period of British union growth was 1905 to 1920. In America the main period was 1935 to 1945. These periods both coincide with recognition of trade unions' legal right to strike. Once trade unions can promise more to their members due to more effective strike threats, the union movement swells. The method of giving legal recognition to strikes makes an interesting contrast in the two countries however.

In Britain the moment came in 1906, with the Trade Disputes Act. The Act conferred immunity on trade unions from being sued civilly if a strike was called during a legal 'trade dispute'. A legal trade dispute was defined at the time to include disputes between employers and workers, or between workers and workers, relating to terms and conditions of employment, membership of trade unions, and machinery for negotiation. This same civil immunity – somewhat narrower – still exists today. It should be noted that the immunity was, and is, limited to trade unions and their officials. Striking workers, as such, have no 'right to strike', and no immunity. They can be dismissed for breach of contract, and so long as the dismissal is not victimisation, this does not infringe the unfair dismissals legislation.

In America the moment came in 1935, with the National Labor Relations Act (Wagner Act) (see Posner, 1984, for a succinct description). The Act was part of Franklin D. Roosevelt's 'New Deal' – it states that 'inequality of bargaining power between employees and employers . . . tends to aggravate recurrent business recessions by depressing wage rates and the purchasing power of wage earners' (cited in Kreps *et al.*, 1981, 148). The Act made it illegal for employers to dismiss or in any way interfere with non-supervisory employees who were organising a union. The National Labor Relations Board, also set up by the Act, polices this rule, and the recognition process. In the process, if there is majority support for a union in a firm, the NLRB grants the union the status of 'sole bargaining agent'. All employees must join the union within thirty days of being hired (union shop), or at least pay union dues (agency shop). The employer is required to negotiate 'in good faith' with that union. Collective agreements are legally enforceable (unlike Britain), and neither side is entitled to call a strike or lockout during the currency of an agreement. In America, as in Britain, strikers can be replaced and their jobs taken by non-strikers.

With the Wagner Act so supportive of trade unions, it is little wonder that

Table 10.1. *Union density in the US and Britain*
(Union members as % of the labour force excluding self-employed)

	US	US excluding agriculture	UK
1900	3%		13%
1905	6		12
1910	6		15
1915	7		24
1920	12		45
1925	8		30
1930	8		25
1935	7		25
1940	13		33
1945	23		39
1950	23		44
1955	25		44
1960	22		44
1965	25		44
1970	25	30	49
1975	24	29	51
1980	20	23	53
1985	16	19	44

Sources: Hirsch and Addison, 1986, table 3.1; Department of Employment, Employment Gazettes, various.

unionisation doubled in the five years up to 1940. The fact that the Act does not protect supervisory employees (foremen were excluded from the definition of employee by the Taft Hartley Act in 1947, and all other managerial workers by an NLRB decision in 1974) explains in part why white-collar unionisation in the US is so much lower than in Britain. Thus table 10.2 shows that, in the private sector, British white-collar workers are 22% unionised, more than twice as large as the US 9% figure. Amongst blue-collar workers the difference is smaller: 48% to 30%.

Though there have been changes, the basic structure of the two countries' labour laws remains to this day. Two changes are worth mentioning. In America there is the 1947 Labor Management Relations (Taft Hartley) Act, which attempted to check union power somewhat – for example, states were allowed to pass 'right to work' laws prohibiting closed shops. Today nineteen states have such laws. A further change in the US case in the 1960s is worth noting. In 1962, two Executive Orders permitted collective bargaining among federal employees. This was followed by a law in 1966 for New York State employees, and other states have followed suit (Lewin and Goldenberg, 1980, 243). Consequently public sector unionism, particularly among teachers, has grown.

In Britain the main change occurred with the long period of Labour rule in the 1960s and 1970s. An Act of 1975, the Employment Protection Act, even made it 'fair' to dismiss workers for non-membership of a trade union, thus expressly encouraging the closed shop. The advent of Mrs Thatcher in 1979 marked a swing of the pendulum back again. No doubt the decline of British trade unionism since then (see table 10.1) has something to do with her legislation restricting the circumstances in which a legal strike can be called – strikes between worker groups (over 'jurisdiction' or 'demarcation' issues) and secondary strikes are no longer protected for example.

The different framework of labour law in the two countries has interesting implications for trade unions. In America a union tends to have a monopoly within a given firm – it is the 'sole bargaining agent'. The difficulty with this concept is that there is only active competition between unions at organising time. Consequently the union need not be so careful to represent its members – particularly where there is a closed shop, so employees cannot even escape into non-unionism. In Britain on the other hand there are often several unions competing within a firm – the phenomenon of 'multi-unionism'. The problem here is that each union then jealously preserves its own patch. 'Jurisdictional' or 'demarcation' disputes are common. In fact the British problem seems worse, and much of the 1968 Donovan Commission on problems of British industrial relations was concerned with the inter-union rivalry caused by multiunionism. Thus Japanese and American firms in Britain today attempt to insist on 'single union' agreements.

It is worth noting that Japan and Germany, like the US, have little competition between unions within firms. The Japanese have 50 or 60 thousand 'enterprise unions', and the Germans have seventeen industrial unions. The Japanese system differs from the American however, because the enterprise unions do not group together into multi-employer units. There has been criticism of the multi-employer bargaining unit in America and Britain, with proposals to limit collective bargaining to the confines of a single firm (see Lande and Zerbe, 1985). Do the 'voice' effects of unions require industry-wide collective bargaining? It is also worth noting that Japanese type enterprise unions have no legal standing in either America or Britain. In both countries legal protection is only extended to 'independent' unions. Unions are thus seen as adversaries of management (see below).

A further consequence of the more regulated industrial relations system in the United States is the different pattern of strikes. In Britain, strikes do not have to occur at the end of a contract, since there is no contract as such. Thus Britain tends to have more frequent, but shorter strikes. Some data are given in

Table 10.2. *Percent of private sector wage and salary employees belonging to labour unions*

	US 1977			UK 1983		
	Blue collar	White collar		Blue collar	White collar	Total incl. govt.
All employees	30%	9		48	22	49
Sex: male	37	10		53	26	56
female	17	8		39	19	40
Race: non-white	30	8		63	19	63
white	31	17		48	22	49
Age: under 25	25	7		32	19	36
25–44	37	9		51	21	50
45–54	42	10		58	25	56
54 plus	34	10		56	14	56
Education:						
not high school graduate	25	11		50	21	51
high school, no post-						
high school	38	11		46	21	45
some post-high school						
education	29	7		52	27	53
Region:						
North East	38	11	North	56	27	57
Central	38	9	Midlands & SW	49	23	47
South	18	5	Wales & Scot.	54	27	59
West	30	11	London & SE	38	17	40
Industry:						
Agriculture	3	2		12	5	13
Mining	47	7		69	17	89
Construction	36	12		28	9	33
Manufacturing	45	10		68	31	57
Trans., communication	61	33		48	30	74
Wholesale & retail trade	14	6		25	15	20
Finance, insurance	17	3		38	29	32
Services	9	9		10	22	58

US total including government, 1983: 20%

Sources: US– Freeman and Medoff, table 2.1; UK – General Household Survey 1983.

table 10.3. It can be seen that the percentage of working time lost due to strikes is similar in the two countries, but US strikes last twice as long – twenty-two days in 1985, compared with ten days in the UK. Note that strikes amount to only a trivial fraction of working days available – in both countries less than one tenth of 1%. Impasse is reached in only a small fraction of labour negotiations because the two sides rationally seek to reach an agreement. It is not strikes as such that matter, but the strike *threat* (see Siebert and Addison, 1981; Cousineau *et al.*, 1986; also Treble, 1990).

Returning to the growth of unions, a further influence to be noted is that of war. Table 10.1 shows how both World Wars have been marked by a large increase in union density. In war, party politics tends to be dropped, and unions become 'incorporated' into the government in return for no strike pledges. In Britain during the First World War, the Secretary of the Steel Smelters Union became Minister of Labour. Similarly in the Second World War, Ernest Bevin, Secretary of the Transport and General Workers' Union (Britain's largest), became Minister of Labour. In both wars all strikes were outlawed, and in return for permitting this and helping with wage restraint union leaders were given power. In the same way in America during the 1914–18 period, a National War Labor Board was established to help settle labour disputes. Though it had no formal powers, it in a sense gave trade unions official recognition. Again in 1940–5, in exchange for a no-strike pledge, the federal government encouraged employers to recognise unions (Kreps *et al.*, 1981, 150). Naturally the union movement prospered.

Economic factors affecting membership

Although industrial relations laws are correlated with union growth, we cannot rely much on these laws to explain union growth. If more people in a country want to be in unions, they will pass the appropriate laws. Another factor, 'pro-union sentiment' – a demand for unions – might cause both the laws and the unionisation.

Thus in the US it has been found that states with 'right to work' RTW laws have lower union density because people prefer not to be in unions, rather than because of the laws. The evidence is simply that, if you ask workers whether they want to be in unions, a smaller proportion answer 'yes' in right to work states (Farber, 1984, 341). The 1977 Quality of Employment Survey of the University of Michigan asked non-union workers whether they would vote for union representation if given the opportunity. About one third said they would. Adding these workers to those already in a union we find that 51% of workers desire union representation in RTW states compared with 65% in non-RTW states. It might well be therefore, that the emphasis usually accorded government intervention in promoting unionisation is overplayed.

Table 10.3. *Industrial disputes*

	US				UK			
			Days lost:				Days lost:	
	Number of stoppages	Workers involved	per striker	% of work time	Number of stoppages	Workers involved	per striker	% of work time
1926	(General Strike in UK)				323	2.7 mill	60 days	5.6%
1960	222	0.9 mill	15 days	0.09%	2,831	0.8	4	0.04
1970	381	2.5	21	0.29	3,906	1.8	6	0.15
1980	187	0.8	26	0.09	1,330	0.8	14	0.14
1985	54	0.3	22	0.03	887	0.6	10	0.08

Note: In the US in 1985, 42 thousand people in any month were employed but not working because they were on strike; 1.3 million were not working because of illness (Statistical Abstract, 1988, 369).
Sources: Statistical Abstract of the United States, 1988, 399; Salamon, 1987.

That other factors than laws affect union density is graphically shown when we compare different industries at a point in time. All industries are subject to the same laws, but they have widely differing levels of union density. This is shown clearly in table 10.2. Taking the blue-collar worker columns, for example, in the US the service industries (wholesale and retail, finance and insurance, and other services) are much less unionised than manufacturing and the utilities. The same is true of the UK, where union levels are generally higher. Indeed, the same pattern pertains even in countries like Sweden, where union levels are higher still.

An explanation for why some industries lend themselves to unionisation is presumably to be found in the costs and benefits of union organising. It is less costly to organise workers in the large firms such as are found in manufacturing and public utilities, because labour turnover in such firms is lower, so new workers do not have to be continually persuaded to join the union (see Zax, 1989 and Trejo, 1991). In addition it is less costly to target a few large firms than many small firms. In a competitive industry many of the small firms might be difficult for the union to find, yet they must be organised lest they undercut the union's bargaining efforts among the firms it has organised.

At the same time the benefits accruing to union members in large firms are greater. Large firms are likely to have some monopoly power – a less elastic demand for labour – and thus have more rent which the union can 'share' via large wage claims. (It is also possible that such firms are less likely to lay workers off when the union demands a wage increase – but we will go into this in more detail later.) Small firms, on the other hand, such as characterise the service sector, are more competitive, and have less rent to share with unions. Finally, if the union wishes to bargain over employment as well as wages (see 'efficient bargains' below), there is no question of setting employment in each firm if there are thousands of firms in the industry. This would be another reason for unions to prefer situations in which only a few firms need to be organised.

The process is illustrated in figure 10.1. The assumption is that a union is deciding how many workers to organise in 'its' industry. The total costs (TC) curve has a fixed cost of organising element which is primarily related to obtaining recognition in the first place. Then the TC curve slopes upwards at an increasing rate, as drawn, reflecting the fact that the cost of organising new members rises as the union expands into less and less suitable firms. The total revenue (TR) curve shows the total dues available from members. These dues should reflect the (present) value of the union to members. Dues will be higher, the higher the wage increment ('mark-up') the union can secure, the better its grievance procedures, and the wider its political influence. The TR curve has been drawn with an 's' shape, reflecting the assumption that there are increasing returns to unionisation, up to a point. The increasing returns derive from the fact that, as non-union competition becomes eliminated, the union mark-up can increase. However, as the competitive fringe of the industry becomes organised the increased mark-up that can be gained presumably begins to taper off, and might even decline. At the optimum size of the union, marginal revenue should equal marginal cost, as indicated.

Unions need not take the TC and TR curves as given, but can try and influence their shape in a way favourable to the union. The most effective way is to change the structure of the industry towards a monopolistic form. Thus unions in Britain have been in favour of 'nationalising' firms, which is effectively to construct a monopoly since the state buys up all firms in the industry. Another way is to 'cartelise' the industry, that is, make it behave as a monopoly by assisting in the control of prices and wages. Some US examples of this in the areas of trucking and airlines will be considered below. A further way is to lobby for tariffs on foreign competition. Tariffs raise prices of the domestic product as well, and thus the wage that the union can press for (the interests of the union and the firm coincide here). All these actions are to be expected if the economic model of unions is correct.

Paula Voos (1983) has made an interesting attempt to implement the above model, using data for twenty-five unions over the period 1964–77. The average cost of organising is found to be about $700 per member, and the marginal cost between $150 and $500 per extra member (in 1967 dollars). The marginal benefit from organising is estimated from the union markup. Taking a markup of 15%, she estimates a marginal benefit of between $126 and $789

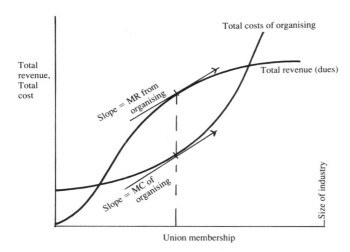

Figure 10.1 Determination of proportion unionised in industry

per extra worker, per year (depending upon industry). The marginal benefit figures are per year, and need to be discounted to give a stock figure which is comparable with the marginal cost figure. Such discounting involves choosing a discount rate, and a time horizon: for example, a rate of 15% and a horizon of five years would convert $126 per year into a present value of $422. According to these results the marginal benefits of union organising are somewhat greater than marginal costs, so unions appear to be somewhat smaller than their optimum. Below we will consider possible reasons why 'business unionism', illustrated here, is oversimplified.

According to the model, industries and firms which offer cheaper organising opportunities to unions, or larger wage gains, should be more highly unionised. Generally speaking, as argued above, we would expect the larger firms to be favoured targets – and the evidence shows this clearly to be the case. Data on the relationship between firm size and union density are given in table 10.4. The British data came from the 1980 Workplace Industrial Relations Survey, a nationally representative survey of 2,000 establishments (that is, plants). The US data are from the Current Population Survey. The table is confined to the private sector, given the difficulty of defining 'firm size' in the government sector. In the US case it can be seen that 6% of workers are unionised in firms employing under twenty-five workers, and the percentage steadily increases to 35% in the 1,000+ firms. In the UK 40% of firms in the 25–99 worker category recognise a union, compared with 93% in the 1,000+ category. Several more formal studies confirm the table, showing that large firms, and firms in concentrated industries, are likely to be highly unionised (see Hirsch and Addison, 1986, 61–2). Thus the cost/benefit model of unionisation receives support.

Alternatively the correlation of firm size with unionism could be due to the fact that large firms are more 'alienating' to work in, so the need for unionisation is greater there. The problem with this view is that it does not seem logical that large firms should be unpleasant to work in. Big firms pay more than small, it is true, but little of this difference seems to be accounted for by reasons of working conditions – even measures of such things as pace of work, and relationships with co-workers (see Brown *et al.*, 1990, 38).

The economic model also has a bearing on who gets to be a member of a union. As shown in table 10.2, females are less likely to be union members, as are young workers. However this is not because they do not want to be union members. When women, or young workers are asked whether they wish to be union members, they are more likely than prime age males to say 'yes'. Thus when a sample of unemployed workers were asked whether they would 'require' a union job, John Heywood found about 13% had this requirement. Holding constant age, education, and unemployment duration, the proportion was only 9% for white men, compared to 14% for minority men, 16% for white women, and 22% for black women (1990b, 125; the Michigan Quality of Employment Survey mentioned above has similar results). Similarly a British study of 1,800 young adults aged eighteen to twenty-four calculates that, had they all been able to obtain jobs in union firms, 61% to 64% would have been unionised; this can be compared with the actual 24% to 27% unionisation figure (Spilsbury *et al.*, 1987, 271).

The fact is that to be a union member one has both to wish to belong to a union *and* be hired by a firm with a union. Yet since unions raise the pay of their members, unionised firms must respond by attempting to raise the productivity of their workforce. One way is to avoid hiring younger workers, or female workers with less labourforce commitment – and indeed, all less experienced, less skilled, workers. There is a queue for union jobs, and the less skilled will be at the back of the queue, driven into the non-union sector. There is a corollary: members of lower paid demographic groups, if they are lucky enough to get a union job, should receive a relatively large increase in pay. This is found. Especially in the case of young workers, those in union jobs earn more than those in non-union jobs. There are signs that this also occurs for female workers and black workers (see Metcalf, 1982, 164 for UK evidence, and Freeman and Medoff, 1984, 48 for US evidence). However, the greater union wage gains for the lower paid demographic groups should be set against the fact that these groups are less likely to find union employment in the first place.

In sum, at a point in time, a cross section of different firms or industries offer different costs and benefits to union organisation, and levels of union density

Table 10.4. *Unionisation by size of firm/establishment*

	Number employed in firm, US 1979				
	1–24	25–99	100–499	500–999	1,000+
Proportion of workers in union	6%	18	26	29	35
	Number employed in establishment, UK 1980			
	25–99	100–499	500–999	1,000+
Proportion of firms recognising union (private sector only)	40%	66%	89%	93%

Source: UK – Daniel and Millward, 1983, 24; US – Mellow, 1982, 497.

vary accordingly. Over the course of time, the time series of union density varies as it becomes more or less difficult to organise. Factors affecting the time series are changes in the law, as already discussed, the rise of the service industries, and also increased international competition. Increased international competition points to a decline in unionisation because unionism does not flourish in a competitive atmosphere. Increased world trade in the 1970s and 1980s might well account for much of the recent decline in unionism.

Economic factors such as unemployment and inflation might also affect union density. Unemployment will have a mechanical link with union membership expressed as a proportion of the total workforce. The reason is that unemployed workers tend to drop their union membership. Total union density is a weighted average of union density among the employed and unemployed:

$$\frac{T_u + T_e}{U + E} = \frac{T_u U}{U L} + \frac{T_e E}{E L},$$

where $T = T_e + T_u$ is total unionised, employed in unions and unemployed in unions respectively; $L = E + U$ is total labourforce, employed and unemployed respectively. If $T_u/U \cong 0$, then $T/L = (T_e/E)(E/L)$, and so as the percentage of unemployed $(1 - E/L)$ rises the fraction unionised, T/L, must fall.

As for inflation, it seems that union membership increases as the rate of inflation increases. The reason might be that unions are credited with wage increases that occur in time of inflation. Union membership consequently increases because the 'benefits' of membership are seen to have increased. But the argument is speculative, because logically it would seem just as difficult to obtain a 1% wage increase when inflation is 1% (that is, maintain one's real wage), as to obtain a 20% increase when inflation is 20%. If a union is needed in one circumstance, it is needed in the other.

The study by Carruth and Disney of British trade union density 1895–84 finds density to increase with inflation and decrease with unemployment. Interestingly, they find only a small political party effect – a Labour rather than a Conservative government is associated with a density level 2.5 percentage points higher (1988, 15). Their results imply that about 3 points, say, of the 10 point decline in union density after 1979 (see table 10.1) can be ascribed to Conservative industrial relations laws. A similar study by Ashenfelter and Pencavel for US unions for the period 1900 to 1960 also finds a pro-cyclical movement of union density, and a small political component to union growth. In particular unions grow faster when the percentage of Democrats in the House is higher (1969, 442–3). Such time series results however tend to vary with the time period chosen (Hirsch and Addison, 1986, 54), and so should not be relied upon too heavily. Nevertheless they support our previous point, that changes in the legal framework should not be given too much emphasis in explaining changes in union density – particularly since the law itself might be a response to, rather than a cause of, unionisation.

10.3 Union wage and employment objectives

Monopoly models

Traditional theory (e.g., Cartter, 1959) views a union as a monopoly that attempts to obtain higher wages for its membership. The union calls out a wage to the firm, and the firm responds by adjusting employment along its demand curve. What wage the union calls out is tricky because it depends on union preferences – and union power. In reality such preferences are not easily modelled.

The simplest starting point is to assume that unions are labour monopolies 'selling' labour to employers. The difference in wages employers pay and the wage at which workers are willing to work (the worker's reservation wage) is defined to be 'rents' (or profits). Demanding a wage that maximises rents can then be taken as one characteristic of union objectives.

Assume a firm with a demand curve for labour such as that labelled MRP in figure 10.2. Points along the curve represent each worker's marginal revenue product (MRP). The extent to which employees are willing to work a given number of hours is measured by the supply curve, assumed horizontal for simplicity. Points along this curve depict worker reservation wages, that is, the minimum wage inducing workers to work. A competitive market yields w_c as the equilibrium wage. At w_c there are enough jobs for all who want to work.

Suppose an entrepreneurial union organiser establishes an employment agency to 'sell' workers to firms. It can employ workers at w_c to sell to firms. But obviously because firms could also employ workers at w_c, the agency would reap no profits. Suppose, however, that the strike threat prohibited firms

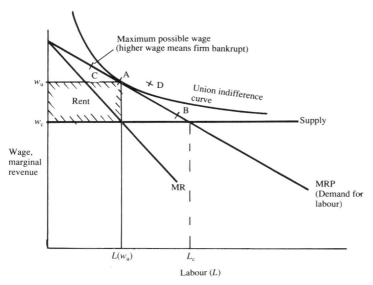

Figure 10.2 The rent maximising union

from buying workers in the free market. Now the agency can sell workers at higher than the competitive wage so that each worker earns a rent. In this case the employment agency's rent maximising wage is determined by seeking the wage, w_u, that maximises:

$$\pi = (w_u - w_c) L(w_u),$$

where $L(w_u)$ is the number of workers rented to the firm. First-order conditions dictate seeking a wage w_u such that the union agency's marginal revenue (MR) based on the industry demand (MRP) curve it faces equals its marginal cost, w_c. This is the case of rent maximisation, and the rent is shown by the shaded rectangle in figure 10.2.

The diagram enables us to show why union organisation in concentrated industries is easier than in competitive industries. The conceptual experiment is as follows. The union organiser says to himself, 'Suppose we were able to raise pay in ALL firms in the competitive sector – either by organising them all, or by getting the government to "extend" union wages to all firms in the industry (as happens in Germany). Should we do this, or would our efforts be better spent in raising pay in the monopolistic industry?' Once the competitive industry is organised, the relevant demand curve for the union is the industry demand curve, and the union will raise wages from w_c to w_u. There is no reason to expect *industry* demand to be more inelastic for a competitive than for a monopolistically structured industry. In any case w_u will be chosen so that the elasticity of labour demand is higher than at w_c – as can be seen, at point A, the elasticity of labour demand is greater than at w_c. Thus despite the fact that unions can be expected to organise firms which have more inelastic demand curves, the union's very success in raising wages causes unionised firms to exhibit greater labour demand elasticity than unorganised firms. The implication is that unions tend to organise concentrated industries not because firms in such industries have more inelastic labour demand (because the union will always set a wage high enough to convert an inelastic labour demand into an elastic one), but rather because it is easier to organise a few large firms than the many firms that make up a competitive industry.

The basic reason that unions are better represented in concentrated industries thus hinges on the fact that it is difficult and expensive to organise many firms (and if this effort fails, the union has no power to raise wages much, because union firms will fear they will be undercut by non-union firms). An extra possibility (see Heywood, 1990a), is that concentrated industries present a better prospect of being able to negotiate over employment as well as wages in each firm. As shown in the next section, this enables the union to attain a more 'efficient' bargain than is possible when negotiating over wages alone.

Rent maximisation requires that the union chooses between wages and employment in a particular way. In other words the union's indifference curves in wage–employment space must have the appropriate shape. One such curve is illustrated in figure 10.2. The downward slope of the indifference curves means that employment as well as wages are 'goods'. That employment is a good is justified on the grounds that the union cares whether its members are unemployed or not. Thus if a representative member's utility in union work is $u(w)$, and in alternative work or welfare is $v(b)$, the union's utility is:

$$U = Lu(w) + (M - L)v(b),$$

where M = total membership (somehow given), and $M - L$ = unemployed members. This is said to be the 'utilitarian' model (Oswald, 1982) because the union's utility is the sum of its members' utilities. Note how if one assumes the union never wants a wage less than w_c, then indifference curves asymptotically approach the w_c line, but do not cross it.

Rent maximisation implies that the 'union' indifference curve be tangent to the MRP curve at the rent maximisation point – and that the union has the power to attain this point. However, if the union were concerned about employment being larger than $L(w_u)$, then the tangency point would be to the right of A, for example at B. If the union were less concerned about employment, the indifference curves would become flatter, and the tangency point would move left of A, up the demand curve. In the limit, if 'the union' were only concerned about wages – wage maximisation – the indifference curves would be

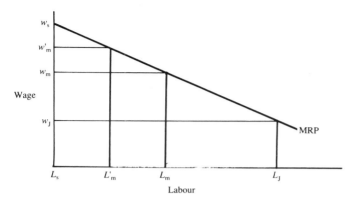

Figure 10.3 Distribution of wage demands if layoff is according to seniority

horizontal straight lines, and equilibrium would be at C. (Providing the firm was breaking even at C – otherwise the wage would be lower.) Thus rent maximisation is not inevitable, it depends on the union's preferences.

The question arises as to how to characterise the union's preferences. The difficulty arises because unions are collections of heterogeneous individuals, who determine union policy in a more or less democratic way. If unions were run by one person, who appropriated the profit from running the union, life would be simpler. The union would then be like any other firm, and the assumption of rent or profit maximisation would be suitable. This was essentially the view taken earlier in figure 10.1.

In practice union preferences must be the outcome of some aggregate of their members' preferences. But members will be different in an essential way, namely, their seniority. Seniority is important because the least senior workers tend to get laid off first – 'last in first out'. Less senior workers will prefer a lower wage claim than more senior workers, so there will be a distribution of wage preferences among members.

A device that is adopted to deal with such a distribution of preferences is the concept of the 'median voter'. In a democratic system, policies will be adopted that command the support of 50% plus one of the members. The member at the 50% + 1 point is the median voter. The position is illustrated in figure 10.3. The workers in the (representative) firm are arranged in order of seniority, with the most junior worker, L_j, preferring the lowest wage, w_j, and the most senior worker is L_s, preferring w_s. The median worker is L_m, preferring w_m. w_m is the highest wage for which a majority can be found. It might therefore be thought that analysis of union wage policy can be based on the median member.

However there are problems with the median voter, too. In the first place, if wage w_m is chosen, then the median member in period 1 becomes the most junior member in period 2. As shown in figure 10.3, the consequence is that wage w'_m is chosen in period 2. The same happens in period 3. Thus the median voter becomes more and more senior with each contract and the union continually shrinks – which is implausible. In the second place the median voter analysis ignores pressure from the employer. The employer might be resistant to the median voter's preferred wage, w_m, for example. Thus an unacceptably long strike could be required to secure that wage. Strike costs need to be incorporated into the analysis (Kaufman *et al.*, 1987). Thirdly, the union leaders might be resistant because w_m implies too small a union in the figure 10.1 sense of equating the marginal revenue from and costs of organising.

Nevertheless it might well be that pressure from senior members for too high a wage accounts for Paula Voos's finding above that unions appear to be too small. On the other hand, empirical research by MacCurdy and Pencavel, attempting to measure the slope of the indifference curves of the International Typographical Union, implies that the indifference curves are quite steep (1986, S33). In particular for the typographical union, at least, membership is greater than is consistent with rent maximisation, i.e., the union is at point B rather than point A in figure 10.2. In sum, while the median voter device is a help in accounting for the preferences of diverse union members, it is not a complete solution. It is useful to continue to use the concept of a 'union' indifference map, though we must be aware that its foundations are somewhat shaky.

Off-the-demand curve models

Up to this point we have assumed that the union sets its workers' wages, and the firm(s) responds by determining employment. However both sides can be made better off by negotiating over both wages and employment. This yields an equilibrium solution that is off the demand curve. For example, instead of being at point A in figure 10.2, we will be to the right of A, say at D, with a wage higher than w_c, and employment not much lower (perhaps even higher) than the competitive level, L_c. This possibility has caused great excitement among some in the economics profession because, if true, it means that trade unions need not cause much unemployment. The argument is as follows.

Firstly, start with the firm side, as illustrated in figure 10.4. The top panel of figure 10.4 shows total revenue product (TRP), and total cost (TC) curves. The bottom panel shows the MRP curve, and two iso-profit curves. The curve π_0 is the zero profit iso-profit curve, and π_1 is a positive profit iso-profit curve.

We want to show why iso-profit curves have an inverted U shape, peaking at the MRP curve. This is best demonstrated using the upper panel. Let us derive the zero profit iso-profit curve, π_0. Take the TRP curve as given by

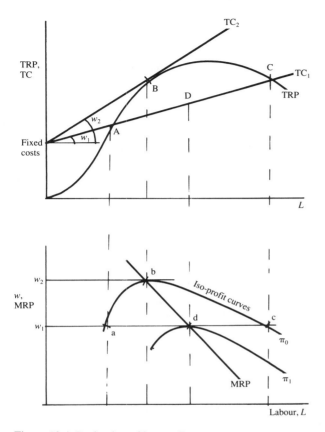

Figure 10.4 Derivation of iso-profit curve

technology, the amount of capital, and product price as usual. The highest wage at which the firm can just break even is w_2. At that wage it will move to point B on the TRP curve, making zero profit. Marginal revenue product will be given by the slope of the total cost line TC_2, and this is graphed in the lower panel as point b. Now let the wage fall to w_1. The firm makes zero profit when it is at points A and C. These are graphed in the lower quadrant as points a and c on the zero profit iso-profit curve π_0, as shown. In fact the firm could make maximum profit with wage w_1 by moving to point D, at which point π_1 profit is made. This corresponds to point d in the lower diagram. By a similar argument, an inverted U iso-profit curve passing through d can be constructed. The MRP curve is the locus of the maxima of all the iso-profit curves – which is why profit maximising firms always aim to stay on the MRP curve.

Alternatively we can derive the iso-profit curves from the profit equation:

$$\pi = pQ(L) - wL,$$

where p is product price (assumed constant), and $Q(L)$ is the production function. Taking the total derivative of profits, which is zero on an iso-profit curve, gives:

$$d\pi = pQ'\, dL - wdL - Ldw = 0,$$

where $Q' = dQ/dP$ is labour's marginal product. Thus the slope of the iso-profit curve is:

$$dw/dL = (pQ' - w)/L.$$

When $pQ' = w$, we are on the demand curve. It can be seen that then $dw/dL = 0$, so the iso-profit curve is horizontal. Also $dw/dL \gtrless 0$ as $pQ' \gtrless w$, that is, dw/dL changes sign according to whether the wage is greater than or less than MRP (McDonald and Solow, 1981).

Now let us consider the bargaining problem. This is shown in figure 10.5. We have to assume a family of 'union' indifference curves, as shown. The union would move to point X if no bargaining over employment was allowed. X is the best the union can do given its preferences and the constraint of the employer's MRP curve. However, the parties could do better than X, since through X passes an iso-profit curve π_0. The union would be better off and the firm no worse off by moving to the contract curve. In fact, anywhere within the shaded bargaining zone, both parties would be better off than at X.

The contract curve CC' marks the locus of wage–employment combinations where the parties are best off. The parties will presumably wish to move to the contract curve, though where they will locate on it we cannot say – that is determined by bargaining strength. In Edgeworth's famous words: 'contract without competition is indeterminate'. Whether indeterminate or not, the important point is that the contract curve, and thus the position to which bargaining would lead the parties, is off the demand curve. The union wants a high level of employment as well as high wages, and the employer is prepared to concede this. The union's 'make work rules' and 'feather bedding' might simply be a way of securing an efficient contract (i.e., on the contract curve), so the argument goes. Moreover it can be seen that efficient contracts generate less unemployment than do on-the-demand-curve contracts. Collective bargaining might therefore merely redistribute income from capitalists to workers, and perhaps leave employment unchanged.

The contract curve in figure 10.5 has been drawn almost vertical, but it need not be so. If the union's indifference curves are horizontal (as would be the case if employment was irrelevant to union decision-makers), then the contract curve would coincide with the demand (MRP) curve. Then the efficient

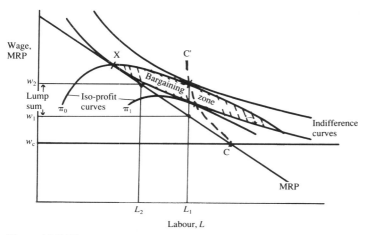

Figure 10.5 The contract curve

contracts argument would be irrelevant. More interesting is where the contract curve is somewhere above point C, as shown, or even bends forward from point C. It is these situations which empirical tests have been designed to detect.

Before looking at empirical tests we should note some logical problems associated with the efficient contracts view of collective bargaining.

1 There is the problem of 'incentive compatibility'. In figure 10.5, suppose the union and the firm agree to wage w_2, and employment L_1. The firm will always then have the incentive to move back to the MRP curve, firing workers until employment level L_2 is reached. The fact is that, while wage levels are easily monitored, employment levels are not. A way around this would be for the union to agree on a lower wage w_1, putting the firm on its MRP curve at the union's desired level of employment L_1. Then every year the firm could pay a lump sum of money to the union equal to the difference between w_2 and w_1 (see Farber, 1986, 1053). This might be more easily monitored. However there are not many instances of firms paying money directly to unions. Firms are geared up to paying money to workers, and once this is done the incentive will again be to move from L_1 to L_2.

2 Collective bargaining does not in practice appear to accord the same emphasis to employment as it does to wages. Collective agreements always specify wage rates but rarely specify employment levels as such. Of nineteen US unions questioned about whether they bargained about employment as well as wages, only two said yes; the equivalent figure for UK unions was three out

of sixteen (Nickell, 1990, 413). It is true it can be argued that the emphasis on 'due process' for dismissals, and for layoffs and redundancies, and the negotiation of feather bedding rules (see Addison and Siebert, 1979, chapter 9) has the same effect as bargaining over employment levels, namely, employment is maintained. On the other hand the employer will foresee that the union restricts freedom to fire, and will slow down the rate of hiring. So the end result of restricting dismissals might not be higher employment levels.

3   The third problem has already been mentioned: layoff by seniority, or last-in-first-out, will mean that the union is less concerned about unemployment. In such a case the contract curve becomes closer to the demand curve, since by definition the union is mainly concerned with wages. The question is how widespread is layoff according to seniority. Surveys of managers show that seniority is emphasised when deciding whom to lay off in union firms, but not in non-union firms. Freeman and Medoff report that 84% of managers in a sample of union firms would never lay off a senior worker in place of a junior; the figure for non-union firms was only 42% (1984, table 8.1). There is a similar emphasis on seniority for promotions in union firms. Thus Quinn Mills reports that 52% of managers in union firms felt required to select the senior bidder for a vacancy, compared to only 4% in non-union firms (1985, 423). Seniority is widespread in the collective bargaining context, therefore, which is an obstacle to off-the-demand curve solutions.

4   Efficient bargaining is unlikely where there are multi-employer and multi-union negotiations. With such a bargaining structure it is simply too difficult to set employment levels, so only wages are collectively bargained. For example in US trucking, union wages are determined by the National Master Freight Agreement, but employment is set by individual firms. In Britain, the largest private sector agreement, that in engineering, at one time set the wages for 1.5 million workers, but employment was determined by the many firms covered. Efficient contracts are thus likely to happen, to the extent they happen at all, in a single union, homogeneous firm context – probably the crafts such as printing, or in the British coal industry where a single (state) employer faces a single union. Indeed it might be because it is easier to negotiate about employment as well as wages that unions – as noted earlier – are more likely to be found in large monopolistic firms.

The importance of off-the-demand curve bargaining in reducing the unfavourable employment effects of collective bargaining is shown in figure 10.6. In the diagram D_u and D_n represent the demand curve for the union and non-union sectors in the economy. The union sector would include manufacturing and government, say. The non-union sector includes services and agriculture, say. Suppose labour is homogeneous, so that without unionisation

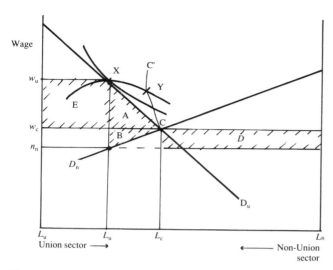

Figure 10.6 Welfare losses and transfers due to unionism

the same wage, w_c, would be established in both sectors. If there is then union-isation, and the resulting bargain is on the demand curve, we will be at a point such as X in the union sector (assuming product prices do not change – they are given by world markets, for example). Wage w_u will rule in the union sector, and union employment will fall to L_u. The displaced workers will move to the non-union sector, and if there is no unemployment, the non-union sector wage will become w_n.

In this orthodox analysis unions have raised the union wage, lowered the non-union wage, reduced union employment and increased non-union employment. Profits in the union sector have declined, but have increased in the non-union sector. In the union sector area E is transferred from profits to union members' wages. In the non-union sector, because labour is cheaper, area D gets transferred from wages to profits. There is also a deadweight loss (fall in national income) equal to areas A plus B, shown shaded. This is calculated as follows. Prior to unionisation, the total of labour and capital income (i.e., national income) is the whole area under the demand curves. After unionisation it is that area less triangles A and B.

Unions help those of their members who remain in a job, but on balance harm other groups because national income is decreased. Some say this welfare loss is small, only 0.2 to 0.4% of GNP (Freeman and Medoff, 1984, 57). Others say it is larger, because we should count not only areas A + B, but also the waste associated with competing for areas E and D (Tullock, 1966).

However if there are efficient, off-the-demand curve bargains, the above analysis is not correct. In such a case the position in the union sector would be more like point Y in figure 10.6. Employment would not change greatly in either sector. There might even be an increase in the labourforce as higher wages induce people to enter the labourforce (for an analysis of this possibility in the context of minimum wages, see Mincer, 1976). There would be no dead-weight loss. And the main transfer would be from capitalists to workers in the union sector. Therefore we have a completely different set of implications, and a much more favourable view of the union. Below we will consider empirical research on off-the-demand curve collective bargaining.

10.4 Union wage and employment effects in practice

Efficient bargains

Attempts have been made to test for efficient bargains in American printing and British coal mining. These are both industries where the bargaining structure is simple enough for the union to be able to monitor employment levels.

The basis of the test is illustrated in figure 10.7. The contract curves have been assumed vertical for simplicity. Take competitive wage w_c; employment will be where MRP $= w_c$, that is, employment will be at L. The negotiated wage will be somewhere above w_c, for example at point A. Where exactly A will be is determined by the parties' bargaining strengths. The point is that there should be no relationship between the negotiated wage and L, and only between L and w_c. Let the competitive wage fall to w'_c. Employment will increase to L'. The negotiated wage will be somewhere above this, on the new contract curve, perhaps at B. Again there should be no systematic relationship between the negotiated wage and L'.

Algebraically the position is as follows. We have already seen that the slope of the iso-profit curve is (normalising product price, p, to unity):

$$dw/dL = (Q' - w)/L,$$

where Q' is labour's MRP. On the union side we have the union's utility function as $U = U(w, L)$ and along indifference curves $dU = 0$, so the slope of indifference curves is:

$$\frac{dw}{dL} = -\frac{U_L}{U_w}.$$

Along the contract curve, iso-profit and indifference curves have the same slope, so:

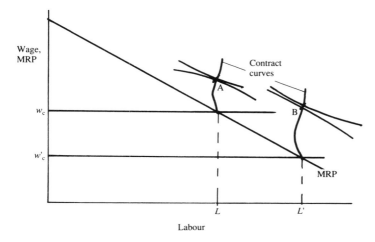

Figure 10.7 Testing for efficient contracts

$$\frac{Q' - w}{L} = \frac{U_w}{U_L}.$$

or

$$Q' = w - \frac{U_L}{U_w} L,$$

In the on-the-demand curve case, $Q' = w$, simply. But in the off-the-demand curve case, Q' is lower than w by the amount:

$$\frac{U_L}{U_w} L,$$

as can be seen. For example, in figure 10.7, MRP is lower than point A (giving the wage).

Let us give the union a particular utility function, so as to bring in the competitive wage explicitly. Let union utility, U, be:

$$U = L^\alpha (w_u - w_c)^\beta.$$

Then:

$$\frac{U_L}{U_w} = \frac{\alpha (w_u - w_c)}{\beta L},$$

and on the contract curve the equation for MRP becomes:

$$Q' = w_u - \frac{U_L}{U_w} L$$

$$= (1 - \frac{\alpha}{\beta}) w_u + \frac{\alpha}{\beta} w_c. \quad \bullet$$

Thus, on the contract curve Q' is higher – and labour demanded, L, is lower (since L varies inversely with Q') – the higher is the union wage, w_u, and the higher is the alternative wage, w_c. In other words, with efficient bargaining, employment in a firm depends not only on the firm's own wage, w_u, but also negatively on the alternative wage, w_c.

It is interesting to find the slope of the contract curve in this case. We do this by taking the total derivative of the equation for MRP, thus:

$$dQ' = d((1 - \alpha/\beta)w + \alpha w_c/\beta) \text{ gives}$$
$$Q''dL = (1 - \alpha/\beta) dw,$$

where $Q'' = d^2Q/dL^2 < 0$ is the rate of change of labour's marginal product. Thus the slope of the contract curve is:

$$dw/dL = Q''/(1 - \alpha/\beta).$$

From this expression we see that, if $\alpha = 0$, so the union's indifference curves are horizontal (L does not enter the utility function) $dw/dL = Q''$, that is, the slope of the contract curve equals Q'', the slope of the MRP curve. In other words we move back to an on-the-demand curve solution. In the case where $\alpha/\beta = 1$ then dw/dL is infinite, that is the contract curve is vertical. Finally, the contract curve slopes forward ($dw/dL > 0$), where $\alpha > \beta$ (that is, $\alpha/\beta > 1$), and backwards where $\alpha < \beta$. In other words where the union puts a bigger weight on employment than wages, the contract curve slopes forward, and where it puts a smaller weight on employment, it slopes backwards, as might be expected.

Tests of whether employment in union firms corresponds negatively to measures of workers' alternative wages give mixed results. The best known results use data for printers organised by the International Typographical Union. The data points correspond to negotiated wages and employment of typesetters in about ten towns made in various years over the post-war period. The ITU conducts local negotiations – so there is no question of a national agreement which would rule out determining both wages and employment at the local level (MacCurdy and Pencavel, 1986, S15). The union is also famous for 'make-work' practices, which could push the firm off the demand curve. For example national advertisements are uneconomically reset by union locals, so-called 'bogus' work. The union also enforces a strict closed shop (pre-entry closed shop), in that all individuals hired for the composing room must already have union cards.

The study by Brown and Ashenfelter of these data finds that employment of typesetters is not negatively related to their 'alternative' wage, however construed. Several different measures of alternative wage are tried such as earnings of production workers in manufacturing, or state average wages of ITU journeymen printers, but none support the theory (1986, table 2A). Generally alternative wages are positively, rather than negatively associated with employment. Walter Wessels (1991), using Canadian data, finds his results to be very sensitive to econometric specification.

On the other hand the study by MacCurdy and Pencavel of the same data, is more supportive of the efficient bargains idea – but the authors are cautious (MacCurdy and Pencavel, 1986, S34). The study of Bean and Turnbull of British coal mining is also supportive. They find that mining employment does respond negatively to alternative wages – here defined to include male manual earnings in manufacturing, and also the value of supplementary benefit (Bean and Turnbull, 1988, tables 1 and 2).

In sum, it is possible that efficient bargaining occurs in some contexts, though the econometric evidence is limited. In any case in most collective bargaining contexts, efficient bargaining would be difficult because of the many parties involved, so the model could not apply. The dramatic implications of figure 10.6, that unions simply share profits without affecting employment, are not borne out.

Insiders and outsiders

While the efficient bargains model sees unions as promoting employment, a new theory of 'insiders and outsiders' sees unions as preventing employment. This is more in line with the traditional view. 'Insiders' are the already employed workers, 'outsiders' are the unemployed who would be prepared to accept lower wages to enter the firm. If insiders are receiving rents, they have to prevent the firm from substituting them with cheaper outsiders. Moreover, when the firm's profits increase, the insiders want to take these profits for themselves, rather than see employment expand.

Labour unions can provide a means of protecting insiders – by raising the costs of firing insiders and of hiring outsiders – for example, by use of the strike threat or the simple closed shop (Lindbeck and Snower, 1986, 238). However, the theory can be made to stretch beyond the union sector. In particular the fixed costs of hiring and firing workers, plus the accumulation of specific human capital investments, act to protect insiders. The theory thus complements the 'internal labour market' view of the world. More broadly, by positing transactions costs when workers are selected or replaced, the insider–outsider theory attacks the neoclassical 'law of one price': the same wage will not rule for workers of given potential productivity. Union power will clearly be an important aspect of the interruption to the competitive process, since unions can only make their members better off by preventing competition.

A way of depicting union insider–outsider effects is given in figure 10.8. The union indifference curves have a special shape, being kinked at the current level of union membership, M (Carruth and Oswald, 1987). M is given in some way, outside the model. To the right of M, indifference curves are horizontal showing that the union will not accept reduced wages to expand beyond M. Also, all indifference curves are kinked at M, showing that whether union utility levels are high or low, it concentrates upon its current members. To the left of M, indifference curves slope upwards in the usual way – perhaps quite steeply – indicating that the union will accept some reductions in membership, so long as wages for remaining members are increased enough.

A problem is how union membership, M, is determined in the first place. The union cannot be a simple 'business' union, as depicted earlier in figure 10.1, maximising the difference between revenue from dues and costs of organising. We might perhaps think of M as initially being determined in this way, after which the existing members become introverted, and concentrate upon the union as it is. This is an example of the problem confronted earlier when discussing the 'median' member concept, of the tension between the aims of the union as an organisation, and that of its members. The union might get a bigger total surplus, and last longer, by being large. But given members might have a larger wage gain by concentrating on themselves – even if, in the longer run, the union disappears. We could have a version of 'short termism' on the part of union members.

Returning to figure 10.8, let us assume that the demand for labour curve is given by MRP_1. With competition, equilibrium would be at A, but with the union it is at C. If we now suppose that demand increases to MRP_2, with competition employment would expand to B, but with the union employment remains fixed at M, and all the advantages of the increased business are taken by existing members in higher wages: equilibrium at point D. If there is symmetry, the opposite should happen when demand decreases: wages fall, but employment remains constant. According to the diagram, insider-union groups' wages should respond to firm profits (movements of the MRP curve) rather than the determinants of w_c. Also insider groups' wages should be sensitive but employment insensitive to business conditions.

To check the above predictions we can look at what unions have actually done in response to changed business conditions. Two case studies are interesting in this connection. The first is the truckers, represented by the International Brotherhood of Teamsters (IBT), and the second the airline workers, represented by the International Association of Airline Mechanics and Aerospace Engineers (IAM). Both unions experienced deregulation in their industries, by the Motor Carrier Act of 1980, and the Airline Deregulation

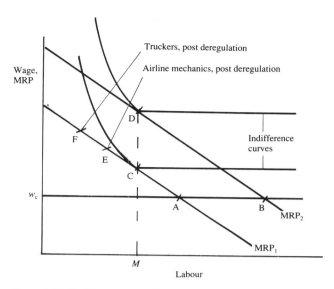

Figure 10.8 Insiders and outsiders

Act of 1978 respectively. Prior to these Acts, entry into interstate trucking was limited by the Interstate Commerce Commission, and into airlines by the Civil Aeronautics Board. For example, the CAB did not grant a single trunk (long distance) route to a new carrier between 1938 and 1978. As for trucking, some idea of the barrier enforced by the ICC is that operating licences had an average price of $530,000 in 1977, $370,000 in 1978, and this collapsed to zero after 1979 (Hirsch, 1988, 303). Deregulation of these industries is the same as a leftward shift of the demand curve for union labour. In terms of figure 10.8, unionised truckers and aircraft workers experienced a movement from MRP_2 to MRP_1.

It is interesting to consider in a bit more detail the effect of regulation and deregulation on unions. Normally we would expect unions to campaign for regulation. This is graphically shown in the case of the Teamsters, whose President went to jail in 1982, after attempting to bribe a senator to vote against deregulation in the 1980 Motor Carrier Act. In Britain as well, the Labour Party has been against privatisation of nationalised industries.

Hendricks *et al.* point out that there are three ways in which unions can gain from regulation (1980, 68). First, note rate of return regulation might encourage overcapitalisation as firms attempt to raise the asset base on which the rate of return is calculated. This could raise labour productivity and wages, but reduce employment, that is, benefit union insiders. Secondly regulation can

Table 10.5. *Truckers' pay before and after deregulation*

	Mean wage of drivers: union/non-union	Proportion union
1974	1.41	62%
1975	1.59	55
1976	1.56	61
1977	1.53	60
1978	1.40	57
1979	1.28	58
1980	1.31	58
1981	1.27	61
1982	No data	
1983	1.35	53
1984	1.41	31
1985	1.19	28

Source: Rose, 1987, 1162.

raise entry barriers and so make for larger firms and a more concentrated industrial structure. Such a structure makes union organisation easier, as we have seen. Thirdly, if the regulators control prices on a 'cost plus' basis, then management will be less interested in keeping costs down, and this will work to the union's advantage. On the other hand if regulators set maximum prices (as in electric utilities) this factor will work against unions since management will be keener to reduce costs. In trucking and airlines however – and in British nationalised industries – regulators encouraged firms to collude in setting prices, amounting effectively to cost-plus pricing.

We therefore summarise the impact of deregulation on unions simply as a leftward shift of the demand curve for union labour. The empirical problem is to establish what happened to union wage rates and union employment. Was there a move similar to that from D to C in figure 10.8?

Figures for trucking and airlines are reported in tables 10.5 and 10.6 respectively. Deregulation can be seen to have had a severe impact on unionised truckers. Prior to 1980, union drivers had a premium of about 50%. After 1980 the premium fell to about 25%. However, the proportion unionised also fell, after holding steady at 60% in the 70s, to only 28% in 1985. Thus although the IBT conceded some ground on wages, it was not enough to preserve union membership. In terms of figure 10.8, the movement in trucking was something like from point D to point F.

For airline personnel the insider model perhaps works better. Table 10.6 shows that with deregulation the number of airlines has increased considerably.

Table 10.6. *Airline industry before and after deregulation*

	1975	1980	1984
Number of airlines in industry	26	30	39
Unionisation of craft workers	47% (1977)		45%
Ratio, airline crafts average wages to craft workers in manufacturing	1.33 (1977)		1.19
Coefficient of variation of mechanics' wages	0.042	0.061	0.144

Sources: US Statistical Abstract; Card, 1986, tables 2 and 4; Peoples, 1990, table 1.

These airlines are less unionised, and their share of employment has increased from 7% in 1975 to 20% in 1980 – so unionisation has fallen somewhat, from 47% to 45%. However union relative wages seem to have fallen considerably. The ratio of craftworkers' pay in airlines to craft pay in manufacturing has fallen from 1.33 in 1977 to 1.19 in 1984 – and even more if changes in personal characteristics are allowed for (Peoples, 1990, table 3). (For airline mechanics however this does not seem true – their premium has been more or less maintained, see Card, 1986.) Thus, in terms of figure 10.8 the move in airlines seems to have been from point D to point E or even C. The airline case study thus appears to give some support to the insider–outsider model.

An interesting study by Blanchflower *et al.* (1988b), using British data, also appears to find support for insider power. The basis of the test here is that insider groups' wages should respond to firm profits more than to external influences such as unemployment. Insider power should logically be lowest in the non-union unskilled sector of the economy, and most in the unionised, skilled sector. Using data from private sector firms in the 1984 Workplace Industrial Relations Survey they do indeed find this pattern. The interesting result (1988, tables 2 and 3) is that for the relation between wages and firms' financial performance: union firms tended to pay more to their skilled or semi-skilled workers (but not to unskilled workers) where managers judged their firms were performing better than others in the same industry. There were similar, but weaker effects, in non-union firms, which is to be expected since insider power is likely to be lower in such firms.

A difficulty with the British results is that firms' financial performance could simply be measuring labour market disequilibrium, not insider power. When firms are performing well financially their labour demand curve shifts right, and wages will increase strongly in the short run, so as to elicit the extra supply of labour. (In the long run wages will fall back, because long-run labour supply is more elastic.) The fact that non-union firms also exhibit wages that are sensitive to firms' profitability is presumably due to this factor. The case for insider power therefore rests on the excess sensitivity of union compared to non-union firms' wages to firm profitability.

In sum, the insider–outsider theory obtains some empirical corroboration in a union context. But there seems to be an asymmetry – as was long ago summed up in Cartter's (1959) 'union wage-preference path' – with unions responding to demand declines by maintaining wages at the expense of employment, and to demand increases by raising wages with employment constant. What the airline and trucking union studies also suggest is that deregulation is bad for unionisation. This is unequivocal. Thus we would expect unions to support regulation and nationalisation, just as we would expect them to lobby for tariffs against foreign competition. Both tactics shift outwards, and perhaps steepen, the demand curve for union workers.

Union effects on non-union workers

If efficient bargain effects are not important, then increased union wages should simply mean reduced union employment (unless unions raise labour productivity – see below). The analysis is then as illustrated above in connection with figure 10.6. Those displaced in the union sector should 'crowd' into the non-union sector putting downward pressure on non-union sector wages. The question is: do union wage increases cause crowding and thereby non-union wage decreases?

The 'crowding' effect is to be distinguished from the 'threat' effect. The latter occurs where non-union firms raise their pay to union levels so as to avert being unionised. IBM, for example, provides very good pay and conditions in order to pre-empt unionisation. The threat effect occurs among union and non-union firms *within* a unionised sector – say manufacturing. The crowding effect primarily occurs *across* sectors: broadly unionised sectors such as manufacturing or utilities (see table 10.2) cause crowding into less unionised sectors such as the service sector.

If union wage increases are paralleled by non-union wage decreases, the picture over time will be as illustrated in figure 10.9. Suppose the main period of unionisation is concentrated in the 1920s. Then union wages, w_u, will increase. If non-union wages, w_n, decrease by as much, the average wage, $\bar{w}$, will be unaffected. If non-union wages do not decrease by as much, perhaps because minimum wages or welfare benefits place a floor under wages, unemployment will ensue. Unemployment will also ensue if displaced workers believe it is worth waiting until a high paying union job becomes available (see Mincer, 1976) – many unemployed workers do seem to have a requirement that any new job they enter must be unionised (Heywood, 1990b, finds 13% of unemployed in his sample have such a requirement). In any case after the once-

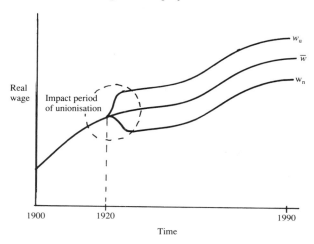

Figure 10.9 Course of union, non-union and average wage over time

for-all union wage effect the wages of the two groups will increase at much the same rate. From the armchair perspective this indeed seems to be very much what has happened. As Milton Friedman has pointed out, the wages of domestic servants have increased as much over time as have the wages of more heavily unionised workers, such as coal miners (Friedman, 1951, 222). On this view unions do not affect the average wage, only distribution given the average. The average wage is thus determined by the deeper forces which influence labour productivity, such as capital accumulation, innovation, education, and secure private property based on stable democracy.

Surprisingly little research has been done into union crowding effects. Results of two interesting US studies (there are no British) are summarised in tables 10.7 and 10.8. Look first at row (a) of table 10.7. The usual earnings functions were calculated, but with the addition of the percentage unionised in the individual's town (standard metropolitan statistical area, SMSA). Crowding effects should be revealed as a fall in non-union workers' pay as percentage unionised in the town increases. Analysis is confined to the sixteen to twenty-four year olds since these are most vulnerable to crowding. Crowding wage effects are found for black non-union workers only. For the white non-union group, the higher the SMSA union density, the higher the non-union wage, which is contrary to the crowding hypothesis.

However if non-union wages are sticky, crowding could be manifested as reduced non-union employment. For example, highly unionised SMSAs might also offer more favourable welfare benefits (e.g., New York City), which would act as a floor beneath non-union pay. The employment effect is

Table 10.7. *Effect of proportion unionised in city on wages and employment of union and non-union workers*

| | Blue-collar males, 16–24 | | | |
| | White | | Black | |
	Union	Non-union	Union	Non-union
Effect of increase in % unionised in SMSA on:				
(a) wage	positive	positive	positive	negative
(b) employment as % of population	negative		negative	

Note: The wage equations include controls for age, education, occupation, industry, region, full-time employment, the growth of average income in the SMSA between 1960 and 1970, proportion of blacks and teenagers in the SMSA population, and the proportion of female headed households in the SMSA.
Source: Holzer, 1982, tables 2 and 3.

considered in row (b) of table 10.7. It can be seen that there is indeed an adverse employment effect: there appear to be fewer employment opportunities for youth in highly unionised towns.

Next, table 10.8 gives results of an interesting case study into crowding. San Francisco is more heavily unionised than Los Angeles, as shown in the top row. However clerical and sales workers are poorly unionised in both cities – see second row. If there is a crowding effect, clerical and sales workers should be more poorly paid in San Francisco. The bottom panel shows this to be the case. Pay levels in general are somewhat higher (5% to 10%) in San Francisco than Los Angeles, but pay levels of clerical and sales workers are 25% lower. A crowding effect is demonstrated.

Also backing up the crowding effect is the finding that increases in industry union density increase non-union workers' pay in large firms, but not small firms (Podgursky, 1986, 283; Moore *et al.*, 1985, 35). Pay in small firms will respond to crowding effects, since such firms are not likely to be targets and hence do not have to respond to threat effects.

Freeman and Medoff, while accepting the above studies, contend they only represent part of the picture (1984, 160–1). The studies, they say, show only that unskilled 'secondary' workers lose from unionism. More skilled non-union workers in large firms gain from unionism due to threat effects. They also contend that in a general equilibrium analysis capital could migrate from the union to the non-union sector, so making non-union workers better off. This amounts to saying that the demand curves in figure 10.6, which we drew on the

Table 10.8. *Effect of proportion unionised on wages of clerical and sales workers in San Francisco and Los Angeles, 1966*

	San Francisco	Los Angeles
Union membership:		
total workforce, average 1954–66	46%	32%
clerical and sales workers, 1966	19%	13%
Wages, Los Angeles = 100:		
all industries	110 (male)	100
	105 (female)	
Clerical and sales*	75	100

Note:
*The wage equation holds constant age, education, colour, sex, and industry.
  Unemployment rates and cost of living are about the same in the two cities.
Source: Kahn, 1978, tables 1, 2, 3, and p. 214.

assumption of given capital stocks, move when w_u changes because capital stocks change in response to unionisation. The simplicity of the diagram is then destroyed. In particular the possibility arises that unions can benefit all labour, union and non-union, at the expense of capital. In terms of figure 10.9, the average wage itself, $\bar{w}$, might be raised by unions. The view that union wage gains come at the expense of non-union workers is therefore 'simplistic' (Freeman and Medoff, 1984, 161).

One way of checking the Freeman and Medoff contention is to look at the effect of unions on capital. In later sections we will summarise research on unions and profitability, investment, and employment. We will find that unions certainly reduce profitability, and they also seem to reduce employment in union firms, which accords with figure 10.6. It might however be argued that unions can increase labour's share in the national income. The determinants of labour's share are not well understood, partly because the share is so difficult to compute accurately (for a discussion see Addison and Siebert, 1979, 285–91). David Metcalf has however pointed to the fact that in Britain in the 1970s when union power increased, there was an increase in the share of wages in national income (Metcalf, 1984, 26). But the 1970s was one of the worst decades ever for British economic performance, with high inflation and a special loan from the International Monetary Fund. The share might have increased, but everyone was worse off. Thus the idea that unions can simply obtain their gains from rich capitalists is itself simplistic.

The average wage depends upon labour productivity, as well as upon labour's share in national income. Phelps Brown and Browne's work on wages in five countries over the last century shows how closely real wages have tracked labour productivity. Table 10.9 gives the results for Germany, Sweden, the UK, and the US for the period 1895–1960. There is a close correlation between periods when productivity increased quickly and real wages increased quickly. To give unions a part to play here, one would have to argue that unions have a role in productivity increase. To assess this argument we look in detail at the effects of unions on firms in the next section, and find the argument unconvincing.

As a final point about the effect of unions on non-union workers, we should note the political role of unions. Even if it were conceded that unions disadvantageously crowd workers into the non-union sector, there is still the political 'pro-labour' role of unions. Freeman and Medoff have performed interesting research here, as well. They contend that unions have pushed for 'social' legislation such as the Public Accommodation Act of 1964, the Civil Rights Act of 1964, anti-poverty legislation, the Occupational Safety and Health Act of 1971, and the minimum wage (1984, 192–9). Similar observations could be made of British trade unions. It could even be argued that unions are more effective in attaining these 'social' goals than labour monopoly goals – British unions have not been able to stop Mrs Thatcher reducing their strike power for example.

The question is whether 'social' legislation helps non-union workers. Minimum wage laws for example cause unemployment. Social legislation might also be said often to have a labour monopoly rather than a social thrust. Thus minimum wage laws act to reduce the competitive threat of low wage non-union labour. Cox and Oaxaca have advanced a model which shows that a minimum wage law raises the wage of skilled union labour, and reduces the real rental rate of capital. It is to be expected therefore that unions will vote for such a law, and firms (and non-union workers) will vote against it. Comparing non-minimum wage law states with minimum wage law states (forty in 1975), they find that the latter do indeed have greater union membership, and less powerful firms (measured as the sum of rents, dividends, and interest as a proportion of state personal income) (1982, 546). Minimum wage laws can thus be explained in terms of the economic self-interest of the major parties. A similar argument can be made for other 'social' legislation. For example safety legislation affects non-union firms disproportionately and thus cuts down non-union competition (see chapter 7). Thus we should be cautious about emphasising union political activities as a means of spreading the benefits of unionisation to non-members.

Effects of unions on firms

Unions have an impact on pay, profitability, productivity, employment, and investment. Let us consider these in turn.

Table 10.9. *Average annual increases in real wages and industrial productivity by country*

	Real wages (increase % p.a.)		Industrial productivity (increase % p.a.)	
Germany				
1895–1913	1.27	(10)	1.93	(8)
1925–38	1.51	(7)	2.60	(4)
1950–9	4.66	(1)	4.86	(1)
Sweden				
1895–1913	1.48	(8)	2.13	(6)
1921–38	1.65	(6)	3.86	(2)
1949–60	3.09	(2)	2.83	(3)
UK				
1895–1913	−0.11	(12)	0.03	(12)
1924–38	1.68	(5)	1.79	(10)
1949–59	2.16	(4)	2.07	(7)
US				
1895–1913	1.33	(9)	1.49	(11)
1920–38	0.65	(11)	1.91	(9)
1946–60	2.46	(3)	2.52	(5)

Note: Figures in brackets are rankings. Correlation of the two rankings is:
 r = 0.720
where r is defined as $r = (1 - 6D)/n(n^2 - 1)$, D = sum of squared rank differences.
Source: Phelps Brown and Browne, 1968, table 30.

Pay

There has been much research on the extent to which unions raise the pay of workers of given potential productivity. The most comprehensive survey of the research is provided by Lewis (1986). The figure he gives for the US union markup for the period 1967–78 is 14% to 17% when computed with cross-sectional data, and 7% to 10% when computed with panel data. The British markup calculated by Mark Stewart for manual workers seems lower than this, about 8% – but varying between 0% for firms with an open shop, and 17% for firms with a closed shop (1987, 153). The approach to obtaining these estimates follows from the earnings function already studied.

Recall the earnings function derived in chapter 4 (appendix 4.1). Individual earnings in any time period are related to accumulated human capital investments:

$$\ln Y_t = a_0 + rs + a_1 t + a_2 t^2,$$

where $\ln Y_t$ is the logarithm of individual earnings after t years of experience, s is years of schooling, and t is years of experience. If unions influence earnings *without* affecting worker human capital investments then the earnings function can be modified by adding a simple union dummy variable U (representing unionisation) thus:

$$\ln Y_t = a_0 + rs + a_1 t + a_2 t^2 + bU,$$

where b approximates the per cent union wage premium. However if union membership affects on-the-job human capital investment then separate equations should be fitted for union and non-union workers. An example is given in table 10.10 using 1987 Panel Study of Income Dynamics Data. Substituting mean values for variables yields a wage gap. As can be seen the results indicate that union earnings profiles are much flatter. For the union sample there is very little increase in pay with experience, or with tenure. Some, such as Freeman (1984), interpret this to mean that unions create greater wage equality among workers, including young and old workers.

Such an interpretation has been called into question. Traditional regression analysis assumes that all regressors including union status are exogenous, so that all sample observations are independently randomly drawn. The problem is that because unionised firms are forced to pay higher wages for workers, they would tend to opt for higher quality workers. However, many aspects of quality are not measurable. If union workers are systematically of higher quality, then single-equation cross-sectional regression models will yield biased results, since unmeasurable quality characteristics describing union workers are omitted.

One solution to unmeasured quality variation is to use panel data. Panel data consist of information obtained by following a given set of individuals annually. One can compare the wage received by a given worker when he is a union member to the wage received by this same worker when he is not in a union. The ability to look at wages before and after a union status change for the same person provides a way of holding constant unmeasurable individual characteristics. Thus using first differences:

$$\Delta \ln Y_t = a_1 \Delta X_t + b_1 U_{t-1} N_t + b_2 N_{t-1} U_t + b_3 N_{t-1} U_t + b_4 N_{t-1} N_t + \epsilon_t,$$

where the Δ denotes the first difference operator, ΔX_t represents changes in variables other than unionisation between $t-1$ and t, and U_t and N_t stand for unionised and non-unionised at time period t. Using this methodology, Freeman (1984) finds about an 8% union effect.

Whereas such a panel data approach appears to represent the perfect solution to cross-sectional estimation biases, statistical problems remain. The first problem, as Freeman (1984, 6) shows, is that even small errors that result in improper reporting of union status can lead to large errors in estimated union

Table 10.10. *Wage regressions by union status, 1987*

	Non-union		Union	
	Mean value	Coefficient	Mean value	Coefficient
Constant		5.165		6.521
Schooling (yrs)	13.7	0.090	13.2	0.038
Experience (yrs)	16.6	0.035	19.7	0.002
Experience^2		−0.0007		−0.0001
Tenure (months)	89.4	0.004	142.3	0.002
Tenure^2		$-0.51 \times 10 - 5$		$-0.22 \times 10 - 5$
Wage ($/hr)	$12.81		15.26	
Sample size	1761		443	

Note: White males 19–66 computed from the 1987 PSID data.

effects. This is because in practice most people do not switch. The chance therefore is that anyone who is misclassified as switching will be put into the switcher category – on which we are relying for our estimate. A way of avoiding such measurement errors is to follow individual one-time union switchers over a sufficiently long time period to be sure there are no errors in classifying union status (Polachek *et al.*, 1987; also Polachek and McCutcheon, 1983).

The second problem is that individuals switching in and out of union membership will differ from those who do not switch. For a start, both joiners and leavers will lose specific human capital when switching union status, since this generally means changing jobs. In addition union joiners are likely to be able younger workers, while union leavers are probably less able, and are likely to have left involuntarily (been fired). In fact we find that union joiners gain 9.1% immediately upon joining, while leavers face a 21.7% loss immediately upon leaving (Polachek *et al.*, 1987, 529). However these figures have to be adjusted for 2% to 9% declines in pay due to change in job (estimated by following job changers). If we therefore add 5%, say, to union joiners and subtract 5% from the loss of union leavers to allow for the loss of specific human capital, a union markup figure of about 14% to 16% is derived – this is the most accurate figure we have at the moment.

Table 10.10 also shows that the coefficients for union workers are lower than for non-union. The question arises as to whether unions are doing this – by negotiating for 'standard rates' for the job – or whether they simply organise the kind of jobs which anyway have a flat profile. An argument for the latter hypothesis is that in some jobs deferred payment schemes and/or specific investments are easier to organise than in others (Polachek *et al.*, 1987). These jobs will attract stable workers whose earnings profile will be steep. At the same time firms will oppose unionisation in these jobs because unions might cause conflict and make the sharing of the gains from these schemes more difficult. The upshot is that jobs with steep earnings profiles are the jobs which are not unionised. Evidence in favour of this hypothesis is the lower unionisation of white-collar workers since more training is required in these jobs (though, as we have seen, there are legal obstacles, too).

Union wage gains should depend on market structure. Higher wage gains should occur where firms are in a position to exert some monopoly power. Such power can arise where the firm has a large enough market share, or where the union is in a position to enforce industry-wide collective bargaining. With industry-wide agreements, wages are 'taken out of competition', presumably making firms less reluctant to concede to the union. A further circumstance is foreign competition, which will act to limit domestic firms' rents, and therefore limit their ability to share these rents with unions.

American results on the market structure issue are not clear-cut. As already noted, the union markup even seems to diminish in larger firms, and more concentrated industries (Mellow, 1982; Green, 1988, 186 presents a similar result for Britain), which is exactly opposite to the rent-sharing hypothesis. This could be simply because small firms are more costly to organise – a bigger markup is needed to cover the costs. The difficulty with the approach is that of selectivity bias: we only observe those unionised firms remaining in business which have been able to survive (or even prosper) with unions. The small unionised firm is quite rare, and it might be that it has exceptional management compared with the small non-union firm. In other words we are not comparing like with like.

An alternative approach is to compare competitive and non-competitive firms. We would expect a lower union markup in the former. Results from the British Workplace Industrial Relations Survey (WIRS) of 2,000 firms suggest that unionised workers in fact do better in firms which face little competition. 'Competition' can be decided on the basis of the answer of the establishment's manager as to how many competitors he has. Unionised firms with many competitors are found to offer no union markup, while in firms with few competitors unions achieve a 9% markup (Stewart, 1990, 1126). Interestingly within the competitive group of firms (many competitors), unions only gain a markup where industry union coverage is high, just as expected (1990, 1132). Within the non-competitive group, there is a markup only where foreign competition is not strong, again as expected (1990, 1134).

US results, despite poor data, also point to unions as sharing in monopoly rents. Freeman and Medoff report that the greater the proportion of union workers in an industry, the bigger the union markup (1984, 51). This is because a high proportion unionised means less room for non-union competition.

Industry level rather than plant level contracts also help the unions for the same reason.

Profitability

Backing the rent sharing view of unions is evidence that unions reduce profit margins more in firms with high market share. Both US and British studies find this. Freeman, for the US, finds unions drive the price–cost margin down 21% in highly concentrated industries, compared to only 7% in less concentrated industries (1984, table 2.2). Also Nancy Rose, in her study of the trucking industry, calculates that truckers were the 'dominant beneficiary' of trucking regulation, taking 65% to 76% of the rents in the industry prior to deregulation (1987, 1175). For Britain, taking a sample of 145 large manufacturing firms in 1984/5, Machin finds that the profit/sales ratio is 9.1% in union firms and 10.8% in non-union. The disadvantage for union firms increases as their market share increases. A union firm with a 20% market share has a ratio of profit to sales about 5 points lower than one with a 10% market share (Machin, 1989, table 3). It is also worth noting that the average market share of union firms in the UK sample was 9%, compared with only 1% for non-union firms – indicating that unions gravitate towards the high market share firms, where there are rents to be gained.

It must be admitted that some studies do not find that the union effect on profits is higher in firms which have market power (according to some measure). Thus Clark (1984), and Connolly *et al.* (1986) find no evidence that unions reduce profits more for firms with market power. One problem with these studies is that they only consider large Fortune 500 firms, so there is little variation in market power – all firms in the sample have power. Another problem is selectivity (which dogs all union studies). The large market share firms will tend to be those with good management – which might be better able to exercise a countervailing force against unions. It would be this special management factor, rather than lack of union power as such, which allows the large market share firm to hold on to its profits as well as the small share firm. If managerial ability could be held constant, the large market share firms should do worse in the face of unions than the small share firms.

At any rate all studies agree that unions reduce profits. Results are reported in tables 10.11 and 10.12. Table 10.11 shows that a firm's market valuation relative to book value (excess value), R and D expenditure, advertising expenditure, and patent activity are all lower if it is highly unionised. A difficulty with the study is that union density is not actually measured for the firms in the sample, but inferred from union density in the industry in which the firm operates. Ruback and Zimmerman's study however shows graphically what happens to a firm's share price when it is unionised. Their data relate to share prices of 253 firms quoted on the New York Stock Exchange between 1962 and

Table 10.11. *Effects of unions on profit and investment, US*
367 firms from 1977 Fortune 500

	Unionisation[b]	
	Less than 30%	Greater than 50%
Excess value[a]/sales	0.17	−0.04
R & D expenditures/sales	0.03	0.01
Advertising exps./sales	0.008	0.002
Number of patents granted in 1977/sales	0.030	0.015

Notes:
[a] Excess value is defined as the difference between the market value of the firm and its book value.
[b] Unionisation was measured by union density in the firm's principal 3-digit census-coded industry.
Source: Connolly *et al.*, 1986, table 1.

Table 10.12. *Effects of unions on firms' financial performance, UK*
933 private sector establishments, 1984

	Unionisation		
	Non-union	Union recognition	Closed shop
Probability of above average performance establishment size:			
25–49 workers	50	34	18
500+ workers	67	51	31

Note: Managers were asked: 'How would you assess the financial performance of the establishment compared to other establishments in the same industry?' They could answer, above, equal, and below average. Estimates come from a profit equation, with control variables set to their means. Controls were: state of product market, labour cost in total cost, presence of profit-related pay.
Source: Blanchflower and Oswald, 1988, table 6.

1980. Unions lost 199 and won fifty-four representation elections in these firms over the period. Using sixty months of data beginning seven years before the election (the last two years are not used in case the stock price already reflects expectations of union organisation), they estimate what the stock price would be in the absence of an election. They find the stock price in firms in which unions are successful fall by about 4% compared to this benchmark (1984,

Table 10.13. *Unions and employment change, UK 1975–84*

	Change in employment (%)			
	Decrease of 20%	−19% to +19%	Increase of 20%	Total
1975–80				
Non-union	14	47	39	100
Recognition, no closed shop	23	49	28	100
Closed shop	21	62	17	100
1980–4				
Non-union	15	62	33	100
Recognition, no closed shop	27	55	18	100
Closed shop	37	35	9	100

Note: Data relate to private sector establishments with over 24 employees. The data are interpreted as follows: the top left 14% figure means 14% of non-union establishments decreased their employment by 20% or more between 1975 and 1980.
Source: Blanchflower and Millward, 1988, table 4.

1149). The average loss per worker comes to about $47,000 in 1980 dollars. This is the stock market's estimate of what unionisation does to a firm's profits (also see Abowd, 1989).

Table 10.12 shows the British evidence. Here the profit variable is profitability as assessed by managers. Profitability is evidently closely related to whether unions are recognised, and particularly to the closed shop. Thus in establishments in the 500+ employees size, there is a 67% chance of a manager in a non-union firm giving an 'above average' estimate for his firm's profitability (as opposed to an average or below average estimate), compared to only a 31% chance if the firm has a closed shop.

British evidence that unions lower profitability is thus consistent with US studies. However if the profitability effect is confined to 'rent capture' in monopolistic firms, unions' adverse effects on jobs and investment will be reduced. In such a case, the economic effect of a union on a firm will simply be to split up the pie differently.

Employment

Unfortunately however it seems that union firms do suffer adverse employment and (less certainly) investment consequences. Striking evidence on union employment effects is contained in table 10.13, which shows a strong relationship between employment decline and whether or not there is a union in the establishment. For example, taking the 1980–4 period, 37% of firms with a closed shop declined by over 20%, compared to only 15% of non-union firms.

It is possible that there might be another, unmeasured factor related to both low unionism and high employment growth, so that the correlation between unionism and low growth need not be causal. For example, British unions tend to be concentrated in 'smoke stack' industries which are declining internationally. However, holding constant firm size, industry, region, and county unemployment, the result remains (Blanchflower *et al.*, 1991, table 4). Unionised plants contract 3% more quickly than equivalent non-union plants.

US results, while not based on a nationwide establishment dataset, also indicate a negative union impact on firm growth. Thus Kaufman and Kaufman (1987), taking the period 1956 to 1982 in Detroit, estimate that UAW organised auto engine and body parts firms have a probability of closing 12% to 33% higher than non-union firms of average size (1987, 347). They attribute this effect to the much higher wages of UAW organised firms – a 29% to 38% markup over equivalent non-union labour (1987, 341) – which is not offset by increased labour productivity. Other evidence is contained in a study of 587 Californian manufacturing plants. It is found that employment growth in union plants over five years is 2% per annum lower than non-union plants (Blanchflower *et al.*, 1991). Finally it has been noted that the decline 1973–84 in durable manufacturing, mining, and construction is solely in the union sectors of those industries; non-union employment increased (Linneman and Wachter, 1986). Also there is a link between those industries experiencing the greatest increase in union wage markup, and those with the largest decline in union employment.

Productivity

The negative relationship between unionisation and firm growth also bears on the argument that unions raise productivity. It is inconsistent with that argument. Freeman and Medoff (1984) have long claimed that the industrial democracy aspect of unions (their substitution of 'voice' for 'exit') will raise labour productivity because morale and cooperation among workers will be improved. In addition they argue that the 'shock' effect of unions will improve management. If productivity were raised enough to offset union pay increases – and reduced labour flexibility – there would be no adverse employment effects. The Freeman and Medoff view has however been criticised (e.g., Reynolds, 1988) as logically inconsistent, because if unions did raise labour productivity by enough to offset the union markup, unit labour costs would fall, and we should observe firms being anxious to be unionised. This we do not generally see.

Nevertheless there has been a widespread investigation into the effect of unions on productivity and productivity growth. Perhaps the fact that productivity is so hard to measure has prolonged the investigation. Allen has found that union productivity in office building contracts is at least 30% higher than non-union, controlling for labour quality, capital–labour ratios, and other factors (1986, 187). However Hirsch and Addison survey the US literature and reach a generally negative conclusion: 'the longer term effects of unionism are not encouraging' (1986, 215). Metcalfe has surveyed the British literature and his conclusion is similar: 'unionization is associated with lower labour productivity or, at best, has no effect' (1988, 6). Thus it cannot be concluded that the union wage markup is offset by extra productivity. Hence average costs of production must rise and firms will be less successful, leading to the adverse employment consequences we have noted in table 10.13.

Investment

If unions lower profits, and employment, and have little effect on labour productivity, there should also be a negative association between unions and investment. Capital investments are vulnerable to collective action by unions because capital, once invested, is illiquid. A higher capital stock promises higher profits, which in turn leads to higher wage demands. The firm, anticipating this type of capture, will not invest, or will invest less. The investments concerned might not only be in tangible capital, but also in intangible capital such as R and D, and even advertising.

Table 10.11 contains some results bearing on the relationship between unionisation and R and D and advertising investment. It can be seen that unionisation is associated with lower levels of both types of investment. The result holds when market structure is controlled as well. However, as we have already noted, firms' unionisation is poorly measured in the study. The study by Clark finds unionisation to be associated with lower profits, but with no difference in the capital/labour ratio, implying unionisation does not reduce investment. Clark in fact interprets his results as being consistent with an efficient bargaining model of the type discussed above (figure 10.5), where the union affects the distribution of profits only, leaving output and employment unchanged (1984, 918).

A similar mixed picture is evident for the British results as well. A study of 133 large manufacturing companies (twenty being non-union) over the period 1972–86 finds no negative effect of unions on investment (Wadhwani and Wall, 1989, 3). On the other hand, a study by Denny and Nickel using changes in investment 1980–4 for seventy-eight 3-digit industries finds that union density is associated with lower investment (1991, table 1).

Given the strong results on profitability and employment in all the studies, the lack of clear investment effects is puzzling, and more research is clearly needed. At any rate, it is clear that the adverse economic effects of unions, based on the strike threat, are important. Thus any beneficial union effects on industrial democracy, to which we now turn, are bought at a cost.

10.5 Industrial democracy

An important aspect of collective bargaining is to restrict 'managerial prerogatives'. Unions aim, through agreed procedures, to regulate the way in which workers can be 'ordered around'. This has been termed the 'sword of justice' effect of collective bargaining (Metcalf, 1988). Basically unions assist in giving workers due process, and a type of property right in their jobs. Unions, in most contexts, have quite small wage effects. The reason that people nevertheless wish to join must be for other reasons: their desire for protection against victimisation. It might be for this reason that disadvantaged groups such as black workers are more pro-union.

Collective bargaining affects almost every aspect of the management of the enterprise. This is shown well in Slichter's famous study of the impact of collective bargaining on management (Slichter *et al.*, 1960). The study has headings under hiring, training, seniority, layoff, promotion, work assignment, sub-contracting, pension plans, discipline, and grievances. Collective bargaining limits managerial discretion in all these areas, and industrial relations policy becomes more important *vis-à-vis* other firm policies, such as marketing. Grievance procedures have costs, in other words, and marketing might well suffer.

Slichter and his colleagues do not conduct empirical research into the consequences of the conflict they hint at between industrial relations and marketing policies. They nevertheless come down strongly in favour of collective bargaining because of 'the sense of participation' it imparts to workers, though they admit that this participation might be bought 'at the expense of the consumer' (1960, 961), that is, raise prices. The rather gloomy economic effects of collective bargaining, reviewed above, should therefore be balanced against the gains in fairness and participation for workers on the factory floor.

However, we must be careful here. It would be wrong to suppose that non-union firms treat their workers without 'due process', and do not recognise property rights in jobs. It does not pay any firm to gain the reputation for treating its workers unfairly. Thus many non-union firms have procedures for dealing with individual grievances. For example among non-union private British firms, 77% had a procedure for grievances, and 80% for health and safety (Milward and Stevens, 1986, table 7.2). Thus union firms do not have a monopoly on fairness – though Freeman and Medoff decry the quality of non-union grievance procedures: less than one in three non-union grievance systems allow outside arbitrators to make the final decision (1984, 109).

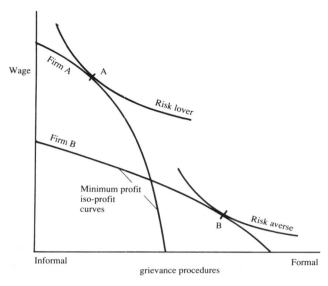

Figure 10.10 Choosing grievance procedures

From the orthodox economic viewpoint the type and formality of grievance procedures a firm chooses depends on its technology, and its workers' preferences, as well as its unionisation. Consider figure 10.10. Two types of firm are depicted. One firm has steep iso-profit curves, indicating that grievance procedures are costly for this firm, so a considerable wage reduction would be required if procedures were to be offered. An example would be a risky business such as dealing on the stock market: jobs cannot be guaranteed, so high wages are offered instead. The minimum (normal) profit iso-profit curve is shown. Risk lovers would be attracted to this type of firm, and locate at point A. At the other end of the scale is the stable firm for which it is quite cheap to offer job property rights – for example, a government department. Low wages and elaborate procedures should characterise such a firm, and it would be peopled by the risk averse, located at a point such as B. This is the basic economic incentive framework underlying the provision of grievance systems (see Ichniowski and Lewin, 1987). Grievance procedures are a non-pecuniary benefit, and workers (and firms) choose whether to be paid in non-pecuniary terms (stable employment for example), or to have higher cash payments. In theory, if firms are unfair, they have to pay more for labour, just as they would if they provided other poor working conditions.

Whether in practice jointly negotiated procedures are 'fairer' than management determined procedures is difficult to determine. Certainly non-union firms have a different order of priorities. We have already seen the emphasis on merit as opposed to seniority, in non-union firms. This translates into a more compressed wage distribution in union firms when compared to non-union firms (Freeman and Medoff, 1984, 85; Metcalf, 1982, 163), and also into lower quit rates in union firms, given wages. The results might indicate greater fairness at the workplace though US results also show higher absenteeism in unionised workplaces (Hirsch and Addison, 1987, 204), which does not square with a more contented workforce. In any case, more fairness within the unionised workplace could be bought at the expense of crowding and unemployment outside it.

The popular assumption seems to be, in Daniel Fischel's words, that 'employers, left to their own devices, will oppress workers' (1984, 1061). For this reason unions are given special privileges, minimum wages are set, health and safety is inspected, redundancy (severance) pay is required, commissions oversee gender and colour hiring policies, maternity leave is required, and the right to dismiss is restricted. Generally more rights are given to full-time than part-time workers – for example in Britain people working less than sixteen hours a week have to have worked with the same firm at least five years before they become eligible for unfair dismissal procedures, whereas those working over sixteen hours a week only have to have worked with the same firm for two years (hence the growth in part-time employment). Freedom of contract is extensively circumscribed.

The need for special protection of workers against employers might be ascribed to several factors. First, it is said that costs of moving between jobs, and ignorance about job characteristics, give firms monopsony power. However the question must be asked, whether the magnitude of the effect is large. Essentially the whole of this book explores issues of the competitiveness of labour markets. Readers can make their own decision. Second it is said that specific capital investments tie workers to firms, and allow firms further monopsony power. But given long-term relationships it is to the advantage of both sides to develop a 'governance structure' to limit opportunistic behaviour. The internal labour market (see chapter 9) has methods of protecting both sides.

Third, it is said the operation of the company pension scheme, or its safety procedures, requires a collective agency, because it is not in the interest of any single worker to monitor company behaviour. 'Free rider' problems require unions. To this we can reply simply that if a company gains a reputation for reneging on pension payments, or safety standards, it will find its cost of labour increasing. Company consultative and information channels are set up precisely so that the firm can ensure that it meets its commitments. This is why the large majority of non-union firms (80%) in the British Workplace Industrial Relations Survey have procedures for dealing with grievances,

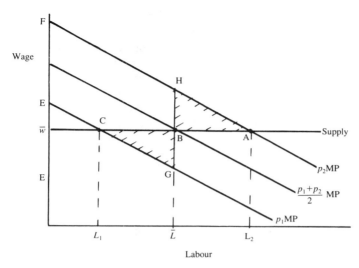

Figure 10.11 Employment protection

dismissals, and health and safety issues (Millward and Stevens, 1986, table 7.3).

Restrictions on freedom of contract can backfire. Employment at will is a case in point. Both America and Britain have laws limiting the right to make contracts terminable at will. These laws are thought to be part of employment 'protection'. A diagrammatic analysis is given in figure 10.11. Suppose price fluctuates between p_1 and p_2, so that MRP moves between p_1MP and p_2MP, as shown (MP = marginal product). Suppose that the supply of labour is horizontal at wage $\bar{w}$ for simplicity. With the ability to hire at will, equilibrium would be at points L_1 and L_2 for low and high demand respectively. The firm surplus will be triangle $EC\bar{w}$ in bad times and triangle $FA\bar{w}$ in good times.

However without the ability to hire at will, the amount of labour hired cannot vary, and the firm will use an 'average' demand for labour to decide how much labour to hire. Profit in the two years will be:

$$\pi_1 + \pi_2 = p_1 Q(\bar{L}) + p_2 Q(\bar{L}) - 2\bar{w}\bar{L},$$

and at maximum:

$$d(\pi_1 + \pi_2)/dL = p_1 Q' + p_2 Q' + 2\bar{w} = 0,$$

where Q' is labour's MP. Thus $\bar{L}$ will be chosen so that:

$$\bar{w} = Q'(p_1 + p_2)/2,$$

in other words $\bar{L}$ will be halfway between L_1 and L_2.

It can be seen that, without employment at will, in good times labour will receive the same wage bill as in bad times – so labour's gains are exactly cancelled out by losses. However firms lose overall due to the policy. In bad times they are at point B, paying workers more than their MRP, which is G, and so losing the cross-hatched triangle CBG. In good times they are still at point B (firms do not expand for fear of not being able to dismiss workers in the downturn) this time paying workers less than their marginal product, which is H, and so losing the cross-hatched triangle HAB. Thus firms lose, and workers do not gain (if the labour supply curve sloped upwards, workers would lose overall as well), which means that employment 'protection' lowers national income, and lowers employment.

10.6 The professions

The professions form union-like bodies such as the American Medical Association and British Medical Association. Professional organisations such as the AMA are not strictly unions, since they are not generally composed of employees but of the self-employed. Consequently they do not usually collectively bargain, though they present a common front to the buyer – and the BMA actually does negotiate with the national health service in Britain. Professional organisations are in some ways more like cartels of firms, enforcing prices and certain business practices such as restrictions on advertising (see Siebert, 1984).

On the other hand, professional organisations are like unions in that there is the same tension between the selfish aims of the organisation, and its social aims. In both cases the organisation receives special legal protection. Doctors, like craft unions, restrict entry via a licensing system. Also only doctors are allowed to provide health care (e.g., prescribe drugs). The selfish aim of restriction of entry is the raising of doctors' earnings (see Weiss, 1985). The social aim, emphasised in public discussion, is to protect the public from quacks. Similarly unions are given special legal privileges because of a social aim: it is thought the worker side is weaker and needs the protection of collective bargaining. Some lessons can therefore be learned about unions by analysing the operation of the professions.

The self-regulating professions (doctors, dentists, lawyers, opticians, accountants, pharmacists, patent agents, surveyors, architects) have in common the fact that they sell commodities with the same basic peculiarity. The peculiarity is that the client knows much less about the commodity being bought than does the vendor. Thus, the client is in the hands of the vendor. The professions all have a more or less arcane body of knowledge. The client cannot easily judge quality of service, how much should be bought, or what 'would have happened' had the service not been bought. The consumer's basic

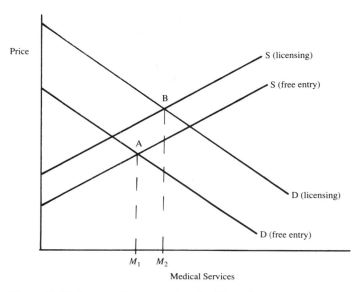

Figure 10.12 Costs and benefits of medical licensing

lack of knowledge weakens his or her bargaining position. It is perhaps for this reason that the markets for professional services have been colonised by self-regulating groups the world over. The consumer's ignorance generates higher fees because it tends to insulate each member of the profession from competition by other practitioners. Each practitioner has a degree of local monopoly power. Just as in the trade union field so in the professions we would expect lower demand elasticity to attract organisation. The fact that limiting entry into a professions assists in maintaining quality standards also facilitates organisation. This aspect of organisation helps the consumer. However we would expect the professions to be more restricted than is needed for consumer protection.

Various empirical tests have been designed to establish whether the professions are too restrictive. A cross-section analysis of US states forms an ideal test bed, because states vary in their degree of restrictiveness. For example, thirty-two states require that dentists qualified out of state have to undergo another in-state examination (Becker, 1986, 225). Can it be shown that the extra restriction has a benefit in terms of increased quality assurance which is greater than its costs in terms of more expensive dental services?

The basis for a test is shown in figure 10.12. The demand curves show demand for, say, medical care with and without licensing. The tests that the Medical Association devises for entrants to the profession increase consumer welfare by raising quality, and so the demand curve shifts rightwards. The tests will also raise the costs of entering the professions, shifting the supply curve leftwards. The upward movement of the supply curve must be sufficient to give a fair return on the increased investment required to become a doctor. As drawn, equilibrium with freedom of entry occurs at point A, with M_1 medical services exchanged. Equilibrium with licensing occurs at B with M_2 medical services exchanged. M_2 will be greater than M_1 if demand shifts upwards more than supply, that is, if the benefits of increased licensing outweigh the costs. Otherwise M_2 will be less than M_1 (see Svorny, 1987, 503). Therefore if licensing requirements help doctors more than their patients, states with strict licensing laws will show a lower per capita consumption of medical services than states with less strict laws, other things equal.

Analysing US states using data for 1965, Svorny finds that there is indeed a lower consumption of medical services in states with strict licensing requirements (Svorny, 1987, 506). While all states require doctors to pass written exams, only twenty-three require basic science certification, and twenty-four require US citizenship. These variables are negatively correlated with the number of physicians per head in a state, the measure of consumption of medical services. The results of the experiment therefore show that organised producer interests tend to dominate consumer interests in the setting of standards.

Another study showing the power of producer interests is that by Becker – on the licensing of dentists (Becker, 1986). As noted above, some states require qualified out-of-state dentists to pass a further in-state examination before being allowed to practise. Such a requirement simply reduces supply and raises in-state dentists' incomes; it amounts to legislative 'capture' by the dentists. This being the case, however, the question arises as to why all State Legislatures are not prevailed upon by dentists to pass such a requirement. The answer is that consumer interests are also represented within the Legislature. The more informed consumers are, the less likely they should be to allow capture. Becker indeed finds that high voter participation in elections, and a more educated population, both make capture by dentists less likely (1986, 227).

In sum, studies of the professions show that there is an economic logic to the actions of interest groups. Professions, like unions, are accorded special legislative protection, because this is thought to be in the public interest. However, vigilance is required if the professions, and the unions, are not to press their privileges to the point where they burden, rather than help, the public.

10.7 Conclusions

Collective bargaining has both benefits and costs. On the benefits side there is greater participation and possibly a sharing of rents from imperfect competition. There are also the democratic benefits of having a well-funded labour movement which – arguably – espouses the interests of the underdog. Many of the policies put forward to help the underdog, such as restrictions on employment at will, have the opposite effect intended, it is true. Nevertheless informed policy-making requires that these views be put, and properly answered, as we try to do here.

On the costs side there is the fact that collective bargaining appears to lessen productivity, profitability, employment, and possibly investment. The evidence is that unions do not simply share in monopoly profits, leaving employment substantially unchanged – so-called 'efficient bargains'. Given the adverse employment effects it follows that non-union wages will be driven down by 'crowding' effects. Certain groups of workers benefit from unions, primarily skilled prime age blue-collar males in large firms. But unskilled secondary workers lose because it is difficult for them to get a union job.

The question is how to get the benefits of greater industrial (and political) democracy with fewer costs. In Scandinavia a 'corporatist' solution is put forward – a partnership between the unions and the state, with wage bargaining highly centralised, and little room for local competitive forces. Both Britain and America have experimented with a form of corporatism back in the days when the unions agreed to incomes restraint in return for a commitment to 'full employment' and higher welfare benefits. Eventually the incomes policies failed, with an increase in inflation and strikes, ushering in a period in which competitive solutions were put forward.

At the macroeconomic level, academic studies of corporatism versus competition give mixed results. The corporatist countries like Austria, Germany, the Netherlands, and Scandinavia seem to do better, according to some criteria, than the competitive countries like the US. Taking the sum of inflation and unemployment rates (Okun's 'misery index'), the sum is lower in consensus countries like Austria and Germany, while low consensus countries like Britain and Italy have poorer performance. The logic behind the results is that a more widespread union organisation means that unions have to be more responsible. The adverse effects of high wages, for example, become inescapable. Against this it might be said that if unions are weak anyway, as in the US, we do not need to be concerned about external effects. From this perspective Britain has the worst of both worlds, with a level of unionism too low to be responsible and too high to be easily managed.

References

Abowd, J. (1989), 'The Effect of Wage Bargains on the Stock Market Performance of Firms', *American Economic Review*, September, 79: 744–800.

Abraham, K. and H. Farber (1987), 'Job Duration, Seniority, and Earnings', *American Economic Review*, June, 77: 278–97.

Adams, J. (1987), 'Intertemporal Wage Variation, Employment and Unemployment', *Journal of Labour Economics*, 5: 106–27.

Addison, J. and P. Portugal (1989), 'On the Costs of Worker Displacement: The Case of Dissipated Firm-Specific Training Investments', *Southern Economic Journal*, July, 55: 166–82.

Addison, J. and S. Siebert (1979), *The Market for Labor*, Los Angeles: Goodyear.
(1991), 'The European Charter of Fundamental Social Rights of Workers: Evolution and Controversies', *Industrial and Labor Relations Review*, 44: 597–625.

Akerlof, G. (1982), 'Labour Contracts as a Partial Gift Exchange', *Quarterly Journal of Economics*, November, 97: 543–59.

Akerlof, G. and W. Dickens (1982), 'The Economic Consequences of Cognitive Dissonance', *American Economic Review*, 72: 307–19.

Alchian, A. and H. Demsetz (1972), 'Production, Information Costs and Economic Organization', *American Economic Review*, December, 62: 777–95.

Aldrich, J. and D. Buchele (1986), *The Economics of Comparable Worth*, Cambridge, MA: Ballinger.

Allen, S. (1986), 'Unionization and Productivity in Office Building and School Construction', *Industrial and Labour Relations Review*, January, 39: 187–201.

Altonji, J. and R. Shakotko (1987), 'Do Wages Rise With Seniority?' *Review of Economic Studies*, July, 54: 437–59.

Anderson, C. (1967), 'The International Comparative Study of Achievement in Mathematics', *Comparative Education Review*, June, 11: 182–96.

Angrist, J. (1990), 'Lifetime Earnings and the Vietnam Era Draft Lottery: Evidence From Social Security Administration Records', *American Economic Review*, 80: 313–36.

Arnould, R. and L. Nichols (1983), 'Wage-risk Premiums and Workers' Compensation', *Journal of Political Economy*, April, 91: 332–40.

Ashenfelter, O. and D. Card (1985), 'Using Longitudinal Structure of Earnings to Estimate the Effect of Training Programs', *Review of Economics and Statistics*, 67: 648–60.

Ashenfelter, O. and T. Hannan (1986), 'Sex Discrimination and Product Market Competition: the Case of the Banking Industry', *Quarterly Journal of Economics*, February, 101: 149–73.

Ashenfelter, O. and J. Pencavel (1969), 'American Trade Union Growth 1900–1960', *Quarterly Journal of Economics*, 83: 434–48.

Baily, M. (1974), 'Wages and Unemployment under Uncertain Demand', *Review of Economic Studies*, 41: 37–50.

Baker, G., M. Jensen and K. Murphy (1988), 'Compensation and Incentives: Practice Versus Theory', *Journal of Finance*, 43: 593–616.

Ball, L. (1990), 'Intertemporal Substitution and Constraints on Labour Supply: Evidence From Panel Data', *Economic Inquiry*, 28: 706–24.

Barro, R. (1989), 'The Ricardian Approach to Budget Deficits', *Journal of Economic Perspectives*, Spring, 3: 37–54.

Barron, J., D. Black and M. Lowenstein (1989), 'Job Matching and On-the-Job Training', January.

Barron, J. and S. McCafferty (1977), 'Job Search, Labor Supply and the Quit Decision: Theory and Evidence', *American Economic Review*, September, 67: 683–91.

Barron, J. and W. Mellow (1979), 'Search Effort in the Labor Market', *Journal of Human Resources*, Summer, 14: 389–405.

Bartrip, P. (1987), *Workmen's Compensation in the Twentieth Century*, Aldershot: Avebury.

Bean, C. and P. Turnbull (1988), 'Employment in the British Coal Industry: A Test of the Labour Demand Model', *Economic Journal*, December, 98: 1092–104.

Becker, G. (1957), *The Economics of Discrimination*, Chicago: University of Chicago Press.

(1974), 'The Theory of Marriage Part 2', *Journal of Political Economy*.

(1975), *Human Capital, A Theoretical and Empirical Analysis with Special Reference to Education*, 2nd edn, New York: National Bureau of Economic Research, Columbia University Press.

(1985), 'Human Capital, Effort, and the Sexual Division of Labor', *Journal of Labor Economics*, 3: S33–58.

(1986), 'The Public Interest Hypothesis Revisited: A New Test of Peltzman's Theory of Regulation', *Public Choice*, 46: 223–34.

Becker, G. and K. Murphy (1988), 'The Family and the State', *Journal of Law and Economics*, 31: 1–18.

Becker, G. and G. Stigler (1974), 'Law Enforcement, Malfeasance and the Compensation of Enforcers', *Journal of Legal Studies*, January, 3: 1–18.

Becker, G. and N. Tomes (1986), 'An Equilibrium Theory of the Distribution of Income and Intergenerational Mobility', *Journal of Political Economy*, Supplement, 91: S1–39.

Becker, M. (1986), 'Barriers Facing Women in the Wage-Labour Market and the Need for Additional Remedies: A Reply to Fischel and Lazear', *University of Chicago Law Review*, 53: 934–49.

Behrman, J. and P. Taubman (1989), 'Is Schooling "Mostly in the Genes"? Nature–Nurture Decomposition Using Data on Relatives', *Journal of Political Economy*, December, 97: 1425–46.

Beider, P., B. Bernheim, V. Fuchs and J. Shoven (1989), 'Comparable Worth in a General Equilibrium Model of the US Economy', *Research in Labor Economics*, 9: 1–52.

Beller, A. and F. Blau (1988), 'Trends in Earnings Differentials By Gender, 1971–1981', *Industrial and Labour Relations Review*, 41: 513–29.

Ben-Porath, H. (1967), 'The Production of Human Capital Over the Life Cycle', *Journal of Political Economy*, July/August, 75: 352–65.

Benham, L. (1974), 'The Benefits of a Woman's Education within Marriage', *Journal of Political Economy*, reprinted in T. W. Schultz (ed.), *The Economics of the Family*, Chicago and London: University of Chicago Press for NBER, 375–89.

Bergmann, B. (1981), 'The Economic Risks of being a Housewife', *American Economic Review Papers and Proceedings*, 71: 81–6.

Bishop, J. (1987), 'The Recognition and Reward of Employee Performance', *Journal of Labor Economics*, October, part 2, 5: S36–56.

Blanchflower, D. and N. Millward (1988a), 'Trade Unions and Employment Change', *European Economic Review*, 32: 717–26.

Blanchflower, D. and W. Oswald (1988b), 'The Economic Effects of Britain's Trade Unions', Centre for Labour Economics Discussion Paper 324.

Blanchflower, D., A. Oswald and M. Garrett (1988c), 'Insider Power in Wage Determination', Centre for Labour Economics Discussion Paper 319, London School of Economics, August.

Blanchflower, D., N. Millward and A. Oswald (1991), 'Unionization and Employment Behaviour', *Economic Journal*, July, 101: 815–34.

Blau, F. and M. Ferber (1986), *The Economics of Women, Men and Work*, Englewood Cliffs: Prentice Hall.

Blau, D. and P. Robins (1991), 'Childcare Demand and Labor Supply of Young Mothers Over Time', *Demography*, August, 28: 333–51.

Booth, A. (1987), 'Extra-Statutory Redundancy Payments in Great Britain', *British Journal of Industrial Relations*, November, 25: 401–18.

(1989), 'Earning and Learning: What Price Specific Training?', unpublished paper, Brunel University, November.

Borjas, G. and S. Bronars (1989), 'Consumer Discrimination and Self-Employment', *Journal of Political Economy*, June, 97: 581–605.

Bouchard, T., D. Lykken, M. McGue, N. Segal and A. Tollegen (1990), 'Sources of Human Psychological Differences: the Minnesota Study of Twins Reared Apart', *Science*, 12 October, 250: 223–8.

Brien, M., J. Cunningham and J. O'Neill (1989), 'Comparable Worth in the Public Sector', *American Economic Review*, May, 79: 305–9.

Brown, Charles (1980), 'Equalizing Differences in the Labour Market', *Quarterly Journal of Economics*, February, 94: 113–34.

Brown, Charles (1990), 'Firms' Choice of Method of Pay', *Industrial and Labor Relations Review*, February, 43: 165S–182S.

Brown, Charles, J. Hamilton and J. Medoff (1990), *Employers Large and Small*, Cambridge, MA: Harvard University Press.

Brown, Colin (1984), *Black and White Britain*, London: Gower.

Brown, Joan (1982), *Industrial Injuries*, London: Policy Studies Institute.

Brown, James (1989), 'Why Do Wages Increase With Tenure?', *American Economic Review*, December, 79: 971–91.

Brown, James and O. Ashenfelter (1986), 'Testing the Efficiency of Employment Contracts', *Journal of Political Economy*, June, 94: S40–87.

Buckley, J. (1985), 'Wage Differences Among Workers in the Same Job and Establishment', *Monthly Labor Review*, 108: 11–16.

Burtless, G. (1986), 'Social Security, Unanticipated Benefit Increases, and the Timing of Retirement', *Review of Economic Studies*, 53: 781–805.

Butler, R. (1982), 'Estimating Wage Discrimination in the Labour Market', *Journal of Human Resources*, 17: 606–21.

Cain, G. (1976), 'The Challenge of Segmented Labor Market Theories to Orthodox Theory: A Survey', *Journal of Economic Literature*, 14: 1215–57.

Cain, G. and M. Dooley (1976), 'Estimation of a Model of Labor Supply, Fertility, and Wages of Married Women', *Journal of Political Economy*, Supp., 84: S179–99.

Card, D. (1986), 'The Impact of Deregulation on the Employment and Wages of Airline Mechanics', *Industrial and Labor Relations Review*, July, 39: 527–38.

Carlson, N. (1982), 'Time Rates Tighten Their Grips on Manufacturing Industries', *Monthly Labor Review*, May, 105: 15–22.

Carruth, A. and R. Disney (1988), 'Where Have Two Million Trade Union Members Gone?', *Economica*, 55: 1–19.

Carruth, A. and A. Oswald (1987), 'On Union Preferences and Labour Market Models: Insiders and Outsiders', *Economic Journal*, June, 97: 431–45.

Cartter, A. (1959), *Theory of Wages and Employment*, Homewood, Illinois: Irwin.

Casey, B. (1986), 'The Dual Apprenticeship System and the Recruitment and Retention of Young Persons in West Germany', *British Journal of Industrial Relations*, March, 24: 63–81.

Chelius, J. (1974), 'The Control of Industrial Accidents', *Law and Contemporary Problems*, Summer-Autumn, 38: 700–29.

(1982), 'The Influence of Workers' Compensation on Safety Incentives', *Industrial and Labour Relations Review*, 35: 235–42.

Chiplin, B. and P. Sloane (1976), 'Male–Female Earnings Differences: A Further Analysis', *British Journal of Industrial Relations*, 14: 77–81.

(1988), 'The Effect of Britain's Anti-Discrimination Legislation: A Comment', *Economic Journal*, 98: 833–8.

Chiswick, B., J. O'Neill, J. Fackler and S. Polachek (1975), 'The Effect of Occupation on Race and Sex Differences in Hourly Earnings', *Proceedings of American Statistical Association Annual Conference*, 219–28.

Chuma, H. and I. Ehrlich (1990), 'A Model of the Demand for Longevity and the Value of Life Extension', *Journal of Political Economy*, 98: 761–82.

Cigno, A. (1989), 'Home Production and the Allocation of Time', in D. Sapsford and Z. Tzannatos (eds.), *Current Issues in Labour Economics*, London: Macmillan, 7–32.

Clark, K. (1984), 'Unionization and Firm Performance', *American Economic Review*, December, 74: 893–919.

Classen, K. (1977), 'The Effect of Unemployment Insurance on the Duration of Unemployment and Subsequent Earnings', *Industrial and Labor Relations Review*, July, 30: 38–44.

Cohen, S. (1975), *Labor in the United States*, 4th edn, Columbus: Charles E. Merrill Publishing Co.

Commission of the European Communities (1989), 'Action Programme Relating to the Implementation of the Community Social Charter of Basic Social Rights of Workers', COM (89) 568 final, Brussels.

Connolly, R., B. Hirsch and M. Hirschey (1986), 'Union Rent Seeking, Intangible Capital, and the Market Value of the Firm', *Review of Economics and Statistics*, November, 68: 567–77.

Corcoran, M., C. Jencks and M. Olneck (1976), 'The Effects of Family Background on Earnings', *American Economic Review*, May, 66: 430–5.

Cornell, J., R. Noll and B. Weingast (1976), 'Safety Regulations', in H. Owen and C. Schultze, *Setting National Priorities*, Washington: Brookings Institution.

Cousineau, J. and R. Lacroix (1986), 'Imperfect Information and Strikes: an Analysis of Canadian Experience 1967–82', *Industrial and Labor Relations Review*, April, 39: 377–87.

Cox, J. and R. Oaxaca (1982), 'The Political Economy of Minimum Wage Legislation', *Economic Inquiry*, October, 20: 533–55.

Current Population Survey (various years), Washington: US Department of Commerce, Bureau of the Census.

Cymrot, D. and J. Dunleavy (1987), 'Are Free Agents Perspicacious Peregrinators?', *Review of Economics and Statistics*, February, 69: 50–8.

Daniel, W. and N. Millward (1983), *Workplace Industrial Relations in Britain*, London: Heinemann Educational Books.

Daymont, T. and P. Andrisani (1984), 'Job Preferences, College Major, and the Gender Gap in Earnings', *Journal of Human Resources*, 19: 408–28.

Denny, K. and S. Nickell (1991), 'Unions and Investment in British Industry', *British Journal of Industrial Relations*, March, 29: 113–22.

Department of Education (1988), 'Top Up Loans, Cm 520', London: HMSO.

Department of Employment (1990), 'Survey of Labour Costs, 1988', *Employment Gazette*, 98 (8), September.

Department of Employment (various years), *New Earnings Survey*, London: HMSO.

Dertouzos, J. and J. Pencavel (1981), 'Wage Employment Determination Under Trade Unionism', *Journal of Political Economy*, December, 89: 1162–81.

Devine, T. and N. Kiefer (1991), *Empirical Labour Economics: The Search Approach*, New York: Oxford University Press.

Dex, S. and P. Sloane (1989), 'The Economics of Sex Discrimination: How Far Have We Come?', in R. Drago and R. Perlman (eds.), *Micro-Economic Issues in Labour Economics*, Brighton: Harvester Wheatsheaf.

Donovan Commission (1968), Royal Commission on Trade Unions and Employers Associations, Cmnd. 3623, London: HMSO.

Dorsey, S. (1983), 'Employment Hazards and Fringe Benefits: Further Tests of Compensating Differentials', in J. Worral (ed.), *Safety and the Workforce*, Cornell: ILR Press.

Dorsey, S. and Walzer, N. (1983), 'Workers' Compensation, Job Hazards and Wages', *Industrial and Labour Relations Review*, 36: 642–54.

Dowd, B. and R. Feldman (1991), 'A New Estimate of the Welfare Loss of Excess Health Insurance', *American Economic Review*, 81: 297–301.

Duncan, G. and Holmlund, B. (1983), 'Was Adam Smith Right After All? Another Test of the Theory of Compensating Wage Differentials', *Journal of Labour Economics*, 1: 366–77.

Duncan, G. and Stafford, F. (1980), 'Do Union Members Receive Compensating Differentials?', *American Economic Review*, 70: 355–71.

Duncan, O. D. (1974), 'Comment on Mincer and Polachek', *Journal of Political Economy*, Supplement, 82: S109–10.

Edwards, L. (1988), 'Equal Employment Opportunity in Japan: A View from the West', *Industrial and Labor Relations Review*, 41: 240–50.

Ehrenberg, R. and M. Bognanno (1990), 'Do Tournaments Have Incentive Effects?', *Journal of Political Economy*, December, 98: 1307–24.

Ehrenberg, R. and R. Oaxaca (1976), 'Unemployment Insurance, Duration of Unemployment and Subsequent Wage Gains', *American Economic Review*, December, 66: 754–66.

Ehrenberg, R. and R. Smith (1987), 'Comparable Worth Wage Adjustments and Female Employment in the State and Local Government Sector', *Journal of Labor Economics*, 5: 43–62.

England, P. (1982), 'The Failure of Human Capital Theory to Explain Occupational Sex Segregation', *Journal of Human Resources*, Spring, 17: 358–70.

EOC (1984), 'Annual Report', Equal Opportunities Commission, London: HMSO.

Farber, H. (1984), 'Right to Work Laws and the Extent of Unionization', *Journal of Labor Economics*, 2: 319–52.

  (1986), 'The Analysis of Union Behaviour', in O. Ashenfelter and R. Layard (eds.), *Handbook of Labor Economics*, vol. II, Amsterdam: North-Holland, 1039–89.

Fearn, R. (1981), *Labor Economics, The Emerging Synthesis*, Cambridge, MA: Winthrop Publishers.

Feinberg, R. (1981), 'Employment Instability, Earnings and Market Structure', *Applied Economics*, June, 13: 257–65.

Fenn, P. and C. Veljanovski (1988), 'A Positive Theory of Regulatory Enforcement', *Economic Journal*, 98: 1055–70.

Fields, G. and O. Mitchell (1984), *Retirement, Pensions, and Social Security*, Cambridge, MA: MIT Press.

336   References

Fischel, D. (1984), 'Labor Markets and Labor Law Compared with Capital Markets and Corporate Law', *University of Chicago Law Review*, 51: 1061–77.

Fischel, D. and E. Lazear (1986), 'Comparable Worth and Discrimination in Labor Markets', *University of Chicago Law Review*, 53: 891–909.

Frank, R. (1978), 'Why Women Earn Less: The Theory and Estimation of Differential Overqualification', *American Economic Review*, June, 68: 360–73.

Freeman, R. (1976), *The Overeducated American*, New York: Academic Press.

(1977), 'The Decline in Economic Rewards to College Education', *Review of Economics and Statistics*, February, 59: 18–29.

(1984), 'Longitudinal Analysis of the Effects of Trade Unions', *Journal of Labor Economics*, 2: 1–26.

Freeman, R. and J. Medoff (1984), *What Do Unions Do?*, New York: Basic Books.

Friedman, M. (1951), 'Some Comments on the Significance of Labour Unions for Economic Policy', in D. Wright (ed.), *The Impact of the Union*, New York: Harcourt Brace.

(1968), 'The Role of Monetary Policy', *American Economic Review*, 58: 1–17.

Friedman, M. and L. Savage (1948), 'The Utility Analysis of Choices Involving Risk', *Journal of Political Economy*, August, 56: 279–304.

Fuchs, V. (1971), 'Differentials in Hourly Earnings Between Men and Women', *Monthly Labor Review*, May, 9–15.

(1988), *Women's Quest for Economic Equality*, Cambridge, MA: Harvard University Press.

Garen, J. (1985), 'Worker Heterogeneity, Job Screening and Firm Size', *Journal of Political Economy*, August, 93: 715–39.

(1988), 'Compensating Wage Differentials and the Endogeneity of Job Riskiness', *Review of Economics and Statistics*, 70: 9–16.

Gaynor, M. and S. Polachek (1991), 'Measuring Ignorance in the Market: A New Method with an Application to Physician Services', mimeo., SUNY-Binghamton.

Ghez, G. and G. Becker (1975), *The Allocation of Time*, New York: NBER: distributed by Columbia University Press.

Gilman, H. (1965), 'Economic Discrimination and Unemployment', *American Economic Review*, December, 55: 1077–96.

Goldin, C. (1986), 'Monitoring Costs and Occupational Segregation by Sex: A Historical Analysis', *Journal of Labor Economics*, January, 4: 1–27.

(1990), *Understanding the Gender Gap: An Economic History of American Women*, New York: Oxford University Press.

Goldin, C. and S. Polachek (1987), 'Residual Differences by Sex: Perspectives on the Gender Gap in Earnings', *American Economic Review*, May, 77: 143–51.

Gordon, D., R. Edwards and M. Reich (1982), *Segmented Work, Divided Workers*, New York: Cambridge University Press.

Green, F. (1988), 'The Trade Union Wage Gap in Britain: Some New Estimates', *Economics Letters*, 27: 183–7.

Greene, K., W. Nenan and C. Scott (1974), *Fiscal Interactions in a Metropolitan Area*, Toronto and London: Lexington Books.

Gregory, R., and R. Duncan (1981), 'Segmented Labour Market Theories and the

Australian Experience of Equal Pay for Women', *Journal of Post-Keynesian Economics*, 3: 403–28.

Gronau, R. (1974), 'Wage Comparisons: A Selectivity Bias', *Journal of Political Economy*, 1119–43.

—— (1986), 'Home Production – a Survey', in O. Ashelfelter and R. Layard (eds.), *Handbook of Labor Economics*, Amsterdam: North Holland.

—— (1988), 'Sex-Related Wage Differentials and Women's Interrupted Work Careers – The Chicken or the Egg', *Journal of Labor Economics*, 6: 277–301.

Hacker, A. (1986), 'Women at Work', *New York Review of Books*, 14 August.

Hall, R. (1972), 'Turnover in the Laborforce', *Brookings Papers on Economic Activity*, 3: 709–56.

—— (1982), 'The Importance of Lifetime Jobs in the US Economy', *American Economic Review*, 72: 716–24.

Hamermesh, D. (1977), 'Economic Aspects of Job Satisfaction', in O. Ashenfelter and W. Oates (eds.), *Essays in Labor Market Analysis*, New York: John Wiley.

—— (1985), 'Expectations, Life Expectancy, and Economic Behavior', *Quarterly Journal of Economics*, 100: 389–408.

Hamermesh, D. and J. Biddle (1990), 'Sleep and the Allocation of Time', *Journal of Political Economy*, 98: 922–43.

Hansen, W. and B. Weisbrod (1969), *Benefits, Costs and Finance of Public Higher Education*, Chicago: Markham Publishing Co.

Hashimoto, M. (1982), 'Minimum Wages Effects of Training on the Job', *American Economic Review*, December, 72: 1070–87.

Hashimoto, M. and J. Raisian (1985), 'Employment Tenure and Earnings Profiles in Japan and the United States', *American Economic Review*, September, 75: 721–35.

Heckman, J. (1979), 'Sample Selection Bias as a Specification Error', *Econometrica*, January, 47: 153–61.

Heckman, J. and S. Polachek (1974), 'Empirical Evidence on the Functional Form of the Earnings-Schooling Relationship', *Journal of the American Statistical Association*, June, 69: 350–4.

Hendricks, W., P. Feuille and C. Szerszen (1980), 'Regulation, Deregulation and Collective Bargaining in Airlines', *Industrial and Labor Relations Review*, October, 33: 67–81.

Heywood, J. (1990a), 'Market Structure and the Demand for Unionised Labour', *Southern Economic Journal*, January, 57: 607–15.

—— (1990b), 'Who Queues for a Union Job?', *Industrial Relations*, Winter, 28: 119–27.

Hicks, J. (1963), *Theory of Wages*, 2nd edn, London: Macmillan.

Hill, M. (1985), 'Patterns of Time Use', in F. Juster and F. Stafford (eds.), *Time, Goods and Well-Being*, University of Michigan, Survey Research Centre.

Hirsch, B. (1988), 'Trucking Regulation, Unionization and Labor Earnings: 1973–85', *Journal of Human Resources*, 23: 296–319.

Hirsch, B. and J. Addison (1986), *The Economic Analysis of Unions*, London: Allen and Unwin.

Holen, A. (1977), 'Effects of Unemployment Insurance Entitlement on Duration and Job Search Outcome', *Industrial and Labor Relations Review*, July, 30: 445–50.

Holzer, H. (1982), 'Unions and the Labor Market Status of White and Minority Youth', *Industrial and Labor Relations Review*, April, 35: 392–405.

(1986a), 'Are Unemployed Black Youth Income-Maximizers?', *Southern Economic Journal*, January, 53: 777–84.

(1986b), 'Reservation Wages and Their Labor Market Effects for Black and White Male Youth', *Journal of Human Resources*, Spring, 21: 157–77.

(1987), 'Informal Job Search and Black Youth Unemployment', *American Economic Review*, June, 77: 446–52.

Hotz, J., F. Kydland and G. Sadlacek (1988), 'Intertemporal Preferences and Labour Supply', *Econometrica*, 56: 335–60.

Hughes, G. and B. McCormick (1981), 'Do Council Housing Policies Reduce Migration Between Regions?', *Economic Journal*, December, 91: 919–37.

Hutchens, R. (1987), 'A Test of Lazear's Theory of Delayed Payment Contracts', *Journal of Labour Economics*, 5: S153–70.

Ichniowski, C. and D. Lewin (1987), 'Grievance Procedures and Firm Performance', in M. Kleiner, R. Block, M. Room and S. Salsburg (eds.), *Human Resources and the Performance of the Firm*, Industrial Relations Research Association.

Idson, T. and D. Feaster (1990), 'A Selectivity Model of Employer-Size Wage Differentials', *Journal of Labor Economics*, January, Part 1, 8: 99–122.

Jackman, R., R. Layard and S. Savouri (1991), 'Labour Market Mismatch: A Framework for Thought', in F. P. Schioppa (ed.), *Mismatch and Labour Mobility*, Cambridge University Press.

Jacoby, S. (1984), 'The Development of Internal Labor Markets in American Manufacturing Firms', in P. Osterman (ed.), *Internal Labor Markets*, Cambridge, MA: MIT Press.

Jencks, C. (1979), *Who Gets Ahead? The Determinants of Economic Success in America*, New York: Basic Books.

Jensen, M. and J. Meckling (1976), 'Theory of the Firm: Managerial Behavior, Agency Costs and Ownership Structure', *Journal of Financial Economics*, October, 3: 305–60.

Jensen, M. and K. Murphy (1986), 'Are Executive Compensation Contracts Properly Structured?', unpublished paper, University of Rochester.

Jiang, F. and S. Polachek (1991), 'Investment-Dependent Labour Supply Over the Life Cycle', *Research in Labour Economics*, 12: 245–67.

Johnson, G. and R. Layard (1986), 'The Natural Rate of Unemployment: Explanation and Policy', in O. Ashenfelter and R. Layard (eds.), *Handbook of Labor Economics*, Amsterdam: North-Holland.

Johnson, G. and G. Solon (1986), 'Estimates of the Direct Effects of Comparable Worth Policies', *American Economic Review*, 76: 1117–26.

Johnson, T. (1978), 'Time in School: the Case of the Prudent Patron', *American Economic Review*, December, 68: 862–72.

Johnson, W. and J. Skinner (1986), 'Labor Supply and Marital Separation', *American Economic Review*, 76: 455–69.

Jones, F. (1983), 'On Decomposing the Wage Gap: A Critical Comment on Blinder's Method', *Journal of Human Resources*, 18: 126–30.

Jones-Lee, M. (1989), *The Economics of Safety and Physical Risk*, Oxford: Basil Blackwell.

Jones-Lee, M., M. Hammerton and P. Philips (1985), 'The Value of Safety: Results of a National Sample Survey', *Economic Journal*, 95: 49–72.

Joshi, H. (1986), 'Participation in Paid Work: Evidence from the Women and Unemployment Survey', in R. Blundell and I. Walker (eds.), *Unemployment, Search and Labour Supply*, Cambridge University Press.

  (1987), 'The Cash Opportunity Costs of Child-Bearing', Economic Policy Research Unit Discussion Paper 208, London.

Joshi, H., R. Layard and S. Owen (1985), 'Why are More Women Working in Britain', *Journal of Labor Economics*, 3: S147–76.

Juster, T. and F. Stafford (1991), 'The Allocation of Time: Empirical Findings, Behavioral Models, and Problems of Measurement', *Journal of Economic Literature*, 29: 471–522.

Kahn, L. (1978), 'The Effect of Unions on the Earnings of Non-union Workers', *Industrial and Labor Relations Review*, January, 31: 205–16.

Kahn, L. and S. Low (1984), 'An Empirical Model of Employed Search, Unemployed Search, and Nonsearch', *Journal of Human Resources*, Winter, 19: 104–17.

Katz, A. (1976), 'The Economics of Unemployment Insurance: A Symposium', *Industrial and Labor Relations Review*, July, 30: 431–6.

Kaufman, R. and R. Kaufman (1987), 'Union Effects on Productivity, Personnel Practices, and Survival in the Automotive Parts Industry', *Journal of Labor Research*, Fall, 7: 332–50.

Kenny, L. (1983), 'The Accumulation of Human Capital During Marriage by Males', *Economic Inquiry*, April, 21: 223–31.

Kiefer, N. and G. Neumann (1979), 'An Empirical Job Search Model, With Test of the Constant Reservation Wage Hypothesis', *Journal of Political Economy*, 87: 89–107.

Killingsworth, M. (1983), *Labor Supply*, Cambridge University Press.

Killingsworth, M. and J. Heckman (1986), 'Female Labour Supply: A Survey', in O. Ashenfelter and R. Layard (eds.), *Handbook of Labor Economics*, Amsterdam: North-Holland, 103-204.

King, A. (1974), 'Occupational Choice, Risk Aversion, and Wealth', *Industrial and Labour Relations Review*, July, 27: 586–96.

Klein, B., R. Crawford and A. Alchian (1978), 'Vertical Integration, Appropriable Rents, and the Competitive Contracting Process', *Journal of Law and Economics*, October, 21: 297–326.

Klerman, J. and A. Liebowitz (1991), 'The Distinction Between Work and Employment of New Mothers', working paper, Rand Corporation.

Kniesner, T. and A. Goldsmith, (1987), 'A Survey of Alternative Models of the Aggregate US Labor Market', *Journal of Economic Literature*, September, 25: 1241–80.

Kniesner, T. and J. Leeth (1989), 'Separating the Reporting Effects From the Injury Rate Effects of Workers' Compensation Insurance: A Hedonic Simulation', *Industrial and Labour Relations Review*, 42: 280–9.

Knight, K. (1987), *Unemployment: An Economic Analysis*, London: Croom Helm.

Korn Ferry (1990), Board of Directors Study UK, Korn Ferry International Ltd.

Kreps, J., P. Martin, R. Perlman and G. Somers (1981), *Contemporary Labor Economics and Labor Relations*, Belmont: Wadsworth.

Krueger, A. and L. Summers (1988), 'Efficiency Wages and the Inter-Industry Wage Structure', *Econometrica*, March, 56: 259–93.

Kuratani, M. (1973), 'A Theory of Training, Earnings and Employment in Japan', Ph.D. Dissertation, Columbia University.

Laband, D. and B. Lentz (1985), *The Roots of Success: Why Children Follow in Their Fathers' Career Footsteps*, New York: Praeger.

Lancaster, T. and A. Chesher (1983), 'An Econometric Analysis of Reservation Wages', *Econometrica*, November, 51: 1661–76.

Lande, R. H. and R. O. Zerbe (1985), 'Reducing Unions' Monopoly Power: Costs and Benefits', *Journal of Law Economics*, May, 28: 297–310.

Landes, W. and L. Solomon (1968), 'Compulsory Schooling Legislation: An Economic Analysis of Law and Social Change in the Nineteenth Century', *Journal of Economic History*, 28: 54–91.

Layard, R. and S. Nickell (1986), 'Unemployment in Britain', *Economica*, 53: S121–70.

Lazear, E. (1977), 'Education: Consumption or Production', *Journal of Political Economy*, 85: 569–97.

(1979a), 'The Narrowing of Black–White Wage Differentials is Illusory', *American Economic Review*, September, 69: 553–64.

(1979b), 'Why is There Mandatory Retirement?', *Journal of Political Economy*, December, 87: 1261–84.

(1981), 'Agency, Earnings Profiles and Hours Restrictions', *American Economic Review*, September, 71: 606–20.

(1988), 'Pensions and Deferred Benefits as Strategic Compensation', mimeo., University of Chicago and Hoover Institution, 17 November.

Lazear, E. and R. Moore (1984), 'Incentives, Productivity and Labor Contracts', *Quarterly Journal of Economics*, May, 99: 275–96.

Lazear, L. and S. Rosen (1981), 'Rank-Order Tournaments as Optimum Labor Contracts', *Journal of Political Economy*, October, 89: 841–64.

Leigh, J. (1983), 'Sex Differences in Absenteeism', *Industrial Relations*, Fall, 22: 349–61.

Leighton, L. and J. Mincer (1981), 'The Effects of Minimum Wages on Human Capital Formation', in S. Rottenberg (ed.), *The Economics of Legal Minimum Wages*, Washington: American Enterprise Institute, 155–73.

Levhari, D. and Y. Weiss (1974), 'The Effect of Risk on the Investment in Human Capital', *American Economic Review*, December, 64: 950–63.

Levitan, S. (1981), Good Jobs, Bad Jobs, No Jobs', *Journal of Economic Literature*, March, 19: 146–8.

Lewin, D. and S. Goldenberg (1980), 'Public Sector Unionism in the US and Canada', *Industrial Relations*, Fall, 18: 239–56.

Lewis, H. G. (1986), *Union Relative Wage Effects: A Survey*, Chicago: University of Chicago Press.

Li, E. (1986), 'Compensating Differentials and Cyclical and Non-Cyclical Unemployment', *Journal of Labour Economics*, 4: 277–300.

Lichtenstein, S., P. Slovic, B. Fischoff, M. Layman and B. Combs (1978), 'Judged Frequency of Lethal Events', *Journal of Experimental Psychology*, 4: 551–78.

Lindbeck, A. and D. Snower (1986), 'Wage Setting, Unemployment, and Insider-Outsider Relations', *American Economic Review*, 76: 235–9.

Lindsay, C. and M. Maloney (1988), 'A Model and Some Evidence Concerning the Influence of Discimination on Wages', *Economic Inquiry*, October, 26: 645–60.

Linneman, P. and M. Wachter (1986), 'Rising Union Premiums and the Declining Boundaries Among Non-Competing Groups', *American Economic Review*, May, 76: 103–8

Lundberg, S. and R. Startz (1983), 'Private Discrimination and Social Intervention in Competitive Labor Markets', *American Economic Review*, 73: 340–7.

Lyttkens, C. (1988), 'Workers' Compensation and Employees' Safety Incentives', *International Review of Law and Economics*, 8: 181–5.

MacCurdy, J. (1981), 'An Empirical Model of Labor Supply in a Life Cycle Setting', *Journal of Political Economy*, 89: 1050–85.

MacCurdy, T. and J. Pencavel, (1986), 'Testing Between Competing Models of Wage and Employment Determination in Unionized Markets', *Journal of Political Economy*, June, Part 2, 94: S3–S39.

Machin, S. (1989), 'Unions and the Capture of Economic Rents: An Investigation Using British Firm Level Data', mimeo., University College, London.

MacIntosh, J. (1987), 'Employment Discrimination: An Economic Perspective', *Ottawa Law Review*, 22: 275–319.

Madden, J. (1981), 'Why Women Work Closer to Home', *Urban Studies*, June, 18: 181–94.

Main, B. (1981), 'The Length of Employment and Unemployment in Great Britain', *Scottish Journal of Political Economy*, June, 28: 146–64.

(1991), 'Top Executive Pay and Performance', *Managerial and Decision Economics*, 12: 219–29.

Malcolmson, J. (1981), 'Unemployment and the Efficiency Wage Hypothesis', *Economic Journal*, December, 91: 848–66.

Mancer, M. and M. Brown (1980), 'Marriage and Household Decision Making: A Bargaining Analysis', *International Economic Review*, 21: 31–44.

Marin, A. and G. Psacharopoulos (1982), 'The Reward for Risk in the Labor Market: Evidence from the United Kingdom and a Reconciliation With Other Studies', *Journal of Political Economy*, August, 90: 827–53.

Marshall, R. (1965), *The Negro and Organised Labor*, Wiley.

Martin, J. and C. Roberts (1984), *Women and Employment*, London: Office of Population Censuses and Surveys.

Marvell, H. (1977), 'Factory Regulation: A Reinterpretation of Early English Experience', *Journal of Law and Economics*, 20: 379–402.

McCaffrey, D. (1983), 'An Assessment of OSHA's Recent Effects on Injury Rates', *Journal of Human Resources*, 18: 131–46.

McDonald, I. and R. Solow (1981), 'Wage Bargaining and Employment', *American Economic Review*, 71: 896–908.

McElroy, M. (1991), 'The Empirical Content of Nash-Bargained Household Behaviour', *Journal of Human Resources*, Fall, 25: 559–83.

McElroy, M. and M. Horney (1981), 'Nash-Bargained Household Decisions: Towards A Generalized Model', *International Economic Review*, June, 22: 333–49.

McNabb, R. (1989), 'Compensating Wage Differentials: Some Evidence for Britain', *Oxford Economic Papers*, 41: 327–38.

Medoff, J. and K. Abraham (1980), 'Experience, Performance and Earnings', *Quarterly Journal of Economics*, December, 95: 703–36.

(1981), 'Are Those Paid More Really More Productive? The Case of Experience', *Journal of Human Resources*, Spring, 16: 186–216.

Melani v. Board of Higher Education, 31 FEP Cases 648, US District Court, Southern District of New York, 1983.

Mellor, E. (1984), 'Investigating the Differences in Weekly Earnings of Women and Men', *Monthly Labor Review*, June, 107 (6): 17–28.

Mellow, W. (1982), 'Employer Size and Wages', *Review of Economics and Statistics*, August, 495–501.

Metcalf, D. (1973), 'Pay Dispersion, Information, and Returns to Search in a Professional Labour Market', *Review of Economic Studies*, October, 40: 491–506.

(1982), 'Unions and the Distribution of Earnings', *British Journal of Industrial Relations*, July, 20: 163–9.

(1984), 'Unions and Pay', *Economic Review*, September, 24–7.

(1988), 'Trade Unions and Economic Performance: The British Evidence', Centre for Labour Economics Discussion Paper 320.

Millward, N. and M. Stevens (1986), *British Workplace Industrial Relations, 1980–84*, Aldershot: Gower.

Mincer, J. (1962), 'Labourforce Participation of Married Women', *Aspects of Labor Economics*, Washington: National Bureau of Economic Research.

(1974), *Schooling, Experience and Earnings*, New York: Columbia University Press for National Bureau of Economic Research.

(1976), 'The Unemployment Effects of Minimum Wages', *Journal of Political Economy*, 84: 587–5104.

(1985), 'Intercounty Comparisons of Labor Force Trends and Related Developments: An Overview', *Journal of Labor Economics*, Supplement, 3: S1–32.

(1989), 'Job Training: Costs, Returns, and Wage Profiles', National Bureau of Economic Research Working Paper No. 3208, December.

Mincer, J. and H. Ofek (1982), 'Interrupted Work Careers: Depreciation and Restoration of Human Capital', *Journal of Human Resources*, Winter, 17: 3–24.

Mincer, J. and S. Polachek (1974), 'Family Investments in Human Capital: Earnings of Women', *Journal of Political Economy*, Supplement, 82: S76–108.

Minford, P. and P. Ashton (1988), 'The Poverty Trap and the Laffer Curve: What Can the GHS Tell us?', Centre for Economic Research Discussion Paper 275.

Minford, P., M. Peel and P. Ashton (1987), *The Housing Morass: Regulation, Immobility and Unemployment*, London: Institute of Economic Affairs.

Mitchell, O. and G. Fields (1984), 'The Economics of Retirement Behaviour', *Journal of Labor Economics*, 2: 84–105.

Montgomery, M. and S. Trussell (1976), 'Models of Marital Status and Child-Bearing', in O. Ashenfelter and R. Layard (eds.), *Handbook of Labor Economics*, Amsterdam: North-Holland, 205–72.

Moore, M. and W. Viscusi (1988), 'The Quantity Adjusted Value of Life', *Economic Inquiry*, 26: 369–88.

Moore, R. (1983), 'Employer Discrimination: Evidence from Self-Employed Workers', *Review of Economics and Statistics*, 65: 496–501.

Moore, W., R. Newman and J. Cunningham (1985), 'The Effect of the Extent of Unionism on Union and Non-Union Wages', *Journal of Labor Research*, Winter, 6: 21–44.

Mortensen, D. (1988a), 'Matching: Finding a Partner for Life or Otherwise', *American Journal of Sociology*, 94: S215–40.

(1988b), 'Wages, Separations, and Job Tenure: On-the-Job Specific Training or Matching', *Journal of Labour Economics*, October, 6: 445–71.

Murphy, K. and Welch, F. (1990), 'Empirical Earnings Profiles', *Journal of Labour Economics*, 8: 202–29.

Nakamura, A. and M. Nakamura (1985), *The Second Paycheck: A Socioeconomic Analysis of Earnings*, London: Academic Press.

Nardinelli, C. and C. Simon (1990), 'Customer Racial Discrimination in the Market for Memorabilia', *Quarterly Journal of Economics*, 105: 575–95.

Narendrenathan, W., S. Nickell and J. Stern (1985), 'Unemployment Benefits Revisited', *Economic Journal*, June, 95: 307–29.

Nelson, P. (1970), 'Information and Consumer Behavior', *Journal of Political Economy*, 78: 311-29.

Neumark, D. (1988), 'Employers' Discriminatory Tastes and the Estimation of Wage Discrimination', *Journal of Human Resources*, 23: 279–95.

Neumark, D. and S. Korenman (1991), 'Does Marriage Really Make Men More Productive?', *Journal of Human Resources*, 26: 282–307.

Nickell, S. (1979), 'The Effect of Unemployment and Related Benefits on the Duration of Unemployment', *Economic Journal*, March, 89: 34–49.

(1990), 'Unemployment: A Survey', *Economic Journal*, June, 100: 391–439.

Oaxaca, R. (1973), 'Male–Female Wage Differentials in Urban Labour Markets', *International Economic Review*, 693–709.

O'Neill, J. (1981), 'A Time Series Analysis of Women's Labor Force Participation', *American Economic Review*, Papers and Proceedings, 71: 76–86.

(1985), 'The Trend in Male–Female Wage Gap in the United States', *Journal of Labour Economics*, 3: S91–116.

O'Neill, J. and S. Polachek (forthcoming), 'Why the Gender Gap in Wages Narrowed in the 1980s', *Journal of Labour Economics*.

O'Reilly, C., B. Main and G. Crystal (1988), 'CEO Compensation as Tournament and A Social Compensation: A Tale of Two Theories', *Administrative Science Quarterly*, June, 33: 257–74.

OECD (1986), *Employment Outlook*, Paris: Organisation for Economic Cooperation and Development, September.

Oi, W. (1962), 'Labor as a Quasi-Fixed Factor', *Journal of Political Economy*, 70: 538–55.

(1974), 'On the Economics of Industrial Safety', *Law and Contemporary Problems*, 38: 669–99.

(1983), 'The Fixed Employment Costs of Specialised Labor', in J. Triplett (ed.), *The Measurement of Labor Cost*, Chicago: University of Chicago Press.

Olson, C. (1981), 'An Analysis of Wage Differentials Received by Workers on Dangerous Jobs', *Journal of Human Resources*, 26: 167–85.

Orazem, P. and J. Mattila (1990), 'The Implementation Process of Comparable Worth: Winners and Losers', *Journal of Political Economy*, February, 98: 134–52.

Oswald, A. (1982), 'The Microeconomic Theory of the Trade Union', *Economic Journal*, September, 92: 576–95.

Paglin, M. and A. Rufolo (1990), 'Heterogeneous Human Capital, Occupational Choice and Male–Female Earnings Differences', *Journal of Labor Economics*, 8: 123–44.

Panel Study of Income Dynamics (various), Ann Arbor, Michigan: Institute for Social Research, Michigan.

Parsons, D. (1986), 'The Employment Relationship: Job Attachment, Work Effort and the Nature of Contracts', in O. Ashenfelter and R. Layard (eds.), *Handbook of Labor Economics*, Amsterdam, North-Holland, 789–848.

Peltzman, S. (1973), 'The Effect of Government Subsidies in Kind on Private Expenditures: the Case of Higher Education', *Journal of Political Economy*, 81: 1–27.

Pencavel, J. (1986), 'Labor Supply of Men: A Survey', in O. Ashenfelter and R. Layard (eds.), *Handbook of Labor Economics*, Amsterdam: North-Holland, 3–102.

Peoples, J. (1990), 'Airline Deregulation and Industry Wage Levels', *Eastern Economic Journal*, January/March, 16: 49–58.

Peters, H. (1986), 'Marriage and Divorce: Informational Constraints and Private Contracting', *American Economic Review*, 76: 437–54.

Phelps, E. (1972), 'The Statistical Theory of Racism and Sexism', *American Economic Review*, 62: 659–61.

Phelps Brown, E. (1977), *The Inequality of Pay*, Oxford: Oxford University Press.

Phelps Brown, E. and M. Browne (1968), *A Century of Pay – the Course of Pay and Production in France, Germany, Sweden, the United Kingdom and the United States of America 1860–1960*, London: Macmillan.

Pike, M. (1985), 'The Employment Response to Equal Pay Legislation', *Oxford Economic Papers*, June, 37: 304–18.

Podgursky, M. (1986), 'Unions Establishment Size and Intra-Industry Threat Effects', *Industrial and Labor Relations Review*, January, 39: 277–86.

Polachek, S. (1975a), 'Differences in Expected Post-School Investment as a

Determinant of Market Wage Differentials', *International Economic Review*, June, 16: 451–70.

(1975b), 'Potential Biases in Measuring Male–Female Discrimination', *Journal of Human Resources*, 6 (10): 205–29.

(1980), 'Secular Changes in Female Job Aspirations', in R. Clark (ed.), *Retirement in an Aging Society*, Durham: Duke University Press.

(1981), 'Occupational Self-Selection: A Human Capital Approach to Sex Differences in Occupational Structure', *Review of Economics and Statistics*, 63: 60–9.

(1984), 'Women in the Economy: Perspectives on Gender Inequality', in *Comparable Worth: Issue for the 80's*, Washington, DC: US Civil Rights Commission, 34–53.

(1987), 'Occupational Segregation and the Gender Gap', *Population Research and Policy Review*, 47–67.

(1990), 'Trends in the Male–Female Wage Gap: The 1980s Compared to the 1970s', Paper Presented at the American Economic Association Conference.

Polachek, S. and Hofler (1991), 'Employee Ignorance in the Labor Market', mimeo., SUNY-Binghamton.

Polachek, S. and F. Horvath (1977), 'A Life-Cycle Approach to Migration: Analysis of the Perspicacious Peregrinator', *Research in Labor Economics*, 1: 103–49.

Polachek, S. and E. McCutcheon (1983), 'Union Effects on Employment Stability: New Estimates Using Panel Data', *Journal of Labour Research*, 4: 273–87.

Polachek, S. and C. Simon (1986), 'Monitoring and the Rate of Unionization', mimeo., SUNY-Binghamton.

Polachek, S., P. Wunnava and M. Hutchins (1987), 'Panel Estimates of Union Effects of Wages and Wage Growth', *Review of Economics and Statistics*, August, 69: 527–31.

Polachek, S. and B. Yoon (1987), 'A Two-Tiered Earnings Frontier: Estimation of Employer and Employee Information in the Labor Market', *Review of Economics and Statistics*, May, 69: 296–302.

Posner, R. (1984), 'Some Economics of Labour Law', *University of Chicago Law Review*, 51: 988–1011.

Prais, S. and K. Wagner (1988), 'Productivity and Management: The Training of Foremen in Britain and Germany', *National Institute Economic Review*, February, 34–7.

Psacharopoulos, G. (1985), 'Returns to Education: A Further International Update and Implications', *Journal of Human Resources*, 20: 583–604.

Quinn, J. (1977), 'Microeconomic Determinants of Early Retirement', *Journal of Human Resources*, 12: 329–46.

Quinn Mills, D. (1985), 'Seniority Versus Ability in Promotion Decisions', *Industrial and Labor Relations Review*, April, 38: 421–5.

Rebitzer, J. (1989), 'Efficiency Wages and Implicit Contracts: An Institutional Evaluation', in R. Drago and R. Perlman (eds.), *Micro-Economic Issues in Labour Economics*, Brighton: Harvester Wheatsheaf.

Reimers, C. (1985), 'Cultural Differences in Labor Force Participation Among

Married Women', *American Economic Review*, Papers and Proceedings, 75: 251–5.

Remick, H. and R. Steinberg (1984), 'Technical Possibilities and Political Realities', in H. Remick (ed.), *Comparable Worth and Wage Discrimination*, Philadelphia: Temple University Press.

Reynolds, M. (1988), 'A Critique of What Do Unions Do', *Review of Austrian Economics*, 2: 359–71.

Robins, P. K. (1984), 'A Comparison of Labor Supply Findings From the Four Negative Income Tax Experiments', *Journal of Human Resources*, 20: 567–82.

Roos, P. (1981), 'Marital Differences in Occupational Distribution and Attainment', Paper presented at the Annual Population Association Meetings.

Rose, N. (1987), 'Labor Rent Sharing and Regulation: Evidence from the Trucking Industry', *Journal of Political Economy*, December, 1146–78.

Rosen, S. (1986), 'The Theory of Equalising Differences', in O. Ashenfelter and R. Layard (eds.), *Handbook of Labor Economics*, Amsterdam: North Holland.

Rosenzweig, M. and T. Schultz (1986), 'The Demand for and Supply of Births', *American Economic Review*, 76: 992–1015.

Ross, A. (1958), 'Do We Have A New Industrial Feudalism?', *American Economic Review*, December, 48: 903–20.

Rothschild, M. (1973), 'Models of Market Organization with Imperfect Information: A Survey', *Journal of Political Economy*, November/December, 81: 1283–308.

Ruback, R. and M. Zimmerman (1984), 'Unionization and Profitability: Evidence from the Capital Market', *Journal of Political Economy*, December, 92: 1134–57.

Ruser, J. (1985), 'Workers' Compensation Insurance, Experience Rating and Occupational Injuries', *Rand Journal of Economics*, 16: 487–96.

Ryan, P. (1981), 'Segmentation, Duality and the Internal Labor Market', in F. Wilkinson (ed.), *The Dynamics of Labor Market Segmentation*, London: Academic Press.

Salomon, M. (1987), *Industrial Relations: Theory and Practice*, Hemel Hempstead: Prentice Hall.

Sandell, S. (1980), 'Job Search by Unemployed Women: Determinants of the Asking Wage', *Industrial and Labor Relations Review*, April, 33: 368–78.

Sandell, S. and D. Shapiro (1980), 'Work Expectations, Human Capital Accumulation, and the Wages of Young Women', *Journal of Human Resources*, 15: 335–53.

Sander, W. (1985), 'Women, Work and Divorce', *American Economic Review*, 75: 519–24.

Sattinger, M. (1991), 'Consistent Wage Offer and Reservation Wage Distributions', *Quarterly Journal of Economics*, 106: 277–88.

Schultz, T. P. (1985), 'Changing World Prices, Women's Wages and the Fertility Transition: Sweden 1860–1910', *Journal of Political Economy*, 93: 1126–54.

Seiler, E. (1984), 'Piece Rate vs. Time Rate: The Effect of Incentives on Earnings', *Review of Economics and Statistics*, August, 66: 363–75.

Seldon, A. (1986), *The Riddle of the Voucher*, Hobart Paperback 21, London: Institute of Economic Affairs.

Shapiro, C. and J. Stiglitz (1984), 'Equilibrium Unemployment as a Worker Discipline Device', *American Economic Review*, June, 74: 433–44.

Shaw, K. (1989), 'Life-Cycle Labour Supply with Human Capital Accumulation', *International Economic Review*, May, 30: 431–56.

Shepela, S. and A. Viviano (1984), 'Some Psychological Factors Affecting Job Segregation and Wages', in H. Remick (ed.), *Comparable Worth and Wage Discrimination: Technical Possibilities and Political Realities*, Philadelphia: Temple University Press.

Shorey, J. (1983), 'An Analysis of Sex Differences in Quits', *Oxford Economic Papers*, 35: 213–27.

Siebert, S. (1984), 'Advertising in the Professions: The Economic Argument', *International Journal of Advertising*, 3: 189–205.

  (1989), 'Inequality of Opportunity: An Analysis Based on the Microeconomics of the Family', in R. Drago and R. Perlman (eds.), *Microeconomic Issues in Labour Economics*, Brighton: Harvester.

Siebert, S. and J. Addison (1981), 'Are Strikes Accidental?', *Economic Journal*, June, 91: 389–404.

  (1991), 'Internal Labour Markets: Causes and Consequences', *Oxford Review of Economic Policy*, January, 7: 76–92.

Siebert, S. and P. Sloane (1981), 'The Measurement of Sex and Marital Status Discrimination at the Workplace', *Economica*, 48: 125–41.

Siebert, S. and A. Young (1983), 'Sex and Family Status Differentials in Professional Earnings: The Case of Librarians', *Scottish Journal of Political Economy*, 30: 18–41.

Sjaastad, L. (1962), 'The Costs and Returns to Human Migration', *Journal of Political Economy*, Supplement, October, 70: 80–93.

Slichter, S., J. Healy and E. Livernash (1960), *The Impact of Collective Bargaining on Management*, Washington: The Brookings Institution.

Sloane, P. (1985), 'Discrimination in the Labour Market', in D. Carline, C. Pissarides, P. Sloane and S. Siebert, *Labour Economics*, London: Longman.

  (1990), 'Sex Differentials: Structure, Stability and Change', in M. Gregory and A. Thomson, *A Portrait of Pay 1970–82*, Oxford: Oxford University Press.

Smith, A. (1776), *Wealth of Nations*, Chicago: University of Chicago (Cannan Edition, 1976).

Smith, J. and M. Ward (1989), 'Women in the Labor Market and the Family', *Journal of Economic Perspectives*, 3: 9–24.

Smith, R. (1979), 'Compensating Wage Differentials and Public Policy: A Review', *Industrial and Labor Relations Review*, April, 32: 339–51

  (1988), 'Comparable Worth: Limited Coverage and the Exacerbation of Inequality', *Industrial and Labor Relations Review*, January, 41: 227–39.

Snow, A. and R. Warren (1990), 'Human Capital Investment and Labor Supply Under Uncertainty', *International Economic Review*, February, 31: 195-206.

Spilsbury, M., M. Hoskins, D. Ashton and M. Maguire (1987), 'A Note on Trade Union Membership Patterns of Young Adults', *British Journal of Industrial Relations*, 25: 267–74.

Sprague, A. (1988), 'Post-war Fertility and Female Labour Force Participation Rates', *Economic Journal*, 98: 682–700.

Stephenson, S. (1976), 'The Economics of Youth Job Search Behavior', *Review of Economics and Statistics*, 58: 104–11.

Stern, S. (1989), 'Estimating A Simultaneous Search Model', *Journal of Labour Economics*, 7: 348–69.

Stewart, M. (1987), 'Collective Bargaining Arrangements, Closed Shops and Relative Pay', *Economic Journal*, March, 97: 140–56.

  (1990), 'Union Wage Differentials, Product Market Influences, and Division of Rents', *Economic Journal*, December, 100: 1122–37.

Stigler, G. (1961), 'The Economics of Information', *Journal of Political Economy*, 69: 213–25.

  (1962), 'Information in the Labor Market', *Journal of Political Economy*, October, 70: 94–105.

Summers, L. (1989), 'Some Simple Economics of Mandated Benefits', *American Economic Review*, May, 79: 177–83.

Svorny, S. (1987), 'Physician Licensure: A New Approach to Examining the Role of Professional Interests', *Economic Inquiry*, July, 25: 497–509.

Tannen, M. (1978), 'The Investment Motive for Attending College', *Industrial and Labor Relations Review*, July, 31: 489–98.

Taubman, P. (1976), 'The Determinants of Earnings: Genetics, Family and Other Environments', *American Economic Review*, September, 66: 858–70.

Topel, R. (1991), 'Specific Capital, Mobility and Wages: Wages Rise With Seniority', *Journal of Political Economy*, February, 99: 145–76.

Thaler, R. and S. Rosen (1976), 'The Value of Saving a Life: Evidence from the Labor Market', in R. Terlekyj, *Household Production and Consumption*, Princeton: BNER.

Trade Union Congress (1985), *Report of the 117th Annual Congress*, London: TUC.

Treble, J. (1990), 'The Pit and the Pendulum: Arbitration in the British Coal Industry, 1893–1914', *Economic Journal*, December, 100: 1095–108.

Treiman, D. and H. Hartmann (eds.) (1981), *Women, Work and Wages: Equal Pay for Jobs of Equal Value*, Washington, DC: National Academy of Sciences.

Trejo, S. (1991), 'Public Sector Unions and Municipal Employment', *Industrial and Labor Relations Review*, October, 45: 166–80.

Tullock, G. (1966), 'The Welfare Costs of Tariffs, Monopolies and Theft', *Western Economic Journal*, July, 5: 224–32.

United Kingdom Annual Abstract of Statistics, London: Central Statistical Office (annual).

United States Statistical Abstract, Washington: Bureau of Statistics (annual).

Van Der Horst, S. (1942), *Native Labour in South Africa*, London: Oxford University Press.

Vanek, J. (1974), 'Time Spent in Housework', *Scientific American*, November, 116–20.

Veljanovski, C. (1981), 'Regulating Industrial Accidents: An Economic Analysis of Market and Legal Responses', D.Phil., Oxford.

(1982), 'Employment and Safety Effects of Employers' Liability', *Scottish Journal of Political Economy*, 256–71.

Viscusi, W. (1978), 'Wealth Effects and Earnings Premiums for Job Hazards', *Review of Economics and Statistics*, 60: 408–13.

(1985), 'Are Individuals Bayesian Decision-Makers?', *American Economic Review, Papers and Proceedings*, 75: 381–5.

(1986), 'The Structure and Enforcement of Job Safety Regulation', *Law and Contemporary Problems*, 49: 127–50.

Viscusi, W. and C. O'Connor (1984), 'Responses to Chemical Labelling: Are Workers Bayesian Decision-Makers?', *American Economic Review*, 74: 942–56.

Viscusi, W. and M. Moore (1987), 'Workers' Compensation: Wage Effects, Benefit Inadequacies, and the Value of Health Losses', *Review of Economics and Statistics*, 69: 249–61.

Vishwanath, T. (1988), 'Parallel Search and Information Gathering', *American Economic Review*, May, 78: 110–16.

Voos, P. (1983), 'Union Organizing: Costs and Benefits', *Industrial and Labor Relations Review*, July, 36: 576–91.

Wachter, M. and R. Wright (1990), 'The Economics of Internal Labor Markets', *Industrial Relations*, Spring, 29: 240–62.

Wadhwani, S. and M. Wall (1989), 'The Effects of Unions on Corporate Investment', Centre for Labour Economics Discussion Paper 354.

Warburton, P. (1987), 'Labour Supply Incentives for the Retired', in M. Beenstock (ed.), *Work, Welfare and Taxation*, London: Allen and Unwin.

Webb, S. (1919), *The History of Trade Unionism 1660–1920*, private publication.

Weiss, Y. (1985), 'The Effect of Labour Unions on Investment in Training: A Dynamic Model', *Journal of Political Economy*, October, 93: 994–1007.

Weisskopf, J., R. Gordon and S. Bowles (1983), 'A Social Model of US Productivity Growth', Brookings Papers in Economic Activity.

Welch, F. (1979), 'Effects of Cohort Size on Earnings: The Baby Boom Babies' Financial Bust', *Journal of Political Economy*, October, 87: S65–97.

Wessels, W. (1991), 'Do Unions Contract for Added Employment?', *Industrial and Labour Relations Review*, October, 45: 181–93.

West, E. (1967), 'The Political Economy of American Public School Education', *Journal of Law and Economics*, October, 10: 101–28.

(1975), *Education and The Industrial Revolution*, New York: Barnes and Noble, 1975.

(1982), 'Education Vouchers: Evolution or Revolution?', *Economic Affairs*, October.

West, E. and M. McKee (1983), 'De Gestibus Est Disputandum: The Phenomenon of "Merit Wants" Revisited', *American Economic Review*, 73: 1110–21.

Williamson, O., M. Wachter and J. Harris (1975), 'Understanding the Employment Relation: An Analysis of Idiosyncratic Exchange', *Bell Journal*, Spring, 6: 250–78.

Wolpin, K. (1977), 'Education and Screening', *American Economic Review*, December, 67: 949–58.

Yoon, B. (1981), 'A Model of Unemployment Duration with Variable Search Intensity', *Review of Economics and Statistics*, November, 63: 599–609.

Zabalza, A. and J. Arrufat (1985), 'The Extent of Sex Discrimination in Great Britain', in A. Zabalza and Z. Tzannatos, *Women and Equal Pay: The Effects of Legislation on Female Employment and Wages in Britain*, Cambridge University Press.

Zabalza, A., C. Pissarides and M. Barton (1980), 'Social Security and the Choice Between Full-time Work, Part-time Work and Retirement', *Journal of Public Economics*, October, 14: 245–76.

Zax, J. (1989), 'Employment and Local Public Sector Unions', *Industrial Relations*, Winter, 28: 21–31.

Subject index

Ability
  and production function for human capital,
    23, 46
  and period in school, 32
  and transfers within the family, 50
  and studies of twins education, 68 ff
  and studies of twins income, 86 ff
  and hiring by small firms, 154, 261
  and measurement of compensating wage
    differentials, 189
  and firm size differentials, 261
  and specific training, 269
Absenteeism, 166, 324
Accidents
  and compensating wage differentials, 175
  and workers compensation, 197
  See also Compensating wage differentials,
  Policy
Acts
  English Education, 63
  Free School, 63
  Equal Pay, 114, 167, 168
  Sex Discrimination, 167
  Title VII of Civil Rights, 167, 312
  Health and Safety at Work, 185
  Factory, 202
  Workman's Compensation, 204
  Trade Union, 279
  Trade Disputes, 280
  National Labour Relations, 280
  Labour Management Relations, 281
  Employment Protection, 282
  Motor Carrier, 304–5
  Airline Deregulation, 304–5
  Public Accommodation, 312
  Occupational Safety and Health, 312
Added worker effect, 107
Adverse selection
  and statistical discrimination, 145
  and industrial accidents, 185 ff

Affirmative action, 89, 167, 170, 207
Age
  and earnings, 3, 18
  and output of human capital, 26, 33
  and participation, 131 ff
  and search, 216, 225
  and unemployment duration, 231
  and investment in information, 244
  and unionisation, 288
  See also Retirement
Age–earnings profile
  and occupational choice, 151
  See also Earnings
Altruism, 49
American Medical Association, 326
Annuity – simplified formula, 35
  See also Present value
Apprentices, 91
Asymmetric information, 272
Atrophy, 147, 158, 167
  and occupational choice, 175
  and wages: theory, 187 ff
  and wages: findings, 199 ff, 202
  and comparable worth, 206
  See also Depreciation
Attitudes
  to staying at home, 118
  to job risk, 184
Auction market, 5 ff, 13
  and long-term contract, 251

Bargaining zone, 297
Birth control, 113, 118, 125, 135
British Medical Association, 326
Budget line
  and within-family transfers, 50
  and labour supply, 98
  for education purchases, 61
  for search, 227
  See also Opportunity set, Choice

Bureaucracy, 66
in the large firm, 274
Business cycle, and unemployment duration,
228
Business unionism, 287, 304

Capital market imperfections, 14
See also Human capital
Capital stock
human capital, life-cycle path for women,
159
life-cycle path in basic model, 28
estimated for men and women, 163 ff, 172
ff
See also Investment, Human capital, Life-
cycle
Cartels, *see* Monopoly
Childcare
and monopsony, 164
subsidised, 170, 172
Choice
in the context of discrimination, 140
of accident rate, 196, 205
of search time and search intensity, 226 ff
City size
and earnings, 83
and employment opportunities, 154, 165
City University of New York, discrimination
case, 147
Closed shop
union shop and agency shop, 280
in printing, 302
and union effects on pay, 313
and profitability, 319
and union effects on employment, 319–20
See also Right to work laws
Coal mining, bargaining in UK, 303
Coase theorem, 204
Collective bargaining
and training, 89
national, in Britain, 236
and enterprise unions, 254, 282, 298
and voice, 278
legal enforceability, 280
and efficient bargains, 297–8, 302–3
and insiders and outsiders, 303 ff
and industrial democracy, 322
See also Unions, Efficient bargains
Collusion, *see* Monopoly
Colour
and earnings function, 83
and value of training, 89
higher participation of black wives, 122
and discrimination, 152
and search, 2, 217, 230, 234 ff

Comparable worth, 168 ff, 206 ff
Compensating and equivalent variation in
income, *see* Surplus
Compensating wage differentials, 174 ff
the facts, 188 ff
and longitudinal studies, 191
and statistical value of life, 192–3, 195,
201
studies of various types, 198
and piece rates, 255–6
and grievance procedures, 323
See also Policy
Competition
and discrimination, 140 ff, 152 ff, 171
and determination of industrial accidents,
176 ff, 197, 207
compared to regulation in context of
industrial accidents, 203
as large numbers exchange, 254
and internal labour markets, 273–4
international, and declines in unionisation,
289
and social policy, 324
Compulsory education, 60, 63, 66
Contraceptive use, *see* Birth Control
Contracts
implicit, 251
enforcement, 272
and wage rigidity, 271 ff, 275 ff
bargaining zone and efficient, 296–7
See also Long-term contracts
Control loss
and discrimination, 154
and piece rates, 257
and efficiency wages, 261 ff
and firm size pay differentials, 261
Corner solution, and labour supply, 98
Correlation
of twins' education levels, 55, 68 ff
defined, 56
of twins income levels, 86
of life-cycle hours worked and wages,
105
between wages and children born, 122
and measurement error, 128
between wage and productivity increases,
312–13
Costs
opportunity, and investment in college,
21
marginal, 31, 40
of college attendance, 58
of having children, 121
of search, 212, 217–18
of union organisation, 286–7, 292, 304

Crowding
    workers into non-union jobs, 308
    case study, in San Francisco, 310
    See also Segregation

Dead-end job, 13, 78
Dead-weight loss
    of minimum wages, 7
    of disallowing statistical discrimination, 145
    and comparable worth, 169
    and union wage claims, 299
    and employment protection, 325–6
    See also Pareto efficiency, Surplus
Deferred compensation, 265 ff
    compared with specific training, 268–9
    See also Efficiency wages theory
Demand
    for labour – *see* Marginal Revenue Product
    for education, 22, 45 ff
    for children, 117, 121
    -side discrimination, 140 ff
    for danger, 177
    -side influences on search, 230
    for unions, 284, 288
Demarcation disputes, *see* Strikes
Democracy, 64
    union democracy and median voter, 293
    and wage determination, 309
    See also Private property, Median voter
Democratic Party, 280
    and increased unionisation, 290
Dentists, *see* Professional associations
Depreciation
    of human capital, 32 ff
    and on-the-job training, 88
    in derivation of earnings function, 92
    and intermittency, 161
    in calculation of human capital stock, 172 ff
    and wage-job atrophy locus, 188
    See also Atrophy
Discount rate, *see* Interest rate
Discrimination
    defined, 140
    attitudes, 118
    and comparisons between single men and women, 137, 147
    and pay differences according to children in family, 138
    and competition, 140 ff, 152 ff
    empirical findings, 146 ff
    wage and employment contrasted, 152
    supply-side factors, 154 ff
    and mathematical abilities, 201
    and efficiency wage theory, 264
    and occupational choice, 208

Dismissal
    'due process' in, 253, 322
    and efficiency wage theory, 261 ff
    and deferred compensation, 267
    of strikers, 280
    and efficient bargains, 298
    See also Grievance procedures
Dispersion of earnings, 211
    and number of searches, 214, 219 ff
    and search, of women, 220
    over the business cycle, 229
    and search, of older workers, 235
    in union firms, 324
Distribution of income, and comparable worth, 170
    See also Equity, Distribution of wages
Distribution of wages
    and search, 213
    uniform, 216
    offer compared to actual, 217, 219
    calculating average maximum wage offer distribution, 248 ff
    under time and piece rates compared, 256–7
Division of labour
    in marriage, 84, 111
    and participation, 97, 117, 119
    and male labour supply, 127, 136
    and travel to work distances, 164
    and intermittency, 166, 167
Divorce
    and participation, 113, 121
    trends, 115
    panel study, 122
    and urbanisation, 124
    no fault, 126
Donovan commission (UK), 282

Earnings
    tabulated by age, colour and sex, 3
    of dead-end and career jobs, 14
    profile, graphed, 17
    potential, defined, 28
    difference between potential and actual, 30
    life-cycle, and hours worked, 105
    by sex, over time, 114
    by sex, 139
    dispersion by occupation, 210
    variance, by age, 236
    and firm size, 261
    and unions, 313 ff
    See also Sex, Marital status, Colour, Tenure, City size, Firm size, Health, Unions

Earnings function
  estimated, 75, 83
  basic derivation, 71
  detailed derivation, 92 ff
  in relation to union wage effects, 314
  See also Earnings
'Eds'
  defined, 20
  production function, 23 ff
  and human capital rental rate, 33
  capitalised value of, 33, 92
  and female human capital investment, 156
Education, *see* Schooling, Capital stock,
  Human capital, Ability
Efficiency
  of education subsidies, 64
  of statistical discrimination, 143
  and over-ruling freedom of contract, 186
  and unemployment insurance, 233
  and enterprise unions, 273
  See also Pareto efficiency, Efficiency wage
    theory
Efficiency wage theory
  in the context of search, 238
  modelled, 261 ff
Efficient bargains, 286, 292
  graphed, 294 ff
  effects in practice, 300 ff
  and union effects on investment, 321
Effort, 96, 250 ff
  and higher wages, 261–3
  and deferred compensation, 266–7
Elasticity
  intertemporal, 105, 128, 135
  of married women compared to men, 112,
    119
  of male labour supply, 119, 127 ff
  in negative income tax experiments, 130
  with respect to pensions, 134
  of executive pay with respect to firm size,
    259
  of industry demand, relevance for
    unionisation, 291
Employment
  and comparable worth, 170
  and sum of producer and consumer surplus,
    178
  and efficient bargains, 298
  effect of unions on, 319
Employment protection
  and cost of capital, 208 ff
  reducing national income, 324–6
  See also Policy, Dismissals, Grievance
    procedures
Engineering, national agreements in UK, 298

Equal opportunity, 171
  and equality of outcome, 172
  See also Affirmative action, Equity
Equal Opportunities Commission, 143
Equity
  and education subsidies, 60, 67
  and workplace accidents, 182
  and health insurance, 186
  and unemployment insurance, 233
European Community, *see* Social Charter
Executive compensation, 258–60
Exit and voice models, 278, 320
  See also Collective bargaining
Experience
  and earnings profiles, 19
  in basic earnings functions, 75
  and general training, 81
  measurement difficulties, for women, 147
Experience rating, *see* Insurance
Externalities
  in context of education, 64
  and workplace accidents, 179, 185 ff

Family background, *see* Family wealth
Family size, 108, 110
  and earnings, 149
  See also Fertility
Family wealth
  and human capital, 24
  relation to interest rate, 32, 47
  and demand for education, 46, 52, 67
  in twins studies, 57, 68 ff, 86 ff
  and college attendance, 58
  and education subsidies, 64
  and earnings function, 85
  See also Poverty
Feather bedding, 296, 298, 302
Fertility
  and participation, 113, 121
  and work interruption – time trends, 117
  and 'fecundity', 121
  changes in, in Sweden, 122
  See also Family size
Firm size
  women's employment by, 150, 154
  and monopsony, 166
  small firms and comparable worth, 170
  small firms and safety standards, 180, 208
  small firms and experience rating, 197
  and choice of piece rates, 257
  and executive pay, 258
  and pay differentials, 261
  and pensions, 267
  small firms and internal labour markets, 273
  and unionisation, 285–8

and crowding, in context of unions, 310
See also Non-union firm, Monopoly,
    Competition, Control loss
Full pay – and value of training, 129

Gender
    unequal occupations and pay, 137–8
    and search, 217–18
    and unionisation, 288
    See also Discrimination, Married women,
        Sex, Divorce, Division of Labour,
        Fertility, Segregation
Genetic variation, 54
    contribution to education differences, 68 ff
    contribution to income differences, 87 ff
Geometric progression, 35
Germany, trainee wages in, 90
    union structure, 383
    extension of union agreements in, 291
Government, employment in and female pay,
    151
Grievance procedures
    and opportunistic behaviour, 254
    determination of, by market forces, 322 ff
    See also Dismissals, Employment
        protection
Guilds, 278
    See also Professional associations

Health
    and earnings function, 83
    of children, 118, 125
    and retirement, 132
Hometime
    used in earnings function, 162
    and wage–job atrophy locus, 187
    See also Intermittency
Household technology, 108, 110, 126
Human capital
    the basic model, 19 ff
    the algebra, 30 ff
    rental rate of, 28, 33
    as loan collateral, 14, 47, 60
    and correlation between unemployment and
        replacement ratio, 129
    and lifetime participation, 157
    See also Capital stock, Specific human
        capital, Eds, Investment, Training, Life
        cycle

Ignorance
    rational, 66, 214, 232
    and education screening, 65
    and search, 211
    graphed, 215

modelled, 238 ff
    See also Information
Implicit contracts, 14, 251
    See also Contracts, Long-term contract
Incentive pay schemes, 250–77
    See also Deferred compensation, Efficiency
        wage theory, Specific human capital,
        Tournaments
Incentives
    and the principal-agent problem, 251
    compatibility, 297
    See also Effort, Principal-agent
Income effect
    and participation, 98
    and transitory non-labour income, 106
    and demand for safety, 182
Incomes policy, 114
    during wartime, and union growth, 284
    and corporatism, 329
Indentured labour, 14
Indifference curves
    for altruist, 49
    as between education and other goods, 61
    for goods and leisure, 97
    for unions, 292–3, 296–7, 300–1
    for unions, and insider-outsider theory, 304–5
Industrial democracy, 278, 322 ff
    See also Collective bargaining
Industry
    and earnings function, 85
    structure of, and participation, 124
    unionisation by, 285
Inflation
    unexpected, and search, 214
    and union density, 289
Information
    and statistical discrimination, 144 ff
    and work, 183 ff
    and wages, 210 ff
    asymmetric, and employment contracts, 272
Insider groups
    and the internal labour market, 274
    and collective bargaining, 303 ff
Insurance
    and accidents, 177
    and adverse selection, 185
    experience rating of, 180, 197, 205
    against workplace accidents, UK and US
        firms compared, 205
    and employment contracts, 271
Interest rate
    and human capital accumulation, 32
    long-term real rate, 38
    market rate of, 43
    See also Investment, Internal rate of return

Intermittency
    and percent female, 151
    and MRP, graphed, 153
    and reduced human capital, 155, 158 ff
    and occupational choice, 158
    and earnings profile, 160
    and comparable worth, 168
    and calculation of human capital stock,
        172 ff
    and wage–atrophy locus: theory, 187 ff
    and wage–atrophy locus: findings, 200 ff
Internal labour market, 10, 14
    and pension schemes, 133
    and workplace accidents, 184
    and payment systems, 250 ff
    characteristics of, 253, 266, 273
    and insider–outsider theory, 303
Internal rate of return
    defined, 35 ff
    and investment in education, 21, 42 ff
    'public' rate, 44, 64
    affected by consumption, 46
    regression estimates, 74
    and training, 78, 95
    and discrimination, 142
    See also Interest rate
International Association of Airline
        Mechanics, 304
International Typographical Union, 294, 302
Investment
    appraisal, 36 ff
    defined, 20
    investment fraction, 23, 40, 72
    and derivation of earnings function, 72
    net investment, 88, 172 ff
    net investment fraction, 93, 172 ff
    requiring a compensating wage differential,
        174
    in information, 244
    union effects on, 321 ff
    See also Internal rate of return, Capital stock
Iso-profit curves, 294–5, 300, 323
Isoquants, for job search, 228

Japan
    women's role, 154
    enterprise unions, 282
Job evaluation, 108
    and internal labour market, 253
Job matches
    and unemployment, 131
    and search, 214, 228, 243
    and effort, 250
    and specific training, 269
Jurisdiction disputes, see Strikes

Labour Party, 279
    and increased unionisation, 290
Labour's share in national income, 311
    See also Unions
Law of one price, 214, 215, 303
Life cycle
    basic model, 16 ff
    human capital stock, 26 ff
    and post-school investment, 71 ff
    effects on labour supply, 104, 127
    wage change, 108
    patterns of time use, 112 ff
    participation and reduced female human
        capital, 155
    and search, 235
    job changing over, 243
    and the efficiency wage hypothesis,
        265
    See also Human capital, Capital stock,
        Training, Investment
Lobbying, see Public choice
Long-term contract, 10, 12 ff, 250 ff
    and deferred compensation, 265
    and specific training, 268
    See also Contracts
Longitudinal studies
    and evidence for compensating wage
        differentials, 191, 195
    to correct for heterogeneity in mobility
        study, 246
    to estimate tenure–wage effect, 270
    of union wage effects, 313–14
Long-term unemployed
    statistics on, 231
    and replacement ratio, 233
Luck, 54, 57, 59, 87
    and 'one-sided error' terms, 240–1

Mandated benefits, 186, 275
Marginal revenue product, 6, 8 ff
    relation to wage in training, 81
    assessment of, 250
    not equal to wage in long-term contract,
        253, 271
    and supervisor's ratings of, 268
    and iso-profit curves, 295
    and insider–outsider theory, 304 ff
    and wage, given employment protection,
        325–6
    See also Demand
Marginal utility of leisure, 98, 102
Marital status
    and earnings function, 83
    and patterns of time use, 113
    and pay by sex, 137–9

and measurement of discrimination, 147 ff
and participation, graphed, 157
and capital stocks, 164
and reservation wages, 238–9
Market failure, *see* Mobility, Adverse
  selection, Externalities
Market forces, *see* Competition
Married women
  labour supply, 108 ff, 113, 135
  participation and husband's income, 107
  pay relative to single women, 84
  elasticity of labour supply, 119, 130
  and reservation wage, 238
  See also Marital status, Single women,
    Participation
Mathematics tests, 155
  and compensating wage differentials, 175,
    200
Measurement error
  and estimates of labour supply elasticity,
    128
  and compensating wage differentials, 189 ff
  graphed, 191
  algebra of, 209
  and tenure-wage effect, 270
  and union wage effect, 314
Median voter model, 293–4
  See also Democracy
Merit, 265
  See also Seniority
Minimum wages
  dead-weight loss of, 7
  and training, 78, 89 ff
  similarities to comparable worth, 170
  and mandated benefits, 186
  and search, 214, 219
  and reservation wages, 234
  and wait unemployment, 300
  and union self-interest, 312
  See also Policy
Mobility
  regional, and divorce, 125
  and discrimination, 142, 146
  and monopsony, 164 ff
  and compensating wage differentials,
    175 ff
  and state-subsidised housing, 236
  over the life cycle, 242 ff
  model of, for geographic migration,
    245 ff
and internal labour markets, 273–4
Monopoly
  and discrimination, 141 ff, 152 ff, 171
  and cartels, 171
  models of unions, 282, 290 ff

encouraging union growth, 285–6, 291
  and efficient bargains, 298
  and union wage effects, 316
  local, and self-regulating professions, 327
  See also Competition
Monopsony, 10 ff, 142
  and travel to work distances, 164
  and social policy, 324
Motivation, of married men, 149

National Labour Relations Board, 280
National Master Freight Agreement (US), 298
Nature versus nurture, 87, *see* Ability
Negative income tax, 107, 130
Negligence, defined, 177
Non-union firms
  and discrimination, 150
  and job evaluations, 169
  and safety standards, 180, 185, 204, 312
  use of merit and seniority pay, 265, 324
  and internal labour markets, 272, 275
  use of seniority in layoff/promotion, 298
  and insider power, 307
  employment trends, compared to union
    firms, 320
  grievance procedures in, 322, 324
  See also Firm size

Occupation
  father's, and demand for education, 53
  and earnings function, 85
  distribution of men and women, 138
  and crowding, 149 ff
  and tastes, 155
  and intermittent participation, 158
  choice and compensating wage
    differentials, 175
  and atrophy, 187
  and correlation between atrophy and
    percent home time, 200–1
  and disease, 204
  wage dispersion in, 211
  and unemployment duration, 231
Occupational safety and health administration,
  202
Off-the-demand curve models, *see* Efficient
  bargains
Omitted variables
  and compensating wage differentials, 189
  algebra of, 209
On-the-job training, *see* Training
Opportunity costs, *see* Costs
Opportunity set
  combining household and market
    production, 109

Opportunity set (*cont.*)
  combining pensions and earnings, 132 ff
  reduced by discrimination, 141
  and travel to work distances, 165
  and compensating wage differentials, 176
  and wage–job risk locus, 180 ff
  and search, 227–8

Panel data, *see* Longitudinal studies
Pareto efficiency, 6 ff
  and health insurance, 186 ff
  and workers compensation, 204–5
  See also Efficiency, Dead-weight loss
Part-time workers
  and internal labour markets, 254, 275
  and social policy, 324
Participation
  time trends for women, 97
  and transitory income change, 107
  determining endogenous and exogenous
    variables, 118, 124
  cross-country correlation with education,
    fertility and divorce, 120
  and fertility, 121
  and divorce, 122 ff
  and child health, 124
  and urbanisation, 124
  by sex and marital status, graphed, 157
  and capital stocks, 164
  See also Married women, Division of
    labour, Atrophy, Minimum wages
Participation, in industry, *see* Industrial
    democracy, Collective bargaining
Pensions
  and labour supply, 128
  and retirement, 132, 136
  and statistical discrimination, 143
  in the internal labour market, 253
  and deferred compensation, 266
  by company size, 266
  and union monitoring, 324
  See also Retirement, Internal labour
    market
Permanent income hypothesis, 106
  and negative income tax, 130
Piece rates, 255–7, 258, 261
  differential overtime rates, 256
  See also Incentive pay, Efficiency wage
    theory
Policy
  for education, 45
  and education subsidies, 48, 58 ff, 135
  and Ricardian equivalence theorem, 52
  free school, 63
  on-the-job training, 88 ff

no-fault divorce, 126
employment protection, 131
and pensions, 134
second guessing firms, 146
on gender equality, 167
comparable worth, 168 ff, 206 ff, 274
to combat sex discrimination, 171 ff
workers compensation, 180, 204 ff
safety standards, 180, 202 ff, 207
and mandated benefits, 186
dismissals protection, 186
employment protection, 208
monetary and fiscal, 212
unemployment counselling and 'job clubs',
  228
state subsidised housing, 236–7
and internal labour markets, 273–4
'social', 312, 324
See also Minimum wages, Affirmative
  action, Acts
Political parties, 280–1
  and union membership, 290
  and 'pro-labour' union role, 312
Post-school investment, 71 ff
  See also Training, Earnings function
Potential earnings
  defined, 28
  relation to actual, 29
  and derivation of earning function, 72
  and calculation of on-the-job training, 85
  See also Earnings
Poverty
  transmission over generations, 46, 49
  and education subsidies, 60
  and choice of risky jobs, 181, 191, 196
  See also Family wealth
Poverty trap, 96, 99 ff, 129, 135
Power
  of men over women, 112
  and discrimination, 142
  of unions, given safety regulation, 185
  of unions in political parties, 280–1
  of unions, and labour's share, 311
Present value
  of earnings, 14
  simple formula, 21
  algebraic derivation, 35 ff
  of earnings stream for young and old
    workers, 25
  of marginal product and wage in training
    context, 80
  of pensions, 132
  of earnings for women, 156
  of returns to search, 218
  of union dues, 287

Pressure group
    and public choice in education, 60
    and medical licensing, 328
    See also Unions, Public choice
Principal-agent problem, 251
    and piece rates, 255 ff
Private property, 9
    and discrimination, 143
    and wage determination, 309
    See also Democracy, Profit maximis-
        ation
Private schools, 65
Privatisation, 305
Production function
    for human capital, 23
    for household goods, 109, 111, 126
    for job offers, 226 ff
Productivity
    and unions, 288
    and average wages, 312–13
    union effects on, 320
Profile, of earnings, *see* Earnings
Professional associations, 326 ff
    See also Unions
Profits
    profit maximisation, 9
    and private property, 9
    and discrimination, 141
    incentive role in capitalism, 251
    maximised, by choice of piece rate,
        256
    and executive pay, 258–9
    correlation with wages, 307
    union effects on, 317 ff
Public choice
    lobbying, 8
    in education, 60, 66 ff
    and cover stories, 66
    and safety standards, 180
    and capture of safety inspectors, 203
    and medical/dental licensing, 328
Public goods
    and workplace accidents, 184
    and information about safety, 206

Quits
    rates, by gender, 166, 212, 230
    to search, 212, 230
    and specific training, 268
    and link between unions and internal labour
        markets, 272

Rate of return, *see* Internal rate of return
Redundancy pay, *see* Severance pay
Regression to the mean, 50, 52

Religion
    and participation, 121, 135
    and divorce, 122, 124
Rent, 7 ff, 285
    maximisation by union, 290–2
    received by insiders, 303
    capture, by unions, 319
Replacement ratio, 101, 129
    time trend in UK, 131
Research and development, effect of unions
        on, 321
Reservation wage, defined, 221 ff
    studies of, 232 ff
    of black and white youths, 234
    and unemployment insurance, 237
    and education, 237
    calculating expected wage, given
        reservation wage, 249
Retirement
    and human investment, 25, 32
    time trends, 131
    analysis, 132 ff
    and deferred compensation, 266
Ricardian equivalence theorem, 52
Right to work laws, 281, 284
    See also Closed shops
Risk
    down-side, and piece rates, 256
    and tournaments, 260

Safety standards, *see* Compensating wage
        differentials, Policy
Schooling
    in human capital theory, 39 ff
    rate of return to, 42
    and father's occupation, 53
    as general training, 79
    trends by sex, 115
    and search, 234
    See also Human capital
Screening, 65
Search
    theories of, 210 ff
    non-sequential model, 216 ff
    sequential model, 220 ff
    and efficiency wage theory, 264
    See also Unemployment, Dispersion
        of earnings, Distribution of
        wages
Segmented labour markets, 142
    and policy with respect to internal labour
        markets, 274
Segregation
    into women's jobs, 137, 149 ff, 153
    and comparable worth, 170

Selectivity bias
  in context of participation, 118
  in the context of compensating wage
    differentials, 181
  and measurement of wage differentials,
    190, 196
  and search, 217
  and studies of union effects, 317
Self-employment
  and tests for education screening, 65
  and tests for discrimination, 154
  and industrial accidents, 197
  and tests for monitoring theories, 266
Seniority
  and promotion, 260
  use instead of merit pay, by firm size,
    265
  and union democracy (median voter), 293
  and efficient bargains, 298
Service sector
  expansion of, related to participation, 117,
    124
Severance pay, and deferred compensation,
  266, 324
Sex, and earnings function, *see* Gender,
  Discrimination
Share price
  and executive pay, 258
  and unionisation, 317
  See also Profits
Shirking, *see* Effort
Single women
  time spent on housework, 113
  participation trends, 113
  elasticity of labour supply, 119, 135
  and negative income tax, 130
  compared with single men, 137
  and crowding, 150
  life-cycle participation, graphed, 157
  occupational choice compared to married
    women, 160
  See also Married women
Skill differential, 114
Small firms, *see* Firm size, Non-union firms
Social Charter of European Community, 91,
  275
Social security, *see* Welfare benefits
South Africa, discrimination in, 152
Specific human capital
  and white/black unemployment, 2
  contrasted with general, 77 ff
  and layoffs, 230 ff
  and internal labour markets, 254, 268 ff
  and labour productivity over the cycle, 264
  studies of, related to training, 270

and insider-outsider theory, 303
  and estimation of union wage effects, 315
  and social policy, 324
  See also Training, Human capital, Capital
    stock
Statistical discrimination, 143 ff
  See also Discrimination
Statistical value of life, *see* Compensating
  wage differentials
Stereotype, by parents in child rearing,
  154
  See also Statistical discrimination
Strikes, right to strike, 280
  demarcation and jurisdictional strikes,
    282
  pattern of, 284–5
  and the median voter model, 294
  and Mrs Thatcher, 312
Subsidies
  for training, 14
  for education, 53
  and withdrawal of private purchases of
    education, 52, 61
  See also Policy
Substitution effect
  and participation, 78
  and temporary wage increase, 104
  and substitutability of market for home
    work, 110
  in male labour supply, 127–8
Supervisor rating, 268
Supply and demand
  and minimum wages, 6 ff
  in white- blue-collar wages, 12
  applied to education, 45 ff
  applied to discrimination, 141
  and comparable worth, 168 ff
  and workplace accidents, 178 ff
  analysis of medical licensing, 327
Supply of labour
  compensated supply, 99
  married women's, 108 ff
  male, 127 ff
  supply-side discrimination, 140, 154 ff
  and workers' compensation, 179
Supply-side policies, 15
  and workplace accidents, 182
Supreme Court of the US, 143, 168, 279
Surplus
  producer and worker, 7, 9
  worker surplus in detail, 102 ff
  and comparable worth, 169
  and choice of accident rate, 178
Tariffs, encouraged by producer groups, 286,
  308

Tastes
for discrimination, 142
women's different from men's, 147 ff,
154 ff
and per cent in female occupation, 152
distribution of, for injury, 181
and mathematical ability, by sex, 200–1
and 'caring', 206
See also Choice, Attitudes
Tax credits, *see* vouchers
Taxation
and education, 52
and labour supply, 100, 127
and subsidised childcare, 172
and subsidised workers compensation, 205
and unemployment insurance, 233, 248
See also Negative income tax
Teenage workers, 90
employment, and unions, 310
Tenure
and specific training, 81 ff, 269 ff
and earnings function, 83
and length of job, 251–2
Threat effects of collective bargaining, 308
Time-equivalent investment, *see* Investment
Time preference, 38
Time use, patterns of, 111 ff
Tournaments, 258 ff
compared with piece rate schemes, 260
Trade disputes, *see* Strikes
Training, 22, 65
policy, 58 ff
general and specific contrasted, 77 ff
training slots, 78
estimated value of, 89
and minimum wages, 90
and full pay, 129
and relative female pay, 151
and atrophy, 158
and comparable worth, 169
studies of on-the-job, 270
See also Specific human capital
Transactions costs, 143
and insurance, 186
and safety regulations, 204
and the role of unions in internal labour
markets, 273
and insider-outsider theory, 303
Transfers within the family, 49 ff
and education subsidies, 61
Twins
studies of education, 54
studies of IQ, 56
models to assess family background, 68 ff
studies of income, 86 ff

Unemployment
graphed over time, for ethnic minorities,
5
and wife's home productivity, 109
and replacement ratio, 129, 131, 233
and structural mismatch, 131
and effects of comparable worth, 169
and mandated benefits, 186
frictional, 210, 248
duration of, 211, 215
and reservation wage, 221
and search costs and offer wages, 224 ff
long-term, and search efficiency, 226
duration, and job offer production function,
227
inflows versus duration, 230–1
and efficiency wage theory, 264
and union density, 289
and efficient bargains, 294
Unemployment benefits, *see* Unemployment,
Welfare benefits, Replacement ratio
Uniform distribution, of wages, 216 ff, 222
See also Distribution of wages
Unions, 278 ff
teachers' union, 45, 60, 67, 282
effect on earnings, 83
and unemployment, 131
and discrimination, 142
in South Africa, 152
and comparable worth, 120–1
and workplace accidents, 184
and compensating wage differentials, 194,
198
safety representatives, 207
wage setting, and search, 214
in the internal labour market, 254, 272-3
and seniority pay, 265
and pay differentials by age, 288
and layoff/promotion by seniority, 298
dues, 304
effects on pay, 313 ff
effects on profits, 317 ff
effects on employment, 319 ff
effects on productivity, 320 ff
effects on investment, 321 ff
professional associations, 326 ff
See also Pressure group, Collective
bargaining, Non-union firms, Union
membership
Union shops, *see* Closed shop
Union membership
time trends, 279
white collar in US and UK, 281
economic factors affecting, 284 ff
by firm size, 285

Union Mermbership (*cont.*)
   and wait unemployment, 308
   See also Unions
Unskilled workers, 90

Vouchers for education, 66 ff

Wage rigidity, 271–2, 275–7
Water and diamond paradox, 5
Wealth
   and inter-family transfers, 51
   and labour supply, 104, 135
   and earlier retirement, 132, 134
   and risk, 182
   See also Family wealth, Poverty
Welfare benefits
   and labour supply, 100, 127–9, 128–30
   and pensions, 134

and search costs, 214
and reservation wages, 239
and efficiency wage theory, 264
and non-unin pay, 309
See also Unemployment, Poverty trap,
   Taxation, Replacement ratio
Workers compensation, 178
   and compensating wage differentials, 180,
      184, 194, 201
   and accident rate, 197
Working conditions
   and compensating wage differentials,
      198
   and unionisation, 288
   See also Compensating wage differentials
Workplace Industrial Relations Survey (UK),
   307, 324

Author index

Abowd, J., 319
Abraham, K., 268, 269
Adams, J., 105
Addison, J., 91, 152, 254, 260, 261, 267, 273, 275, 281, 284, 288, 290, 298, 311, 321, 324
Akerlof, G., 183, 262
Alchian, A., 251, 254 (*see* Klein)
Aldrich, J., 152
Allen, S., 321
Altonji, J., 269
Anderson, C., 155
Andrisani, P., 86, 147, 155
Angrist, J., 86
Arnould, R., 195
Arrufat, J., 147
Ashenfelter, O., 86, 142, 153, 290, 303
Ashton, D., 288 (*see* Spilsbury)
Ashton, P., 129

Baily, M., 271
Baker, G., 259, 260
Ball, L., 105
Barro, R., 52
Barron, J., 212, 234, 270
Barton, M., 134 (*see* Zabalza)
Bartrip, P., 180, 204
Bean, C., 303
Becker, G., 49–52, 61, 104, 105, 117, 120, 124, 126, 128, 142, 152, 244, 265, 268, 327, 328
Becker, M., 170
Behrman, J., 57
Beider, P., 207
Beller, A., 137
Ben Porath, Y., 22–30
Benham, L., 84
Bergmann, B., 112
Bernheim, B., 207 (*see* Beider)
Biddle, J., 108

Bishop, J., 268
Black, D., 270 (*see* Barron)
Blanchflower, D., 307, 318, 319, 320
Blau, D., 110
Blau, F., 137 (*see* Beller)
Bognano, M., 260 (*see* Ehrenberg)
Booth, A., 267, 270
Borjas, G., 142
Bouchard, T., 57, 69, 70
Bowles, S., 264
Brien, M., 170
Bronars, S., 142
Brown, Colin, 5
Brown, Charles, 191, 192, 265, 288
Brown, James, 271, 303
Brown, Joan, 206
Brown, M., 112
Browne, M., 311, 313
Buchele, D., 152
Buckley, J., 210
Burtless, G., 134
Butler, R., 146

Cain, G., 121, 124, 140
Card, D., 86, 307
Carlson, N., 257
Carruth, A., 289, 304
Cartter, A., 290, 308
Casey, B., 90
Chelius, J., 177, 197
Chesher, A., 237, 238, 239
Chiplin, B., 114, 127
Chiswick, B., 150
Chuma, H., 132
Cigno, A., 112
Clark, K., 317, 321
Classen, K., 232
Cohen, S., 279
Combs, B., 183 (*see* Lichtenstein)
Connolly, R., 317, 318

Corcoran, M., 57, 69
Cornell, J., 204
Cousineau, J., 284
Cox, J., 312
Crawford, R., 254 (*see* Klein)
Crystal, G., 259 (*see* O'Reilly)
Cunningham, J., 170 (*see* Brien), 310 (*see* W. Moore)
Cymrot, D., 246

Daniel, W., 289
Daymont, T., 147, 155
Demsetz, H., 251
Denny, K., 321
Dertouzos, J., 302
Devine, T., 232
Dex, 153
Dickens, W., 183
Disney, R., 289
Dooley, M., 121, 124
Dorsey, S., 185, 193, 194–5, 205
Dowd, B., 66
Duncan, G., 142, 184, 193, 195, 198, 198–9
Duncan, O. D., 118
Dunleavy, J., 246 (*see* Cymrot)

Edwards, L., 155
Edwards, R., 142 (*see* Gordon)
Ehrenberg, R., 232–3, 235, 260
Ehrlich, I., 132
England, P., 160, 199

Fackler, J., 150 (*see* Chiswick)
Farber, H., 269, 284, 297
Fearn, R., 157
Feaster, D., 261
Feinberg, R., 198
Feldman, R., 66 (*see* Dowd)
Fenn, P., 203 (*see* Veljanovski)
Ferber, M., 137 (*see* F. Blau)
Feuille, P., 305 (*see* Hendricks)
Fields, G., 133
Filer, R., 206
Fischel, D., 171, 324
Fischoff, B., 183 (*see* Lichtenstein)
Frank, R., 166
Freeman, R., 12, 283–9, 288, 298, 310, 311, 312, 314, 314–15, 316, 317, 320, 322, 324
Friedman, M., 198, 215, 309
Fuchs, V., 161, 207 (*see* Beider)

Garen, J., 154, 193, 196, 261
Garrett, M., 307 (*see* Blanchflower)
Gaynor, M., 242

Ghez, G., 104, 105, 128
Gilman, H., 232
Goldenberg, S., 282
Goldin, C., 114, 123
Goldsmith, A., 6
Gordon, D., 142
Gordon, R., 264
Green, F., 316
Greene, K., 66
Gregory, R., 142
Gronau, R., 108, 120, 217, 218

Hacker, A., 138
Hall, R., 238, 252, 253
Hamermesh, D., 108, 198
Hamilton, J., 288 (*see* Charles Brown)
Hammerton, M., 184 (*see* Jones-Lee)
Hand, L., 177
Hannan, I., 142, 153
Hansen, W., 66
Harris, J., 251, 254 (*see* Williamson), 268 (*see* Williamson)
Hartmann, H., 150
Hashimoto, M., 90, 252
Healy, J., 322 (*see* Slichter)
Heckman, J., 97, 104, 118, 119
Hendricks, W., 305
Heywood, J., 288, 292, 308
Hicks, J., 174
Hill, M., 113
Hirsch, B., 281, 288, 290, 317 (*see* Connolly), 318 (*see* Connolly), 321, 324
Hirschey, M., 317 (*see* Connolly), 318 (*see* Connolly)
Hofler, R., 243
Holen, A., 235
Holmlund, B., 193, 195
Holzer, H., 230, 234, 235, 237, 238, 310
Horney, M., 112
Horvath, F., 247
Hoskins, M., 288 (*see* Spilsbury)
Hotz, J., 105
Hughes, G., 236
Hutchens, R., 267
Hutchins, M., 315 (*see* Polachek)

Ichniowski, C., 323
Idson, T., 261

Jackman, R., 231, 237
Jacoby, S., 272
Jaing, F., 105
Jencks, C., 57, 69, 86
Jensen, M., 251, 258, 259 (*see* Baker), 260 (*see* Baker)

Johnson, G., 131, 236
Johnson, T., 94
Johnson, W., 122–7
Jones, F., 146
Jones-Lee, M., 182, 184, 201
Joshi, H., 116, 119, 124, 156
Juster, T., 113

Kahn, I., 230, 311
Katz, A., 232
Kaufman, Robert, 294
Kaufman, Roger, 294
Kenny, I., 84
Keynes, J., 215
Kiefer, N., 232, 237
Killingsworth, M., 97, 104, 118, 119
King, A., 198
Klein, B., 254
Klerman, J., 115
Kniesner, T., 6, 196
Knight, K., 212
Korenman, S., 84 (*see* Neumark)
Kreps, J., 280, 284
Krueger, A., 265
Kuratani, M., 80
Kydland, F., 105 (*see* Hotz)

Laband, 86
Lacroix, R., 284
Lancaster, T., 237, 238, 239
Lande, R., 282
Landes, W., 64
Layard, R., 116 (*see* Joshi), 131, 231, 236
Layman, M., 183 (*see* Lichtenstein)
Lazear, I., 47, 89, 90, 134, 171, 258, 259, 266
Leeth, J., 196
Leibowitz, A., 115
Leigh, J., 166
Leighton, L., 90
Lentz, 86 (*see* Laband)
Levhari, D., 25
Levitan, S., 65
Lewin, D., 282, 323
Lewis, H. G., 313
Li, E., 182, 209
Lichtenstein, S., 183
Lindbeck, A., 303
Lindsay, C., 154
Linneman, P., 320
Livernach, E., 322 (*see* Slichter)
Low, S., 230
Lowenstein, M., 270 (*see* Barron)
Lundberg, S., 142
Lykken, D., 57
Lyttkens, C., 197

Machin, S., 317
MacIntosh, J., 143
MaCurdy, J., 105, 128, 294, 302, 303
Madden, J., 165
Maguire, M., 288 (*see* Spilsbury)
Main, B., 252, 258, 259, 259 (*see* O'Reilly)
Malcolmson, J., 264
Maloney, M., 154
Mancer, M., 112
Marin, A., 183, 185, 192, 194, 196
Marshall, R., 142
Martin, J., 115, 117
Martin, P., 280 (*see* Kreps), 284 (*see* Kreps)
Marvell, H., 202
Mattila, J., 170 (*see* Ozarem)
McCaffrey, D., 203–4, 212
McCormick, B., 236
McCutcheon, E., 315
McDonald, I., 296
McElroy, M., 112
McGue, M., 57
McKee, M., 140
McNabb, R., 198, 199
Meckling, J., 251
Medoff, J., 268, 283, 288 (*see* Charles
    Brown), 288, 298, 299, 310, 311, 312,
    316, 320, 322, 324
Mellor, E., 3, 139
Mellow, W., 234, 261, 289, 316
Metcalf, D., 220, 288, 311, 321, 322, 324
Millward, N., 289, 319, 320 (*see*
    Blanchflower), 322, 325
Mincer, J., 18, 19, 71–4, 74–7, 90, 92–5, 106,
    107, 110, 116, 118, 119, 120, 121, 124,
    155, 235, 300, 308
Minford, P., 129, 236
Mitchell, O., 133
Montgomery, M., 122
Moore, M., 193, 195, 196
Moore, R., 154, 266
Moore, W., 310
Mortensen, D., 244
Murphy, K. J., 258, 259 (*see* Baker), 260 (see
    Baker)
Murphy, K. M., 73, 124, 126

Nakamura, A., 114
Nakamura, M., 114
Nardinelli, C., 142
Narendrenathan, W., 233, 235
Nelson, P., 220
Nenan, W., 66 (*see* Greene)
Neumann, G., 232, 237
Neumark, D., 84, 146
Newman, R., 310 (*see* W. Moore)

Nichols, L., 195
Nickell, S., 131, 212, 226, 233 (*see* Narendrenathan), 235, 298, 321
Noll, R., 204 (*see* Cornell)

O'Connor, C., 183
O'Neill, J., 119, 120, 124, 137, 150 (*see* Chiswick), 170 (*see* Brien)
O'Reilly, C., 259
Oaxaca, R., 146, 232–3, 312
Ofek, H., 155
Oi, W., 230, 254, 261, 268
Olneck, M., 57, 69
Olson, C., 192, 194, 203
Orazem, P., 170
Oswald, 292, 304, 307 (*see* Blanchflower), 318, 320 (*see* Blanchflower)
Owen, S., 116 (*see* Joshi)

Paglin, M., 200
Pareto, W., 6, 7, 186, 204, 205
Parsons, 257, 268
Peel, M., 236 (*see* Minford)
Peltzman, W., 61–4
Pencavel, J., 127, 290, 294, 302, 303
Peoples, J., 307
Perlman, R., 280 (*see* Kreps), 284 (*see* Kreps)
Peters, H., 127
Phelps, E., 143
Phelps Brown, E., 147, 256, 311, 313
Philips, P., 184 (*see* Jones-Lee)
Pike, M., 170
Pissarides, C., 134 (*see* Zabalza)
Podgursky, M., 310
Polachek, S., 84, 105, 118, 121, 137, 146, 150 (*see* Chiswick), 155, 163, 165, 172–3, 187–9, 201, 240, 242, 243, 247, 315
Portugal, P., 269 (*see* Addison)
Posner, R., 280
Prais, S., 90
Psacharopoulos, G., 44, 183, 185, 192, 194, 196

Quinn, J., 132, 134
Quinn Mills, D., 298

Raisian, J., 252
Rebitzer, J., 265, 272
Reich, M., 142 (*see* Gordon)
Reimers, C., 123
Remick, H., 274
Reynolds, M., 320
Roberts, C., 115, 117
Robins, P., 107, 110, 130
Roos, P., 160

Roosevelt, F., 280
Rose, N., 306, 317
Rosen, S., 180, 182, 190, 258, 259
Rosenzweig, M., 121, 122, 124, 125
Ross, A., 272
Rothschild, M., 211
Ruback, R., 317–19
Rufolo, A., 200
Ruser, J., 180, 197
Ryan, P., 273

Sadlacek, G., 105 (*see* Hotz)
Salamon, M., 285
Sandell, S., 160, 232, 237
Sander, W., 124
Sattinger, M., 211
Savage, L., 198
Savouri, S., 231
Schultz, T. P., 121, 122, 124, 125
Scott, C., 66 (*see* Greene)
Segal, N., 57
Seiler, E., 256, 257
Seldon, A., 67
Shakotko, R., 269
Shapiro, C., 264, 266
Shapiro, D., 160
Shaw, K., 105
Shepela, S., 154
Shorey, J., 166
Shoven, J., 207 (*see* Beider)
Siebert, S., 48, 91, 148, 152, 166, 254, 261, 267, 273, 275, 284, 298, 311, 326
Simon, C., 142, 315
Skinner, J., 122–7
Slichter, S., 322
Sloane, P., 114, 127, 150, 153 (*see* Dex)
Slovic, P., 183 (*see* Lichtenstein)
Smith, A. [Adam], 4, 64–5, 174, 175, 194, 198
Smith, J., 115
Smith, R., 170, 203, 253
Snow, A., 25
Snower, D., 303
Solomon, I., 64
Solow, R., 296
Somers, G., 280 (*see* Kreps), 284 (*see* Kreps)
Spilsbury, M., 288
Sprague, A., 126
Stafford, F., 113, 184, 198–9
Startz, R., 142
Steinberg, R., 274
Stephenson, S., 234, 237
Stern, J., 233 (*see* Narendranathan), 235
Stern, S., 245
Stevens, M., 322, 325
Stewart, M., 313, 316

Stigler, G., 154, 210, 210–11, 216–20, 221, 224, 261, 265
Stiglitz, J., 264, 266
Summers, L., 185, 265
Svorny, S., 328
Szerszen, C., 305 (*see* Hendricks)

Tannen, M., 58–9
Taubman, P., 57, 86
Thaler, R., 182
Tollegen, A., 57
Tomes, N., 49–52, 61
Topel, R., 270
Trade Union Congress, 180
Treble, J., 284
Treiman, D., 150
Trejo, S., 285
Trussell, S., 122
Tullock, G., 299
Turnbull, P., 303

Van Der Horst, S., 152
Vanek, J., 108
Veljanovski, C., 192, 194, 197, 203
Viscusi, W. K., 183–4, 193, 195, 196, 197, 203
Vishwanath, T., 226
Viviano, A., 154
Voos, P., 286

Wachter, M., 251, 254 (*see* Williamson), 268 (*see* Williamson), 320
Wadhwani, S., 321
Wagner, K., 90
Wall, M., 321
Walzer, N., 186, 193, 194–5, 205
Warburton, P., 134
Ward, M., 115
Warren, R., 25
Webb, S., 279
Weingast, B., 204 (*see* Cornell)
Weisbrod, B., 66
Weiss, Y., 25, 326
Weisskopf, J., 264
Welch, F., 12, 73
Wessels, W., 303
West, E., 60, 62, 63, 64, 67, 140
Williamson, O., 251, 254, 268
Wolpin, K., 65
Wright, R., 254
Wunnava, P., 315

Yoon, B., 240, 242
Young, A., 148, 166

Zabalza, A., 134, 147
Zax, J., 285
Zerbe, R. O., 282
Zimmerman, M., 317–19